Individualization

Theory, Culture & Society

Theory, Culture & Society caters for the resurgence of interest in culture within contemporary social science and the humanities. Building on the heritage of classical social theory, the book series examines ways in which this tradition has been reshaped by a new generation of theorists. It also publishes theoretically informed analyses of everyday life, popular culture, and new intellectual movements.

EDITOR: Mike Featherstone, *Nottingham Trent University*

THE TCS CENTRE

The *Theory, Culture & Society* book series, the journals *Theory, Culture & Society* and *Body & Society*, and related conference, seminar and postgraduate programmes operate from the TCS Centre at Nottingham Trent University. For further details of the TCS Centre's activities please contact:

Centre Administrator
The TCS Centre, Room 175
Faculty of Humanities
Nottingham Trent University
Clifton Lane, Nottingham, NG11 8NS, UK
e-mail: tcs@ntu.ac.uk
web: http://tcs.ntu.ac.uk

Individualization

Institutionalized Individualism and its Social and Political Consequences

Ulrich Beck *and*
Elisabeth Beck-Gernsheim

SAGE Publications
London • Thousand Oaks • New Delhi

First published 2002

SAGE Publications Ltd
6 Bonhill Street
London EC2A 4PU

SAGE Publications Inc
2455 Teller Road
Thousand Oaks, California 91320

SAGE Publications India Pvt Ltd
32, M-Block Market
Greater Kailash - I
New Delhi 110 048

British Library Cataloguing in Publication data

A catalogue record for this book is available from the British Library

ISBN 0 7619 6111 9
ISBN 0 7619 6112 7 (pbk)

Library of Congress Control Number available

Typeset by SIVA Math Setters, Chennai, India
Printed and bound in Great Britain by Athenaeum Press, Gateshead

Contents

Foreword by Scott Lash:
Individualization in a Non-Linear Mode

Ulrich Beck's Risk Society, and indeed the theory of 'reflexive modernization' is characterized by two theses: an environmental thesis or the 'risk thesis', and an 'individualization thesis'. Beck's work has, from the mid 1980s, been understood in Germany in terms of a balance of these two theses. In Anglo-Saxon sociology the risk thesis has been enormously influential. The individualization thesis, for its part, has passed virtually ignored. That is the shortcoming that this book, *Individualization*, addresses. In the original German the individualization thesis is found across a range of articles and books. English readers have better fortune. In this single volume this thesis receives the exclusive attention of Ulrich and Elisabeth Beck. This book represents the other half of Beck's work. And this half today may be the most important half.

At stake in this book is a notion of the individual and a process of 'becoming-individual' that is clearly from another space than the possessive and ego-istic individualism of Thatcher, Reagan, George W. and contemporary global free-market liberalism. Perhaps more importantly it is also a notion of the individual that is vastly different from even the ethical and altruistic individualism of the Enlightenment. Indeed Enlightenment individualism is more about 'being-individual' than becoming-individual at all. And this is because Enlightenment individualism takes place in what Beck understands as 'the first' or 'simple modernity', while the individualism at stake in this book is a phenomenon of 'the second', 'reflexive' modernity. If the first modernity comprises predominantly a logic of structures, then the second modernity, if we are to follow Manuel Castells, involves a logic of flows. Beck's notions of unintended consequences, of ever-incomplete knowledge, of not irrationality but a rationality that is forever indeterminate is comfortable in the logic of flows. Beck's chronic indeterminacy of risk and risk-taking, of living with risk is of much more a piece with not the determinacy of structure but with the partial, the elusive determinacy of flow.

So we need to ask ourselves, along with Ulrich and Elisabeth Beck-Gernsheim, what can individualization and individualism mean in an age of flows. There are two issues at stake here. One is what Durkheim saw as an anomic individualism. In the shift from one set of social arrangements to another, there is a necessary period of movement, of unsettling that is understood as anomie. Thus in the move from the traditional Gemeinschaft and the *ancien regime* there is a transition phase of rootlessness until the first, industrial modernity develops its own normativities and classic Enlightenment individualism becomes routinized. Thus Hegel understood the shift from the anomic excesses of the French Revolution to the institutionalized individualism of property, contract, the bourgeois family and civil society of The Philosophy of Right. The same sort of process is at stake in the transition from industrial to the second, informational modernity. First an anomic individualism. The point for Beck is that even after the transition to reflexive modernity, the new individualism does not become routinized. It is, even in its mature phase indeterminate, full of risk and precarious freedom.

In order to come to grips with Beck's notion of individualization and individualism I do not think it is helpful to make comparisons with either Habermas or Anthony Giddens. This is because German sociology has a markedly different genealogy than its Anglo-American counterpart. In many respects both Habermas and Giddens wrote from a dissatisfaction with the structural functionalism, the linear systems theory of Talcott Parsons, and the dominance of Parsonsian sociology in the post-war decades. Both Habermas and Giddens had affinities with Marxism. Both featured a stress on the importance of agency in contrast to structure. This was the position from the late 1970s when the two theorists came to hegemonic positions in German and Anglo-Saxon sociology. Beck comes effectively from another generation. He came to a position of predominance in the 1990s in Germany. This was a decade of intellectual history that defined itself against Habermas and corporatist and Marx-influenced social democracy. Indeed Beck came to prominence among a generation for whom no longer Habermas, but Niklas Luhmann was the guiding figure. It is significant that Giddens's two most influential younger colleagues and co-workers have been John Thompson and David Held, two Habermas-influenced sociologists who have produced indeed an impressive corpus of work. Beck in contrast came to prominence against the grain of Habermas and with Luhmann. Surely in the early years of the present millennium the outbreak of dogmatic Luhmannism in Germany is something Beck feels distinctly uncomfortable with. Beck is clearly not a Luhmannianer. Yet a generation of German students have come to maturity in an ambience that is given shape to by both Beck and Luhmann, and this ambience is not characterized less by conflict than by convergence of their respective conceptual frameworks.

At stake in this, and the defining thematic of this book, is a decidedly non-linear notion of the individual and individualization. In the first modernity, the modernity of structure, society is conceived as a linear system. Talcott Parsons's social system is such a linear system. Linear systems have single points of equilibria, and only external forces can disturb this equilibrium and lead to system change. The reflexive individualization of the second modernity presumes the existence of non-linear systems. Here system dis-equilibrium and change is produced internally to the system through feedback loops. These are open systems. The point is that the feedback loop, that is the defining property of non-linear systems, passes through the individual. Individualization now is at the same time system destabilization. Complex systems do not simply reproduce. They change. The individual is the point of passage for the unintended consequences that lead to system dis-equilibrium. Beck does not use this sort of language, but this sort of non-linearity is at the heart of individualization in the second modernity. It breaks with the linear individualism – both possessive and ethical-moral – of simple modernity. Indeed it might be fair to suggest that Parsonsian systems-linearity was in many respects the other side of Habermas's linearity of agency.

By the same token Luhmann's second-modernity non-linearity of system finds its parallel in Beck's non-linear individualism.

In this sense also the individual of the first modernity is reflective while that of the second modernity is reflexive. The idea of reflective belongs to the philosophy of consciousness of the first modernity. And, to be fair, Habermas was one of the first to note this. To reflect is to somehow subsume the object under the subject of knowledge. Reflection presumes apodictic knowledge and certainty. It presumes a dualism, a scientific attitude in which the subject is in one realm, the object of knowledge in another. Beck's work from the very start has presupposed a critique of such objectivist knowledge, a critique of such dualisms, be they Cartesian or Kantian. Beck's very first book, well before *Risk Society* (1992), stemming from his doctoral work, addressed issues of knowledge and science. This work was already implicitly phenomenological, breaking with assumptions of the subsumptive (possessive) individualism of the Enlightenment and positivism. For Beck, as for phenomenology, the knowing individual was already in the world with the objects of his/her knowledge. This subject could only grasp a certain portion of the object, in connection with what Husserl called the subject's 'attitude', in Beck's case the interest-constituted attitude of the knower. Thus the objectivity of simple-modernity individualism is replaced by the intentionality of knowledge in the second modernity. This intentionality is again at centre stage in *Risk Society*, now tied up with the ecological problematique. Science and industry for all their claims to objectivity, and to being somehow objective and outside of the world, are indeed in the world with their own proper interest constituted intentionality. The problem here, although it is at the same time its saving grace, is that what is intended leads to the most extraordinary unintendedness, to side effects, to unintended consequences.

The Cartesian subject of simple modernity, of Descartes' Metaphysical Meditations is reflective. So is the Kantian subject of determinate judgement. Beck often describes today's non-linear individual in terms of, not the 'I think therefore I am', but instead in terms of 'I am I'. 'I think, therefore I am' has to do with reflection. 'I am I' has more to do with reflex. And Beck often indeed works from the contrast of 'reflex' with reflection. Reflexive he argues has more to do with reflex than reflection. Reflexes are indeterminate. They are immediate. They do not in any sense subsume. Reflexes cope with a world of speed and quick decision-making. The contemporary individual, Beck never tires of saying, is characterized by choice, where previous generations had no such choices. What Beck often omits to say is that this individual must choose fast, must – as in a reflex – make quick decisions. Second-modernity individuals haven't sufficient reflective distance on themselves to construct linear and narrative biographies. They must be content, as Ronald Hitzler has noted, with *Bastelbiographen*, with bricolage-biographies in Levi-Strauss's sense. The non-linear individual may wish to be reflective but has neither the time nor the space to reflect. He is a combinard. He puts together networks, constructs alliances, makes deals. He must live, is forced to live in an atmosphere of risk in which knowledge and life-changes are precarious.

So what is at stake here? The second modernity and its non-linear individualism is a result of the retreat of the classic institutions: state, class, nuclear family, ethnic group. The roles that reproduced linear individuals and systems in the first modernity are transgressed. Yet the result is not the disappearance of the subject, or a general irrationality. The subject relating to today's fragmented institutions instead has moved from a position of reflection to one of being reflexive. Yet this subject is so constantly in motion that it makes little sense to talk about a subject-position. The subject is still with us and so is knowledge. Only knowledge itself is of uncertainty. What happens now is not non-knowledge or anti-reason. Indeed the reflexive-modern individual is better educated, more knowledgeable than ever. Instead the type of knowledge at stake changes. It is itself precarious as distinct from certain, and what that knowledge is about is also uncertain – probabilistic, at best; more likely 'possibilistic'.

Beck has written extensively about globalization, about cosmopolitanism, in the years since the publication of *Risk Society* and *Reflexive Modernization* (1994). But Individualization and the individualization thesis more generally is not about the extensivity of the global, but instead the intensivity of the individual. Cosmopolitanism is in fact as much a property of the individual as it is of the global system. Indeed cosmopolitanism itself presumes a certain movement of strategic locus both extensively and intensively away from the nation-state. A number of chapters of this book thus address the family. What happens to the family in the second and reflexive modernity? What happens is to a certain extent a generalized outsourcing. In Beck's *Risk Society* or what John Urry and I at about the same time called 'disorganised capitalism', there is a generalized outsourcing of functions, of operations. The hierarchical economic organization begins to regularly make decisions, not to 'make' but to 'buy'. A whole host of functions of the firm are outsourced in this age of vertical disintegration. The welfare state begins to outsource functions onto private and charitable sector organizations. There is it seems also an outsourcing of the family. At stake here is first an anomic disorganization but then a new normalization, which again is a normalization that institutionalizes abnormality, institutionalizes not the normal but the state of exception (as Carl Schmitt might have it). It is in a sense a rou-tinization of Weberian charisma that winds up not as bureaucracy but instead as somewhat more regularisable charisma.

What is happening however is not just an outsourcing but also an insourcing. Anthony Giddens of course has always been well aware of this. A number of pro-perties, functions and activities previously attributable to the nation-state, the welfare state, the hierarchical firm, the family, and the centralized trade union have been otherwise located. Some of them have been extensively displaced onto global instances, while others have been intensively displaced, onto the individual, to conscious or unconscious subjectivity: in any sense more private instances. Even the shift of activities onto small forms have been such an inten-sification. Today's start-ups – not so much the dot.coms, but patent-generating technology firms and copyright-generating new media firms, have very private, personal and intense characteristics. They are not so to speak paternalistic as they were in the bygone days, not the least because women now run a number of them. It has to do with the fact that so many of the employees are freelance and sub-contractors and hence eminently individualize. It has to do with the individual not the paternalist charisma of firm leaders. These are not so to speak 'leaders of men', but risk takers and innovators.

So there is in our times an outsourcing of governance functions of the state, of national rights to become global rights, of accountancy organizations, of economic functions onto supra-national economic bodies, and supra-national cultural instances like the world-wide spread of biennales. There is just as much an offloading of functions onto private instances. Thus we have globalization, on the one hand, paralleled by individualization on the other – both as the constitutive features of the second modernity. In the first modernity the individual was constituted in consonance with a set of roles in a variety of institutions. Now these institutions are in crisis, and functions which were once taking place at the interface of institution and individual in the role are now taking place much more intensively and closer to the individual. What has happened is that there has been a de-normalization of roles. The individual has become, and Beck too uses this word, 'nomadic'. There has been a move toward complexity, indeed towards 'chaos'. But it is somehow a regularizable chaos. The 'roles' of the first modernity depended very much on what Kant called determinate judgement; on prescription, on determinate rules. Now the individual must be much more the rule finder himself. Determinate judgement is replaced by 'reflective judgement'. Reflective judgement is not reflection because there is now no universal to subsume the particular. In reflective judgement the individual must find the rule. Reflective judgement is always a question of uncertainty, of risk, but it also leaves the door open much more to innovation. Thus Beck and Beck *Der ganz normale Chaos der Liebe* has appeared perhaps misleadingly in English as *The Chaos of Love* (1995). The German title translates literally as 'The Totally Normal Chaos of Love' and this need to be taken seriously. Love here becomes dissociated from roles and hence chaotic. Yet this chaos becomes totally normal. Becomes regularized in a fashion. Becomes even more or less predictable. Yet at the same time it remains nonetheless chaos. Chaotic love, regularizable chaotic love is non-linear love to parallel the Beck's non-linear individualization.

This all leads to the question of institutions. Today's debates about globalization and cosmopolitanism have led to a considerable literature on the extensive outsourcing of, in this case, sovereignty. The pursuing for example of governance as discussed by Held, of economic functions as discussed by Sassen, of rights (Homi Bhabha). But what about institutions that regulate the above mentioned insourcing of functions. What kind of institutions can regulate what Beck and Beck since the early 1980s have understood under the heading of 'a life of one's own' (Eigenes Leben). What kind of institutions can regulate an individual whose differentia specifica is precisely not to be determined by the rules of institutions. What institutions can enable individuals to be reflexive in the sense of being rule-finders. At issue here is an individual that is not so much anomic as auto-nomic. And this is the 64-dollar question. Governance of second-modernity flows is always going to be a lot different than governance of first modernity structures. Perhaps at stake is a question of institutions so different that for us they are almost unrecognizable as institutions. It may make sense in this context to think in terms of two types of institutions: of institutions that proffer us two types of rules. Let us go back to the distinction between constitutive and regulative rules. Constitutive rules are those that let us play the game, much akin to constitutional law. Without them there is no playing field. Regulative rules are more prescriptive. What kind of constitutive rules, we may ask, are consistent with a set of regulative rules that do not regulate? What type of constitutive rule is consistent with a set of rule-finding, as distinct from rule-determining, activities? Perhaps new second modernity institutions must be comprised primarily of not regulative, but constitutive, rules. And in this sense they may not be recognizable to us as institutions.

It has become commonplace to say that in the global information age, in the second modernity, that power and inequality operate less through exploitation than exclusion. Beck is very cognisant of this with his notion of 'Brazilianization'. The point I am trying to make here is that exploitation takes place through regulative rules while exclusion take place through constitutive rules. This is consistent with Hardt and Negri's argument in *Empire* that the transition from one mode of production to another is governed less by class struggle than by 'lines of flight'. Here the subordinate class escapes literally as flight, flow, or flux away from the dominant class and its institutions. So perhaps the key institutions at stake in the second modernity are those that govern exclusion. And here is where I have my strongest quibble with Beck's work. I think that a great number of these characteristically second-modernity institutions, if that is the word for them, are now not solely social, but socio-technical. Now this is completely consistent with the technologization of science thesis that has been so prominent in Beck's work. Pivotal for me among the socio-technical (constitutive more than regulatory) institutions that govern contemporary power relations are platforms, operating systems, communications protocols, standards, intellectual property and the like. There is a certain awareness of such socio-technical institutions also in Elisabeth Beck's work on genetic databases in this book. But I do not think that the technological dimension is sufficiently taken on by the Becks. Nor the dimension and extent to which social relations are mediated through the (now interactive) mass and non-mass media of communications. Individualization, the Becks in this book argue, is a question of 'place-polygamy'. My point is that such place-polygamy is always necessarily technologically mediated, by cheaper air flights, by mobile phones, by microprocessors in various smart boxes, by protocols and channels enabling communication at a distance between individuals.

This brings me back to the centrality of non-linearity in Beck's notion of the individual. The first modernity was linear, the second non-linear. The first modernity a question of determinate judgement and rule following, the second a matter of rule finding and reflective judgement. There is as I argued above a very loose and implicit notion of complex (open in both senses) and non-linear systems in Beck's work. But these are always social systems. The point I want to make in this preface is that there has been a shift here, which again is implicitly addressed in Beck's work. In the fist modernity we were faced with relatively mutually exclusive and exhaustive systems: of (Parsonsian) social systems, on the one hand, and engineering-like technical systems, on the other. The second modernity's totally normal chaos is regulated by non-linear systems. It is also regulated by an extraordinarily powerful interlacing of social and technical systems: by, precisely, socio-technical systems. It is at the interface of the social and the technical that we find the second-modernity's individual. It is at this interface that we take on the precarious freedom of a 'life of our own'; that we 'invent the political', that we take on ecological responsibility. The individual in the second modernity is profoundly a socio-technical subject.

Scott Lash
April 2001
London

This introduction draws on a number of long discussions with Jakob Arnoldi and June Hee Jung. I am grateful to them for a number of points here. The judgements here however are my own, and they should not be held responsible for them.

To be fair to Giddens, his notion of agency has important dimensions of non linearity, especially with the centrality of unintended consequences and the individual as experiment in his work.

Foreword by Zygmunt Bauman:
Individually, Together

The title given by Norbert Elias to his last, posthumously published study, 'Society of individuals', flawlessly grasps the gist of the problem which has haunted social theory since its inception. Breaking with the tradition established with Hobbes and reforged by John Stuart Mill, Herbert Spencer and the liberal orthodoxy into the *doxa* – the unexamined frame for all further cognition – of our century, Elias replaced the 'and' and the 'versus' with the 'of'; and by so doing he shifted the discourse from the *imaginaire* of the two forces locked in a mortal, yet unending battle of freedom and domination, into that of 'reciprocal conception': society shaping the individuality of its members and the individuals forming society out of their life actions while pursuing strategies plausible and feasible within the socially woven web of their dependencies.

Casting members as individuals is the trademark of modern society. That casting, however, was not a one-off act. It is an activity re-enacted daily. Modern society exists in its activity of 'individualizing', as much as the activities of individuals consist in that daily reshaping and renegotiating of their mutual engagements which is called 'society'. Neither of the two partners stays put for long. And so the meaning of 'individualization' keeps changing, taking on ever new shapes – as the accumulated results of its past history set ever new rules and turn out ever new stakes of the game. 'Individualization' now means something very different from what it meant 100 years ago and what it conveyed in the early times of the modern era – the times of extolled human 'emancipation' from the tightly knit web of communal dependency, surveillance and enforcement.

Ulrich Beck's 'Jenseits von Stand und Klasse ?' (1983),[1] and a few years later his *Risikogesellschaft: Auf den Weg in eine andere Moderne*, as well as Elisabeth Beck-Gernsheim's *Vom Dasein für andere zum Anspruch auf ein Stück 'eigenes Leben' – Individualisierungsprozesse in weiblichen Lebenszusammenhäng* (1983),[2] opened a new chapter in our understanding of the 'individualization process'. The works presented this process and an ongoing and unfinished history with its distinct stages – without a 'telos' or preordained destination but with an erratic logic of sharp twists and turns instead. It can be said that just as Elias 'historicized' Sigmund Freud's theory of the civilized individual, exploring civilization as an event in (modern) history, so Beck historicized Elias's account of the birth of the individual by representing that birth as an aspect of the continuous and continuing, compulsive and obsessive *modernization*. Beck also set the portrayal of individualization free from the time-bound, transient accoutrements that now becloud the understanding more than they clarify the picture (first and foremost, from the vision of linear development or 'progress' plotted along the axes of emancipation, growing autonomy and freedom of self-assertion), thereby opening to scrutiny the variety of historical tendencies of individualization and their products and allowing a better comprehension of the distinctive features of its current stage.

To put it in a nutshell, 'individualization' consists in transforming human 'identity' from a 'given' into a 'task' – and charging the actors with the responsibility for performing that task and for the consequences (also the side-effects) of their performance: in other words, it consists in establishing a *de jure* autonomy (although not necessarily a *de facto* one). No more are human beings 'born into' their identities; as Jean-Paul Sartre famously put it: it is not enough to be born a bourgeois, one must live one's life as a bourgeois. (The same did not need to be said, nor could it have been, about the princes, knights, serfs or townsmen of the pre-modern era!) Needing to *become* what one *is* is the hallmark of modern living – and of this living alone (not of modern 'individualization' – that expression being evidently pleonastic; to speak of individualization and of modernity is to speak of the same social condition). Modernity replaces determination of social standing with compulsive and obligatory self-determination.

This holds for 'individualization' in all its renditions and for the whole of the modern era; for all periods and all sectors of society. Yet within that shared predicament there are significant variations, which set apart denizens of successive periods as well as various categories of actors co-inhabiting the same historical stage. The task of 'self-identification' set before men and women of the early modern era, once the stiff frames of estates had been broken, boiled down to the challenge of living 'true to kind' ('up with the Joneses'); of actively conforming to the established social types and models of conduct; of imitating, following the pattern, 'acculturating', not falling out of step, not deviating from the norm. 'Estates' came to be replaced by 'classes'. While the former were a matter of ascription, membership of the latter contained a large measure of achievement; classes, unlike estates, had to be 'joined' and the membership had to be constantly renewed, reconfirmed and documented in day-to-day conduct.

One may say in retrospect that the class division (or gender division for that matter) was a by-product of unequal access to resources required to render self-assertion effective. Classes differed in the range of identities available and in the facility of choice between them. People endowed with fewer resources, and thus with less choice, had to compensate for their individual weakness by the 'power of numbers' – by closing ranks and engaging in collective action. As Claus Offe pointed out, collective, class-oriented action came to those lower down the social ladder as 'naturally' and 'matter-of-factly' as individual pursuit of their life-goals came to their employers.

Deprivations, so to speak, 'added up' and congealed in 'common interests' – and were seen as amenable solely to a collective remedy: 'collectivism' was a first-choice strategy for those on the receiving end of individualization yet unable to self-assert as individuals deploying their own, individually owned, blatantly inadequate resources. The class orientation of the better-off was, contrariwise, partial and, in a sense, derivative; it came to the fore mostly when the unequal distribution of resources was challenged and contested. It can be said, however, that by and large the 'disembedded' individuals of the classic 'modernity' era deployed their new empowerment and the entitlements of autonomous agency in the frantic search for 're-embeddedment'. And there was no shortage of 'beds' waiting and ready to accommodate them. Class allocation, though formed and negotiable rather than inherited or simply 'born into' as the *Stände* used to be, tended to become as solid, unalterable and resistant to individual manipulation as the pre-modern assignment to the estate. Class and gender hung heavily over the individual range of choices; to escape their constraint was not much easier than to contest one's place in the 'divine chain of being'. To all intents and purposes, class and gender were 'facts of nature' and the task left to the self-assertion of most individuals was to 'fit in' – that is, fit into the allocated niche by behaving as the other occupants did.

This is, precisely, what distinguishes the 'individualization' of yore from the form it has taken in *Risikogesellschaft*, in terms of 'reflexive modernity' or 'second modernity' (as Ulrich Beck variously calls the contemporary era). No 'beds' are left to 're-embed' – not for long at any rate. There are instead 'musical chairs' of various sizes and styles as well as of changing numbers and positions, forcing men and women to be constantly on the move and promising no rest and no satisfaction on 'arrival', no comfort on reaching the destination where one can disarm, relax and stop worrying. There is no 're-embeddedment' prospect at the end of the road taken by (now chronically) disembedded individuals.

Let there be no mistake: now, as before, individualization is a fate, not a choice; in the land of individual freedom of choice, the option to escape individualization and to refuse participation in the individualizing game is emphatically *not* on the agenda. That men and women have no one to blame for their frustrations and troubles does not mean, any more than it did in the past, that they can protect themselves against frustration by using their own domestic appliances or pull themselves out of trouble, like Baron Münchhausen, by their bootstraps. If they fall ill, it is because they were not resolute or industrious enough in following a health regime. If they stay unemployed, it is because they failed to learn the skills of winning an interview or because they did not try hard enough to find a job or because they are, purely and simply, work-shy. If they are not sure about their career prospects and agonize about their future, it is because they are not good enough at winning friends and influencing people and have failed to learn as they should the arts of self-expression and impressing others. This is, at any rate, what they are told and what they have come to believe – so that they behave '*als ob*', 'as if', this were indeed the truth of the matter. As Beck aptly and poignantly puts it: 'How ones lives becomes a *biographical solution to systemic contradictions.*' Risks and contradictions go on being socially produced; it is just the duty and the necessity to cope with them that is being individualized.

To cut a long story short: there is a growing gap between individuality as fate and individuality as practical capacity for self-assertion (as 'individuation', the term selected by Beck to distinguish the self-sustained and self-propelled individual from a merely 'individualized' individual, that is, a human being who has no choice but to act as if the individuation had not been attained); and bridging that gap is, most crucially, *not* part of that capacity.

The self-assertive ability of individualized men and women falls short, as a rule, of what a genuine self-constitution would require. As Leo Strauss observed, the other face of unencumbered freedom is insignificance of choice – the two faces conditioning each other: why bother to prohibit what is anyway of little consequence? A cynical observer would say that freedom comes when it matters no more. There is a nasty fly of impotence in the ointment of freedom shaped through the pressures of individualization; that impotence is felt as all the more odious and upsetting in view of the empowerment that freedom was expected to deliver.

Perhaps, as in the past, standing shoulder and marching step would offer a remedy? Perhaps if individual powers, however wan and meagre, are condensed into a collective stand and action, things will be done jointly which no man or woman on their own could dream of doing? The snag is, though, that the most common troubles of the individuals-by-fate are these days *not additive*. They simply do not sum up into a 'common cause'. They are shaped from the beginning in such a way as to lack the edges allowing them to dovetail with other people's troubles. Troubles may be similar (and the increasingly popular chat-shows go out of their way to demonstrate their similarity and to hammer home the message that their most important similarity lies in being handled by each sufferer on his or her own), but they do *not* form a totality 'greater than the sum of its parts', and acquire no new, easier to handle quality through being confronted together. The sole advantage the company of other sufferers may bring is to reassure each one that fighting troubles alone is what all the others do daily – and so to reinvigorate the flagging resolve to go on doing just that. One may perhaps also learn from other people's experience how to survive the next round of 'downsizing', how to handle children who think they are adolescents and adolescents who refuse to become adults, how to get fat and other unwelcome 'foreign bodies' 'out of one's system', how to get rid of a no longer satisfying addiction or a no longer pleasurable partner. But what one learns in the first place from the company of others is that the only service which company can render is advice about how to survive in one's own irreparable solitude and that everyone's life is full of risks which need to be confronted and fought alone.

So there is another snag as well. As de Tocqueville long suspected, setting people free may make them *indifferent*. The individual is the citizen's worst enemy de Tocqueville suggested. The individual tends to be lukewarm, sceptical or wary of 'common good', 'good society' or 'just society'. What is the sense of 'common interests' except allowing each individual to satisfy his or her own? Whatever else individuals may do when coming together portends constraint on their freedom to pursue what they see fit for themselves and won't help such pursuit anyway. The only two useful things one would expect, and wish, from the 'public power' to deliver are to observe human rights (that is, to let everyone go his or her own way) and to enable everyone to do it in peace – by guarding the security of his or her body and possessions safe, locking up criminals in prison and keeping the streets free of muggers, perverts, beggars and obnoxious and malevolent strangers.

With his usual inimitable wit, Woody Allen unerringly grasps the fads and foibles of late-modern individuals-by-decree, when browsing through imaginary leaflets advertising 'adult summer courses' which Americans would be eager to attend. The course in economic theory includes the item 'Inflation and depression – how to dress for each'. The course in ethics entails 'the categorical imperative, and six ways to make it work for you' and the prospectus for astronomy informs one: 'The sun, which is made of gas, can explode at any moment, sending our entire planet system hurtling to destruction; students are advised what the average citizen can do in such a case.'

To sum up: the other side of individualization seems to be the corrosion and slow disintegration of citizenship. Joël Roman, co-editor of *Esprit*, points out in his recent book (*La Démocratie des Individus*, 1998) that 'vigilance is degraded to the point of surveillance, engaging collective emotions and fear of the neighbour' – and urges people to seek a 'renewed capacity for deciding together', a capacity now conspicuous mostly by its absence.

If the individual is the citizen's worst enemy and if individualization spells trouble for citizenship and citizenship-based politics, it is because the concerns and preoccupations of individuals qua individuals fill the public space, claiming to be its only legitimate occupants and elbowing out from public discourse everything else. The 'public' is colonized by the 'private'; 'public interest' is reduced to curiosity about the private lives of public figures and the art of public life is tapered to the public display of private affairs and public confessions of private sentiments (the more intimate the better). 'Public issues' which resist such reduction become all but incomprehensible.

The prospects for a 're-embedding' of individualized actors in the republican body of citizenship are dim. What prompts them to venture onto the public stage is not so much a search for common causes and ways to negotiate the meaning of the common good and the principles of life in common, as a desperate need for 'networking'. The sharing of intimacies, as Richard Sennett keeps pointing out, tends to be the preferred, perhaps the only remaining, method of 'community-building'. This building technique can spawn 'communities' only as fragile and short-lived, scattered and wandering emotions, shifting erratically from one target to another and drifting in the forever inconclusive search for a secure haven; communities of shared worries, shared anxieties or shared hatreds – but in each case a 'peg' community, a momentary gathering around a nail on which many solitary individuals hang their solitary individual fears. As Ulrich Beck puts it (in his essay 'On the mortality of industrial society'[3]): 'What emerges from the fading social norms is naked, frightened, aggressive ego in search of love and help. In the search for itself and for an affectionate sociality, it easily gets lost in the jungle of the self... Someone who is poking around in the fog of his or her own self is no longer capable of noticing that this isolation, this "solitary confinement of the ego", is a mass sentence.'

Individualization is here to stay; all thinking about the means to deal with its impact on the way we all conduct our lives must start from acknowledgement of this fact. Individualization brings to the ever growing number of men and women an unprecedented freedom of experimenting – but (*timeo danaos et dona ferentes…*) it also brings an unprecedented task of coping with the consequences. The yawning gap between the right of self-assertion and the capacity to control the social settings which render such self-assertion feasible or unrealistic seems to be the main contradiction of the 'second modernity' – one which, through trial and error, critical reflection and bold experimentation, we must collectively learn to tackle collectively.

In *The Reinvention of Politics*,[4] Ulrich Beck suggests that nothing less than 'another Reformation' is needed and that this calls for the 'radicalization of modernity'. He proposes that 'this assumes social inventions and collective courage in political experiments' – only to add at once that these 'inclinations and qualities… are not exactly frequently encountered, and are perhaps no longer even capable of garnering a majority'. Yet here we are: we have no other conditions in which to act. And in these conditions, like it or not, act we will, bearing the consequences of our actions or our failure to act.

Zygmunt Bauman
February 1999

Notes

1 See Chapter 3 in this volume.
2 See Chapter 5 in this volume.
3 In U. Beck, *Ecological Enlightenment: Essays on the Politics of the Risk Society*. Atlantic Highlands, NJ: Humanities Press, 1995.
4 U. Beck, *The Reinvention of Politics*. Cambridge: Polity Press, 1997.

Authors' Preface:
Institutionalized Individualism

An international dispute about fundamental principles is raging beneath the surface in the social sciences. One side starts from the idea that the social and political landscape has fundamentally changed, at the latest since the collapse of the Berlin Wall and the Soviet empire in 1989, but that this has not been reflected in sociology and political science. The other side, the majority, sees no sign of an 'epochal shift' and argues that modernity has always been another word for crisis; feeling outraged and insulted, it continues as before, only with still more figures and still better methods. There is no doubt that, when this dispute breaks into the open and rouses the national and international sociological congresses from their Sleeping Beauty world, it will revitalize the discipline and help it to regain public attention.

The essays collected in this volume document the position of two authors who *do* think there has been a categorical break. In our view, the suppression of the new is one of the great traumas of modern capitalism; it has brought forth a huge structure of postponement and denial, which claims that everything remains as it was. As the result of a more radical process of 'reflexive modernization',[1] however, a fundamental change is occurring in the nature of the social and political – an erosion of anthropological certitudes which compels the social sciences to modify their theoretical tools and even to reinvent the social sciences themselves, in a collaborative division of labour with history, geography, anthropology, economics and natural science.[2] This is a far-reaching supposition, of course. But the crucial question is how, beyond the mere assertion of an epochal break, sociology can strengthen its theoretical, methodological and organizational foundations by making them more concrete or focused, and in this way ultimately renew its claim to another enlightenment.

The keyword in this international controversy is *globalization*. The consequences of this for society (and sociology) have been spelt out most clearly in the English-speaking countries, but above all in Britain, where it has been forcefully argued that conventional social and political science remains caught up in a national-territorial concept of society. Critics of 'methodological nationalism' have attacked its explicit or implicit premise that the national state is the 'container' of social processes and that the national framework is still the one best suited to measure and analyse major social, economic and political changes.[3] The social sciences are thus found guilty of 'embedded statism',[4] and thought is given to a reorganization of the interdisciplinary field.

Within a different perspective, a comparable critique of the conceptual bases of social science has been conducted since the mid-1980s in the German-language area under the keyword *individualization*, although its empirical and theoretical scope has not yet been registered in the English-speaking countries. The discussion of *Risk Society*,[5] for example, has centred mainly on the risk argument (Part 1) and little or not at all on the individualization argument (Part 2).[6] The present volume is an attempt to remedy this gap. If the globalization debate took up the territorial bias, the individualization debate has probed and criticized the *collective* bias of the social sciences.

One can hardly think of a word heavier with misunderstandings than 'individualization' has proved to have in the English-speaking countries. To prevent the discussion of this book from running aground on these misunderstandings, it is necessary to establish and keep in view the distinction between the *neoliberal idea of the free-market individual* (inseparable from the concept of 'individualization' as used in the English-speaking countries) and the concept of *Individualisierung* in the sense of *institutionalized individualism*, as it will be developed in this book.

Neoliberal economics rests upon an image of the autarkic human self. It assumes that individuals alone can master the whole of their lives, that they derive and renew their capacity for action from within themselves. Talk of the 'self-entrepreneur' makes this clear. Yet this ideology blatantly conflicts with everyday experience in (and sociological studies of) the worlds of work, family and local community, which show that the individual is not a monad but is self-*in*sufficient and increasingly tied to others, including at the level of world-wide networks and institutions. The ideological notion of the self-sufficient individual ultimately implies the disappearance of any sense of mutual obligation – which is why neoliberalism inevitably threatens the welfare state. A sociological understanding of *Individualisierung* is thus intimately bound up with the question of how individuals can demystify this false image of autarky. It is not freedom of choice, but insight into the fundamental incompleteness of the self, which is at the core of individual and political freedom in the second modernity.

The *social-scientific* sense of 'individualization' should thus be distinguished from the neoliberal sense. A history of sociology could be written in terms of how its principal theorists – from Marx through Weber, Durkheim and Simmel to Parsons, Foucault, Elias, Luhmann, Habermas and Giddens – have varied the basic idea that individualization is a product of complex, contingent and thus high-level socialization.[7] For although they tell quite different – some optimistically, many pessimistically tinged – narratives of individualization, and although some see it as a danger to society and/or individuality itself, the red thread running through them all is that individualization (a) is a structural characteristic of highly differentiated societies and (b) does not endanger their integration but actually makes it possible. The individual creativity which it releases is seen as creating space for the renewal of society under conditions of radical change. In developed modernity – to be quite blunt about it – human mutuality and community rest no longer on solidly established traditions, but, rather, on a paradoxical collectivity of reciprocal individualization.

In this book, the concept of 'individualization' will be deployed in this sociological sense of institutionalized individualism. Central institutions of modern society – basic civil, political and social rights, but also paid employment and the training and mobility necessary for it – are geared to the individual and not to the group. Insofar as basic rights are internalized and everyone wants to or must be economically active to earn their livelihood, the spiral of individualization destroys the given foundations of social coexistence. So – to give a simple definition – 'individualization' means disembedding without reembedding.

But what then is specific about individualization and second modernity? In second modern society the separation between subjective and objective analysis, consciousness and class, *Überbau* and *Unterbau* is losing its significance. Individualization can no longer be understood as a mere subjective reality which has to be relativated by and confronted with objective class analysis. Because individualization not only effects the *Überbau* – ideology, false consciousness – but also the economic *Unterbau* of 'real classes'; the individual is becoming the basic unit of social reproduction for the first time in history.

To put it in a nutshell – individualization is becoming *the social structure of second modern society itself*. Institutionalized individualism is no longer Talcott Parsons' idea of linear self-reproducing systems; it means the paradox of an 'individualizing structure' as a non-linear, open-ended, highly ambivalent, ongoing process. It relates to a decline of narratives of given sociability. Thus the theoretical collectivisms of sociology ends. A 'microfoundation of macrosciology' (Collins) may not be possible. But sociology as an institutionalized rejection of individualism is no longer possible either.

So what does individualization *beyond* the collective bias of the social science mean? An institutionalized imbalance between the disembedded individual and global problems in a global risk society. The Western type of individualized society tells us *to seek biographical solutions to systemic contradictions*. For example, the tension in family life today is the fact that equality of men and women cannot be created in an institutional family structure which presupposes and enforces their inequality.

But does this not mean that everyone just revolves around themselves, forgetting how much they rely on others for the assertion of their own push-and-shove freedom? Certainly the stereotype in people's heads is that individualization breeds a me-first society, but, as we will try to show, this is a false, one-sided picture of what actually happens in the family, gender relationships, love and sex, youth and old age. There are also signs that point towards an ethic of 'altruistic individualism'. Anyone who wants to live a life of their own must also be socially sensitive to a very high degree.

To adapt Habermas's concept of an 'ideal speech situation', we might speak here of an 'ideal intimacy situation'. If the former refers to general norms, the latter establishes specific rules for the intimate interactions involved in relationships, marriage, parenthood, friendship and the family – a normative horizon of expectations of reciprocal individuation which, having emerged under conditions of cultural democratization, must be counterfactually assumed and sustained.[8] The result is that 'natural' living conditions and inequalities become political. For example, the division of labour in the family or workplace can no longer claim to be a 'natural' matter of course; like much else besides, it must be negotiated and justified. But part of the same phenomenon is the right to a life of one's own (space, time and money of one's own) within relationships and the family. The issues of fairness and recognition of the other's identity thus become highly charged or 'jinxed' as they get caught up in the partners' distribution of daily tasks and career chances, and as the 'family' more and more becomes the rubbish bin for all the social problems around the world that cannot be solved in any other way.

The French sociologist Jean-Claude Kaufmann once asked what actually constitutes a couple now that it is no longer a marriage certificate. His answer was that a couple arises when two people buy one washing-machine together, instead of two separate ones. It is then that the long-term breakdown over the 'dirty washing' begins.[9] What counts as dirty? Who washes when and for whom? Does it have to be ironed? What if he says yes and she says no? Everything can be negotiated – but then again not. By the same token, any kind of discussion presupposes shared meanings that cannot simply be placed in doubt; limits must therefore be set to argument and confrontation if you want to live with somebody on a daily basis. The 'dirty washing' issue, however, makes people feel bad. The partner who shuts up and washes is swallowing the fact that the pain of injustice will ultimately suffocate the love.

The separation which then becomes necessary (and is always there as a danger) often does not take place in a 'socially sensitive' manner. But it involves an awakening of, or a fight for, co-operative individualism, which presupposes that each has a right to a life of his or her own and that the terms of living together have to be renegotiated in each case. The twofold search for individuation, which is often unsuccessful, might be termed the *freedom culture*. This daily culture of freedom also has political implications, for it stands in blatant contradiction with the global victory of neoliberalism. The smouldering conflict is called 'capitalism or freedom' (in an inverted allusion to the old conservative election motto: 'Freedom or Socialism!'). The freedom culture is in danger of being destroyed by capitalism.

Many will notice that the dimension of power, of the relationship between power and subjectivity, is missing from this book. The idea comes from Hegel that people at the top of society also develop a richer subjectivity. In modern management, this takes the sharper form that anyone climbing the career ladder not only knows better what he wants, but forgets that he depends on those he has left behind; he lives in the illusion that he can do the job of anyone else working for him. At the same time, the new capitalism intensifies social inequalities throughout the world and changes their historical characteristics. Marx spoke of the proletariat and had in mind the need of capital for cheap labour power. But today this seems to be less and less the case: global capital, in bidding farewell to unskilled labour, dismisses more and more people into a state beyond society in which their services are no longer needed (by the labour market).

This suggests the following objection. The farewell to class conceptualized by individualization theory may have been applicable yesterday, but it is no longer applicable today and will be invalid tomorrow. The concept of class, so often pronounced dead, has been undergoing a renaissance in the new global context. For the new inequalities growing worldwide are also a collective experience.

That is precisely the question. For paradoxically, it is the individualization and fragmentation of growing inequalities into separate biographies which is a collective experience.[10] The concept of class actually *plays down* the situation of growing inequalities *without* collective ties. Class, social layer, gender presuppose a collective moulding of individual behaviour – the old idea that, by knowing that someone was a Siemens apprentice, you also knew the things he said, the way he dressed and enjoyed himself, what he read and how he voted. This chain syllogism has now become questionable. Under conditions of individualization, the point is rather to work out if and when new collective forms of action take shape, and which forms they are. The key question, therefore – to which this book also knows no answer – is how the bubbling, contradictory process of individualization and denationalization can be cast into new democratic forms of organization.

It would be a big mistake, however, to equate the crisis of the concept of class with a denial of increasing inequalities. In fact basing ourselves on individualization theory, we investigate and think out the opposite notion: that social inequality is on the rise precisely because of the spread of individualization. Instead of suppressing the question of how collectivity can be generated in global modernity, or shifting it into the premises of a sociology based upon uncertain class collectives, the non-class character of individualized inequalities poses it in a more radical way. There are further questions that stand out in individualization theory, even if it often has no answer to them.

No doubt the question of the *frontiers* of individualization is becoming ever more pressing. Many think that objective limits of collectivity are set in advance, rather as there are natural limits to growth, and this suggests that the limits of individualization should be sought in the individualization process itself – that, to put it mechanically, the more people are individualized, the more they produce de-individualizing consequences for others. Take the case of a woman who files for divorce and whose husband finds himself facing a void. In the tussle over the children, each one tries to impose on the other the dictates of his or her life. Not only is there a positive sum game of co-individualization; probably more often there is also a negative sum game of contra-individualization. It would seem reasonable to suppose that the irritation caused by the other's resistance strengthens the urge for a new, and perhaps seemingly 'democratic', authoritarianism.

If we now circle back to our starting-point – the coming sociological dispute over continuity or discontinuity – the point at issue can be identified more clearly. To the extent that modern society and modern sociology are experiencing a change in their foundations, the suspicion arises – in relation to *all* social science and all special areas of sociology – that they are largely operating with *zombie* or living-dead categories which blind them to the realities and contradictions of globalizing and individualizing modernities. This idea is developed here in a concluding interview, which could just as well be read as an introduction.

A few of the essays contained in this book were written in the 1980s, but most of them date from the 1990s and have been taken up in the still heated debate on individualization. Chapter 1, 'Losing the traditional: Individualization and "precarious freedoms"' and Chapter 2, 'A life of one's own in a runaway world', introduce the theme of the book. Chapters 3 and 4 – 'Beyond status and class?' and 'The ambivalent social structure' – then develop and discuss the connection between individualization and growing social inequalities. Chapters 5 to 7 – 'From "living for others" to "a life of one's own"', 'On the way to a post-familial family' and 'Division of labour, self-image and life projects' – turn the individualization argument in a feminist direction and apply it to such issues as the family, love and the male-female division of labour. Chapters 8 and 9 – 'Declining birthrates and the wish to have children' and 'Apparatuses do not care for people' – discuss some of the implications for birthrates, the wish to have children and associated dilemmas in the planning of everyday life. Chapters 10 and 11 – 'Health and responsibility in the age of genetic technology' and 'Death of one's own, life of one's own' – illustrate the individualization thesis from the points of view of human genetics and death. Chapters 12 and 13 – 'Freedom's children' and 'Freedom's fathers' – discuss and reinterpret the individualization argument as it has a bearing on young people and investigate its intellectual roots in the past.

Notes

1 See U. Beck, A. Giddens and S. Lash, *Reflexive Modernization*. Cambridge: Polity Press, 1994; U. Beck, *The Reinvention of Politics*. Cambridge: Polity Press, 1997, Chapter 1; U. Beck (in conversation with J. Willms) *Freiheit oder Kapitalismus – Gesellschaft neu denken*. Frankfurt/M.: Suhrkamp, 2000; and U. Beck and W. Bonß, *Die Modernisierung der Moderne*. Frankfurt/M.: Suhrkamp, 2001.

2 P. J. Taylor, 'Embedded statism and the social sciences: opening up to new spaces'. *Environment and Planning*, 28, 1996, pp. 1917–1995; and *British Journal of Sociology*, 1, 2000.

3 See U. Beck, *What Is Globalization?* Cambridge: Polity Press, 2000.

4 Taylor, 1996; N. Brenner, 'Global cities and glocal states'. *Review of International Political Economy*, 5, 1,1998.

5 U. Beck, *Risk Society: Towards a New Modernity*. London: Sage, 1992.

6. See also Beck, *The Reinvention of Politics*. Chapters 2 and 4.

7 M. Schroer, *Die Individuen der Gesellschaft*. Frankfurt: Suhrkamp, 2001.

8 U. Beck and E. Beck-Gernsheim, *The Normal Chaos of Love*. Cambridge: Polity Press, 1995; A. Giddens, *The Transformation of Intimacy*. Cambridge: Polity Press, 1992.

9 J. -C. Kaufmann, *Schmutzige Wäsche*. Konstanz: Universitätsverlag, 1992.

10 L. Leisering and S. Leibfried, *Time and Poverty in Western Welfare States*. Cambridge: Polity Press, 1999.

We shared the writing of this book between vs as follows: Chapter 1 was written jointly. Chapters 2, 3, 4, 11, 12, 13, and 14 were written by Ulrich Beck, and Chapters 5, 6, 7, 8, 9, and 10 were written by Elisabeth Beck-Gernsheim.

1

Losing the Traditional

Individualization and 'Precarious Freedoms'

What does 'Individualization of Lifestyles' Mean?

'Only the day before yesterday, only four years ago, a grand experiment for humanity that had lasted forty years came to an end here.' These words were spoken in Luther's town of Wittenberg by Friedrich Schorlemmer at the end of 1993.

> Seventeen million Germans lived in the walled province in enforced collectivization. A one-party state was seen as the highest form of freedom, individualization was damned as subjectivism. A risk-taking approach to the future was rejected in the name of 'scientific' optimism. The 'victors of history' were to set the norms and strive towards a unitary society (the socialist community). Human beings, understood as ceaselessly active communal creatures, were fed on the safe goal of communism, which was guaranteed by scientific laws. People were not allowed to decide anything because there was nothing left to decide, because history had already decided everything 'up there'. But they did not need to decide, either.
>
> Now, in freedom, they may and must decide for themselves; all the existing institutions have collapsed, all the old certainties are gone . The joy of freedom is at the same time a falling into a void. Now let everyone look after himself. What are the rules? Who's in charge? Those who have, and who know how to increase what they have. Seventeen million people have reached this point, but the West's caravan moves on, calling out: 'Come with us. We know the way. We know the goal. We don't know any way. We don't know any goal. What is certain? That everything's uncertain, precarious. Enjoy our lack of ties as freedom.' (1993: 1)

The development in China is different, yet in many ways similar. There, too, the collective system that provided a guaranteed income, the 'iron rice-bowl', is breaking down. Earlier, people had hardly any scope for choice in private or professional life, but the minimal safety net of Communism offered them state-subsidized accommodation, training and health care. It is this state care from the cradle to the grave, tied to the work collective in the factory or on the land, that is now disintegrating. Its place is being taken by contracts linking income and job security to ability and performance. People are now expected to take their lives into their own hands and to pay a market price for services they receive. 'The constant refrain among urban Chinese is that they can no longer keep up with the quickened pace of life. They are confused by shifting values and outlooks on such fundamentals as careers, marriage and family relations' (Sun, 1993: 5).

Whatever we consider – God, nature, truth, science, technology, morality, love, marriage – modern life is turning them all into 'precarious freedoms'. All metaphysics and transcendence, all necessity and certainty are being replaced by artistry. In the most public and the most private ways we are helplessly becoming high-wire dancers in the circus tent. And many of us fall. Not only in the West, but in the countries that have abruptly opened their doors to Western ways of life. People in the former GDR, in Poland, Russia or China, are caught up in a dramatic 'plunge into modernity'.

Such examples, seemingly remote to citizens of the old Federal German Republic, point nevertheless to a dynamic that is familiar to us, too. Schorlemmer's address contains the catch-word 'individualization'. This concept implies a group of social developments and experiences characterized, above all, by two meanings. In intellectual debate as in reality these meanings constantly intersect and overlap (which, hardly surprisingly, has given rise to a whole series of misunderstandings and controversies). On the one hand, individualization means the disintegration of previously existing social forms – for example, the increasing fragility of such categories as class and social status, gender roles, family, neighbourhood etc. Or, as in the case of the GDR and other states of the Eastern bloc, it means the collapse of state-sanctioned normal biographies, frames of reference, role models. Wherever such tendencies towards disintegration show themselves the question also arises: which new modes of life are coming into being where the old ones, ordained by religion, tradition or the state, are breaking down?

The answer points to the second aspect of individualization. It is, simply, that in modern societies new demands, controls and constraints are being imposed on individuals. Through the job market, the welfare state and institutions, people are tied into a network of regulations, conditions, provisos. From pension rights to insurance protection, from educational grants to tax rates: all these are institutional reference points marking out the horizon within which modern thinking, planning and action must take place.

Individualization in this sense, therefore, certainly does not mean an 'unfettered logic of action, juggling in a virtually empty space'; neither does it mean mere 'subjectivity', an attitude which refuses to see that 'beneath the surface of life is a highly efficient, densely woven institutional society'.[1] On the contrary, the space in which modern subjects deploy their options is anything but a non-social sphere. The density of regulations informing modern society is well known, even notorious (from the MOT test and the tax return to the laws governing the sorting of refuse). In its overall effect it is a work of art of labyrinthine complexity, which accompanies us literally from the cradle to the grave.

The decisive feature of these modern regulations or guidelines is that, far more than earlier, individuals must, in part, supply them for themselves, import them into their biographies through their own actions. This has much to do with the fact that traditional guidelines often contained severe restrictions or even prohibitions on action (such as the ban on marriage, in pre-industrial societies, which prevented members of non-property-owning groups from marrying; or the travel restrictions and the recent obstructions to marriage in the Eastern bloc states, which forbade contact with the 'class enemy'). By contrast, the institutional pressures in modern

Western society tend rather to be offers of services or incentives to action – take, for example, the welfare state, with its unemployment benefit, student grants or mortgage relief. To simplify: one was born into traditional society and its preconditions (such as social estate and religion). For modern social advantages one has to do something, to make an active effort. One has to win, know how to assert oneself in the competition for limited resources – and not only once, but day after day.

The normal biography thus becomes the 'elective biography', the 'reflexive biography', the 'do-it-yourself biography'.[2] This does not necessarily happen by choice, neither does it necessarily succeed. The do-it-yourself biography is always a 'risk biography', indeed a 'tightrope biography', a state of permanent (partly overt, partly concealed) endangerment. The façade of prosperity, consumption, glitter can often mask the nearby precipice. The wrong choice of career or just the wrong field, compounded by the downward spiral of private misfortune, divorce, illness, the repossessed home – all this is merely called bad luck. Such cases bring into the open what was always secretly on the cards: the do-it-yourself biography can swiftly become the breakdown biography. The preordained, unquestioned, often enforced ties of earlier times are replaced by the principle: 'until further notice'. As Bauman (1993) puts it:

> Nowadays everything seems to conspire against… lifelong projects, permanent bonds, eternal alliances, immutable identities. I cannot build for the long term on my job, my profession or even my abilities. I can bet on my job being cut, my profession changing out of all recognition, my skills being no longer in demand. Nor can a partnership or family provide a basis in the future. In the age of what Anthony Giddens has called 'confluent love', togetherness lasts no longer than the gratification of one of the partners, ties are from the outset only 'until further notice', today's intense attachment makes tomorrow's frustration only the more violent.

A kind of 'vagrant's morality' thus becomes a characteristic of the present. The vagrant:

> does not know how long he will remain where he is, and it is not usually he who decides the length of his stay. He chooses his goals as he goes along, as they turn up and as he reads them off the signposts. But even then he does not know for sure whether he is going to take a rest at the next stopping-point, or for how long. He only knows that his stay is unlikely to be a long one. What drives him on is disappointment with the last place he stopped at, and the never-dying hope that the next, as yet unvisited place, or perhaps the one after that, will be free of the defects which have spoiled the ones up to now. (Bauman, 1993: 17)

Are such portrayals, as some suspect, signs of egoism and hedonism, of an ego fever rampant in the West? Looking more closely, we find that another feature of the guidelines of modernity is that they act against, rather than for, family cohesion. Most of the rights and entitlements to support by the welfare state are designed for individuals rather than for families. In many cases they presuppose employment (or, in the case of the unemployed, willingness to work). Employment in turn implies education and both of these presuppose mobility or willingness to move. By all these requirements individuals are not so much compelled as peremptorily invited to constitute themselves as individuals: to plan, understand, design themselves and act as individuals – or, should they 'fail', to lie as individuals on the bed they have made for themselves. The welfare state is in this sense an experimental apparatus for conditioning ego-related lifestyles. The common good may well be injected into people's hearts as a compulsory inoculation, but the litany of the lost sense of community that is just now being publicly intoned once more, continues to talk with a forked tongue, with a double moral standard, as long as the mechanism of individualization remains intact and no one either wishes or is able to call it seriously into question.

Here, again, we find the same picture: decisions, possibly undecidable ones, within guidelines that lead into dilemmas – but decisions which place the individual, as an individual, at the centre and correspondingly penalize traditional lifestyles and behaviour.

Seen in this way, individualization is a social condition which is not arrived at by a free decision of individuals. To adapt Jean-Paul Sartre's phrase: people are condemned to individualization. Individualization is a compulsion, albeit a paradoxical one, to create, to stage manage, not only one's own biography but the bonds and networks surrounding it and to do this amid changing preferences and at successive stages of life, while constantly adapting to the conditions of the labour market, the education system, the welfare state and so on.

One of the decisive features of individualization processes, then, is that they not only permit but they also demand an active contribution by individuals. As the range of options widens and the necessity of deciding between them grows, so too does the need for individually performed actions, for adjustment, co-ordination, integration. If they are not to fail, individuals must be able to plan for the long term and adapt to change; they must organize and improvise, set goals, recognize obstacles, accept defeats and attempt new starts. They need initiative, tenacity, flexibility and tolerance of frustration.

Opportunities, dangers, biographical uncertainties that were earlier predefined within the family association, the village community, or by recourse to the rules of social estates or classes, must now be perceived, interpreted, decided and processed by individuals themselves. The consequences – opportunities and burdens alike – are shifted onto individuals who, naturally, in face of the complexity of social interconnections, are often unable to take the necessary decisions in a properly founded way, by considering interests, morality and consequences.

It is perhaps only by comparing generations that we can perceive how steeply the demands imposed on individuals have been rising. In a novel by Michael Cunningham (1991), a daughter asks her mother why she married her father:

> 'You knew that, of all the people in the world, he was the one you wanted to marry?' I asked. 'You never worried that you might be making some sort of extended mistake, like losing track of your real life and going off on, I don't know, a tangent you could never return from.'

But her mother 'waved the question away as if it were a sluggish but persistent fly. "We didn't ask such big questions then," she said. "Isn't it hard on you, to think and wonder and plan so much?"' (1991: 189f).

In a novel by Scott Turow (1991), a meeting between father and daughter is described in similar terms:

Listening to Sonny, who was twisted about by impulse and emotion – beseeching, beleaguered, ironic, angry – it struck Stern that Clara [his wife] and he had had the benefit of a certain good fortune. In his time, the definitions were clearer. Men and women of middle-class upbringing anywhere in the Western world desired to marry, to bear and rear children. Et cetera. Everyone travelled along the same ruts in the road. But for Sonny, marrying late in life, in the New Era, everything was a matter of choice. She got up in the morning and started from scratch, wondering about relationships, marriage, men, the erratic fellow she'd chosen – who, from her description, still seemed to be half a boy. He was reminded of Marta, who often said she would find a male companion just as soon as she figured out what she needed one for. (p. 349)

To some, such examples sound familiar. To others they seem alien – tales from a distant world. It is clear that there is no such thing as 'the' individualized society. Unquestionably, the situation in cities like Munich or Berlin is different from that in Pomerania or East Friesland. Between urban and rural regions there are clear differences, which are empirically demonstrable with regard, for example, to lifestyle and family structure.[3] What has long been taken for granted in one as a part of normal life, seems odd, irritating, threatening in the other. Of course, lifestyles and attitudes from the town are spreading to the country – but refractedly, with a different gloss. Individualization means, implies, urbanization. But urbanization carries the role models of the world out there into the village living room – through the expansion of education, through tourism, and not least through advertising, the mass media and consumerism. Even where seemingly unaltered lifestyles and traditional certainties are chosen and put on show, they quite often represent decisions against new longings and aroused desires.

It is necessary, therefore, to check each group, milieu and region to determine how far individualization processes – overt or covert – have advanced within it. We do not maintain that this development has achieved blanket coverage of the whole population without differentiation. Rather, the catch-word 'individualization' should be seen as designating a trend. What is decisive is the systematic nature of the development linked to the advance of modernity. Martin Baethge (1991) writes: 'Something which points towards tomorrow can hardly be representative of today' (p. 271). Individualization has elements of both – it is an exemplary diagnosis of the present and the wave of the future.

What is heralded, ultimately, by this development is the end of fixed, predefined images of man. The human being becomes (in a radicalization of Sartre's meaning) a choice among possibilities, *homo optionis*. Life, death, gender, corporeality, identity, religion, marriage, parenthood, social ties – all are becoming decidable down to the small print; once fragmented into options, everything must be decided.[4] At best, this constellation reminds us of Baron Münchhausen, who reputedly solved what has now become a universal problem: how to pull oneself out of the swamp of (im)possibilities by one's own pigtail. This artistic state of civilization has been summed up perhaps most clearly (with a pessimistic twist) by the poet Gottfried Benn (1979): 'In my view the history of man, of his endangerment, his tragedy, is only just beginning. Up to now the altars of saints and the wings of archangels have stood behind him; his weaknesses and wounds have been bathed from chalices and fonts. Now is beginning the series of his great, insoluble, self-inflicted dooms' (pp. 150f).

On the Impossibility of Living Modern Life:
the De-Routinization of the Mundane

It is easily said: certainties have fragmented into questions which are now spinning around in people's heads. But it is more than that. Social action needs routines in which to be enacted. One can even say that our thoughts and actions are shaped, at the deepest level, by something of which we are hardly or not at all aware. There is an extensive literature which stresses the relief afforded in this way by internalized, pre-conscious or semi-conscious routines – or more precisely, the indispensable role they play in enabling people to lead their lives and discover their identities within their social coordinates. As Hartmann Tyrell (1986) shows, everyday life is concerned primarily with:

> the temporal order of doing… But it is not only the temporal order as such which matters, but the associated stratum of experiences repeated over and over again, the normal, the regular, the unsurprising. At the same time, daily life is a sphere of reduced attention, of routinized activity, of safe, easy availability, and thus of actions that can be repeated 'again and again'. It is about 'what is done here', sometimes in a decidedly particularist sense, in the family circle, the village, the region, etc. It is about the commonplace and familiar… what 'everyone does here'. (p. 255)

It is precisely this level of pre-conscious 'collective habitualizations', of matters taken for granted, that is breaking down into a cloud of possibilities to be thought about and negotiated. The deep layer of foreclosed decisions is being forced up into the level of decision making.

Hence the irritation, the endless chafing of the open wound – and the defensive-aggressive reaction. The questions and decisions rising up from the floor of existence can be neither escaped nor changed back into a silent ground on which life can be lived. At most, such pacification is achieved temporarily, provisionally; it is permeated with questions that can burst out again at any time. Think, calculate, plan, adjust, negotiate, define, revoke (with everything constantly starting again from the beginning): these are the imperatives of the 'precarious freedoms' that are taking hold of life as modernity advances. Even not deciding, the mercy of having to submit, is vanishing. Sometimes its place is taken by a hybrid, simulating what has been lost: the decision in favour of chance, of not deciding, an attempt to banish doubt which yet is pursued by doubt even in its interior dialogues:

> I thought I'd be pregnant soon. I'd stopped taking precautions. But I couldn't seem to tell anyone, not Bobby or Jonathan. I suppose I was ashamed of my own motives. I didn't like the idea of myself as calculating or underhanded. All I wanted, really, was to get pregnant by accident. The unexpected disadvantage of modern life is our victory over our own fates. We're called on to decide so much, almost everything… In another era I'd have had babies in my twenties, when I was married to Denny. I'd have become a mother without quite deciding to. Without weighing the consequences. (Cunningham, 1991: 203)

Life loses its self-evident quality; the social 'instinct substitute' which supports and guides it is caught up in the grinding mills of what needs to be thought out and decided. If it is correct that routines and institutions have an unburdening function which renders individuality and decision making possible, it becomes clear what kind of encumbrance, exertion and stress is imposed by the destruction of routine. Ansgar Weymann (1989) points to the efforts the individual makes to escape this 'tyranny of possibilities' – such as flight into magic, myth, metaphysics. The overtaxed individual 'seeks, finds and produces countless authorities intervening in social and psychic life, which, as his professional representatives, relieve him of the question: "Who am I and what do I want?" and thus reduce his fear of freedom' (1989: 3). This creates the market for the answer factories, the psycho-boom, the advice literature – that mixture of the esoteric cult, the primal scream, mysticism, yoga and Freud which is supposed to drown out the tyranny of possibilities but in fact reinforces it with its changing fashions.

It is sometimes claimed that individualization means autonomy, emancipation, the freedom and self-liberation of humanity.[5] This calls to mind the proud subject postulated by the philosophy of the Enlightenment, who will acknowledge nothing but reason and its laws. But sometimes anomie rather than autonomy seems to prevail – a state unregulated to the point of lawlessness. (Emile Durkheim, in his classic study of anomie, sees it as the 'evil of missing boundaries', a time of overflowing wishes and desires, no longer disciplined by social barriers (1993: 289, 311). Any generalization that seeks to understand individualized society only in terms of one extreme or the other – autonomy or anomie – abbreviates and distorts the questions that confront us here. This society is characterized by hybrid forms, contradictions, ambivalences (dependent on political, economic and family conditions). It is also characterized, as we have said, by the 'do-it-yourself biography' which – depending on the economic situation, educational qualifications, stage of life, family situation, colleagues – can easily turn into a 'breakdown biography' (Hitzler, 1988; Beck and Beck-Gernsheim, 1993). Failure and inalienable freedom live in close proximity and perhaps intermingle (as in the 'chosen' lifestyle of 'singles').

At any rate, the topics that individuals wear themselves out on project into the most diverse spheres of life. They may be 'small' questions (such as the allocation of housework), but also include 'large' questions of life and death (from prenatal diagnosis to intensive medical care). The abolition of routine thus releases questions of very different social and moral weight. But they all bear on the core of existence. One can even say that decisions about lifestyles are 'deified'. Questions that went out of use with God are re-emerging at the centre of life. Everyday life is being post-religiously 'theologized'.

A secular line can be drawn: God, nature, social system. Each of these categories and horizons of meaning to an extent replaces the previous one; each stands for a particular group of self-evident assumptions and provides a source of legitimation for social action, which can be seen as a sequence of secularized necessities. As the dams become permeable and are breached, what was once reserved for God or was given in advance by nature, is now transformed into questions and decisions which have their locus in the conduct of private life.

(With the successes of reproductive medicine and human genetics the anthropology of the human species is even being drawn quite literally into the area of decision making.) To this extent, from the viewpoint of cultural history, it can be said that modernity, which dawned with the subject's claim to self-empowerment, is redeeming its promise. As modernity gains ground, God, nature and the social system are being progressively replaced, in greater and lesser steps, by the individual – confused, astray, helpless and at a loss. With the abolition of the old coordinates a question arises that has been decried and acclaimed, derided, pronounced sacred, guilty and dead: the question of the individual.

What is New in Individualization Processes?
The Example of the Social History of Marriage

In his book *The Civilization of the Renaissance in Italy*, published in 1860, Jakob Burckhardt writes that in the Middle Ages human consciousness lay:

> dreaming or half awake, beneath a collective veil. The veil was woven of faith, illusion and childish prepossession, through which the world and history were seen clad in strange hues. Man was conscious of himself only as a member of a race, people, party, family, corporation – only through some general category. In Italy, this veil first melted into air, an objective treatment and consideration of the state and of all the things of this world became possible. The subjective side at the same time asserted itself with corresponding emphasis; man became a spiritual individual, and recognized himself as such. (1987: 161)

Paradoxically, Burckhardt's description of the Renaissance has features of post-modernism. Everything is taken over by fashions; the politically indifferent private person comes into being; biographies and autobiographies are written and invented; women are educated according to masculine ideals. 'The highest praise which could then be given to the great Italian women was that they had the mind and the courage of men.' From the standpoint of the nineteenth century, Burckhardt notes, something emerged which 'our age would call immodesty' (1987: 428).

Anyone reading this and similar accounts will ask: what is new and specific in the individualization processes of the second half of the twentieth century?[6] To give a concise and direct answer, what is historically new is that something that was earlier expected of a few – to lead a life of their own – is now being demanded of more and more people and, in the limiting case, of all. The new element is, first, the democratization of individualization processes and, second (and closely connected), the fact that basic conditions in society favour or enforce individualization (the job market, the need for mobility and training, labour and social legislation, pension provisions etc.).

This history of the spread to pre-eminence of individualizations can be illustrated by various social phenomena and formations. Such will now be done by means of an exemplary sketch of the social history of marriage. To state our thesis at the outset: whereas marriage was earlier first and foremost an institution sui generis raised above the individual, today it is becoming more and more a product and construct of the individuals forming it. Let us now trace this historical curve in more detail.

As late as the seventeenth and eighteenth centuries, marriage was to be understood not from below to above but from above to below, as a direct component of the social order. It was a socially binding mode of living and working which was largely inaccessible to individual intervention. It prescribed to men and women what they had to do and not to do even in the details of daily life, work, economic behaviour and sexuality. (Of course, not everyone complied. But the social mesh of the family and village community was tight, and possibilities of control were omnipresent. Anyone who infringed the prevailing norms therefore had to reckon with rigorous sanctions.) To overstate slightly: marriage was a kind of internalized 'natural law' which – hallowed by God and the authority of the church, secured by the material interests of those bound together within it – was, so to speak, 'executed' in marriage. This emerges clearly through what seems to be an example of the contrary, a hard-won divorce reported by Gisela Bock and Barbara Duden (1977):

> In the early 18th century, in the Seine/Maine region of France, two people appeared before the responsible church court: Jean Plicque, a vintner in Villenoy and Catherine Giradin, his wife. Seven months earlier she had with difficulty achieved a separation of bed and board on grounds of absolute incompatibility. Now they came back and declared that it would be not only better but 'much more advantageous and useful for them to live together than to remain apart'. This couple's realization is typical of all rural and urban households: husband and wife were dependent on each other because and as long as there was no possibility of earning a livelihood outside joint family work. (1977: 126)

This couple's realization points up a situation that (despite all the diversity) seems to have been typical of pre-industrial society. Apart from church and monastery, there was no basis for material existence outside marriage. Marriage was not held together by the love, self-discovery or self-therapy of two wage-earners seeking each other and themselves, but was founded on religious obligation and materially anchored in the marital forms of work and life. Anyone who wishes to understand the meaning of this institution of marriage must leave aside the individuals and place at the centre the overarching whole of an order finally founded on God and the afterlife. Here marriage did not serve individual happiness, but was a means for achieving succession, hereditary family rule in the case of the nobility and so on. The stability of the social order and hierarchy depended on it in a very tangible way.

With the beginning of the modern age the higher meanings superimposed on forms of social existence were loosened. The trend towards individuality – first in the middle-class 'market individual' founded on private capital – called into question the gravity of collective identities and action units, at least latently. With the separation of the family from the economic sphere, the working, economic unit of husband and wife was ruptured. Characteristically, the response to this dissolution of the material basis of the marriage community was a heightening of the moral and legal underpinnings of marriage. Here, again, marriage is justified 'deductively', that is from above to below, but now with a moral exclamation mark, as a cornerstone of the bourgeois–Christian world order. A draft of the German Civil Code, published in 1888, states: 'A German Civil Code, following the general Christian view among the people, will have to start from the assumption that in marital law it is not the principle of the individual freedom of the spouses that prevails, but that marriage should be seen as a moral and legal order independent of the will of the spouses' (cited by Blasius, 1992: 130f).

'Not the principle of ... individual freedom', but an 'order independent of the will of the spouses': the threatening possibility resonates implicitly in the negation. However, the community is a one-sided one. The wife is expressly forbidden to use her own name. The surname thus becomes that of the husband. In exemplary fashion, the general element is equated with power – here, that of the husband. As late as 1956 we read in a judgement: 'Rather, Article 6 GG allows equal rights to come into play in family law only to the extent that our traditional concept of the family, as determined by Christianity, remains intact. All exaggerated individualistic tendencies are thereby denied an effect on marital law... This must also apply to marital law as it relates to names' (cited by Struck, 1991: 390). Here we already find the exorcising formulation about the 'exaggerated individualistic tendencies' that has lost nothing of its topicality. By it the Beelzebub of individualism was supposed to be sprinkled and driven out with the holy water of tradition.

Family registers are an unopened treasure trove of idealized family images proclaimed, as it were, *ex cathedra*. Two of them will be juxtaposed here: one from the time of National Socialism and one from the 1970s in the German Federal Republic. The contrast could hardly be more radical. The prefatory remarks make clear the individualistic conversion that has taken place in Germany – even officially – within three decades.

In the register from the early 1940s we read: 'Prefatory note: Marriage cannot be an end in itself, but must serve a greater goal, the increase and survival of the species and the race. Adolf Hitler.'[7] This sounds like a command and is no doubt intended as one. The racial doctrine of National Socialism is an extreme example of the 'counter-modernization' which stages a masquerade of the past in order to push back the 'decadent' tendencies of modernity (Beck, 1993: Chapter 4). It aims – using every means – to establish the unquestioned world of a re-integrated blood community. Marriage thus becomes a branch office of the state, a miniature state, the 'germ-cell of the state'. It is the place where the 'German race' is reproduced.

The commentary in the family register from the 1970s seems expressly to countermand the one just quoted. Here we read that 'the task of marriage under private law is not to see itself primarily as serving other aims beyond it, but to find its main purpose in marriage itself.'[8] Today's marriage manual no longer talks about the 'Christian world order and its values' or of 'state goals', and still less of the 'survival of the race'. Instead, it makes explicit the switch that has taken place from a view directed at the whole to one focused on people. The state even seems to slap its own wrist in warning the spouses entrusted to it not to do what up until then had been state law and policy regarding marriage, namely to follow 'traditional models':

> Caution is advised in face of the dangerous temptation to accept traditional models of marriage and of the family without question as 'natural', causing them to become fossilized in law. The rapid development of our modern industrial

society, the increasing number of working women, the expected further reduction of working hours, the changing character of professions, etc. compel the legal system to adopt an open-minded, unprejudiced attitude towards new embodiments of marriage and the family.[9]

The voice of sociology is audible here. This may even be a case of the (legendary) 'trickling down', the 'disappearance' of sociology – here, in the family register – which indicates its successful effect.

However, the newly weds also find the following 'blessing' quoted in their marriage manual in a chapter on 'The Dissolution of Marriage': 'Once their disputes have reached a certain stage, they (the spouses) seem to each other like two surgeons operating on each other without anaesthetic, who "get better and better at knowing what hurts".'[10] This is witty and apt and could hardly contrast more dramatically with the 'racial marriage' or the 'Christian marriage' still legally binding in the 1950s. Furthermore it could not show more clearly the radical change from the interpretation of marriage as something beyond the individual to the exclusively individual interpretation. Here, not only does an official text mention the dissolution of marriage in the same breath as the contract; marriage is also institutionalized as an individualized programme. The why, what and how long of marriage are placed entirely in the hands and hearts of those joined in it. From now on there is just one maxim defining what marriage means: the script is the individualization of marriage. The individual code of marriage is, so to speak, legally ordained.

This makes two things clear. First, even the old forms of marriage, now that they have been bureaucratically disowned, must be chosen and lived at one's personal risk. Even the marriage guidance manual contains, in effect, the warning that marriage – like excessive speed on a winding road – is a risky personal undertaking for which no insurances are valid. And second, no one now can say what goes on behind the oh-so-unchanging label 'marriage' – what is possible, permitted, required, taboo or indispensable. The world order of marriage is from now on an individual order which must be questioned and reconstructed by individuals as they go along.

To forestall any misunderstanding: even the new, individual order of marriage is not a mere product of individualization and its wishes. Rather, it is bound to institutional edicts – for example those of the legal system, which are central. It depends on the requirements of the educational system, the labour market, old-age pensions (the last today presupposing that both partners – and not just the husband, as earlier – have their own independent biographies, as earners and their own financial security). Even with regard to the twosome, therefore – that seemingly completely private, intimate sphere – individualization does not by any means imply that the increased freedom of choice is the same thing as a breakdown of order.[11] Rather, what we see here, as elsewhere, is what Talcott Parsons has called 'institutionalized individualism' (1978: 321). Freely translated, this means that in modern life the individual is confronted on many levels with the following challenge: You may and you must lead your own independent life, outside the old bonds of family, tribe, religion, origin and class; and you must do this within the new guidelines and rules which the state, the job market, the bureaucracy etc. lay down.

In this sense marriage, too, in its modern version, is not merely an individual order but an 'individual situation dependent on institutions' (Beck, 1986: 210).

Perspectives and Controversies of an Individual-Oriented Sociology

All sociology splits into two opposed views of the same thing. The social dimension can be regarded either from the standpoint of individuals or from that of the whole (society, state, the common good, class, group, organization etc.) (cf. Bolte, 1983). Both standpoints are founded on the structure of social action, which can be analysed either in terms of the agents or in terms of the social structure. However, that both standpoints are equally possible, equally necessary or equally original does not mean that they are equally valuable or have equal rights; still less does it mean that they are identical. Rather, each of these viewpoints relativizes, criticizes the other (subtly, but with abundant consequences): anyone who analyses society from the standpoint of the individual does not accept its form at a particular time as a preordained, unalterable datum, but calls it into question. Here, sociological thought is not far from the 'art of mistrust', to use a formulation of Berger (1977: 40), adapted from Nietzsche. Indeed, it tends to 'destabilize' existing power relationships, as Bauman (1991: 17), for example, puts it. By contrast, where the so-called 'operational requirements' of society (or subdivisions of it) provide the framework of reference, they are often presented to the outside world simply as the inner happiness of the ego. To apply this happiness there are funnels – known as 'duties' – and institutions for pouring it through these funnels, for purposes of intimidation: schools, courts, marriages, organizations etc.

The prevailing sociology has usually made things easy for itself by cutting off the questions that arise here with the strict injunction, backed up by thick volumes, that individuals can only be or become individuals within society. In this way they continually repress the idea: what would happen if these individuals wanted a different society, or even a different type of society?

The old sociology, still well endowed with university chairs, is armed against this idea: the general interest, congealed as structure, is condensed and glorified as Parsonian 'functional prerequisites'. From such prerequisites – as from a cornucopia of secularized ethical duties – pour forth 'role patterns', 'functions', 'demands', 'subsystems', equally remote from God and the earth, divorced from action and yet its precondition, which are to be applied as a standard to the confusion and refractoriness of individuals, to yield judgements such as 'normal', 'deviant', 'erroneous' and 'absurd'.

Accordingly, the 'individualistic' perspective on society has up to now been usually dismissed as presumptuous and self-contradictory. There is talk – using an up-to-date idiom – of 'demand inflation' and the 'ego society'. The decay of values is deplored, while it is forgotten that such decay is as old as Socrates. The GDR had exemplary experience of the inverse question and foundered on it: what happens to institutions without individuals? What does it mean when individuals withdraw their assent from the institutional elite? The same question was urgently posed in Italy in 1993 (and in France, Sweden, Finland, Germany, the USA etc.) and the answer was the same: the political systems tremble. Where the functionalist viewpoint, based on system theory, is dominant, a 'subject-oriented' sociology often appears not only deviant but subversive. For it can sometimes reveal that the party and institutional elites are riders without horses.

Neither is it true, of course, that both conceptions of the social order are incomplete in themselves and need to supplement each other. But before such a need for harmony smoothes over a conflict which has not yet been fought out openly, it should be pointed out here that for some centuries the view of the totality has suppressed that of individuals. In view of this it is time to turn the tables and ask what kind of society comes into being after the demise of the great political camps and the party political consensus.

In other words: the two points of view remain until further notice incompatible; they are even becoming, through a modernization which is setting individuals and their demands and dilemmas free, more and more irreconcilable, and are giving rise to antithetical explanations, methods, theories and intellectual traditions.

It will be objected that this is not a meaningful antithesis. Entities which presuppose each other analytically, individuals and society, cannot be described as a social conflict. Moreover, both viewpoints lay claim to both viewpoints. He who embraces the 'whole' (of society) – the functionality of social formations – in his field of vision, self-evidently claims to include the standpoint of individuals as well. If necessary, this is presented as the morally correct standpoint, that which must be asserted against the false self-consciousness of individuals in their own well-understood interests. Whereas, conversely, every variant of subject- or individual-oriented sociology naturally also offers statements and explanations about the intrinsic reality of social formations and systems, their structure, stage management etc.

What was shown in the preceding section through the example of marriage applies generally: the antithesis between the individual- and system-based viewpoints should be understood as a historical development. If, in traditional, pre-industrial societies, we can still, perhaps, assume a fairly balanced relationship between the two frames of reference, this pre-established harmony breaks down with the unfolding of modernity. This is the central theme of sociology in Emile Durkheim and Georg Simmel. But both still assume that it is possible to integrate individualized society, as it were transcendentally, through values. Such a possibility, however, became more unrealistic the more individuals were released from classical forms of integration in groups, including family and class. What is emerging today can be called, with Hans Magnus Enzensberger, 'the average exoticism of everyday life':

> It is most obvious in the provinces. Market towns in Lower Bavaria, villages in the Eifel Hills, small towns in Holstein are populated by figures no one could have dreamed of only thirty years ago. For example, golf-playing butchers, wives imported from Thailand, counter-intelligence agents with allotments, Turkish Mullahs, women chemists in Nicaragua committees, vagrants driving Mercedes, autonomists with organic gardens, weapons-collecting tax officials,

peacock-breeding smallholders, militant lesbians, Tamil ice-cream sellers, classics scholars in commodity futures trading, mercenaries on home leave, extremist animal-rights activists, cocaine dealers with solariums, dominas with clients in top management, computer freaks commuting between Californian data banks and nature reserves in Hesse, carpenters who supply golden doors to Saudi Arabia, art forgers, Karl May researchers, bodyguards, jazz experts, euthanasists and porno producers. Into the shoes of the village idiots and the oddballs, of the eccentrics and the queer fish, has stepped the average deviationist, who no longer stands out at all from millions like him. (1992: 179)

Under such conditions, institutions are founded on antiquated images of individuals and their social situations. To avoid endangering their own power, the administrators of these institutions maintain the status quo at all costs (supported by a sociology operating with the old conceptual stereotypes). An amusing consequence of this is that the political class regards the individuals 'out there' as no less stupid and brazen than the society of individuals considers the political class. The question as to which of them is right can, in principle, be easily decided. The idea that only the party elite and the bureaucratic apparatus knows what is what and that everyone else is imbecilic is one that characterized the Soviet Union – until it collapsed.

'This society', Enzensberger writes of the German Federal Republic:

is no longer capable of being disappointed. It registered very early, very quickly what's going on in Bonn. The way the parties present themselves also contributes to this cynical view. The politicians try to compensate for the loss of their authority, the erosion of power and trust, by a huge expenditure on advertising. But these wasteful battles are counter-productive. The message is tautologous and empty. They always say only one thing, which is, 'I am I' or 'We are we'. The zero statement is the preferred form of self-presentation. That naturally confirms people's belief that no ideas can be expected from this caste... When the posters say: 'It's Germany's future', then everyone knows that these are empty words, at most it's about the future of the milk subsidy to farmers, of the health insurance contributions or benefits. The Federal Republic is relatively stable and relatively successful not because of, but despite being ruled by the people who grin down from the election posters. (1992: 233, 228)

The theory of individualization takes sides in political debate in two ways: first, it elaborates a frame of reference which allows the subject area – the conflicts between individuals and society – to be analysed from the standpoint of individuals. Second, the theory shows how, as modern society develops further, it is becoming questionable to assume that collective units of meaning and action exist. System theories, which assume an existence and reproduction of the social independence of the actions and thoughts of individuals, are thereby losing reality content. To exaggerate slightly: system theory is turning into a system *metaphysics* which obstructs the view of the virulent social and political process whereby, in all spheres of activity, the content, goals, foundations and structures of the 'social' are having to be renegotiated, reinvented and reconstructed.[12]

A sociology which confronts the viewpoint serving the survival of institutions with the viewpoint of individuals is a largely undeveloped area of the discipline. Almost all sociology, through a 'congenital bias', is based on a negation of individuality and the individual. The social has almost always been conceived in terms of tribes, religions, classes, associations, and above all, recently, of social systems. The individuals were the interchangeable element, the product of circumstances, the character masks, the subjective factor, the environment of the systems, in short: the indefinable. Sociology's credo, to which it owes its professional identity, states over and over again that the individual is the illusion of individuals who are denied insight into the social conditions and conditionality of their lives.

The works of world literature, the great narratives and dramas that have held the epochs in thrall, are variations of this doctrine of the higher reality and dignity of the general, social dimension, the indivisible unit of which – as the term *individere* itself implies – is the individual. But is a science of individere actually possible? Is not a 'sociology of the individual' (unless it contents itself with the social history of that concept, in the context of discourse theory) a self-contradiction, a pig with wings, a disguised appeal for sociology to abolish itself?

One does not need to go to the opposite extreme to see that many of the main concepts of sociology are on a war footing with the basic idea of individualization theory: that traditional contexts are being broken up, reconnected, recast; are becoming in all cases decidable, decision dependent, in need of justification. Where this historical development is asserting itself, the viewpoints from 'above' and 'below', from the social whole and from the individual, are diverging. At the same time, the questions stirred up by system theory's perspective are still in force and even take on increased importance as they become more unmanageable. Take, for example, the declining birthrate, which can only be deciphered if seen against the background of the changed wishes, hopes and life plans of men and women. On the level of society as a whole, it brings with it a whole string of secondary consequences and questions (education policy, labour market management, pensions, local planning, immigration policy etc.). Individuals, their preferences and aversions, are becoming the interference factor, that which is simply incalculable, a constant source of irritation, because they upset all calculations – education quotas, study plans, pension calculations etc. Among politicians and administrators, and the academic experts who prepare their texts, this heightens the suspicion of irrationality, since it keeps turning the current legal, administrative and computing formulae into waste paper. Where hitherto-accepted assumptions are found wanting, the clamour about 'mood democracy' and the 'elbow society' begins. Norms and moral standards are set. But the tidal wave of new life designs, of do-it-yourself and tightrope biographies, cannot be either held back or understood in this way. The scurrying of the individualized lifestyles, elaborated in the personal trial-and-error process (between training, retraining, unemployment and career, between hopes of love, divorce, new dreams of happiness), is unamenable to the need for standardization of bureaucratized political science and sociology.

No one denies that important matters are thought about and initiated by these disciplines, too. But what was previously regarded as background noise to be neglected, is now being seen, more and more undeniably, as the basic situation. The frame of reference of institutionalized state politics and administration, on one hand, and that of individuals trying to hold together their biography fragments, on the other, is breaking apart into antagonistic conceptions of 'public welfare', 'quality of life', 'future viability', 'justice' and 'progress'. A rift is opening between the images of society prevalent in politics and institutions and those arising from the situations of individuals struggling for viable ways of living.

In this tension-laden field, sociology must rethink its concepts and its research routines. In the face of Enzensberger's 'average exoticism of everyday life', together with what is now formulated with scholarly caution as the 'pluralization of lifestyles', old classifications and schemata are becoming as ideologically suspect as they are necessary to the institutional actors. Take, for example, the studies which 'prove' that the increasingly numerous non-marital partnerships are really pre-conjugal communities and that post-conjugal communities are actually only a preliminary form of the next marriage, so that marriage can be proclaimed the transcendental victor throughout all this turbulence. Such consolations have their market and their grateful customers: the turmoils of individualization, their message runs, are a storm in surviving marriage's teacup.

This confirms the old adage that the echo coming back out of the wood is the same as the shout that went into it. Anyone who 'maritalizes' alternative ways of living should not be surprised if he sees marriages wherever he looks. But this is a prime example of blind empiricism. Even methodical brilliance, that is able to avoid calling its categorical framework into question, becomes a second-hand bookshop stocked with standard social groups, which only exist as an ideal: though as such they are very much alive.[13]

Prospect: How can Highly Individualized Societies be Integrated?

Individualization has a double face: 'precarious freedoms'. Expressed in the old, wrong terms, emancipation and anomie form together, through their political chemistry, an explosive mixture. The consequences and questions erupting in all parts of society are correspondingly deep reaching and nerve deadening; they increasingly alarm the public and preoccupy social scientists. To mention only a few: how do children grow up when there are fewer and fewer clear guidelines and responsibilities in families? Can connections be made with the growing tendency towards violence among young people? Is the age of mass products and mass consumption coming to an end with the pluralization of lifestyles and must the economy and industry adapt themselves to products and product fashions that can be combined individually, with corresponding methods of production?

Is it at all possible for a society in the drifting sand of individualization to be registered statistically and analysed sociologically? Is there any remaining basic unit of the social, whether the household, family or commune? How could such units be defined and made operational? How should the various political spheres – for example, local politics, traffic policy, environmental policy, family or welfare policy – react to the diversification and transitoriness of needs and situations? How must social work (and its educational content) change when poverty is divided up and, as it were, distributed laterally among biographies? What architecture, what spatial planning, what educational planning does a society need under the pressure of individualization? Has the end come for the big parties and the big associations or are they just starting a new stage of their history?

Behind all these irritating questions, a basic question is making itself more and more clearly heard: is it still at all possible to integrate highly individualized societies? As is shown by the rebirth of nationalism, of ethnic differences and conflicts in Europe, there is a strong temptation to react to these challenges with the classical instruments of encapsulation against 'aliens': which means turning back the wheels of social modernization. No doubt the acceptance of violence against foreigners in the streets (for example) may indeed be explained in this way. In Germany as in other Western European states an uprising against the 1970s and 1980s is in progress, a *Kulturkampf* of the two modernities. Old certainties, just now grown fragile, are again proclaimed – from everyday life to politics, from the family to the economy and the concept of progress. The highly individualized, find-out-for-yourself society is to be replaced by an inwardly heterogeneous society outwardly consolidated into a fortress – and the demarcation against 'foreigners' fits in with this calculation.

To put the matter ironically: since men can no longer, 'unfortunately', deny the right of women to vote, since women's desire for education can only with difficulty be held in check, since everything that might be useful in this regard proves awkward, a perhaps quite serviceable alternative route is being taken – not quite consciously but not quite unconsciously either. It involves achieving the same goals through the dramaturgy of violence and nationalism. Here the breaching of the taboo on violence by right-wing extremists has a basis of which little account has been taken: namely, the counter-revolt, pent up in the West too, against the individualization, feminization and ecologization of everyday life. Quite incidentally, violence reinstates the priorities of orthodox industrial society – economic growth, the faith in technology, the nuclear family, gender hierarchy – banishing the tiresome spirits of permanent questioning; or seeming to do so.

But nailing down the status quo or even doing a backward *salto mortale* could not, at the end of the twentieth century, provide a basis of legitimacy. The same is true of the three ways of integrating highly industrialized societies that are mentioned again and again in the debate. They, too, are becoming uncertain, fragile, unable to function in the longer term.

The first is the possibility of what might be called a transcendental consensus, an integration through values, which was the driving force of classical sociology from Durkheim to Parsons. Opposing this today is the realization that the diversification of cultural perceptions and the connections people have to make for themselves eat away the very foundations on which value communities can feed and constantly renew themselves.

Others, second, contrast to this integration through values an integration founded on joint material interests. If an avowal of common values (which, of course, always has a narrowing, repressive side) is no longer possible, it is replaced in highly developed society by the share in prosperity that is felt by broad sections of the population, binding them into that society. According to this theory, the cohesion of the old federal republic rested primarily on the growing 'economic cake', whereas the new, enlarged republic – where recession, shortage and poverty are starting to take control – faces severe tests. But even disregarding this topical development, the basic assumption is itself questionable. To hope that only material interests and institutional dependence (consumption, job market, welfare state, pensions) create cohesion, is to confuse the problem with the solution, making a virtue (desired by theory) out of the necessity of disintegrating groups and group allegiances.

Third, national consciousness, too, is no longer able to provide a basis for stable integration. This is not only shown by the polarizations generated by the 'national project'. It is also, as René König wrote as early as 1979, 'much too abstract in relation to real and very tangible fissures' (p. 364); it is simply no longer able to reach and bind these splits. In other words, with the mobilization of ethnic identities, it is precisely national integration which breaks down:

> This can be called a 'relapse into the middle ages', and the disintegration of the existing large societies into separate, opposed local powers can be seen as the decay of the old 'nations' – a process which has been a reality in some parts of the old and new worlds for some time now. Here, the old path from alliances to empires is reversed; the great empires sometimes split up into federative formations, or the individual parts split off along lines determined by political, ethnic or other factors. (ibid.: 364f)

So what is left? In conclusion, we would like to indicate at least the possibility of a different kind of integration and to put it forward for discussion. To summarize our basic idea: if highly individualized societies can be bound together at all, it is only, first, through a clear understanding of precisely this situation and second, if people can be successfully mobilized and motivated for the challenges present at the centre of their lives (unemployment, destruction of nature etc.). Where the old sociality is 'evaporating', society must be reinvented. Integration therefore becomes possible if no attempt is made to arrest and push back the breakout of individuals. It can happen if we make conscious use of this situation and try to forge new, politically open, creative forms of bond and alliance. The question of whether we still have the strength, the imagination – and the time – for this 'invention of the political' (Beck, 1993) is, to be sure, a matter of life and death.

In one of his last major essays, König sketched a positively utopian role for sociology in this connection. He believed it could contribute to integration through enabling the highly complex society to reflect and observe itself creatively and methodically. He criticized the 'ruling class of today' in the strongest terms because it had 'lived entirely on a legitimacy borrowed from old elites and had added nothing of its own'. In this situation, König goes on, 'sociology could make this highly complex thematic context transparent... Admittedly, integration could not then be achieved on the institutional level' – either ethnically, socially, economically or through state nationalism. 'To an extent, it can only be implemented "in thought".' Therefore, it could be achieved 'only within the framework of a new philosophy, which no longer revolved around "being" and "becoming", but around the chances for human beings under the conditions that have been described' (pp. 367ff; cf. Peters, 1993).

What König proposes is in fact very topical – an integration to be attained 'in thought', in the struggle for new existential foundations for industrial civilization. Post-traditional societies threatening the cohesion of this civilization can only become integrable, if at all, through the experiment of their self-interpretation, self-observation, self-opening, self-discovery, indeed, their self-invention. Their future, their ability to have and shape a future, is the measure of their integration. Whether they can succeed in this is, of course, questionable. Perhaps it will turn out that individualization and integration are in fact mutually exclusive. And what of sociology? Is it really able to make an intellectual contribution to pluralist societies? Or will it remain stuck in its routines, obliterating the big outlines of change and challenge with its minute calculations of developmental trends?

In his novel *The Man without Qualities* (1961), Musil distinguishes between a sense for reality and a sense for possibility. He defines the latter as 'the capacity to think how everything could "just as easily" be, and to attach no more importance to what is than to what is not'. Someone who sees possible truths, Musil goes on, has, 'at least in the opinion of their devotees... something positively divine, a fiery, soaring quality, a constructive will... that does not shrink from reality but treats it, on the contrary, as a mission and an invention... Since his ideas... are nothing else than as yet unborn realities, he too of course has a sense of reality; but it is a sense of possible reality' (pp. 12f). Undoubtedly, sociology, too, ought to develop such a sense of possible reality – but that is another matter.

Notes

1 Respectively, this is how Ostner and Roy (1991, p. 18) and Karl Ulrich Mayer (1991, pp. 88f) understand individualization; for a summary of the debate on individualization, see Beck (1994).

2 Ronald Hitzler (1988) writes about 'do-it-yourself biography' (*Bastelbiographie*), Anthony Giddens (1991) about 'reflexive biography' and Katrin Ley (1984) about 'elective biography' (*Wahlbiographie*).

3 Hans Bertram and Clemens Dannenbeck (1990); Hans Bertram, Hiltrud Bayer and Renate Bauereiss (1993); Günter Burkart and Martin Kohli (1992).

4 Peter Gross refers to the multi-options society (1994). *Multioptionsgesellschaft*. Frankfurt: Suhrkamp.

5 E.g. Günter Burkart (1993).

6 Cf., for example, Dumont (1991); Macfarlane (1979); Morris (1972); Foucault (1984).

7 *Familienstammbuch mit Ahnenpass*, Paul Albrechts Verlage, Stulp and Berlin, no date (c. 1940), cf. p. 3; for the interrelations between individualization, family, sex roles and love, see Beck and Beck-Gernsheim (1994).

8 *Stammbuch*, published by Bundesverband der Deutsches Standesbeamten, e.V., Verlag für Standesamtwesen, Berlin and Frankfurt, no date (c. 1970), no page references.

9 Ibid.

10 Ibid.

11 Zapf (1992) expressly opposes this widespread misunderstanding (cf. pp. 190f).

12 Cf. the theory of reflexive modernization in Beck (1993), esp. Chapter 3; and Beck, Giddens and Lash (1994).

13 The pragmatic a priori method of mass data sociology is worth noting: quantitative methods presuppose pre-formed categories and concepts (even if they are nominally deactivated). However, a society which is individualizing itself eludes these standardizations imposed by research method (which is already giving rise to unmanageable complications in the introduction of flexible working time and work contracts, for example). It is therefore difficult for a sociology proud of its technical virtuosity to jump over its own shadow and address questions of a self-individualizing society. But at the same time it becomes clear, here again, how woefully sociology has so far neglected the question of what kind of sociological empiricism, of scholarly and social self-observation, is appropriate to a society caught in the draught and sand drift of individualization. Cf. Beck and Allmendinger (1993).

Bibliography

Baethge, M. (1991) 'Arbeit, Vergesellschaftung, Identität – zur zunehmenden normativen Subjectivierung der Arbeit', in W. Zapf (ed.), *Die Modernisierung moderner Gesellschaften*. Frankfurt/M.: Campus.

Bauman, Z. (1991) *Thinking Sociologically*. UK: Oxford: Blackwell; USA: Cambridge.

Bauman, Z. (1993) 'Wir sind wie Landstreicher – die Moral im Zeitalter der Beliebigkeit', *Süddeutsche Zeitung*, 16–17 November 1993.

Beck, U. (1986) *Risikogesellschaft. Auf dem Weg in eine andere Moderne*. Frankfurt/M.: Suhrkamp; *Risk Society*. London: Sage, 1992.

Beck, U. (1993) *Die Erfindung des Politischen*. Frankfurt: Suhrkamp; translation (1997): *The Reinvention of Politics*. Cambridge: Polity Press.

Beck, U. (1994) 'The debate on the "individualization theory"', in B. Schäfers (ed.), *Sociology in Germany – Development, Institutionalization, Theoretical Disputes*. Opladen: Leske Verlag. pp. 191–200.

Beck, U. and Allmendinger, J. (1993) *Individualisierung und die Erhebung sozialer Ungleichheit*. Munich: DFG research project.

Beck, U. and Beck-Gernsheim, E. (1993) 'Nicht Autonomie, sondern Bastelbiographie', *Zeitschrift für Soziologie*, 3, June, pp. 178–87.

Beck, U. and Beck-Gernsheim, E. (1994) *The Normal Chaos of Love*. Cambridge: Polity Press.

Beck, U., Giddens, A. and Lash, S. (1994) *Reflexive Modernization – Politics, Tradition and Aesthetics in the Modern Social Order*. Cambridge: Polity Press.

Benn, G. (1979) *Essays und Reden um der Farsung der Eastdrucke*. Frankfurt/M.: Fischer.

Berger, P. L. (1977) *Einladung zur Soziologie*. Munich: Deutsche Taschenbuch Verlag.

Bertram, H. and Dannenbeck, C. (1990) 'Pluralisierung von Lebenslagen und Individualisierung von Lebensführungen. Zur Theorie und Empirie regionaler Disparitäten in der Bundesrepublik Deutschland', in P. A. Berger and S. Bradil (eds), *Lebenslagen, Lebensläufe, Lebensstile*. Göttingen: Schwartz. pp. 207–29.

Bertram, H., Bayer, H. and Bauereiss, R. (1993) *Familien-Atlas, Lebenslagen und Regionen in Deutschland*. Opladen: Leske und Budrich.

Blasius, D. (1992) *Ehescheidung in Deutschland im 19. und 20. Jahrhundert*. Frankfurt: Fischer Taschenbuch Verlag.

Bock, G. and Duden, B. (1977) 'Arbeit aus Liebe – Liebe als Arbeit', in *Frauen und Wissenschaft. Beiträge zur Berliner Sommeruniversität für Frauen*, July 1986. Berlin: Courage Verlag. pp. 118–99.

Bolte, K. M. (1983) 'Subjektorientierte Soziologie – Plädoyer für eine Forschungsperspektive', in K. M. Bolte and E. Treutner (eds), *Subjektorientierte Arbeits- und Berufssoziologie*. Frankfurt/M.: Campus. pp. 12–36.

Burckhardt, J. (1987) *Die Kultur der Renaissance in Italien*. Stuttgart: Reclam.

Burkart, G. (1993) 'Individualisierung und Elternschaft – das Beispiel USA', *Zeitschrift für Soziologie*, 3, June 1993, pp. 159–77.

Burkart, G. and Kohli, M. (1992) *Liebe, Ehe, Elternschaft*. Munich: Piper.

Cunningham, M. (1991) *A Home at the End of the World*. Harmondsworth: Penguin.

Dumont, L. (1991) *Individualismus – Zur Ideologie der Moderne*. Frankfurt/M.: Campus.

Durkheim, E. (1993) *Der Selbstmord*. Frankfurt: Suhrkamp; *Suicide: A Study in Sociology*. New York: Free Press.

Enzensberger, H. M. (1992) *Mediocrity and Delusion, Collected Diversions* (trans. Martin Chalmers). London: Verso.

Foucault, M. (1984) *Le Souci de Soi*. Paris: Gallimard.

Giddens, A. (1991) *Self-Identity and Modernity*. London: Polity.

Hitzler, R. (1988) *Kleine Lebenswelten – Ein Beitrag zum Verstehen von Kultur*. Opladen: Westdeutscher Verlag.

König, R. (1979) 'Gesellschaftliches Bewusstsein und Soziologie', in G. Lüschen (ed.), *Deutsche Soziologie seit 1945*. Special edition 21, Opladen: Westdeutscher Verlag. pp. 358–370.

Ley, K. (1984) 'Von der Normal – zur Wahlbiographie', in M. Kohli and G. Robert (eds), *Biographie und Soziale Wirklichkeit*. Stuttgart: Metzler. pp. 239–60.

Macfarlane, A. (1979) *The Origins of English Individualism. The Family, Property and Social Transition*. New York: Cambridge University Press.

Mayer, K. U. (1991) 'Soziale Ungleichheit und Lebensläufe', in B. Giesen and C. Leggewie (eds), *Experiment Vereinigung*. Berlin: Rotbuch. pp. 87–99.

Morris, C. (1972) *The Discovery of the Individual, 1050–1200*. Toronto: University of Toronto Press.

Musil, R. (1961) *The Man without Qualities*. London: Secker & Warburg.

Ostner, I. and Roy, P. (1991) *Späte Heirat – Ergebnis biographisch unterschiedlicher Erfahrungen mit 'Cash' und 'Care'*. Project proposal to Deutsche Forschungsgemeinschaft (DFG), Bremen.

Parsons, T. (1978) *Religion in Postindustrial Society. In Action, Theory and the Human Condition*. New York: Free Press.

Peters, B. (1993) *Die Integration moderner Gesellschaften*. Frankfurt/M.: Suhrkamp.

Schorlemmer, F. (1993) 'Der Befund ist nicht alles'. Contribution to debate on Bindungsverlust und Zukunftsangst in der Risikogesellschaft, 30 October 1993, in Halle. Manuscript.

Struck, G. (1991) 'Die mühselige Gleichberechtigung von Mann und Frau in Ehenamensrecht, *Neue Justiz*, 9, pp. 390–2.

Sun, L. H. (1993) 'Freedom has a price, Chinese Discover', *International Herald Tribune*, 14 June.

Turow, S. (1991) *The Burden of Proof*. Harmondsworth: Penguin.

Tyrell, H. (1986) 'Soziologische Anmerkungen zur historischen Familienforschung', *Geschichte und Gesellschaft*, 12, pp. 254–73.

Weymann, A. (1989) 'Handlungsspielräume im Lebenslauf', in A. Weymann (ed.), *Handlungs- spielräume. Untersuchungen zur Individualisierung und Institutionalisierung von Lebensläufen in der Moderne*. Stuttgart: Enke.

Zapf, W. (1992) 'Entwicklung und Sozialstruktur moderner Gesellschaften', in H. Korte and B. Schäfers (eds), *Einführung in Hauptbegriffe der Soziologie*. Opladen: Leske and Budrich.

Losing the Traditional: Individualization and 'Precarious Freedoms'. First published in Heelas, Lash, Morris (eds), *Detraditionalization* (1996). Published here by kind permission of Blackwell Publishers.

2

A Life of One's Own in a Runaway World

Individualization, Globalization and Politics

There is hardly a desire more widespread in the West today than to lead 'a life of your own'. If a traveller in France, Finland, Poland, Switzerland, Britain, Germany, Hungary, the USA or Canada asks what really moves people there, what they strive and struggle to achieve, the answer may be money, work, power, love, God or whatever, but it would also be, more and more, the promise of 'a life of one's own'. Money means your own money, space means your own space, even in the elementary sense of a precondition for a life you can call your own. Love, marriage and parenthood are required to bind and hold together the individual's own, centrifugal life story. It would be only a slight exaggeration to say that the daily struggle for a life of one's own has become the collective experience of the Western world. It expresses the remnant of our communal feeling.

What drives people to reach for the stars in their lives? Why is this new direction emerging which, although seemingly meaningful only at the level of the individual, is really unfolding in accordance with a schematic pattern? What explains the zeal, the fear and enthusiasm, the cunning and determination, with which large numbers of people fret and fight for their 'own lives'? For many, the answer obviously lies within the people themselves – in their individual wills, their inflated expectations, their insatiable hunger for new experience, their decreasing preparedness to obey commands, to get into lane, to make sacrifices. Such hasty explanations, however, throw up a new series of questions. How are we to explain the fact that people in many countries suddenly and simultaneously want to take control of their lives? Everything is acted out in the personalized costumes of the individual – independently, in the world's most varied cultures, languages and cities. Is this a kind of epidemic of egoism, an ego fever, to be overcome through daily doses of ethics and references to the public good? Or are individuals, despite all the glitter of the campaign for their own lives, perhaps also in the vanguard of a deeper change? Do they point to new shores, towards a struggle for a new relationship between the individual and society, which still has to be invented? This is what the present chapter will argue.

We live in an age in which the social order of the national state, class, ethnicity and the traditional family is in decline. The ethic of individual self-fulfilment and achievement is the most powerful current in modern society. The choosing, deciding, shaping human being who aspires to be the author of his or her own life, the creator of an individual identity, is the central character of our time. It is the fundamental cause behind changes in the family and the global gender revolution in relation to work and politics. Any attempt to create a new sense of social cohesion has to start from the recognition that individualism, diversity and scepticism are written into Western culture. The importance of a life of one's own in a runaway world may be outlined in the following 15 points.

1: The compulsion to lead a life of one's own and the possibility of doing it, emerge when a society is highly differentiated. To the extent that society breaks down into separate functional spheres that are neither interchangeable nor graftable onto one another, people are integrated into society only in their partial aspects as taxpayers, car drivers, students, consumers, voters, patients, producers, fathers, mothers, sisters, pedestrians and so on. Constantly changing between different, partly incompatible logics of action, they are forced to take into their hands that which is in danger of breaking into pieces: their own lives. Modern society does not integrate them as whole persons into its functional systems; rather, it relies on the fact that individuals are not integrated but only partly and temporarily involved as they wander between different functional worlds. The social form of your own life is initially an empty space which an ever more differentiated society has opened up. It becomes filled with incompatibilities, the ruins of traditions, the junk of side-effects. The space left behind as once dominant certainties lose their power becomes a junkyard for the wreckage of people's own lives. Many Westerners could say: 'My life is not a continuum. It is not merely broken by day and night into black and white pieces. It is different versions of me which go to the station, sit in the office and make bookings, stalk through groves, write; I am the thinker-of-all-trades, of broken-up trades, who runs, smokes, kills, listens to the radio, says "Yes, sir" to the chief officer.' Such a person has been called 'a tray full of sparkling snapshots' (Arno Schmidt, *Aus dem Leben eines Fauns*).

2: The life of one's own is not a life peculiar to oneself. In fact the opposite is true; a standardized life is produced that combines both achievement and justice and in which the interest of the individual and rationalized society are merged. The expansion of the nation-state produced and affirmed individualization, with doctrines of socialization and institutions of education to match. This is what I call the paradox of 'institutional individualism'. The legal norms of the welfare state make individuals (not groups) the recipients of benefits, thereby enforcing the rule that people should organize more and more of their own lives. People used to be born into traditional societies, as they were into social classes or religions. Today even God himself has to be chosen. And the ubiquitous rule is that, in order to survive the rat race, one has to become active, inventive and resourceful, to develop ideas of one's own, to be faster, nimbler and more creative – not just on one occasion, but constantly, day after day. Individuals become actors, builders, jugglers, stage managers of their own biographies and identities and also of their social links and networks.

3: The life of one's own is thus completely dependent on institutions. In the place of binding traditions, institutional guidelines appear on the scene to organize your own life. The qualitative difference between traditional and modern life stories is not, as many assume, that in older corporate and agrarian societies various suffocating controls and guidelines restricted the individual's say in his or her own life to a minimum, whereas today hardly any such restrictions are left. It is, in fact, in the bureaucratic and institutional jungle of modernity that life is most securely bound into networks of guidelines and regulations. The crucial difference is that modern guidelines actually compel the self-organization and self-thematization of people's biographies. In earlier times in Europe very precise rules governed wedding ceremonies, for example, so that in some regions and periods nearly half the population of marriageable age remained single. Today, by contrast, many sets of guidelines – in the educational system, the labour market or the welfare state – involve demands that individuals should run their own lives, on pain of economic sanction.

4: Living a life of one's own therefore means that standard biographies become elective biographies, 'do-it-yourself biographies', risk biographies, broken or broken-down biographies. Even behind façades of security and prosperity, the possibilities of biographical slippage and collapse are ever present. Hence the clinging and the fear, even in the externally wealthy middle layers of society. So there is a big difference to be made between individualization where there are institutional resources like human rights, education and the welfare state to cope with the contradiction of modern biographies and 'atomization' where there are not. The neoliberal market ideology enforces atomization with all its political will.

5: In spite or because of the institutional guidelines and the often incalculable insecurity, the life of one's own is condemned to activity. Even in failure, it is an active life in its structuring of demands. The other side of this obligation to be active is that failure becomes personal failure, no longer perceived as class experience in a 'culture of poverty'. It goes hand in hand with forms of self-responsibility. Whereas illness, addiction, unemployment and other deviations from the norm used to count as blows of fate, the emphasis today is on individual blame and responsibility. Living your own life therefore entails taking responsibility for personal misfortunes and unanticipated events. Typically, this is not only an individual perception, but a culturally binding mode of attribution. It corresponds to an image of society in which individuals are not passive reflections of circumstances but active shapers of their own lives, within varying degrees of limitation.

6: Your own life – your own failure. Consequently, social crisis phenomena such as structural unemployment can be shifted as a burden of risk onto the shoulders of individuals. Social problems can be directly turned into psychological dispositions: into guilt feelings, anxieties, conflicts and neuroses. Paradoxically enough, a new immediacy develops in the relationship between the individual and society, an immediacy of disorder such that social crises appear as individual and are no longer – or only very indirectly – perceived in their social dimension. This is even true of the darker side of still integrated societies: the new collective positions of underclass and exclusion. These are collectively individualized. Here is certainly one of the sources, both present and future, for the outbreaks of violence for its own sake that are directed against shifting victims ('foreigners', the disabled, homosexuals, Jews). Researchers distinguish between 'life story' as a chain of actual events and 'biography' as the narrative form of events – which by no means necessarily coincide with each other. Thus, if biographies spoke only of 'blows of fate', 'objective conditions' and 'outside forces' that 'overwhelmed', 'predetermined' or 'compelled', that would refute our formulated theory, for it has been argued that individuals have to perceive themselves as at least partly shaping themselves and the conditions of their lives, even or above all in the language of failure. A rough pragmatic indicator for the 'living one's own life' theory is thus the presence of elements of an individualistic and active narrative form in people's own biographies. Life's events are ascribed not mainly to 'alien' causes, but to aspects of the individual (decisions, non-decisions, omissions, capacities, incapacities, achievements, compromises, defeats). This does not, of course, rule out the possibility of false consciousness.

7: People struggle to live their own lives in a world that increasingly and more evidently escapes their grasp, one that is irrevocably and globally networked. Even the most natural action of all – the inhaling of clean air – ultimately presupposes a revolution in the industrial world order. This brings us to the concept of the globalization of biography. In the global age, one's own life is no longer sedentary or tied to a particular place. It is a travelling life, both literally and metaphorically, a nomadic life, a life spent in cars, aeroplanes and trains, on the telephone or the internet, supported by the mass media, a transnational life stretching across frontiers. The multilocal transnationality of the life of one's own is a further reason for the hollowing out of national sovereignty and the obsolescence of nation-based sociology. The association of place and community or society is coming unstuck (Beck, 1999a). Whether voluntarily or compulsorily or both, people spread their lives out across separate worlds. Globalization of biography means place polygamy; people are wedded to several places at once. Place-polygamous ways of living are translated biographies: they have to be constantly translated both for oneself and for others, so that they can continue as in-between lives. The transition from the first to the second modernity is also a transition from place monogamy to place polygamy. To understand the social figure of globalization as it applies to the life of one's own, it is necessary to keep in view the different conflicting places across which that life is spread out. In this sense, not only global players but also Indian taxi drivers in Chicago or Russian Jews in Israel live transnational lives. Globalization of biographies means a very complex, contradictory process that generates novel conflicts and forms of separation. Thus, the upsurge of local nationalisms and the new emphasis on local identity should be seen as an unmistakable consequence of globalization, and not, as they may first appear, as a phenomenon that contradicts it. This seventh thesis therefore implies that the life of one's own is a global life. The framework of the national state has become too big and too small. What happens within your own life has a lot to do with worldwide influences, challenges and fashions or with protection against them.

8: The other side of globalization is detraditionalization. The life of one's own is also a detraditionalized life. This does not mean that tradition no longer plays any role – often the opposite is the case. But traditions must be chosen and often invented, and they have force only through the decisions and experience of individuals. The sources of collective and group identity and of meaning which are characteristic of industrial society (ethnic identity, class consciousness, faith in progress), whose lifestyles and notions of security underpinned Western democracies and economies into the 1960s, here lose their mystique and break up, exhausted. Those who live in this post-national, global society are constantly engaged in discarding old classifications and formulating new ones. The hybrid identities and cultures that ensue are precisely the individuality which then determines social integration. In this way, identity emerges through intersection and combination and thus through conflict with other identities.

How does this differ from the historical and theoretical analyses of Georg Simmel, Emile Durkheim and Max Weber in the early part of the twentieth century? The main difference is that today people are not discharged from corporate religious-cosmological certainties into the world of industrial society, but are transplanted from the national industrial societies of the first modernity into the transnational turmoil of world-risk society (Beck, 1999b). People are expected to live their lives with the most diverse and contradictory transnational and personal identities and risks. Individualization in this sense means detraditionalization, but also the opposite: a life lived in conflict between different cultures, the invention of hybrid traditions. It is hardly surprising that various idylls – grandma's apple cake, forget-me-nots and communitarianism – are experiencing a boom. Even traditional (for example, religious) systems of interpretation cannot shut themselves off from what is happening; they collide with one another and end up in public competition and conflict, at both a global and a local level. Fundamentalism too, in its European and non-European variants, is in this sense a reaction to both individualization and globalization. The crucial point here is that the public realm no longer has anything to do with collective decisions. It is a question not of solidarity or obligation but of conflictual coexistence.

9: If globalization, detraditionalization and individualization are analysed together, it becomes clear that the life of one's own is an experimental life. Inherited recipes for living and role stereotypes fail to function. There are no historical models for the conduct of life. Individual and social life – in marriage and parenthood as well as in politics, public activity and paid work – have to be brought back into harmony with each other. The restlessness of the age, of the Zeitgeist, is also due to the fact that no one knows how or whether this can be achieved.

10: The life of one's own is a reflexive life. Social reflexion – the processing of contradictory information, dialogue, negotiation, compromise – is almost synonymous with living one's own life. Active management (and that does seem the right word) is necessary for the conduct of life in a context of conflicting demands and a space of global uncertainty. Self-realization and self-determination are by no means merely individual goals; they are often also public stopgaps, the reverse side of the problems that all partial systems unload onto citizens by suddenly deeming them 'mature and responsible'. This compulsion to self-realization, this departure for the foreign continent of the life of one's own, goes hand in hand with integration into worldwide contexts. Something like individual distinctiveness really appears for the first time through the combination of social crises in which individuals are forced to think, act and live. It becomes normal to test out a number of different mixes; several overlapping identities are discovered and a life is constructed out of their combination. The social structure of the global life of one's own thus appears together with continual differentiation and individualization – or, to be more precise, with the individualization of classes, ethnic groups, nuclear families and normal female biographies. In this way, the nationally fixed social categories of industrial society are culturally dissolved or transformed. They become 'zombie categories', which have died yet live on. Even traditional conditions of life become dependent on decisions; they have to be chosen, defended and justified against other options and lived out as a personal risk. Not only genetically modified food but also love and marriage, including the traditional housewife marriage, become a risk.

11: Living a life of one's own is, in this sense, a late-modern form which enjoys high esteem. This has not always been so. In traditional, nationally closed societies, the individual remains a species concept: the smallest unit of an imagined whole. Only detraditionalization, global opening and a new multiplicity of functional logics give social space and meaning to the emphasis on the individual. The positive evaluation of the individual is thus a truly modern phenomenon, which at the same time continues to be vigorously combated even today (as talk of the 'me-first' or 'push-and-shove' society shows). All through history, individualist behaviour has been equated with conduct that is deviant or even idiotic. When individuality features in the consciousness of a world picture, it is tainted with a flaw or defect. This was true in ancient Greece or during the early Middle Ages in Europe, when individuality was mainly interpreted as deviant or sinful behaviour to be avoided. This deprecatory sense of individuality persisted in the sciences and 'the bourgeois world, up to the epigraph of Sartre's *La Nausée*: "Ce type n'a aucune valeur pour la société, il n'est qu'un individu." A mere individual – that is the most concise formula expressing the opposition to the early Romantic rehabilitation (and redefinition) of the essence of individuality' (Frank, 1988: 611). Interestingly enough, this revaluation of individuality succeeded precisely because that which had for centuries been the reason for its low value now became the reason for its high value: namely, that the individual cannot be derived from the general. The point now was that the general could only be surmised and thus paled beside the verifiability and indeed immemoriality of the individual. The 'essence of individuality' may therefore be understood as 'radical non-identity'.

12: The life of one's own, seen in this way, is a radically non-identical life. While culture was previously defined by traditions, today it must be defined as an area of freedom which protects each group of individuals and has the capacity to produce and defend its own individualization. To be more specific, culture is the field in which we assert that we can live together, equal yet different.

13: Living your own life therefore can mean living under the conditions for radicalized democracy, for which many of the concepts and formulae of the first modernity have become inadequate. No one knows how the conflicting transnational identities can be politically integrated. No one knows how the ever growing demands for family intimacy can be linked to the new demands for the freedom and self-realization of men, women and children. No one knows how the need of mass organizations (political parties, trade unions) to obligate individuals can be made compatible with claims for participation and self-organization. People are better adapted to the future than are social institutions and their representatives.

14: The decline of values which cultural pessimists are so fond of decrying is in fact opening up the possibility of escape from the creed of 'bigger, more, better', in a period that is living beyond its means ecologically and economically. Whereas, in the old value system, the self always had to be subordinated to patterns of collectivity, these new 'we' orientations are creating something like a co-operative or altruistic individualism. Thinking of oneself and living for others, once considered a contradiction in terms, is revealed as an internal connection. In fact, living alone means living socially. The politics based on the defence of life as a personal project is the rejection of its adversaries: a powerful market system on the one hand and a communalism that imposes purity and homogeneity on the other.

15: The dominance of the life of one's own thus leads to an opening and a sub-politicization of society, but also to a depoliticization of national politics. Two of the basic conditions for national representative democracy are being especially called into question. The first of these conditions is the general trust that enables parties (and other collective actors) to mobilize citizens and party members, to some extent blindly and independently of their personal preferences, around certain issues of the day. The second is the limited number of collective actors and their internal homogeneity. Both these premises are becoming questionable as a result of individualization processes. It cannot be assumed either that citizens are party members and party members are party troops or that parties and trade unions are intrinsically capable of achieving consensus – because large organizations are also pluralized in respect of their content. In the wake of the processes of individualization and globalization, collective actors are themselves being hollowed out and summoned to programmatic revolutions behind an unchanging façade (New Labour, for example). Unpredictable dilemmas arise, however, for the organization of politics at the level of the national state. Here we see the impetuous development of what Kant already noted in his critique of representative democracy: namely, the contradiction that democracy appeals to the individual as the subject of law making, yet filters out, glides over and holds down the expression of individual will in the forms of representativity. On the one hand, the 'living your own life' society validates at the heart of national politics the basic proposition that the individual – and only the individual – counts as the source of democratic legitimacy. On the other hand, the corporate and representative organization of the mediation of interests rests precisely upon the fact that it is not individuals but collective actors, constructed in accordance with the constitution, who take political decisions of major importance and scope. Conversely, it is not possible to admit more and more actors into the game of political power, because that would multiply the arenas of conflict without increasing the potential for consensus. The number of negotiating systems cannot grow indefinitely, and it is by no means the case that many individual negotiations add up to a single all-integrating power of decision. It thus becomes apparent that the politicization of society in the wake of cultural democratization does not at all translate into an activation of politics. This takes the steam out of the frequent objection that the numerically larger involvement of modern individualists in a wide range of local initiatives or (to use the fashionable expression) networks – from sports clubs to campaigns against xenophobia – integrates or socializes modern society in a way that is functionally equivalent to that of the traditional political forms of large organizations or the national state. Even the widespread talk of a 'networking of networks' cannot obscure the fact that the increasingly fragmented political structure of society, which is expressed in the individualization of political behaviour and the waning capacity of the old large organizations for integration and aggregation, weakens the potential of political societies for purposive mobilization and direction. (Greven, 1997: 246ff.). The ideal of integration through conflict, which is the basis of national democracy, here breaks down. It becomes ever more difficult to guarantee the two sides of democracy: consensus among individuals and groups based upon free agreement and representation of conflictual interests. But this is where a real political dilemma of the second modernity becomes palpable. On the one hand, political imagination and political action are confronted with challenges of a quite unprecedented scale. We need only think of the sweeping reforms needed to give the social state a new foundation with regard to insecure forms of employment and the working poor; or of what is required to reorganize the nationally calibrated key institutions of parliamentary democracy so that they are more open to transnational identities, life situations and economic link-ups; not to speak of the once totally neglected question of ecologically reforming the autonomous and ever faster world industrial dynamic. On the other hand, processes of individualization are eroding the social-structural conditions for political consensus, which until now have made possible collective political action. The paradox is that this happens because political involvement is increasing at the microcosmic level and subpolitical society is governed from below in more and more issues and fields of action. The closed space of national politics no longer exists. Society and the public realm are constituted out of conflictual spaces that are at once individualized, transnationally open and defined in opposition to one another. It is in these spaces that each cultural group tests and lives out its hybrid.

Bibliography

Beck, U. (1999a) *What is Globalization?* Cambridge: Polity Press.

Beck, U. (1999b) *World Risk Society*. Cambridge: Polity Press.

Beck, U. and Beck-Gernsheim, E. (2001) *Individualization*. London: Sage.

Frank, M. (1988) 'Einleitung in Fragmente einer Schlussdiskussion', in M. Frank and P. Haverlcamp (eds), *Individualität, Poetik und Hermeneutik*, vol. 13. Munich: Fink.

Greven, Michael T. (1997) 'Politisierung ohne Citoyens', in H. Klein and G. Schmalz-Bruns (eds), *Politische Beteiligung und Bürgerengagement in Deutschland*. Opladen: Westdeutscher Verlag.

Translated from the German version © **Eigenes Leben. Ausflüge in die unbekannte Gesellschaft, in der wir leben** von Ulrich Beck, Wilhelm Vossenkuhl and Ulf E. Ziegler. 105 Fotos von Timm Rautert, München, 1995.

3

Beyond Status and Class?

Are we now witnessing a historic change whereby people are 'released' from the forms of industrial society (class, social layer, occupation, family, marriage), as they were released during the Reformation from the secular domination of the Church? Is it possible that, amid the waning of traditional ways of life, new ones are taking shape for which we simply have no concept and therefore no perception? Are the forceful demands for self-determination and participation as much a sign of this as are the boundary crossing and new combinations of the private and the public?

Today, anyone who poses the key question of the reality of classes in Germany or other advanced societies is faced with an apparent contradiction. On the one hand, the structure of social inequality in the developed countries displays a surprising *stability*; research findings tell us that, despite all the technological and economic changes and all the attempts at reform, there has been no major change in the relations of inequality between major groups in our society – leaving aside isolated shifts and grey areas.

On the other hand, questions concerning inequality are no longer perceived and politically handled as class questions. In the wake of the unification of the two German states, unemployment and poverty have sharply increased and such phenomena as the struggle for women's rights, movements against nuclear power stations, and inter-generational, inter-regional and inter-religious conflicts also centrally involve issues of inequality. But if the public political debate is taken as a measure of real developments, the general conclusion would seem to be that we live in a country already *beyond* class society, in which the imagery of class is preserved only for want of a better alternative.

This contradiction is resolvable if we examine more closely the extent to which the *social significance* of inequalities has changed over the past three decades – a change that has largely escaped the attention of the relevant research. Our thesis is precisely that in the wealthy industrial heartlands of the West – and most plainly in the Federal Republic of Germany – the post-war development of the welfare state brought with it a social impetus toward individualization of unprecedented scale and dynamism, beneath the cover of largely constant relations of inequality. Against the backdrop of a comparatively high standard of living and social security, a break in historical continuity released people from traditional class ties and family supports and increasingly threw them onto their own resources and their individual fate in the labour market, with all its attendant risks, opportunities and contradictions.

A process of individualization has long been considered a feature of the newly developing bourgeoisie, but in another form it was also distinctive of the 'free wage labourer' of modern capitalism and of the labour market dynamic under the conditions of welfare state mass democracies. Entry into the labour market has repeatedly released people from fixed ties of family, neighbourhood and occupation, as well as from ties to a particular regional culture and landscape. These individualizing thrusts *compete* with such collective aspects of a labour market destiny as the social risks of wage labour (unemployment, deskilling etc.). But it is only insofar as these risks are reduced – through relative affluence and social protection – that individualization actually leads to a *dissolution* of lifeworlds associated with class and status group subcultures.

The implications for social structure are thus ambivalent. On the one hand, stratification theorists (and Marxist class theorists) may consider that nothing essential has changed, for distances in the income hierarchy and fundamental coordinates of wage labour have remained much the same. But on the other hand, ties to a social class (in Max Weber's sense) have typically been pushed into the background. A tendency to individualized lifestyles and life situations forces people – for the sake of material survival – to make themselves the centre of their own life plans and conduct.

Consequently, individualization should here be understood as a historically contradictory *process of socialization*. The standardized collective character of these individualized life situations is certainly difficult to comprehend. Yet it is precisely the breaking out of this contradiction and the consciousness of it as a contradiction, which can lead to the emergence of new socio-cultural commonalities: whether new class situations spanning different income and skill groups become visible along with the intensification of social risks; or whether, in the wake of individualization processes, expectations of 'a life of one's own' (conceived materially, spatially, temporally and as a pattern of social relations) are systematically awakened yet brought up against social-political limitations and resistances. This constantly gives rise to new quests, which may involve extreme experiments with social relations and with people's own lives and bodies in the various alternative scenes and youth subcultures (including the excesses of far-right violence). Commonalities are here cultivated not least in aggressive protest actions, sparked off by bureaucratic-industrial encroachments on people's own 'private lives'.

We may say that a wide-ranging social and cultural *process of erosion and evolution* has been unleashed by the ongoing individualization. The course and the consequences of individualization processes within society are therefore of general interest for an understanding of major social shifts in the phase of advanced modernity. There are strong indications that they tend to bring about a change in the social meaning and pattern of such central lifeworld structures as the family (marriage, parenthood), gender roles, community relations, labour relations and party affiliations and that they help to explain the 'new social movements' and political behaviour in general, including the question of consensus and governability in modern societies.

The Labour Market as 'Motor' of Individualization

'Individualization of social inequality' – does this not suggest that everything important is being forgotten, misunderstood or simply dismissed, including everything we have learned about the class character of society, its nature as a system, about mass society and the concentration of capital, about ideological distortions and alienation, about unchanging human traits and the complexity of social and historical reality? And does not the concept of individualization also spell the premature end of sociology, leading to the tolling of its bell?

This calls for a number of clarifications. The existence of individualization has been empirically verified in numerous qualitative interviews and studies. They all point to one central concern, the demand for control of one's own money, time, living space and body. In other words, people demand the right to develop their own perspective on life and to be able to act upon it. However illusory and ideological these claims may turn out to be, they are a reality which cannot be overlooked. And they arise from the actual conditions of life in Germany as they have developed in the past three decades. But today it is also becoming apparent that such processes of individualization can be quite precarious, especially where groups are suddenly hit or threatened by unemployment and forced to confront radical disruptions of their lifestyle precisely because of the individualization they have experienced and despite the protections provided by the welfare state.

How do such trends differ from the rise of bourgeois individualism in the eighteenth and nineteenth centuries? Processes of individualization among the bourgeoisie derived essentially from the ownership and accumulation of capital. The bourgeoisie developed its social and political identity in the struggle against feudal structures of domination and authority. In late modernity, by contrast, individualization is a product of the labour market and manifests itself in the acquisition, proffering and application of a variety of work skills. This argument can be elaborated by looking at three dimensions of the labour market – education, mobility and competition.

Education

As schooling increases in duration, traditional orientations, ways of thinking and lifestyles are recast and displaced by universalistic forms of learning and teaching, as well as by universalistic forms of knowledge and language. Depending on its duration and content, education makes possible at least a certain degree of self-discovery and reflection. Education, furthermore, is connected with *selection* and therefore requires the individual's expectations of upward mobility; these expectations remain effective even in cases where upward mobility through education is an illusion, since education is little more than a protection against downward mobility (as to some extent happened during the period of expansion of educational opportunities). For it is after all only possible to pass through formal education by individually succeeding by way of assignments, examinations and tests. Formal education in schools and universities, in turn, provides individual credentials leading to individualized career opportunities in the labour market.

Mobility

As soon as people enter the labour market, they experience mobility. They are removed from traditional patterns and arrangements and, unless they are prepared to suffer economic ruin, they are forced to take charge of their own life. The labour market, by way of occupational mobility, place of residence or employment, type of employment, as well as the changes in social location it initiates, reveals itself as a driving force behind the individualization of people's lives. They become relatively independent of inherited or newly formed ties (e.g. family, neighbourhood, friendship, partnership). By becoming independent from traditional ties, people's lives take on an independent quality which, for the first time, makes possible the experience of a personal destiny.

Competition

Competition rests upon the interchangeability of qualifications and thereby compels people to advertise the individuality and uniqueness of their work and of their own accomplishments. The growing pressure of competition leads to an individualization among equals, i.e. precisely in areas of interaction and conduct which are characterized by a shared background (similar education, similar experience, similar knowledge). Especially where such a shared background still exists, community is dissolved in the acid bath of competition. In this sense, competition undermines the equality of equals without, however, eliminating it. It causes the isolation of individuals within homogeneous social groups.

Education, mobility and competition, however, are by no means independent of one another. Rather, they supplement and reinforce one another – and it is only by doing this that they have led to the distinctive impetus towards individualization of the past three decades.

Individualization and Class Formation: Marx and Weber

The thrust toward individualization in the welfare state can be understood more precisely by examining Karl Marx's and Max Weber's theories of social inequality. It is quite possible to regard Marx as one of the most resolute theorists of 'individualization'. Marx often stressed that an unparalleled process of emancipation had been set in motion as a result of the development of industrial capitalism. In his view, emancipation from feudal relations was a precondition for the establishment of capitalist relations of production. But even within capitalism itself people are uprooted in successive waves and wrested loose from tradition, family, neighbourhood, occupation and culture.

Marx never followed up on this variant of a class society caught in the process of individualization. For him the capitalist process of isolation and 'uprooting' had always been cushioned by the collective experience of immiseration and the resulting class struggle. Marx thought that it was precisely the process of emancipation and uprooting and the deterioration of the living conditions of workers under capitalism that led to the transformation of the working class from a 'class in itself' into a 'class for itself'. He dismissed as irrelevant the question of how individual proletarians, qua market subjects, could ever form stable bonds of solidarity, given that capitalism systematically uprooted their lives. Marx always equated processes of individualization with the formation of classes. This still appears to be the basic position of many contemporary class theorists.

The thesis of the individualization of social inequality may be regarded as precisely mirroring the Marxian position. Processes of individualization, as already described, can only become entrenched when material immiseration, as the condition for the formation of classes predicted by Marx, has been overcome. Trends toward individualization are dependent on complex structural conditions which up to now have been realized in very few countries and even then only during the most recent phase of development. Among such trends are economic prosperity, the construction of a welfare state, the institutionalization of interests represented by trade unions, the legal underpinning of labour contracts, the expansion of education, the growth of the service sector and associated opportunities for mobility and the shortening of the working week.[1]

These analyses may now be at once broadened and clarified if we turn to a second tradition associated with the name of Max Weber. On the one hand, as is well known, Max Weber laid much greater stress than Marx on the wide range of modern lifestyles. On the other hand, he ignored the latent tendencies toward individualization within market society. Weber, in fact, argued that these could not succeed, but without sharing Marx's belief in class formation resulting from immiseration. Tendencies toward individualization were blocked, according to Weber, by the continuity and the authority of traditions and subcultures based on status. In industrial capitalism traditional 'status-bound' attitudes, Weber argues, have been combined with expertise and market opportunities into substantively differentiated 'social class positions'. Thus Weber's work already contained the basic arguments spelled out in detail by Marxist labour historians at the end of the 1960s: namely, that the characteristic norms governing lifeworlds, value orientations and lifestyles during the expansion of industrial capitalism are less the product of 'class structures' and 'class formation' (as understood by Marx) than remnants of *pre*-capitalist and *pre*-industrial traditions. 'Capitalist culture' is consequently a less autochthonous creation than is often assumed. It is rather of pre-capitalist origins, modernized and assimilated by a system of industrial capitalism which recasts and consumes it. Thus, although Weber recognized various trends toward 'disenchantment' and 'demystification' of traditional lifestyles, he still regarded the social dynamic of individualization processes as following the principle of community formation linked to status.

Historical studies suggest that this indeed applied up to the early 1950s, but I do not believe that it still held for post-war developments in Germany at least. At that point the unstable unity of shared life experiences mediated by the market and shaped by status, which Max Weber brought together in the concept of social class, began to break apart. Its different elements (such as material conditions dependent on specific market opportunities, the effectiveness of tradition and of pre-capitalist lifestyles, the consciousness of communal bonds and of barriers to mobility, as well as networks of contact) have slowly disintegrated. They have been changed beyond recognition by the increasing standard of living and the increasing dependence on education as well as by an intensified mobility, competition and the juridification of labour relations. The traditional internal differentiations and social environments, which were still real enough for industrial workers in Imperial Germany and in the Weimar Republic, have been increasingly dissolved since the 1950s. At the same time, differences within the industrial labour force and between rural and urban populations have been levelled. Everywhere educational reform is accompanied by a dependence on education. More and more groups get caught up in the race for educational credentials. As a result there emerge new *internal* differentiations. While these may still respond to traditional differences between groups, the impact of education makes them fundamentally different from traditional ones. Here we can employ Bernstein's distinction that the new generation must move from a 'restricted' to an 'elaborated' code of speech. In conjunction with novel patterns of upward and downward mobility and increasing local labour mobility as well, new hierarchies and differentiations develop which are internal to social classes.

During the same period, traditional forms of settlement have frequently been replaced by new urban housing projects. These changes have also generated new forms of individualization. They affect patterns of interaction dependent on housing and living arrangements. The modern metropolis as well as urban developments in the smaller towns replace traditional settlement patterns. People from a great variety of cultural backgrounds are mixed together and social relations in the neighbourhood are much more loosely organized. Thus traditional forms of community beyond the family are beginning to disappear. Often, the members of the family choose their own separate relationships and live in networks of their own. This need not imply that social isolation increases or that relatively private family life prevails – although this may happen. But it does imply that already existing (ascriptively organized) neighbourhoods are shattered, together with their limitations and their opportunities for social control. The newly formed social relationships and social networks now have to be individually chosen; social ties, too, are becoming *reflexive*, so that they have to be established, maintained and constantly renewed by individuals.

This may mean, to take an extreme example, that interaction is no longer present, that social isolation and loneliness become the major pattern of relationships, as often happens with elderly people. It may also mean, however, that self-selected and self-created hierarchies and forms of stratification develop in relationships with acquaintances, neighbours and friends. These relationships are no longer primarily dependent on 'physical' proximity. Whether they transcend the local sphere or not, they are formed by individuals who regard themselves as organizers of their own circles of contacts and relationships. In the passage from one generation to the next, this may also entail that opportunities arise for people to experiment and test out new modes of living with one another.

The ability to choose and maintain one's own social relations may explain, for example, the emergence of many different layers and aspects of the private sphere, including the new phenomenon of *political privatism*. By this I mean an internally consistent, externally provocative stretching of the social and legal limits to people's freedom of action; a way of experimenting with social relations and lifestyles at the edge of what is culturally 'permissible' which generates political disturbances as well as processes of identity formation and identity attribution. This may result in a division into culture and counterculture, society and alternative society (including a growth of far-right violence), such as we have repeatedly seen in the last 20 years.

These and other developments suggest that the unstable association of community and market society which Max Weber had in mind when he spoke of social class has been partially transformed or even dissolved in the course of post-war developments. People at any rate no longer seem to understand or to experience it. The new ways of living reveal dynamic possibilities for a reorganization of social relations, which cannot be adequately comprehended by following either Marx or Weber.

As a result, the following questions become paramount. What actually happens when, in the course of historical development, the identity of social classes rooted in the lifeworld melts away – that is, when class loses its basis in subcultures and people's own experience of the world, even as the conditions and risks of wage labour are becoming generalized? Is a class identity no longer shaped by status even conceivable? Can the inequalities persisting under conditions of individualization still be grasped by means of the concept of class or by means of even more general hierarchical models of social inequality? Perhaps all these hierarchical models categorically depend on traditional status dependency? But are there interpretations which can replace these models? It may, of course, also be the case that processes of individualization are embedded in contradictions which in turn produce new social groupings and conflicts. How then are processes of individualization transformed into their opposite, into a quest for new social identities and ties and the development of new ways of living? One can imagine three extreme variants which are by no means mutually exclusive and indeed may even overlap.

First, the waning of traditional lifestyles does not bring the end of class, but rather *emancipates* classes from regional and particularist limitations. A new chapter in the history of classes is beginning, but we still need to comprehend its historical dynamics. It can in any case no longer be said without further qualification that this still is a history of the formation of class solidarities.

Second, in the course of the developments just described, both the firm and the workplace lose their significance in conflict and identity formation. A new site arises for the formation of social bonds and for the development of conflicts: namely, the sphere of private social relations and of personal modes of work and life. It is here that new social formations and identities are moulded beyond class society.

Third, the end of class society is not some revolutionary 'big bang'. It is a collectively experienced process of individualization within a post-traditional society of employees.

The Emergence of Non-Corporate Class Identities

Discussion about the working class and the workers' movement in the second half of the twentieth century was marked by a false alternative. On the one hand, more and more arguments are adduced to show that the situation of working people under capitalism has significantly improved (material prosperity, greater educational opportunities, trade union and political organization resulting in the acquisition of rights and social security). On the other hand, it is said that the lot of the working class – that is, the wage relationship with its associated dependence, alienation and risks – has remained the same as before or even grown sharper as a result of unemployment, deskilling and so on. The point of the argument is to demonstrate, in the former case, that the working class is being *dissolved* and in the latter case that it displays *continuity* – with all the political consequences that flow from this. What both sides fail to recognize, however, is that the symbiosis of occupation and class is being shattered, with the result that corporate sub-cultures melt away while basic features of class are generalized. Once this fact is grasped, the question arises of how far the detachment of classes from corporate rigidities marks the beginning of a new type of class formation.

With the waning of the corporate reality of social classes, it is less and less pos-sible to relate the development of forms of solidarity in society to the historical model of the 'proletarian productive worker'. Talk of the working class, or the class of employees, no longer appears a matter of course in people's lifeworlds, so that the basic references cease to apply for arguments about whether the pro-letariat is becoming 'bourgeoisified' or employees 'proletarianized'. At the same time, the dynamic of the labour market – or unemployment! – has been encom-passing ever wider layers; the group of those not dependent on a wage becomes ever smaller and the group of those dependent on a wage ever larger. For all the differences, common features – especially common risks – increasingly stretch across groups defined by income or education.

Consequently, the potential and actual clientele of the trade unions has markedly *increased*, while at the same time it is *endangered* in new ways. The image of proletarianization also involved the coming together of those affected by it through the facts of material impoverishment and alienation. Wage labour risks, however, do not necessarily set up *any* commonality.They call instead for social, political and legal measures which in turn bring about the individualization of demands; people have to be specifically made aware of the collective character of these demands, in contrast to individual-therapeutic ways of handling problems. Thus, trade unionist and political modes of perception and action enter into com-petition with individually centred legal, medical or psychotheraputic remedies and compensations, which may sometimes appear much more apposite to those upon whom the harm has been inflicted.

From the Family to Political Privatism

In the 1950s and 1960s, a lot of social research in the industrialized West demon-strated that the way in which people related to their job could be understood only in the context of their family life and their general situation vis-à-vis work. It became apparent that, even for industrial workers, the central focus of life was their family and not their experience of industrial wage labour.

This thoroughly ambivalent development of the private sphere, intensified by means of the culture and leisure industry, is not only an ideology but a *real* process and a *real* opportunity for people to fashion the conditions of their own life. The process only began with the family-centred privatism so characteristic of the 1950s and 1960s. As can now be seen more clearly, it could assume many dif-ferent forms and acquire an independent dynamic that eventually gave privatism a political charge or dissolved it from within (for example, through the altered significance of family and sexuality, marriage and parenthood, but also in the emergence of fast changing alternative cultures). In a completely new manner that perhaps cut more ice than attempts at political reform, the constant erosion and evolution of lifestyles placed the social-political structure under pressure to change and adapt in the most detailed ways. In this sense, the detraditionalization of the last few decades has unleashed a learning process whose historical effects (on children's upbringing or gender relations, for example) may be tensely awaited.

In the 1950s and 1960s, people gave a clear and unambiguous answer to the question of their goal in life: it was a 'happy' family home, a new car, a good education for their children and a higher standard of living. Today many speak a different (inevitably less clear-cut) language, which revolves around issues of individuality and identity, the 'development of personal capacities' and 'keeping things moving'. This does not, however, apply equally to all sections of the population. It is essentially a change on the part of the better educated and more affluent younger generation, whereas older, poorer and less educated groups remain clearly tied to the value system of the 1950s. In the eyes of many, the conventional symbols of success (income, career, status) no longer fulfil their need for self-discovery and self-assertion or their hunger for a 'fuller life'.

People therefore end up more and more in a labyrinth of self-doubt and uncertainty. The (infinite) regress involved in this self-questioning – 'Am I really happy?', 'Am I really fulfilled?', 'Who exactly is the I saying and asking this?' – leads to ever new kinds of response, which then often provide a market niche for experts, industries and religious movements. In their quest for self-fulfilment, people scour the travel brochures and go to the four corners of the earth; they throw away the best marriages and rapidly enter new ties; they undergo retraining, diet and jog; they shift from one therapy group to another and swear by quite different therapies and therapists. They pull themselves up by the roots, to see whether the roots are really healthy.

This value system of individualization also contains the elements of a new ethics, which is based on the principle of 'duty to oneself'. Of course, this completely contradicts the traditional view of ethics, in which duties are necessarily social in character and adjust the individual to the whole. The new value orientations are thus often seen as an expression of egoism and narcissism. But this is to misunderstand the essence of what is new about them: namely, their focus on self-enlightenment and self-liberation as an active process to be accomplished in their own lives, including the search for new social ties in family, workplace and politics.

The political strength of the labour movement rests upon its capacity to stop work in the organized form of the strike. By contrast, the political potential of the newly developing private sphere lies in the realization that it enables a degree of self-fashioning of people's lives which, through the direct act of making things different, challenges and overcomes deep-rooted cultural beliefs. To take one example, the strength of the women's movement also rests on the remoulding of everyday routines and certainties in all areas of formal work, the legal system and the various centres of decision making, where its policy of pinpricks is felt as painful by the closed male 'corporation'. In general, then, the trigger for today's social conflicts and movements (unlike in lifeworlds shaped by class cultures) is a perceptible threat to spaces of action and decision that were once confidently held in a spirit of expansion.

Toward an Individualized Society of Employees

There are a great many different attempts to develop new social groupings, but however strong the convulsions triggered by them may be, they are invariably qualified by the fact that they, too, are exposed to ever new thrusts toward individualization. The motor of individualization is going at full blast and it is not at all clear how new and lasting social arrangements, comparable in depth of penetration to social classes, can even be created. On the contrary, especially in the immediate future, it is very likely that, as a way of coping with unemployment and economic crises, social and technological innovations will be set in motion which will open up new opportunities for individualization processes, in particular with regard to greater flexibility in labour market relations and new regulations governing working hours. But this also applies to the new forms of communication. These technological and social revolutions, which either still lie ahead or are already in full swing, will unleash a profound individualization of lifestyles.

If this assessment is correct, a variant of social structure which neither Marx nor Weber foresaw will gain in importance. Class society will pale into insignificance beside *an individualized society of employees*. Both the typical characteristics as well as the dangers of such a society are now becoming increasingly clear. In contrast to class society, which is defined essentially in terms of tradition and culture, a society of employees must be defined in terms of labour law and by means of socio-political categories. The result is a peculiar stage of transition, in which persisting or intensifying inequalities coincide with elements of a no longer traditional, individualized post-class society (which bears no resemblance to Marx's vision of a classless society). This transitional society is distinguished by a variety of typical structures and changes.

First, processes of individualization deprive class distinctions of their social identity. Social groups lose their distinctive traits, both in terms of their self-understanding and in relation to other groups. They also lose their independent identities and the chance to become a formative political force. As a result of this development, the idea of social mobility (in the sense of individual movement between actual status classes), which until very late in the twentieth century constituted a social and political theme of considerable importance for social identity formation, pales into insignificance.

Second, inequalities by no means disappear. They merely become redefined in terms of an *individualization of social risks*. The result is that social problems are increasingly perceived in terms of psychological dispositions: as personal inadequacies, guilt feelings, anxieties, conflicts, and neuroses. There emerges, paradoxically, a new immediacy of individual and society, a direct relation between crisis and sickness. Social crises appear as individual crises, which are no longer (or only very indirectly) perceived in terms of their rootedness in the social realm. This is one of the explanations for the current revival of interest in psychology. Individual achievement orientation similarly gains in importance. It can now be predicted that the full range of problems associated with the achievement society and its tendency toward (pseudo-)legitimations of social inequalities will emerge in the future.

Third, in attempting to cope with social problems, people are forced into political and social alliances. These, however, need no longer follow a single pattern, such as the class model. The isolation of privatized lives, shielded against all other privatized lives, can be shattered by social and political events and developments of the most heterogeneous kind. Accordingly, temporary coalitions between different groups and different camps are formed and dissolved, depending on the particular issue at stake and on the particular situation. In this way, risks and risk conflicts, as far as they are personally experienced, are becoming an important issue as well. It is possible cheerfully to embrace seemingly contradictory causes, for example, to join forces with local residents in protests against noise pollution by air traffic, to belong to the metalworkers' union, and yet – in the face of impending economic crisis – to vote conservative. Such coalitions represent pragmatic alliances in the individual struggle for existence and occur on the various battlefields of society. A peculiar multiplication of areas of conflict can be observed. The individualized society prepares the ground for new and multi-faceted conflicts, ideologies and alliances, which go beyond the scope of all hitherto existing schematizations. These alliances are generally focused on single issues, are by no means heterogeneous and are oriented toward specific situations and personalities. The resulting so-called structure is susceptible to the latest social fashions (in issues and conflicts) which, pushed by the mass media, rule the public consciousness just as the spring, autumn and winter fashion shows do.

Fourth, permanent conflicts tend to arise along the lines of ascribed characteristics, which now as much as ever are undeniably connected with discrimination. Race, skin colour, gender, ethnicity, age, homosexuality, physical disability – these are the major ascribed characteristics. Under the conditions of advanced individualization, such quasi-natural social inequalities lead to the development of quite specific organizing effects. These attempt to gain political muscle by focusing upon the inescapability and permanence of such inequalities as well as upon their incompatibility with the achievement principle, their tangibility, and the fact that – as a result of their direct visibility – they make possible independent social and individual processes of identification. At the same time, individual fate is increasingly determined in a new way by economic trends and by historical necessity, as it were, – for example, by economic crisis or boom, restricted admission to universities and to the professions, the size of age cohorts and so on.

Will it be possible to choose as a point of departure the claims and the promises of the process of individualization now under way together with its impulse toward social emancipation, thereby in a new way – beyond status and class – uniting individuals and groups as self-conscious subjects of their own personal social and political affairs? Or will the last bastions of social and political action be swept away as a result of that very process? Would the individualized society then not fall, torn apart by conflicts and displaying symptoms of sickness, into the kind of political apathy that precludes virtually nothing, not even new and insidious forms of a modernized barbarism?

Notes

1 Under conditions of growing poverty and unemployment, 'individualization' means that poverty and unemployment less and less affect one group for a long period of time, but are distributed across society at particular phases of people's lives. To put this somewhat schematically, the conflicts involved in social inequality appear as conflicts between parts of a single life history. People's lives become more varied and discontinuous – which also implies that a growing section of the population is at least temporarily exposed to poverty and unemployment. Cf. U. Beck, *Risikogesellschaft*. Frankfurt/M. Suhrkamp 1986, pp. 143–51; Leisering and Zwick, 'Heterogenisierung der Armut?', *Zeitschrift für Sozialreform*, 1990, 11/12, pp. 715–45; P. A. Berger, *Individualisierung, Statusunsicherheit und Erfahrungsvielfalt*. Opladen: Westdeutscher Verlag 1996.

Translated from the German version, **Jenseits von Stand und Klasse? Zur Entraditionalisierung industriegessellschaftlicher Lebensformen**, in Ulrich Beck, and Elisabeth Beck-Gernsheim (eds.) *Riskante Freiheiten* (1994). Published here, in English, by kind permission of Suhrkamp Verlag, Frankfurt.

4

The Ambivalent Social Structure

Poverty and Wealth in A 'Self-Driven Culture'

Where individualization has been carried through, there arises what we would call an 'own life culture' or 'self-culture'. This should be understood in a twofold sense: it involves both recognition of the self (indeterminacy of the self and of the ensuing conflicts, crises and developmental opportunities) and a binding or bonding of self-oriented individuals to, with and against one another. 'Self-culture' thus denotes what was at first negatively addressed with the concept of a *post*-traditional lifeworld: that is, the compulsion and the pleasure of leading an insecure life of one's own and co-ordinating it with the distinctive lives of other people.

Proletarian Culture, Bourgeois Culture and 'Self-Culture'

The concept of a 'self-culture', understood as the adventurous search of the many for a 'life of their own', should first be distinguished from the concepts of *proletarian* and *bourgeois* culture that marked the features and the conflicts of the first (industrial) modernity. The latter's characteristic hopes and quirks, its habits in life, work, love and consumption, its styles of politics, its self-destructive rituals for sleeping, living, bathing, learning, relaxing and so on: all these are visible in the literature of every field, from the sciences through the novel to music. The self-culture develops to the extent that both proletarian culture and bourgeois culture fade and disappear. What then emerges is not, as sociologists have often suspected, a uniform middle-class culture and society (Schelsky, 1965), but precisely a self-culture that is unpredictable both for one-self and for others, a cross between civil society, consumer society, therapy society and risk society.

One crucial difference from proletarian and bourgeois culture is that here it is no longer class categories but the very cultural and political dynamic of 'one's own life' which puts its stamp on society. The lines of conflict are more diffuse but no less profound. New imaginaries of morality and responsibility take shape and develop; poverty, marriage, youth and political commitment assume new countenances. And along with the basic distinction between fixed corporations and elective communities in which a reference to individuals is the norm, a number of other features may serve to define what is meant by a self-culture.

First there are external, *demographic* criteria: the growing number of single-person households (where individuals live the contradiction of being at once young and old, single, widowed and divorced etc.) and the correspondingly high value placed on separateness in every lifestyle. This is expressed in the basic need (developed and established historically) for 'space' and 'time of one's own', and in the numerous consequences which this has for such things as the architectonics and infrastructure of late-modern cities. Another social-demographic feature of the self-culture is the high divorce figures and the related plethora, both open and concealed, of pre-marital, non-marital, extra-marital and post-marital lifestyles which we have grown used to lumping together under the veil of 'pluralization'.

Staging of the Self, the Practice of Freedom and Self-Organization

In addition to these and other external characteristics, three further ones are of major significance for the self-culture. First, *the staging of the self in processes of aesthetic lifestyle creation*. The goal of making one's own life a work of art has become a guiding idea for the generation of 18 to 35 year olds; research findings about global (or 'glocal') culture are here materially relevant to the sociology of life histories.

Second, *an internalized, practising consciousness of freedom*. Only with difficulty, if at all, can this be circumscribed and directed from above into certain goals and forms of commitment (party, trade union or church membership etc.); this presupposes certain reforms – basic rights, citizenship, the rule of law – as well as educational facilities and much else besides, so that the cultural consciousness of freedom can develop in all its contradictions and be put to the test of practice.

Third, *self-organization geared to action and not just to the ballot box*. This differs from mere *participation*, which assumes a hierarchical division of jurisdiction and authority and sorts out who should be involved in what. Self-organization demands what is still denied in participation – namely, the right of citizens to take charge of matters they deem important.

We must be careful not to equate this with *emancipation* and all the other fine things proclaimed by theorists of democracy. For it *may* quite easily appear together with xenophobia, violence and all manner of panic movements in which people turn nasty and abandon not only their duty as 'good citizens' but also their role as election fodder for political parties. Whereas, in the model of parliamentary democracy, the political activity of citizens is largely conceived as empowering someone else to represent them, self-organization is centred on the citizens' own activity. It is a question not just of occasionally voting people in and out, but of complaining, campaigning and acting about all things possible and impossible.

In this way a self-authorizing, self-referential sphere distinct from those of politics and economics, a kind of third sector of self-culture, develops through the centrifugal dynamic of 'a life of one's own'. Its autonomous logic of self-organization sets it apart from the money economy as much as from ballot-box democracy.

This third sector does not live off initiatives taken elsewhere but itself produces initiatives. It requires *institutional props and resources* – for example, basic social and political rights – which are internalized through education and practised in areas of free activity. A self-culture presupposes what it also demands: preparedness for conflict, capacity for compromise, civil courage, curiosity, tolerance of ambiguity and so on, even in relation to the uglier aspects of the self-culture. That there are signs of this (as well as of dissolution and decay) may be appreciated if we simply mention a few key phrases: first, the *new social movements* which keep discovering new issues and forms of expression and thereby display the power of resistance within civil society; then the many kinds of moral and aesthetic *experimentation* that people practise with their own lives and space, in relationships, parenthood, sex and love; the great unfinished experiment with *healthy eating*, in which a new and quite personal relationship is achieved with nature and with people's own bodies; the forms of active *empathy* expressed in protests against animal transport or in a commitment to the welfare of homeless people, asylum seekers or drug addicts; the minor and major *conflicts between men and women* in their own everyday life and in the economy, politics and the public arena; the wide-ranging disputes over *urban and regional planning, global identity* or *the powers of reason*; and last but not least, the new *'vigilante forces'* that spring up to protect niches of prosperity from anything that appears to threaten them – whether ecological destruction, noise pollution, foreigners, drug addicts or bureaucratic interference. The political dynamic that has created the ecological worldview is due not to the urgency of ecological questions, but to the institutional opening of a social space of 'self-culture' and 'self-organization'.

Self-Politics and State Politics

All these trends converge in what Giddens (1991) has termed 'life politics'. With the disappearance of physical and social nature, many new aspects become matters for decision. These concern the very foundations of people's lives (genetics, reproductive medicine), as well as various publicly contentious issues where the political bursts into the centre of the private.

Everything that counts in the left–right political schema of industrial society as a sign of loss, danger or decay – for example, concern with the question of who I am and what I want, or with shopping and what's on the menu – leads to a different kind of definition of the political. At key moments of a person's biography, for example, it becomes necessary to discuss and agree on matters connected with work and life (who will do the washing-up, change the baby's nappy or give up their career), as well as on policies to do with transport, labour, technology or any of the other everyday issues of a risk-filled civilization. As the Shell and 'British beef' controversies show, a directly political field of decision making can suddenly arise in what appear to be purely private matters of everyday life – for example, filling the petrol tank or cooking dinner. Here citizens discover the act of shopping as one in which they can always cast their ballot – on a world scale, no less. Are consumer society and *direct* politics thus beginning to come together and to bypass parties, parliaments and governments? Can this work in the long run?

Certainly it is necessary to distinguish between this kind of *direct* self-culture politics and the capacities and reach of state-organized parliamentary politics. And, of course, protests against Shell's plan to sink one of its oil platforms in the Atlantic do not add up to an effective environmental politics. It might even be asked whether actions of that kind are not spectacles that distract attention from the truly important questions of environmental politics.

But that would be to confuse self-culture politics with establishment politics, failing to see that it is, for example, both expressionist and impressionist. Self-culture politics is expressionist because it feels and develops its power and identity by dealing in symbolically generated mass media effects. It is impressionist because it consists of many isolated 'ad hoc actions' (in which both the activists and the issues are ad hoc), because it can politically assert its mass individualism only in publicly staged lightning flashes. Political action appears possible only as publicly organized collage.

In other words, the successes of self-culture politics should be measured by quite different yardsticks from those of governmental and parliamentary politics. Here success means a direct and tangible link-up between private actions that may have little meaning by themselves (filling a petrol tank, for example) and outcomes in which individuals can feel themselves to be authors of global political acts that would otherwise not have happened. Here the politicians, statesmen and other leaders sit in the spectators' area. The fascination of self-culture politics is precisely this inversion whereby the non-political becomes political and the political non-political, in such a way that individuals feel themselves to be originators of political intervention and (perhaps quite illusorily) political subjects crossing boundaries and breaching the system. Insofar as the self-culture becomes conscious of itself politically, a new kind of competitive relationship thus arises between self-organized and representative forms of political action.

This means that the political system is losing its monopoly of politics in the emphatic sense of the term, its claim to be the only legitimate site and subject for bargaining and decisions about the weal and woe. Alongside the forms and forums of parliamentary democracy, forms and forums of a politically self-active culture are taking shape. State politics and self-politics can neither copy nor replace one another: each has its characteristic ways of influencing events; they compete with one another (although by no means on equal terms) for the space of the political.

The power of system politics waxes and wanes with the resources it has at its disposal, but it also varies negatively with the growth of an independent self-culture politics. The latter's weakness is its lack of resources (money, time, law etc.). But its relative strength derives from its combination of universality (it can intervene anywhere on any issue) with ad hoc forms of commitment that shield it from outside control – its *impressionist imperialism*, we might call it.

Self-politics gains ground when system politics has long failed to suffice in *all* spheres of society: family, economy, church, clubs and associations and so on. Self-politics *may* also show off the superiority of republican over democratic claims. For, as Kant already noted, democracy is 'despotic'; it is based on representation and therefore on disempowerment of individuals and their political freedom. This is precisely why, if there is a conflict, it may be legitimate to deploy self-politics against the politics (or lack of it) of politicians – whatever the prospects of success. It can be seen from this that republican morality is a function of spontaneity; it cannot be organized by state action as something on the side. There is one very simple rule for the facilitation of self-cultures: make rights and minimal resources available and then *leave people alone*. There is no way in which voluntary activity can ever be forced on people.

A paradoxical relation therefore arises between self-active politics and state politics or control. *The more a self-culture is planned and promoted by the state, the weaker and punier it is likely to be.*[1] This is an expression of freedom, which can only be grasped and practised but never manufactured.

We live, as Giddens says, in a world of 'clever citizens'. Their cleverness is also a response to the destabilization of their situation. It does not denote academic intelligence, for example, but rather the practical ability to cope in a world where contradictory information and impossible decisions are the stuff of daily life.

And yet Giddens (1994) gives a guardedly optimistic answer to the question of what holds modern society together: namely, 'active trust' which ultimately requires a democratization of democracy. Active trust is the basis of the self-culture. It assumes not a clinging to consensus, but the presence of *dissent*; it rests upon recognition (not demonization) of the claim to 'a life of one's own' in a cosmopolitan world. It is true that active trust does not exclude inequality, but it does presuppose equal rights for all and is incompatible with feverish talk about duties and insistence on pre-given roles.

The declining credibility of political parties, but also of experts, academic disciplines, parents, teachers and so on, entails that many do not understand the independent logic of a self-active culture or its possible ups and downs. They still ask for consent when conscious dissent prevails. They should learn from this to develop and preserve an attitude of trust – although no one knows how this can succeed in a global culture marked by insoluble contradictions. Constantly bombarded with information and with appeals to take sides, everyone must also learn how to switch off (which should not be confused with indifference). Whether and when they will 'switch on again' – an absorbing question for all who would seduce others into buying things or into giving their consent – cannot be answered from above or outside in the case of a self-active culture. All commitment is (or is becoming) self-commitment – and is therefore unpredictable.

Individualization as a Sharpening of Social Inequality

But is not all this a rosy picture of a society in which gathering storm clouds (more than four million *registered* unemployed in Germany in summer 1996) have made niches of prosperity seem peculiarly old fashioned? Is it not the case that talk of a 'self-culture', although perhaps once applicable, no longer holds up in the face of growing poverty and urban decay? Does a life of your own not assume money and a job of your own, as well as a modicum of space and an assurance that you won't be mugged or stabbed at the next corner? Is not a life of one's own fundamentally threatened? Is this not why irrationalism and violence are no longer marginal phenomena but exist at the core of society?

Does talk of a 'self-culture' perhaps correspond to how the winners see things, while the silent losers go downhill with the violence born of despair? Are today's winners anyway not tomorrow's losers? And is it not a fear of plunging downward which makes them too tremble for the future? In the 1970s and 1980s it was doubtless possible to speak of individualization based on affluence, but since the early 1990s the starting-point has rather been an individualization based on the precarious conditions of life in a *capitalism without work*. But the idea of a 'self-culture' anyway signifies not the overcoming but the *sharpening* of social inequality. Here is some of the evidence:

- In the last 15 years income from work has risen in real terms by two per cent (virtually not at all), while income from capital has increased by 59 per cent (Kommission für Zukunftsfragen, 1996) and this is just the beginning of a phase of development in which the productivity of capital grows *without* labour.

- More and more groups in society are at least temporarily afflicted with poverty and unemployment. The industrial heartlands of the West are witnessing the emergence of a new and ever larger Lumpenproletariat of the *excluded*. Exclusion is the sociological term for the poverty trap at the heart of modern society: *Without a home no work. Without work no home. Without work and a home, no democracy.*

  Over the last two decades global output has risen from $4 trillion to $23 trillion – and at the same time the numbers of the poor have increased by more than 20 per cent. The share of world income enjoyed by the poorest fifth of humanity sank from four per cent to one per cent between 1960 and 1990 and today 358 dollar billionaires own more than a half of humanity combined.[2] Even if this does not raise too many eyebrows, more than 35,000 children die *every day* around the world – not from typhoons or floods or other natural disasters, but from diseases of civilization which, with the right means, are *relatively easy to prevent or cure* (pneumonia, dysentery, chicken pox, malaria, tetanus, whooping cough). In two days, then, more children die than Americans were killed in the Vietnam war (58,000) (Bradshaw and Wallace, 1996: 16f.).

  Meanwhile, in Germany more than seven million people live in the shadow of prosperity and even the apparently secure middle layers are threatened with decline. Managers evicted from the middle rungs of the hierarchy, bank employees rationalized out of a job, engineers whose services are no longer required: these are the threatened and the insecure who at first carefully conceal their fall from grace behind a façade of affluence. It would be hard to overstate the social and political drama of this widening gap between rich and poor within and between countries in Europe and North America. Indeed, the guessing game has begun in the upper reaches of the economy and politics as to how much poverty democracy can withstand.

- Since poverty and unemployment correspond less and less to class stereotypes, it is becoming increasingly difficult to identify them and to organize a strong political movement around them. Not only unemployment but also divorce, sudden illness, denial of credit or loss of affordable housing are typical trapdoors through which people fall into poverty and homelessness.

- In the form of their own lives, people must take individual responsibility and blame for – and often cope alone with – what used to be handled collectively as a class destiny. 'People are no longer human, the loss of face is indescribable': this is how an unemployed East German expresses in words the wretchedness of his present existence. In the new lands of the Federal Republic, the spectre of unemployment now has a majority of people directly or indirectly in its grip. The equation of losing a job with 'losing face' applies there in an even deeper sense, for the GDR was most emphatically a 'work society', where people were integrated into the community via the workplace (often even after they had retired from it).

Self-culture means detraditionalization, release from pre-given certainties and supports. Your life becomes in principle a *risky venture*. A normal life story becomes a (seemingly) elective life, a *risk* biography, in the sense that everything (or nearly everything) is a matter for decision. And yet, faced with the opaque and contradictory character of modern society, the self-focused individual is hardly in a position to take the unavoidable decisions in a rational and responsible manner, that is, with reference to the possible consequences.

Risk and Danger Biographies

It is essential to distinguish here between classical industrial society and world risk society. Both differ from traditional societies in having to deal with uncertainty *produced through decisions* in the modernization process (decisions concerning technology, economics and politics, but also the conduct of life). In the industrial era, rules such as those governing insurance cover were supposed to predict the (at least theoretically) unpredictable consequences of industrial production; but this social 'insurance contract' (Ewald, 1993) is virtually rescinded in the atomic, chemical and genetic age. Many industries of the future pick their way precariously across the limits of (private) insurance, negating the economic yardsticks of controllability. For 'life of one's own' sociology, it is now similarly important to distinguish between situations of biographical uncertainty which *still* appear to individuals as open to calculation and control and those which *no longer* appear to be so. I use the term *risk* biography for the former and *danger* biography for the latter.

It is a difficult business to identify the various degrees of socially produced existential insecurity. The grey areas are large and obscure, for the boundaries are ultimately nothing other than the *boundary perceptions* of individuals. It is possible to study objective indicators such as resource availability or measures of normality, but none of those can get around the fact that the boundary between still calculable risk biography and no-longer-calculable danger biography is wide open to subjective opinion, supposition, expectation, hope and prophecy.

It must be said, however, that when a growing number of people feel – for whatever reason – overwhelmed by conditions that they are unable to grasp, tame or ignore with the limited means and capacities available to them, this fact is of great significance for society and for social theory. The compulsion to self-activity and self-organization may turn into *desperation* and therefore perhaps into blind *rage*. Biographies of perceived danger are the breeding ground for violence, neonationalism and revolution.

The core of the problem is not just the waning of traditions or the ominous collapse of values or even the enticements of a life of one's own, but rather the constant overburdening to which that life is subjected. In many areas of breakdown individualization (the former East Germany) and poverty individualization (mass unemployment), this situation already seems to have gone beyond a critical threshold.

Dynamic Poverty and Unemployment

There are a number of reasons why the verdict is so imprecise. One of the most important – as we have already seen – is that unemployment and poverty under conditions of individualization are distributed not so much by group as by *phase in a person's life*. The conflicts associated with social inequality thus appear as conflicts *between parts of an individual biography*. Lives become more varied, discontinuous, heterogeneous. This also means that a growing part of the total population is at least temporarily exposed to unemployment and poverty – as the case of the United States shows most clearly. In 1978, 6.8 per cent of the population had an income below the officially defined poverty level. But according to a long-range study, only 54 to 65 per cent of people considered poor in one year are still below the poverty threshold in the following year. Over the relevant ten-year period only 0.7 per cent of those interviewed had been continually poor, while more than 24 per cent had been affected by poverty in at least one of the years (Berger, 1996). Sociologists speak of *dynamic* poverty and unemployment – by which they mean that, although the number of excluded may be growing, there is a lot of coming and going in respect of poverty and unemployment (e.g. Leibfried and Voges, 1992; Zwick, 1994; Habich, 1996).

This makes it necessary to clarify the notion of a 'two-thirds society' (cf. Glotz, 1985), according to which a third of society is permanently underprivileged. Many researchers suggest that it is more appropriate to speak of a '75–15–10 society' (Habich et al., 1991): three-quarters never having been poor in the period in question, some 15 per cent having been poor for a short time (once or twice) and the other ten per cent or so having been poor for a long time (three or more times).

The size and constancy of the percentages thus obscure the fact that poverty and unemployment first enter people's lives not as permanent facts but as a less forbidding temporary condition, coming and going and only at certain times becoming more settled. To borrow an image from Joseph Schumpeter, we might say that the bus of mass unemployment contains one group who have remained stuck to their seats, but that most faces keep changing as people get on and off for a few stops. From an external vantage point, it may well be possible to identify certain trends and frequencies. Seen by an observer on the spot, however, the passengers are a mass of individuals thrown together as they wait to get off the bus. They are already thinking of this when they get on – and of the fact that everyone else wants to get off, just as everyone has their own story to tell of how they came to be in the bus in the first place. People are rather embarrassed to meet one another there. The new poverty is usually hidden away behind the four walls of the home, so scandalous that it is *actively* concealed. It is not clear which is worse: to be discovered or not to be discovered, to be forced onto benefit or to hold out a little longer. The figures exist. But we do not know where the actual people are. They leave traces: the disconnected telephone; the surprising termination of a club membership; the schoolteacher who uses her own money to buy a classroom refrigerator and keeps it well stocked so that the hungry children can eat their fill for once. But all these traces conjure up the allure of temporariness with which poverty is surrounded even when it has become definitive.

This tendency is highly double-edged. It demonstrates that, in the social optic of 'a life of one's own', the systemically generated fate of mass unemployment breaks up into millions of pieces. The scandal of rising mass unemployment, which looks set to become a long-term phenomenon, has the political consequences one might expect. For it is 'individualized' out of existence. Indeed, the way it is spread around even allows one to think of a redistribution of scarcity, a levelling of opportunity (equal wrongs for all!) as 'those at the top' find they are less and less safe from poverty and unemployment.

It is not only the poor but also the rich – leaving aside the handful of super-rich – who are getting on and off. As Berger has shown, only four per cent continually earn more than one and a half times the average monthly income. 'But in West Germany between 1984 and 1989, nearly a quarter of men and women found themselves at least once in the relatively privileged position of earning more than one and a half times the average income. Thus both wealth and poverty can be broken down into a stable but fairly small "core" and a considerably larger and unstable "periphery"' (Berger, 1996: 21; cf. Sopp, 1994).[3]

Situations Subject to Cancellation: the Concept of 'Ambivalent' Inequality and Ways of Investigating it

What this means is that the self-culture involves historically specific forms of both poverty and wealth, each of which has a characteristic significance and way of being perceived. Whereas relatively clear criteria for when someone was rich or poor existed in the proletarian and the bourgeois culture, this is less and less the case in the situations and optics of the self-culture. Thus, someone may own expensive consumer goods that used to denote a successful career and yet still be poor – for example, if he or she lives off benefits and has to look after several children who arrive hungry at school – or else may live in a bungalow, have large debts and be threatened with the abyss as a result of unemployment or divorce or both. Is this a case of being still-rich or already-poor? With the advent of a self-culture, the multiple faces of an *unambiguously ambivalent* social structure take shape – that is, of momentary wealth overlapping with momentary poverty, continued or renewed wealth with continued or renewed poverty, so that what used to be part of clearly distinct positions in life is now in one way or another jumbled up. Someone who lives as a rich man today (with a high level of debt, for example) may become poor tomorrow. And someone who is poor may in some respects (leisure time, video ownership etc.) appear to be well off. Above all, there remain hardly any unambiguous criteria of poverty or wealth. A second look is required – a methodical, analytical look at the precarious and the ambivalent.

The face of society is thus changing dramatically. In some small areas, extreme clarity can suddenly appear – at the very top and also at the very bottom, which is no longer really a bottom but an outside. In between, ambivalences develop and intermesh with one another. More and more people live, as it were, between the categories. But this intercategorial existence can perfectly well be identified or reconstructed. In this sense, it is a question of *unambiguous* ambivalence. The self-culture, understood as a situation or milieu of inequality – in a different way from the old proletarian and bourgeois cultures – is not a 'neither-nor' culture but a 'both-and' culture. This means, first, that top and bottom do not simply form two separate spheres; they overlap and merge in such a way as to constitute a wealth *aspect* or a poverty *aspect* or wealth *for a time*, as well as matching forms of combined existence. Hence *insecurity prevails* at nearly every location within society.

Such categories as the *ambivalence, endangerment, opportunity* or *contingency* of a life of one's own identify *risk* as the basic feature of this society in general – to which should be added the central category of *self-attribution*. Of course, there are still unambiguous social structures, perhaps more than ever, especially on the margins of society. But it is questionable whether they still belong (either in their own or in other people's estimation) to a *single* social world. Nevertheless, this is the premise of all theories of class, stratification, lifestyle or individualization – that is, of all social-structural analyses.

With the emergence of a self-culture, it is rather a *lack* of social structures which establishes itself as the basic feature of the social structure. As whole sections of the population are separated off and are in danger of breaking away – that is, of being 'dismissed' not only from their job but from society – the image develops of an *ambivalent* society *without* social structures. The self-culture ultimately calls into question, both empirically and theoretically, a basic idea of the sociology of inequality: namely, the idea of social structures handed down from one generation to another that remain constant in spite of political change and biographical variation (cf. Berger, 1996).

Concepts and research methods need to be developed instead for an *ambivalent* sociology of inequality. They should address typologically and empirically the new hybrids of rich and poor, top and bottom (in relation to such variables as income, education, housing, employment variation, temporal horizons, family relations, housework and support networks). The *stable* and *predictable* characteristics of all concepts of social location (class, occupational group, social layer) would thus give way to typologies of *the precarious*, *the ambivalent* and *the provisional*, of social locations *subject to cancellation*, of 'both-and' locations. More generally, concepts of location would themselves eventually be replaced with concepts of *movement* and *fusion*. The 'tightrope' might serve as a metaphor for the corresponding biographies. Everyone is in constant danger of falling to the ground but attempts, with greater or less artistic skill and awareness, to get control of their own life; a few are very lucky, many others much less so. A society in which tightrope biographies become the norm is characterized by the fact that mental stress, artistic appeal and *fear* cast their spell over everyone – and many fall down.

To sum up, we may say that societies with a 'both-and' structure develop in the self-culture; rising and falling are always possible and *appear* to be somehow connected. Consequently:

1   The concept of location (in all its manifestations) has a semblance of stability in time, space and content which is *everywhere* being lost.
2   Instead of locations that are constantly up above or down below, others emerge that are subject to cancellation, hybrid locations that bind together what appear to be mutually exclusive.
3   To move up in one respect may mean to move down in another respect. Images of up-down or down-up movement therefore need to be developed.

The precariousness of a location, when seen from above, means:

1   A continual balancing act is required to ward off the danger of a fall.
2   Seen from below, this is expressed in a hope of moving back up with the *next* job application or the *next* marriage.
3   A consciousness of guilt or shame takes the place of class consciousness. In the 'own life' optic, a structurally determined and perfectly transparent collective destiny is transformed into guilt. *Your own life = your own poverty: such is the Calvary of self-consciousness.* In this way unemployment, something external and social, becomes an attribute of individuals.

The new precarious poverty vanishes *and* grows in an atmosphere of silence. This is a scandalous and dramatic state of affairs which calls for urgent political action. For poverty, once removed from the social-structural focal points of classes and political organizations, does not in the least disappear but intensifies amid the mutations of an individualized life. It becomes the expression of a *widespread liability of the conditions of life* that stretches into externally affluent middle layers and whose political impact is as new as it is unpredictable and global.

Notes

1 See the discussion of this principle in Saunders (1993).

2 All figures are taken from the OECD Report published in summer 1996 (in *The Independent*, 4 April 1996).

3 On the action orientation of benefit recipients, see Leisering's contribution to U. Beck and P. Sopp (eds), *Individualisierung und Integration*. Opladen: Leske und Budrich 1997.

Bibliography

Berger, P. A. (1996) *Individualisierung, Statusunsicherheit und Erfahrungsvielfalt*. Opladen: Westdeutscher Verlag.

Bradshaw, Y. W. and Wallace, M. (1996) *Global Inequalities*. London: Sage Publications Ltd.

Ewald, F. (1993) *Der Vorsorgestaat*, Frankfurt/M.: Suhrkamp.

Giddens, A. (1991) *Modernity and Self-Identity: Self and Society in the Late Modern Age*. Cambridge: Polity.

Giddens, A. (1994) *Beyond Left and Right: The Future of Radical Politics*. Cambridge: Polity.

Glotz, P. (1985) *Manifest für eine Neue Europäische Linke*. Berlin: Siedler.

Habich, R. (1996) 'Problemgruppen und Armut: Zur These der Zwei-Drittel-Gesellschaft', in W. Zapf and R. Habich (eds), *Wohlfahrtsentwicklung im vereinten Deutschland. Sozialstruktur, sozialer Wandel und Lebensqualität*. Berlin: Ed. Sugma. pp. 161–85.

Habich, R., Headey, B. and Krause, P. (1991) 'Armut im reichtum – ist die Bundesrepublik Deutschland eine Zwei-Drittel-Gesellschaft?', in U. Rendtel and G. Wagner (eds), *Lebenslagen im Wandel – Zur Einkommensdynamik in Deutschland seit 1984*. Frankfurt, New York: Frankfurt/M. m.a.: Campus. pp. 488–509.

Kommission für Zukunftsfragen der Freistaaten Bayern und Sachsen (1996) *Erwerbstätigkeit und Arbeitslosigkeit in Deutschland. Entwicklung, Ursachen und Maßnahmen. Teil 1: Entwicklung von Erwerbstätigkeit und Arbeitslosigkeit in Deutschland und anderen frühindustrialisierten Ländern*. Bonn.

Leibfried, S. and Voges, W. (eds) (1992) *Armut im modernen Wohlfahrtsstaat*. Special issue no. 32 of *KZfSS*. Opladen: Westdeutscher Verlag.

Leisering, L. (1995) 'Zweidrittelgesellschaft oder Risikogesellschaft?', in K. J. Bieback and H. Milz (eds), *Neue Armut*. Frankfurt, New York: Frankfurt/M. m.a.: Campus. pp. 58–92.

Mutz, G., Ludwig-Mayerhofer, W. Koemeni, E., Eder, K. and Bonr, B. W. (1995) *Diskontinuierliche Erwerbsläufe. Analysen zur postindustriellen Arbeitslosigkeit*. Opladen: Leske und Budrich.

Saunders, P. (1993) 'Citizenship in a liberal society', in B. S. Turner (ed.), *Citizenship and Social Theory*. London: Sage Publications Ltd. pp. 82ff.

Schelsky, H. (1965) *Auf der Suche nach Wirklichkeit. Gesammelte Aufsätze*. Düsseldorf: E. Duederichs Verlag.

Sopp, P. (1994) 'Das Ende der Zwei-Drittel-Gesellschaft?', in M. M. Zwick (ed.).

Zwick, M. M. (ed.) (1994) *Einmal arm, immer arm? Neue Befunde zur Armut in Deutschland*. Frankfurt, New York: Frankfurt/M. m.a: Campus.

Translated from the German version, **Die uneindeutige Sozialstruktur: Was heißt Armut, was heißt Reichtum in der "Selbst-Kultur"**, published in Beck & Sopp (eds): *Individualisierung und Integration. Neue Konfliktlinien und neuer Integrationsmodus?* (1997). Published here, in English, by kind permission of Leske & Budrich, Opladen.

5

From 'Living for Others' to 'A Life of One's Own'

Individualization and Women*

Women in the Individualization Process: between 'No Longer' and 'Not Yet'

To try to assess the position of women in German society is like asking whether a glass filled halfway up is 'half full' or 'half empty'. On the one hand, as the women's movement has repeatedly shown, social *inequalities* between men and women have by no means been eradicated in the Federal Republic or other industrialized countries but persist at a number of different levels; indeed, they may in future grow sharper as a result of economic problems, rising unemployment and the crisis of the welfare state. On the other hand – and without this background the emergence of the women's movement cannot be understood – fundamental changes in the context of women's lives have occurred over the last few decades, both in the family and in relation to education, work, legislation, public life and so on, which have brought the normal life story of women closer to that of men. In themselves, both perspectives – the comparison with men and the historical comparison – involve characteristic foreshortening and bias.

When the position of men is taken as the yardstick, one may fail to recognize the specificity of changes in women's lives or the social and politically explosive dynamic of the new awareness of women's interests. Paradoxically enough, it would in a sense involve adopting that very way of thinking in terms of status, income and career which the women's movement has criticized as an expression of a one-sided and economically narrow 'male world'. And such an approach might also fit in with a tendency not unknown in women's groups to 'keep going on' about derogatory attitudes and discrimination, instead of focusing on signs of change and how they can be extended and actively utilized.

When the present generation of women is compared with earlier ones, the danger is that continuing material and social inequalities between men and women will be pushed out of the picture by a *bien pensant* image of ever advancing 'progress'. This may suggest a 'thankfulness for small favours', itself part of women's traditional role of adapting and fitting in. And its emphasis on 'blessings already

---

* This text was first published in 1983 and as it is one of the reference points in the German 'individualization debate' it is reproduced here without change.

achieved' may even supply arguments to those who are seeking to defuse the issues raised by the women's movement.

Each of the two comparative perspectives, then, has a different 'political valency'. Insofar as women researchers see their analyses as an element in the social context of which they are part – as one way of helping women to develop their abilities – they are especially sensitive to the different comparative yardsticks and often look with suspicion on a cross-generational perspective that refers only to women.

Nevertheless, the theme of this article is 'generations of women in change' and it will deliberately focus on inconspicuous everyday changes in women's lives which are today often taken for granted. This is an area that women's studies has not previously taken up – and has perhaps avoided taking up, for the understandable reason that such changes are ambivalent by nature. For they contain an aspect of adaptation, while *also* having a momentum of their own which tends to challenge existing conditions. The watchword for this second aspect might be Ebner-Eschenbach's: 'The women's question came into being when a woman learnt how to read.'[1] Or, freely translated: it is not the major systemic changes, power struggles and revolutions on which history and sociology have long concentrated, but rather the *many little steps* in education, work and the family, which have given the women's movement of the last two decades its momentum and brought about palpable changes in society. For these little steps have been creating an awareness of traditional inequalities which – measured by society's own principles of equality – can hardly be legitimated and are therefore politically explosive. There will be much talk of 'trivial matters' in what follows – but it will be argued that these trivial matters are what make history and society. Our historical frame of reference here may be briefly outlined as follows.

In the period of a century, and especially in the last two decades, rapid changes have taken place in the context of women's lives. They have occurred not in an even, linear fashion, but in peculiarly wave-like movements of progress and regress. A general line of movement is discernible, however, away from 'living for others' towards 'a bit of a life of our own'. This implies a complex, multi-layered and contradictory process, whose significance will be identified here from different angles. First, a descriptive presentation:

> With the collapse of the traditional social order a glimmer of something like freedom of choice appeared – for most women, of course, still very distant... Inclusion in the market as a female worker might bring low wages and wretched working conditions, loneliness and insecurity. But it also brought a chance that was inconceivable in the traditional social order – the chance of freeing oneself from the clutches of the family.[2]

Thus, as women were increasingly released from direct ties to the family, the female biography underwent an 'individualization boost' and, connected to this, what functionalist theory calls a shift from 'ascribed' to 'acquired' roles. It opened up new scope for action and decision and new chances for women. But just as plainly it brought new uncertainties, conflicts and pressures. For now women had to face risks to which only men had previously been exposed – as well as further risks resulting from the fact that for women the individualization process was 'incomplete', was trapped in a peculiar *intermediate stage*. Women today are no longer defined as much as they used to be in terms of family life and a male provider, but they still take much more responsibility than do men for family tasks and are still much less protected by a stable position in the labour market. This 'no longer' and 'not yet' generate numerous ambivalences and contradictions in women's lives. While old restrictions have receded and many new possibilities have opened up, new types of dependence and compulsion have appeared whose consequences are not yet visible. There is no longer any 'model' that defines women's life prospects – they are both more open and less protected than before.

The Demand for a Bit of 'A Life of One's Own'

In the nineteenth century, it should be briefly recalled, women had scarcely any opportunity to shape their lives.[3] Among the 'lower classes', material constraints were so severe that all efforts and energies had to go into the task of daily survival. Among the bourgeoisie, it was the new model of a woman's role confined to the home, with all the associated expectations and dependences, which excluded women from almost any autonomous development. Their vocation was the gentle and ever ready 'living for the family', its highest commandment: *self-abnegation and self-sacrifice*:

> Independence and manly ways are a deformation of woman; her greatest honour is artless femininity – and that means glad-hearted submission and modest humility; it means not wanting to be anything different or more than she is meant to be... Man was created before woman and in order to be independent; woman was given to him for his sake. (*Löhe*, b. 1808, quoted from Ostner and Krutwa-Schott, 1981: 25)

'From her early years, a woman's vocation is one great sacrifice... She renounces herself; she has no joy and no pain other than that of those closest to her' (*Feuerbach*, 1839, quoted from Behrens, 1982: 69f.).

The situation looks rather different today. True, it is still women who bear the brunt of family tasks, but they more and more display expectations and wishes that extend beyond the family. This begins with the 'little freedoms' of a more independent everyday life and leads on to the big words: autonomy, self-realization and 'emancipation'. The degree to which expectations are conscious and the degree to which they are expressed and fulfilled, varies according to the woman's social and educational level. But they constantly make their appearance in everyday language as well as sociological surveys – not only among so-called 'career women', but also among working-class women and the 'average' suburban housewife:

> [T]hen through marriage... I gave up all that [own interests]... The stupid thing is that I would never do it again today... Since then I have been only what everyone else wanted, never what I myself wanted to be. (Interview with a housewife, from Münz and Pichler, 1982)

> Well, in ten years I shall be forty-seven. But then I won't yet be old... too old to travel everywhere I'd like to go. Then I'll enjoy my life for the first time... You

can virtually say: twenty years of planning every weekend, all your free time,
just for the children. Then that's it – then it's my turn! (Interview with a female
industrial worker, from Becker-Schmidt et al., 1982: 67).

What we have to investigate is how this shift came about from 'living for
others' to big or small hopes for 'a life of one's own'; how, in three or four generations spanning roughly a century, a claim that had earlier been scarcely permissible or possible took shape and spread among women. What social trends
triggered this and pushed it further? Such a question will take us into many different areas – from work, the law and education to public life, politics and the
media – where particular tendencies overlap, interact and reinforce one another.
To make this tangle easier to grasp, we shall concentrate on education, work and
sex and relationships and thus on the phases in young women's lives when the
crucial shifts occur.

The method will be to combine two levels of observation:[4] first, an overview
of material recording 'objective' trends in the three areas in question; then a
change of perspective to consider the underlying 'subjective' effects that have not
previously been given sufficient attention. The aim of this 'dual-track' procedure
will in each case – education, work, sexuality and relationships – be to ask how
far the external framework of women's lives has changed and then to pose the
really central questions: Where precisely, across these generations of women, did
new lines of biographical development emerge? How did they bring about a new
stage: the hope, but also the compulsion, to achieve some kind of 'life of one's
own'?

Changes in Education

Until late in the nineteenth century, there were hardly any educational opportunities for girls. Those from the lower classes were given basic training in 'the three
Rs', while the daughters of the bourgeoisie were schooled chiefly in the fine arts.
Such education was designed to promote not the girl's individual interests and
abilities, but a life lived for the family and her future husband.[5] The skills a
woman expected to acquire should be 'appropriate to her station',[6] so that they
helped her advance to a 'suitable' marriage. Any hint of independent interests
was suspect because it damaged her marriage prospects; a girl's education
stopped when she began to master a subject for herself.[7]

Only towards the end of the nineteenth century did signs of change begin to
appear. In 1889 the first courses to prepare girls for the Abitur were introduced
in Germany,[8] and in 1896 the first girls left school with this higher certificate.[9] In
the same year women were permitted to attend some university courses, although
only as non-registered students under highly unfavourable conditions,[10] and in
1900 the first regular female students matriculated in Baden.[11] This hesitant
spread of educational opportunities was brought to a halt when the Nazis came to
power and introduced measures to prevent women from studying.[12] Even in the
years after the Second World War, there was only slow improvement: women
were clearly underrepresented in post-secondary education,[13] and they encountered widespread reservations and prejudice in the universities.[14]

The great change appeared with the educational expansion of the 1960s. The number of compulsory years at school was increased.[15] Whereas tuition fees had previously been payable, a system of grants and subsidies was now increasingly deployed.[16] The educational disadvantage suffered by girls, which had long been considered natural, was now recognized as a social problem.[17] Girls became one of the main target groups of new educational measures[18] and the results were not slow in coming. The number of uneducated young women fell sharply[19] as the proportion of girls or women in upper levels of education increased to a degree that exceeded all expectations.[20] The change has been especially marked across generations: girls stay much longer today in the educational system than they did two decades ago.[21] It may be said, then, that the changes which have taken place in Germany are almost tantamount to a 'quiet revolution'.[22] *Whereas in the 1960s there was still a marked gender gap in opportunities, the chances of entry to all sectors of the educational system are today almost equal.*[23]

Furthermore, although sexism at school has by no means disappeared,[24] *qualitative changes have led to fairer treatment and entitlement than in the past.* There is more coeducation instead of division into girls' and boys' schools and the basic principle is a single syllabus rather than separate ones for 'male' and 'female' domains. There is greater awareness of the problem of traditional role clichés in course material and a greater preparedness on the part of teachers to treat boys and girls equally, to offer girls the same encouragement and to make the same demands of them.

So much for the 'objective' trends that can be verified by empirical data. But the really decisive, and much more difficult, question concerns the biographical, social and political potential contained in them. No more vivid formula can be given than that of the nineteenth-century American suffragette Mary Harris Jones: 'Sit yourself down and read. Prepare for the coming conflicts.'[25] In other words, the objective changes in education are a crucial foundation for a process of consciousness raising that enables women to deal actively with their own situation. Their explosive force comes from the fact that they do not take place in isolation, but *historically coincide with major changes in what is considered a normal female biography*. Women used to be completely focused on 'living for others' and the social structure *denied* possibilities of becoming conscious of their situation. Today, the bonds to family life have loosened somewhat and through the expansion of educational opportunities women have *gained* a greater capacity to recognize the specificities and restrictions of the context in which they live their lives. Precisely here, at the intersection of these lines of development, *women may develop a new private and political self-awareness*. Typically enough, this new awareness starts from educationally privileged women, but it also acts as a signal – not least because it is converted into tangible action by encounter groups, women's literature and publishing houses and the establishment of women's sections in political parties, trade unions and professional organizations.

After this very general overview, let us look more closely at some aspects of the equalization of educational opportunities. Let us begin with the longer period of compulsory schooling. Measured against ideal learning conditions, today's schooling may well be 'neither liberatory nor educative' (Ilich, 1973), but it does afford some respite from the early physical and mental rigours of factory work and defence against pressures that virtually destroy any possibility of further development.[26] Next there is the rising proportion of girls in middle and higher education and their rejection of the ghetto of so-called 'women's subjects'; the teaching on offer is no longer geared mainly to the training of wives and mothers, but breaks out of the radius of the family and leads into other areas of human experience, other ways of thinking, other traditions. These new, more 'elevated' subjects do not merely involve passive learning; they both permit and encourage a more 'active' approach. Finally, this is all bound up with practice in ways of speaking and thinking that allow of abstraction and reflection: that is, in socio-logical terms, a quiet shift from a 'restricted' to an 'elaborated' code (Bernstein). For now, instead of a context-bound, and in many ways, prelinguistic mode of expression based upon a shared lifeworld, it is necessary to develop modes of speech and thought in which meanings are consciously worked out and indivi-dually given their final shape. This presupposes a greater *personal contribution* – and not least a distance between the individual and the surrounding world.[27] The general conclusion, then, is that for all the defects of the existing schools system, the improvement of educational opportunity has had a major function in shaping the context of women's lives. For it opens *access to the kind of courses that challenge women to stand up for themselves and actively to confront their own situation.*

The greater educational opportunity is perceptible not only at a directly cogni-tive level, but also indirectly in many areas of everyday life. One result is that the average educational level of girls and young women is today considerably higher than that of their parents, especially of their mothers.[28] In many respects, they have left behind the horizon of expectations and experience typical of their social class and of previously customary female roles. Their life plans are different from those of their parents, especially of their mothers. *This gap between the genera-tions requires young women to make their own projects and actions, to work out their own ideas about the future, with little support from any model or tradition.*

The improvement of educational opportunities, however, entails *a growth in knowledge and therefore in power on the many battlefields of everyday life.* When opportunities in education become more equal, inequalities in the job market lose their legitimacy, so that the expansion of female education has a politicizing effect in the employment system and career hierarchies. With appropriate infor-mation and communication skills, women can combat violations of the rules and actively assert their own interests, whether against employers or against land-lords. In personal relations too, the equalization of educational opportunities means an end to the advantage which underpinned male superiority and cemented female subordination ('You don't understand about these things'). Finally, women no longer unconditionally set their sights on marriage as a goal to be achieved as quickly as possible. For the better educated they are, the greater chance they have to find an intrinsically satisfying activity from which they can earn their own living; whereas uneducated women stuck at the lower end of the hierarchy often see marriage as the only possible escape from monotonous and wretchedly paid work.

In another respect too, developments in the educational system have given a fresh boost to individualization, especially since the 1960s. Already before then, the educational system was strongly oriented to *individual performance*: the decisive hurdles were tests and marks organized along individual rather than collective lines; and the evaluation of performance served not only to reveal the individual's progress or backwardness in learning, but integrated him or her as an individual into a visible hierarchy.

Since the 1960s, this trend has further intensified.[29] For the introduction of a numerus clausus, the shortage of university places, the growing unemployment and the pressing of baby boomers into education and employment bottlenecks have all entailed a struggle over the distribution of fewer and fewer opportunities, a kind of trickle-down 'competition for places'. In the educational system, this sets up a *growing pressure to perform and to compete*. More than in the past, educational institutions become places where everyone must learn to make individual judgements and to win through against others. The socialization conditions have thus decisively changed for boys and girls alike. But for girls, this goes together with another change. Whereas they used to be assigned to 'female' courses where little was offered, but also little was required, now they are exposed to similar – and increasingly the same – pressures as those that face boys. Taken together, these changes have had a 'dual effect', creating a deep divide between yesterday and today. *Within just a few decades, the protected space of girls' education has given way to an early pressure to perform.*

Furthermore, the characteristic tendency of all industrial societies towards rationalization, technocratization and 'legalization' of more and more areas of life and towards standardized measures of success and effectiveness, has taken hold of schools at a number of different levels[30] and found many a point of contact with the educational euphoria and reforms of the late 1960s. The examples are well known: standard curricula and the scientific organization of teaching material; the replacement of small local schools with larger centralized institutions; specialization of teachers in particular subjects from a very early stage; weakening of the school class as a bond among pupils, to the advantage of subject-based ties. The character of the school has gradually changed as a result. Whereas it used to be a space fairly similar to that of the family, an 'extension of the family' in some respects, its rules and demands, procedures and patterns of behaviour are becoming much more impersonally abstract and akin to those of the adult world. This is the school as 'workplace',[31] and here too the change in conditions, although affecting boys as well, has been much more radical for girls. As the education of girls used to be much more restricted and family bounded than that of boys, in a sense always remaining more 'childish', the change is all the greater now that the school system educates them for 'early adulthood'.

Changes in the World of Work

When the pre-industrial unity of work and life broke up, the model of a new division of labour between the sexes came into being: the man as outside breadwinner, the woman freed to look after the private world at home. From the start, fissures appeared in this new division of labour and by the late nineteenth century they were becoming quite conspicuous. The bourgeois role model had always been unattainable in the lower classes, because the man's wage barely sufficed for the family's support and his wife and children also had to earn something.[32] For the wife this meant either regular employment outside the home or work in one of the many 'niches' outside the official labour market.[33]

Among the bourgeoisie too, where work in the family increasingly lost its productive functions, the family was less and less able to offer employment and a livelihood to unmarried women; more and more of those without property of their own had to find some form of paid work. So it was that the late nineteenth century witnessed the birth of various associations that sought to improve women's lot and to demand their right to work.[34] And yet occupational activity among bourgeois women continued only until the time of marriage; the married woman's place remained in the home.[35] In many occupations, this role allocation was formally established by a clause requiring women to give up their job at marriage and the effects could be seen especially in the various cities of the early twentieth century. During the First World War there was a huge leap in the numbers of women employed,[36] but officially ordered redundancies soon put an end to this trend.[37] Again in the economic crisis of the 1920s unemployment first of all hit married women, who were exposed to additional forms of discrimination.[38] An intense polemic against female employment in general, and 'dual earners' in particular, developed in the post-1929 Depression.[39] And in 1933 the Nazis presented a series of measures to reduce female employment,[40] although rearmament and then the Second World War led to labour shortages and a revival in the number of women at work.[41]

Only since the 1950s have there been clear signs of a new turn in women's biographies. *First, in Germany as in other industrialized countries, there has been a sharp rise in female employment:*[42] more and more women stay at work not only until they marry but until the birth of their first child[43] and some return after their children have grown up. It was during the 1950s that a 'three-phase model' of a woman's biography (Myrdal and Klein, 1956) took shape: the period until the birth of a first child, then ten to 15 years in the family, then a resumption of occupational activity. But what then appeared as an innovative programme has in many ways been subsequently overtaken by reality. For *second, both in Germany and elsewhere, there have been marked shifts in the relationship between motherhood and paid work*, which have crystallized not least in rising employment among mothers.[44] Women wait longer to have their first child[45] and have fewer children than before;[46] they tend more to keep working after the birth of their first child and to leave only once they are expecting a second; and those who give up work tend to do so only for a relatively short time.[47] For more and more women, then, paid employment is today much more than an intermediate phase: 'Not to have a job has become an exceptional situation for women, ever more clearly restricted to the phase of bringing up young children' (Willms, 1983: 111).[48]

There is a lot of evidence that this trend is continuing among the younger generation. One reason is the improvement in educational opportunities: the higher the qualification, the greater the job motivation. Another reason is the reform in marriage and family law: whereas the so-called traditional division of labour was a legally established norm as late as 1957 – the husband as 'breadwinner', the wife as 'heart of the family'[49] – this model has been replaced since 1977 with a principle of 'free choice', whereby husband and wife decide how to share their tasks at work and in the family.[50] At the same time, the basic principle governing maintenance in cases of divorce has changed in such a way that women now have to be responsible for their own livelihood. A third reason is the fact that young women, according to recent research, plan for lifelong work, with only some interruptions for the care of young children and part-time employment during subsequent years (Seidenspinner/Burger, 1982).[51] All these tendencies show how, in little more than 100 years, paid work has acquired ever greater significance in women's lives, shifting from the nineteenth-century model of confinement within the inner world of the family to ever longer (and potentially lifelong) paid employment towards the end of the twentieth century.

Consequently, more and more women have *money which they have earned themselves*. If one compares this with the late-nineteenth century situation of extremely low female wages[52] – and with the widespread use of non-monetary remuneration in typically female areas such as domestic service, agriculture or nursing care[53] – it is clear that especially since the economic boom of the 1960s the real income of women has considerably increased. Moreover, whereas young women once often had to use their pay as a contribution to their family's upkeep,[54] they now have more available to spend themselves.[55] Not only does work today bring young women more money, *it brings them more money 'of their own'*.

The biographical potential of this is far reaching; money allows and educates for greater autonomy than women could achieve while financially dependent on parents or a husband. This is true especially for those who have been locked into dependence because of their youth or gender. 'To be financially independent through work... is a general goal for young people' (Fuchs, 1981: 197). The availability of money creates the basis for escaping parental control; it is an entry ticket to 'the world outside', to experiences and contacts beyond the family, to the things on offer in the leisure and consumption society (if only a trip to the cinema or a Coke in a youth club). Money makes it possible to have plans and desires that relate to one's own person, but it also requires budgeting and therefore weighing up pros and contras, deferring certain needs, imposing self-discipline. Conversely, as a study of 'unemployed girls' has shown (Diezinger et al., 1982), to be unemployed and penniless means to remain confined within the family's internal space, dependent on parents or boyfriend, limited in one's choice of contacts; it means reversion to, or rather, never learning to escape from, the traditional model of a female biography:[56]

> [W]hen I had no money, I always had to go with him [boyfriend]... When I said let's go somewhere else, it would be: No, I don't like it there, you can go by yourself! But I didn't have any money and had to go with him. (From an interview in Diezinger et al., 1982: 213)

Money is also a kind of 'objective indicator' of the importance of what one does. Whereas work in the family is invisible, outside employment has a tangible result that can be seen every month on your bank statement. Money that you have earned yourself demonstrates in a direct way the value of your work and output; it awards *self-confirmation and self-confidence and recognition by others*.

> When you work, you know you've earned all your money. When you don't work, you can be sure the state will have to feed you – to put it bluntly. And that wouldn't make me proud... So I think, man: if I do something myself, I know I'll get something for it. And that's better, it gives you a boost, to know you're capable of doing something. (Interview in Diezinger et al., 1982: 184f.)

Money also gives people a certain *power and ability to assert themselves* in their immediate environment: 'The one who buys is the one who decides.' Women who contribute to the family budget have more of a say in shaping its lifestyle. This is especially true of women whose money is an important or even an indispensable part of the family income:[57] they gain legitimacy from their foothold in the world of work outside the home, even if the husband is fundamentally unsympathetic; they derive feelings of pride, strength and independence from their awareness of also being a family breadwinner; and they can expect more consideration and help from the rest of the family, who directly rely upon their fitness for work. The importance of money becomes all the greater in the event of sharp conflicts, because it allows women to escape more easily from disputes in the parental home or from a failed marriage.[58] At all these levels, money that women earn for themselves works against the old ties of dependence and gives them a greater possibility of asserting their rights and demands.

At work women experience other claims on their time, which may in many respects be more demanding than those in the family but which may also afford them something in the way of *leisure time*. Here lies a crucial difference between a job and work in the family. The latter is daily service for the physical and psychological needs of various family members, performed on an open-ended basis; the wife–mother does not have to be active all the time, but she must be *available* 'round the clock' – which hardly leaves her any time really to plan any activity of her own.[59] Work at a job, however, sets up a clear boundary between fixed working hours and a 'private life' of evenings, weekends and holidays. This distinction introduces at least the possibility of *time that belongs not to work but to women themselves, 'personal time' at their own disposal*. In the past, of course, not only were working hours extremely long – above all in typically female occupations[60] – but girls were expected to help a lot at home[61] and any remaining time was subject to strict parental regulation. So it is not just the jobs themselves but also other changes – shorter working hours, fewer demands in the parental home, shifts to more liberal ways of bringing up children – which have made leisure time a tangible reality in women's lives. As a result of changes in outside work, domestic labour and education, a historically new phase has emerged for women in which youth is 'a time of one's own'.

If one considers that women's lives used to be almost totally absorbed in living for the family, it is clear that this represents a major turning point. For even the apparently passive and undemanding models of the leisure industry call for a minimum of activity and for a *choice* between the competing possibilities on offer. Despite the seductive calls of advertising and the mass media, despite the signals of peer groups, this choice is ultimately linked to the subject of action herself; it presupposes that she has at least some idea of her own desires and interests, arouses those desires and steers them in one direction or another. Moreover, the shaping of leisure time takes place in a 'goal-free space', where it is possible to discover various aspects of one's environment and personality without running any great risk. It also allows young people to get away from home into new areas of the world outside.[62] All this means that time of one's own involves freedoms which, although perhaps objectively modest, are important for a person's biography and encourage her to become independent and to take initiatives of her own.

Furthermore, the growth in female work outside the home since the end of the nineteenth century, and especially since the Second World War,[63] has led to *greater spatial mobility in women's lives*. The significance of this may again be gauged by looking back at an earlier time. Here is how Virginia Woolf recalled the world of the Brontës:

> I read how Jane Eyre used to go up on to the roof... and looked over the fields at the distant view. And then she longed... 'then I longed for a power of vision which might overpass that limit; which might reach the busy world, towns, regions full of life I had heard of but never seen;... then I desired more of practical experience than I possessed; more of intercourse with my kind, of acquaintance with variety of character than was here within my reach.'... In those words she [Charlotte Brontë] puts her finger exactly not only upon her own defects as a novelist but upon those of her sex at that time. She knew, no one better, how enormously her genius would have profited if it had not spent itself in solitary visions over distant fields; if experience and intercourse and travel had been granted her... All those good novels were written by women without more experience of life than could enter the house of a respectable clergyman. (Woolf, 1929: 102–105)

For the middle-class woman of the nineteenth century, everyday life was nearly always a fenced-off preserve of family and neighbours, a smoothly functioning network of social relations. By going out to work, she might escape the confines of this world but also lost the protection associated with it (Tilly and Scott, 1978). She then had to grapple with an external world where she was mainly regarded not as a member of a family (daughter, sister, wife) but as an individual person, where her days were no longer directly regulated by parental instructions or the specific duties of 'living for others', where she faced new pressures, demands and manners and often new conflicts – in short, where the system of co-ordinates of the family world was immobilized at various points and different forms of perception, thought and action had to be developed. *Released from the 'bosom' of the family, she had to survive as an individual person; behaviour 'of her own' was not only permitted but demanded.*

By way of contrast, an outside job increases women's opportunities for new contacts and experience. This is why women who do not go out to work often feel 'cut off from life'.[64] For at various levels – directly or indirectly, modestly or extensively, even simply through dealings with customers from different backgrounds and groups – a job is a door to the public world. New experiences may also trigger a *process of comparison* that makes women more aware of things they used to take for granted, so that they become more open to question. Other ways of living cast one's own way of life in a new light, making its limitations and burdens no longer seem such a rigid destiny and creating a focus for new hopes, expectations and desires. A *politicization effect* may set in here, since the unjust and discriminatory treatment of women is more sharply felt in the workplace.

In the switching backwards and forwards from one area of life to another, from work to family, an *experiential gulf* eventually emerges: on the one side are family members with whom the woman does not share her experiences of the outside world; on the other side are people from the outside world with whom she does not have in common her experiences in the family. In fact, the processes described here have considerably strengthened in the last few decades, as a result of several factors:

- *Geographical mobility.* The greater the distance between workplace and home, and the more the job requires the woman to move or to be at times away from home, the more it takes her out of her familiar milieu and leads her to meet people from other backgrounds and social groups.
- *Opening up of new occupations*, together with increasing job differentiation and specialization. The more occupations are opened up to women, and the more specialized new jobs emerge, the more are women from the same background exposed to different demands and experiences. They undergo different disappointments, satisfactions and difficulties; they have more or fewer chances, face more or fewer obstacles to their career; and their expectations and plans differ accordingly, determined less than before by their background and more by particular experiences in their job.
- *Social mobility.* The improvement of educational opportunities contributes to the fact that some women manage to rise above the social status of their original family. To be sure, the educational opportunities do not translate into equally improved job opportunities and so the advancement is usually rather modest. Nevertheless, it means leaving the familiar context for a new world marked by different experiences and habits, different convictions, rules and norms, as can be immediately felt in many details from clothing and food to child-rearing customs and leisure pursuits.
- *Generational change.* As the model of a longer (even lifelong) working life has become increasingly normal, a considerable distance – to some extent, even a gulf – has emerged between the older and the younger generation of women. Things that their mothers took for granted – life plans and associated expectations and attitudes – have become questionable for many daughters. To exaggerate a little, one might say that it is 'a generation without role models', without the supportive strength of given references and orientations.

Geographical mobility, differential job chances, social mobility and generational change: an experiential gulf mediated by work thus divides women from women at a number of levels. Women are increasingly confronted with new situations for which the conventional repertoire of rules and forms of behaviour no longer suffices. When such 'gaps' appear and new models are not immediately ready to fill them, women feel 'thrown back on themselves' and have to come up with their own solutions, ways of behaving and reference points. *The lack of models, which is tangible in many areas of everyday life, not only permits but compels attempts to establish personal independence.*

Until now we have been discussing historical changes in the relationship between women and work outside the home. But the picture is incomplete if we do not remember that *the old structures persist alongside the new*. As many studies have shown, the dual, gender-divided labour market continues to involve the well-known forms of discrimination for women: lower pay, less chance of promotion, greater job insecurity. And behind these stand the less obvious double standards and contradictory demands resulting from the opposition of job and family, which married women in particular come to experience. Jobs are designed in such a way that employees are supposed to be relieved of everyday chores by someone else working silently in the background – but women who go out to work, instead of being relieved of these chores, have to perform them not only for themselves but to a large extent also for their husband and children. Working people are expected to be geographically mobile – but in any relationship it is usually the wife who follows the husband. Working people are expected to be self-assertive and successful – but if a woman is more successful than her husband, this may endanger their relationship. Since the mid-1970s, moreover, there has been a tendency for changes to be partly reversed and older structures to be revived. The economic crisis has been exacerbating labour market risks for women: from rationalizations in commerce and administration to the recent changes in labour law,[65] from the shortage of trainee positions[66] and the growing number of jobs without security[67] to disproportionately high rates of female unemployment.[68] Changed political constellations have also been placing more emphasis on 'freedom of choice' than job-based integration and even urging compulsory limitation of female employment as a response to falling birthrates.[69] Such forces have turned sharply against what they call 'the false doctrine of women's liberation through integration into the production process',[70] made a programme out of the 'new motherhood', cut back on public child care provision and rediscovered the honour of voluntary tasks for the second half of women's lives.

It is precisely this juxtaposition of new and old elements, this 'simultaneity of the non-simultaneous', which is now having biographical effects of a special kind. In education young women increasingly face the same demands and opportunities as men and not least for this reason they develop increasingly similar expectations and demands for their career. A number of studies have shown much evidence of their strong levels of motivation. Thus, girls take even more care than boys in choosing their career;[71] they no longer gear this choice so much to the needs of a future family as to their own current interests;[72] and, whereas for women of the older generation, the wish to leave the parental home was often the motive for an early marriage, girls now direct this wish more towards a job and the independence that it brings.[73] But in the early years of transition to the world of work, they come to feel the uncertainty and partly even futility of their life plans as they encounter the difficulties of finding training and a job, or as they discover the reality of women's jobs which – in content, organization and pay – are not meant for the long term, offer no secure livelihood and destroy any original interest in them (Weltz et al., 1978; Bilden, 1982). 'In education doors are open to girls which are later slammed shut again in the labour market.'[74] The outcome is a historically new kind of discrepancy. Discrimination against women in the labour market *today occurs at a time when young women's level of demands has changed and their motivation and interest in a job has grown stronger. The gulf between demand and reality is continually widening* (Bilden, 1982).

This tense relationship between women's life plans and their actual chances of fulfilling them is a breeding ground for insecurity, anxiety and disappointment. And given the lack of models, young women are again thrown back on themselves in trying to come to terms as best they can with the contradictions of their work situation. One may assume that, depending on family background, education, occupation, personal relationships and biographical features or accidents, they will pursue various strategies in this individual quest: from a streamlined career to alternative types of employment, from full-time employment for life to short-term contracts, part-time work, job sharing and successive temporary jobs. This obviously carries a high risk of failure and even of a (mostly involuntary) retreat into family life. *Incomplete integration into the world of work thus entails contradictions in women's lives, which cause differentiation and division among women* – not only between different generations, but also within the younger generation itself. It is this differentiation which often produces misunderstandings or a lack of any understanding among women – sometimes even leading to a 'sisterly quarrel'[75] among those in different situations in life.

Alongside such troubles, the economic crisis has resulted in severe risks that may be summed up in the expression 'feminization of poverty' (Diana Pearce). This trend first appeared in the United States, but it is increasingly visible in the Federal Republic as well:[76]

> Two out of three adults who come under the official definition of poverty are women... The harsh new trends in the economy belie the notion that the seventies were 'the decade of women's liberation'. For some women it was that in one way or another... But beneath such glittering images of upward mobility, women as a class... were constantly losing ground... The fastest-growing group among the female poor are single women – divorced or never married – who are bringing up children alone... The first [reason for this] has to do with jobs. To be sure, more women go out to work today than ever before this century. But for women a job is not necessarily a cure for poverty. The jobs open to them are part of the problem... It is currently estimated that, whether as a result of divorce, desertion or death [of a husband], 85 per cent of American women have to count on providing for themselves (if not for themselves and their children) at some time in their life. And that is the second main reason for the feminization of poverty. (Ehrenreich and Stallard, 1982: 217–21)

In conclusion, we may say that this new situation of risk has a twofold root: in 'the economic fact that women themselves earn very little'; and in 'the social fact that they are much more likely than before to be thrown back on their own resources' (ibid.: 222). Quite unmistakably, then, the feminization of poverty is the other side of the coin of 'a life of one's own' – or of a process of individualization caught between 'no longer' and 'not yet'.

Changes in Sexuality and Relationships

The catch-phrase of a 'sexual revolution' is much too crude and general, but it does highlight what scientific studies have also identified as a tendency. In comparison with the sexual morality of the late nineteenth century, a far-reaching liberalization has certainly occurred and a greater 'permissiveness' has asserted itself in many areas of behaviour. The outward signs of this change, which has been especially noticeable since the 1960s, range from waves of sex education material to the student revolution, 'flower children' and the challenging slogan: 'Make love not war!' The shifts in attitude and behaviour are perhaps most remarkable among young women. Whereas in the early 1960s virginity was for many still a value, and premarital sex was either taboo or linked to a firm intention to marry,[77] in the 1970s and early 1980s the situation was almost the reverse.[78] Only few then thought it important 'to wait until marriage' and a majority of 15- to 19-year-old girls had sex with their boyfriend.

The situation then was nevertheless somewhat *transitional* with regard to sexual norms, especially as far as women were concerned. For although the traditional values were no longer taken for granted, the contours of new values were still blurred and uncertain. The old *dual morality* which allowed men to have sexual relations before and outside marriage but categorically forbade them to 'decent' girls and women was disappearing – but persisted in a changed form.[79] Moreover, although sex was no longer taboo for young people or limited to dark and secret spaces, it had become 'normalized' in a peculiarly contradictory form. For, on the one hand (as one sees from the mass media and modern educational theory), youth sexuality was often understood as part of 'normal' development and to some extent openly discussed in school lessons or advice columns in magazines for young people. But, on the other hand, it was still often condemned in traditional groups such as the churches and parts of the upper strata of society; warnings and contradictory advice were given about contraception and health risks; demands for new standards in sexual behaviour, or new competitive pressures to perform, often threw young people (who were especially dependent on outside recognition) into a state of disorientation and uncertainty;[80] and in the family, parents who neither strictly forbade nor openly permitted their children to have sexual relations maintained a kind of tolerant 'conspiracy of silence' (Furstenberg).[81] In the wake of 'liberalization', moreover, girls and women were subject to *far more sexual demands* than in the past – ranging from the peremptory expectations of a peer group to the stronger pressure of boyfriends.[82] This resulted in a peculiar inversion. Whereas sexual relations used to be strictly forbidden as a general norm, there was now a pressure on girls to have sex even if they really did not want to; it was a question of 'keeping up with others', because it was supposedly 'the done thing', so as not to lose a boyfriend. Under such conditions, the right to 'autonomy' turns into another form of heteronomy and the 'new freedom' becomes a new compulsion. In the end it is still the woman who bears the *greater risk* – the risk of a bad reputation, of health troubles (because reliable methods of contraception interfere with *her* body) and of an unwanted pregnancy.

All this means that in today's 'liberal transition' girls are confronted in new ways with the issue of sexuality; their situation has become not only simpler but also, on the contrary, more complicated. For whereas, in the late nineteenth century, at least middle-class daughters were still strictly 'protected' and supervised, whereas two or three decades ago they still received clear commands and prohibitions from their parents, now a *more open and diffuse space* has emerged which contains more freedoms but also grey areas, contradictory instructions and considerable risks, requiring 'individual responsibility' and in any event forcing individuals to make decisions for themselves. The need for tenderness and intimacy is closely bound up with 'if', 'from when' and 'how far' questions, with the confusion of feelings, desires, fears and doubts. Girls are thus left more to their own devices. *Without a strict 'no' imposed from outside, they must increasingly find their own rules and behaviour.*

The last few decades have also seen a decisive change in the 'consequences' of sex – or, to be more precise, in the control of those consequences. Contraceptive methods (above all the 'pill') have become more reliable and readily available and in many countries changes to the law have made it easier for a pregnancy to be terminated. Here too there is a certain ambivalence as far as women's lives are concerned, with a possible strengthening of both autonomy and heteronomy. For as the women's movement and researchers have often stressed, women become more easily (because more 'inconsequentially') available, while men are freed of responsibility even more than before. This often reinforces the pressure of sexual expectation, with women becoming a 'disposable' object. (More rarely one sees the opposite pattern, in which a woman's 'new freedom' is asserted at the expense of the male partner.) The pill and other contraceptive improvements have also faced women with *a new dilemma*, with a classic 'double bind' of irreconcilable demands.[83] At the start of a new relationship the man often expects or tacitly assumes that the woman is taking the pill or using some other device. But since neither the pill nor other safe means of contraception can be simply used on an ad hoc basis, but require something to be done in advance, some *agreement on sexual activity* is needed or at least some prior willingness. And so, in a new kind of double morality, the dubious impression may arise that the woman is all too willing. Contraception, then, requires *unromantic, consciously planned behaviour*, which both conflicts with the spiritual ideal of love imparted through female socialization and may be interpreted (also with male irritation) as a sign of cold calculation contradicting the passive waiting traditionally expected of women:

> The ideal image of femininity includes such features as passivity and a willingness to fit in with male supremacy. The male is the hunter who pursues the woman – for her attention, for a date, for sex. After she has played along with this ritual in which the man takes the leading role, the young woman has suddenly to change her behaviour. She is supposed to display confidence in her own sexuality and to take responsibility for controlling the 'consequences' – thus showing the man that she obviously has enough sexual experience to plan in a cold-blooded manner. (Woodhouse, 1982: 14 – retranslated)

The woman therefore falls between two changing and even contradictory demands, according to the situation, her reference group and her partner. She is exposed to diverse, ambiguous expectations but is required to make a decision that is ultimately unambiguous: for or against contraception. And this is all played out in an area that essentially lives on unexpressed signals, where feelings often overrun reason and everyone is particularly vulnerable – that is, the quest for intimacy, tenderness and closeness. This constellation is particularly well suited to produce misunderstandings between the sexes, which weigh most heavily upon the woman and force her into difficult balancing acts, confusing and often overtaxing her if she is young and inexperienced. Evidence of 'contraceptive embarrassment' (Herold, 1981) are the still numerous cases of unwanted pregnancy. They may appear irrational if one considers only the availability of reliable methods of contraception; but interviews with young women who have had an abortion show that what is involved is in a sense thoroughly rational: namely, an attempt to avoid the dilemma of incompatible demands. This very dilemma makes it clear that women's autonomy and improved contraception are related to each other in a way that is highly complicated and far from unambiguous. For if the new possibilities are to expand a woman's autonomy, they assume a considerable degree of strength and self-assurance on her part. But when women learn consciously to use these possibilities, they also learn a new self-understanding and a new relationship to their partner: active planning instead of passive waiting; responsibility for themselves instead of dependence on a man.

This casts light on what has long been known: that contraception and birth control face women with new problems, but also bring them a release from old and still difficult constraints. They may set in train changes which concern women's lives not only at the margin but right at the core. For so long as it is women who not only bear children but also have the main responsibility for caring for them and bringing them up – which ties them to the life of a housewife or the burdens of the 'dual role' – then the biological fact of having children is associated with far-reaching social consequences. Motherhood then nearly always means a considerable restriction of everyday movement and future possibilities. And not infrequently, unintended motherhood pushes them into a chain of risks that keeps growing stronger: from the ending of education to 'having to get married' in unfavourable circumstances or social discrimination as a single mother. Precisely because the burdens of having children fall only on women and decisively affect the course of their lives, the women's movement has repeatedly raised the demand for 'reproductive freedom'[84] (even though this has very soon brought with it new risks) and stubbornly fought through political debate, demonstrations and spectacular actions for the right to control their fertility. The typical formulations are crystal clear: 'We alone decide/Whether to have children or not', 'My body belongs to me'. And not by chance is the standard feminist work on birth control entitled *Woman's Body, Woman's Right* (Gordon, 1977). Basically one idea stands behind this: 'Without the full capacity to limit her own reproduction, a woman's other "freedoms" are tantalizing mockeries that cannot be exercised' (Cisler, 1970: 276).

If this is the case, then today's widespread birth-control facilities may not be enough, because the medical risks fall only on the woman and the law still does not allow her complete freedom of choice. In historical comparison, however, it is true that the freedom of choice has grown considerably in a short space of time. Much more than before, women today are free from conflicts and often lifelong consequences of an unwanted pregnancy. They thereby gain a greater *right to autonomy – not only over their own body, but much more over the shaping of their life and future perspectives*.

The changed sexual norms, combined with improved methods of contraception, find perhaps their clearest expression in the emergence and spread of a new model of relationship: *living together without a marriage certificate, or 'trial marriage'*. Here public attitude changed dramatically from one generation to the next.[85] For whereas, in the early 1960s, young women rejected sex before marriage or at most practised it in secret (Pfeil, 1968), by the 1980s they took more or less for granted an open, non-legalized relationship and mostly saw it as a meaningful option for their own life.[86] The usual reason given for this was: 'until I know whether he's the right one'[87] – an expression which announced a new attitude to men friends. Clearly the point was no longer to find a man come what may, or – more precisely – to be found by him; no longer to view marriage as the overriding goal in life. Rather, the attitude was much more considered: the wish for a stable relationship or even marriage was still predominant, but always on condition that 'we get on together'. Neither was this seen any longer mainly as a one-sided willingness on the woman's part to adapt her interests and life plans to those of a man:[88] now she wanted to test in advance whether he really was 'the right one'; and part of her idea of partnership was that she should sometimes do things *without* her husband.[89] A sizeable group of women were prepared to take the initiative in getting to know a man.[90] Finally, a growing number were consciously deciding to have a child without getting married. They 'only' wanted a child without being tied to a man.[91]

Another important change in recent decades is the rapid rise in the number of *divorces*. As historical research on the family has shown, this is essentially due to the fact that the significance of marriage has fundamentally altered in the course of industrialization – a trend often presented in the form of well-known polarities: from a community of work to a community of feeling; from part of an encompassing family bond to a relationship between two individuals.[92] If we look more closely, however, we can see not two but *three* distinct stages. First, there is the pre-industrial marital relationship, mainly determined by *material* tasks such as common economic activity to assure the existence of a craft or peasant family, or the tasks of status representation and the bequeathing of property and titles in the case of the nobility. Then came the spread of the bourgeois family in the age of industrialization, with a distinctive marital combination of *material and emotional tasks*. According to the new division of labour, the husband was financially responsible for the family livelihood, while the wife was defined as 'the heart of the family' responsible for 'relationship work' – that is, not only for obvious domestic tasks and child care, but also for the maintenance of a climate of security and contentment. This kind of marital relationship obviously still exists today, especially among the older generation, but the further development of industrialization – not least the improved educational opportunities for girls and the increasing employment of women outside the home – has led to a third type.

71

Here marriage is primarily a source of *emotional support*, a tie between two persons who each earns their own living and seeks in their partner mainly the fulfilment of inner needs. Thus marriage is increasingly seen as free of objective goals and geared to subjective expectations.[93] This shift in what counts as a 'good' marriage means that its central focus is now the *individual person* with her own desires, needs, ideas and plans, in short, *personal happiness*. Or to put it in another way, the newly emerging form of the couple always has behind it *a claim of one's own on life*.[94] Of course, this makes the relationship more vulnerable and even prone to breakdown. For if life together cannot satisfy what is expected of it, the logical conclusion is to live alone. 'The burden of proof has been reversed – from what the individual can do for the family, to what the family can do for the individual... Divorce is the understandable outcome if individual contentment becomes the touchstone of what a good marriage is.'[95]

Unlike in the past, there are more women than men who file for divorce.[96] This may be interpreted on the one hand as a sign of greater independence, as a consequence of those objective changes which have increasingly distanced women from the traditional model of a female biography. So long as 'living for others' was all there was to life, the woman was more or less unconditionally tied to marriage. But insofar as she is regarded as an independent person, it becomes possible for her to conceive of being alone rather than living unhappily in a couple. And if she has a job that makes her no longer completely dependent on her husband financially, it is also easier for her to make up her mind and act. Nevertheless, it is important to realize that her job is only a 'facilitator'; the deep cause is the presence of certain desires, whatever they may be exactly. Thus there are certainly a small number of women who develop very strong wishes in relation to work and who, if these meet with the man's resistance, choose their career over marriage.[97] More important, however, because much more typical, are those women who have high hopes of a 'good', emotionally fulfilling family life and are therefore more dissatisfied than men with their marital relationship.[98] Both cases – career hopes or marital ideals – indicate strongly developed *ideas for a personal life their own*, which, if it cannot be lived with the existing partner, may result in divorce:

> I was the one who walked out. I said I'd had enough. It wasn't how I wanted to live, and I simply stood up and left... It was the smartest thing I've ever done. (From an interview in Holmstrom, 1973: 146)

> He just kept saying: clear off, I want my peace and quiet... So I said to myself, if I'm anyway alone with the children in my marriage, why shouldn't I be alone without the marriage. (From an interview in Fischer, 1983: 53)

In interviews with divorced women, expressions often appear to the effect that a new life began with the divorce – a life of their own for the first time:[99]

> When I got divorced, life really began for me. They were the best years of my life – and still are. For only then did I really have the guts to say that now I come first and I'll do what I think I should... At first it was pure euphoria for me. When I came home from work at the weekend, I switched off the bell and thought that now I have a day and a half just for myself. It was heaven on earth. (From an interview in Wagnerova, 1982: 151f.)

But the rising divorce figures are not only an expression and consequence of increasing independence; they are at least as much a trigger, a *compulsion* for women to become more independent. For through divorce women give up the traditional model of female biography, directed at marriage as the 'main goal in life'. Whether or not they wanted the divorce, they find themselves in the position of a 'single woman' and have to organize their daily life accordingly; they must look for a job if they do not have one already; they must have dealings, often for the first time in their life, with various public bodies (not least in court over the divorce settlement); and they must find new ways of structuring their leisure time (e.g. going out alone or taking a 'singles' holiday). Now they have to face alone various practical tasks, issues and decisions which their partner used to sort out or which they used to tackle together. But although they must develop elements of an independent lifestyle, divorced women have hardly been prepared for this by the previous course of their life – especially if they used to stick closely to the 'living for others' model. 'Their experience and training reinforced nurturant, affiliative, and domestic skills, not skills that would enable them to assume the responsibilities of heading a family' (Kohen, 1981: 232). The result is a 'forced independence' – potentially a challenge but in reality often too much to cope with. Interviews with divorced women also bring out this aspect, as a loss of security or in extreme cases a loss of identity:

> The immediate post-divorce period – that is, the year or so after marital breakdown – was clearly a separate period in the reorganization of the self-identities of the divorced mothers... Of the 30 women, 18 described themselves during this period as 'nonpeople', not part of life, or depersonalized. Bea, deserted by her husband and having to find full-time work to support the family, said, 'I've suppressed the whole first year. I didn't believe it. I felt shattered. Your whole life drops out.' Josie, a young mother... described herself as being 'numb' after the divorce. Then she said, 'I don't know how I felt. I was depersonalized'. (Kohen, 1981: 232).

Another consequence of forced independence is the fact that, after a divorce, the woman usually has much greater financial problems than the man.[100] The new German divorce law, which hinges upon equal rights between the sexes, expects that the woman will earn her living herself. But since the world of work is far from equal, there is little chance of her finding that 'reasonable' employment corresponding to her former living standard which the law anticipates, especially if she has no educational qualifications, has not had a job for a long time, is less able to compete because of child care responsibilities, or finds herself in a period of high unemployment. In cases where the former husband does have to pay maintenance, it is by no means guaranteed that he will carry out his obligations correctly.[101] All in all, therefore, the rising divorce rate means two quite different yet closely related things: on the one hand, a self-confident demand (just as much on the part of women as of men) for a life of their own in association with their partner; on the other hand (if this demand is not satisfied), new risks and constraints that affect women harder than men. We might sum this up in the phrase: *independence without adequate preparation.*

Not least under the pressure of such risks, a tendency arises toward lifestyles that already plan for the risks and at the same time are supposed to safeguard against them. The more common divorce becomes, the more lifestyles develop which *keep open the possibility of a later life on one's own*. This helps to explain a number of phenomena: parents who are willing to help their daughter get an educational qualification; women who plan on being out at work as constantly as possible;[102] couples who prefer to live together without getting married, postpone having children or give up the idea altogether.[103] A complex interrelationship thus exists between rising divorce rates and growing independence. *Planning a life of one's own and being forced into a life of one's own*: the two are interlocked with each other.

A powerful example of this connection may be found in the interviews with single mothers and their daughters. When asked what they would have done differently in hindsight, divorced women significantly talk of 'more independence'. And their daughters learn the lesson; they want to build their life more independently right from the start.

A divorced woman: 'Whoever my partner was and whatever the situation, I'd try to have a career and get myself better educated, so that I was really independent. I'd even ditch my partner if he didn't agree to it.'[104]

A daughter after her parents' divorce: 'What does it all mean for me? That I mustn't give up on myself. That I shouldn't give up things which I enjoy and my partner maybe doesn't enjoy. I should say: okay, then I'll do it alone. I should simply have my own space and not become anyone's appendage.'[105]

This connection, illustrated here with concrete examples, is statistically confirmed by the research of Seidenspinner and Burger (1982), which compares daughters of single mothers with girls from 'complete' families and establishes that the former later show more detachment in their lives and greater scepticism toward the traditional model of female biography. The daughter inherits her mother's compulsion to independence, but converts it into the active form of a life's project:

> They want to rely on their own efforts and achievements. Another crucial factor in this is their mother's compelling necessity to earn money. Every fourth respondent thought that she would like to have a job which, unlike her mother's, was enjoyable and made her a lot of money. With their mother's lives before their eyes, a large number of them are sure they do not want to marry. When they do want to marry, they think of it as taking place later in life. Accordingly, their wish to have children is markedly less strong and less certain than in other girls and, insofar as they have given it any thought, they would mostly like to keep the number of children to one. (Seidenspinner and Burger, 1982: 60f.)

A Bit of 'A Life of One's Own': from Private Demand to Political Effect

The previous sections have shown how, in the context of women's lives, historical shifts have occurred from 'living for others' to a bit of 'a life of one's own'. Measured by the radical feminist vision of a society in which women have full autonomy, such changes appear inconsiderable – no more than variations on a familiar theme that still involve forms of 'repression', now becoming more veiled than before. An assessment which is different in approach but partly similar in its results arises in the system theory paradigm, where the stronger participation of women in education and work and their resulting possession of time and money of their own, are 'in conformity with the system' and have anyhow got stuck halfway. The parallel is with the working class, where the same developments (upward educational and occupational mobility, better wages, more leisure etc.) are interpreted as a tendency to 'integration' and 'bourgeoisification'.

Are biographical changes of the kind discussed here therefore insignificant and unpolitical, or to be dismissed as 'social-democratic reform politics in the private sphere'? Or conversely, where is what we began by calling the 'revolutionary impulse' of these expanded opportunities for release and participation?

First of all, the objectively similar content – expanded opportunities in education, work and income – *has quite a different meaning for men and for women* (which is why the parallel with the working class is inaccurate). Whereas, in men's lives, advances in education and work are compared with the previous situation either of themselves or of their father, and are thus an incremental variation of what remains fundamentally the same, similar advances in women's lives are experienced against the traditional background of 'living for others' and are thus *both new and different*. The two frames of reference are quite distinct. What appears incriminating from the point of view of a lifelong assignment to the education and employment system may, in the context of women's lives, signify a new and challenging experience. In the space of a few generations, women have made a leap between these two frames of reference which men have never experienced in the same way. The 'petty' educational and work opportunities and 'petty' freedom and independence which women have won in the historical process may be a route into the burdens, alienations and illusions of the male world and may look to men like simply 'more of the same', but in the experiential horizon of those concerned they represent a major turning point.

Second, the continuing allocation of women to the sphere of the family means that they have a direct field of practice in *private life* and their relationship to husband and children. This field was, of course, hardly perceived as active so long as women were mainly practised in acceptance, adaptation and dependence. But as they become more aware, the consequences can be felt in attempts to discover and demand new kinds of relationship that allow some space for a life of their own. The broad and diverse field of women's literature may be read as a call for new forms of relationship. It begins with a demand for greater male involvement in housework – a demand which sounds so tame and modest but which still has sharp repercussions in everyday family life. Then it moves on to a refusal to take the demands of the husband's career as the unconditional priority for the family, through postponement or renunciation of the wish to have a child, then a wish to have a child alone, without the husband or a traditional couple set-up, and finally the development of a feminist subculture completely built around relations, ties and feelings among women. These are all experiments, projects and demands which change the shape of society. For 'society' is not only macro-bodies and institutions; it is also the tangible everyday reality directly surrounding us, 'the enormous and mundane, subtle and not so subtle, delightful, painful, immediate, far-reaching, paradoxical, inexorable and probably irreversible changes in women's lives – and in men's'.[106] Over the past 100 years, women have not seized the reins of power in politics, economics and public life. But at this other, 'merely' private level, women's groups have for some years played a kind of leading role.

Is it 'merely' a private level? No, of course not. The formulation is characteristically false. It leaves out of account a key watchword of the women's movement: 'The personal is the political.' It leaves out of account what, at a more theoretical level, is the fundamental idea of a subject-oriented approach, such as this contribution has tried to develop. Just as changes in society as a whole produce new developmental models of what constitutes, for example, a normal female biography, *so do new normal biographies react back upon the structures of society as a whole*, producing tensions and conflicts there and triggering changes in their turn. The relationship, then, is reciprocal. As the fierce public debate on falling birthrates has made clear, changes in this sphere do not remain private but may have important effects for the economy, state and society. In this process of interaction and repercussions, women no longer remain passive and mute – especially not those with high or very high educational qualifications who have gained some degree of self-awareness. It is precisely women in skilled positions who are beginning to construct their own reference groups and forming 'networks' within particular institutes, departments or professional organizations. In this way they seek to carry the experiences and needs of women into the most diverse fields of practice, from the media and art to architecture, medicine and law and even into the realm of science (especially the social sciences). 'Women are looking for their history' (Hausen, 1983) and behind 'history' they are discovering 'herstory', the officially forgotten, omitted, suppressed story of the way in which women have lived their lives. Examples could be listed at random, but all that counts here is that such categories do not emerge by chance. They reflect at a theoretical level the same historical trend that has been discussed here – namely, the growing demand of women for a life of their own.

Not the least important development is the way in which women are directly carrying this demand into politics. For so long as a life of one's own remains an individual quest, it is dependent on the goodwill of partners, colleagues and others in the surrounding world, always threatened by political movements that come and go, by government austerity programmes and economic crises. This is why women are hardly content any longer with the offer of individual 'freedom of choice', a formula so beloved by politicians. The demand now is for something 'beyond freedom of choice',[107] for changes at the level of the law, the world of work, public institutions and the basic principles of society. 'Beyond mere equal rights', the women's movement 'strives for women's autonomy, and beyond a critique... of discrimination it calls modern power structures as a whole into question.'[108] It seems that this kind of political consciousness is as yet characteristic only of a minority. But there are increasing signs that, in the less established, less power-encrusted political groups – from citizens' action groups through the peace movement to the Greens – women have a visible share and influence and that even in political parties and trade unions the pressure from the 'women's corner' is steadily mounting. In the United States, where present economic and social policies are accentuating the feminization of poverty, a 'gender gap' has meanwhile emerged so that the government finds considerably less support among women than among men.[109] It may be that the following claim is too boldly formulated: Women's liberal-feminist consciousness of their equality of rights is the great radical political force of the eighties. But the words with which Betty Friedan concluded her balance sheet of two decades of the new women's movement will certainly be realized: 'To be continued.'[110]

Notes

1 Quoted from Brinker-Gabler, 1979, p. 5.

2 Ehrenreich and English, 1976, p. 12.

3 Leaving aside, that is, the 'ruse of powerlessness' (Honegger and Heintz, 1981) and strategies of passive withdrawal and refusal such as the 'flight into illness' (Ehrenreich and English, 1976).

4 See the development of a 'subject-oriented' approach in Bolte, 1983.

5 See, for example, the mid-nineteenth-century catch-phrase about 'the education of future mothers in the people' which the Prussian minister in charge of such matters took as his guiding idea (Bäumer, 1902, p. 104). An oft-quoted phrase from a memorandum written in 1872 was meant to introduce a call for girls' high schools: 'Women should be enabled to have an intellectual education on a par with that of men... so that German men will not be bored by their wife's petty and blinkered vision and held back in their dedication to higher things' (quoted from ibid., p. 111).

6 Zinnecker, 1973, p. 54.

7 Bäumer, 1902, p. 105.

8 Ibid., p. 123.

9 Ibid., p. 124.

10 Schenk, 1980, p. 29.

11 Bavaria followed in 1903, Württemberg in 1904, Saxony in 1906, Thuringia in 1907, Hesse in 1908, Prussia in 1908, Alsace-Lorraine in 1908–1909 and Mecklenburg in 1909 (Nave-Herz, 1972, p. 107).

12 Schenk, 1980, p. 73.

13 Pross, 1969.

14 See Anger, 1960.

15 'A ninth school year was gradually introduced in the 1960s and became compulsory by the end of the decade. In the 1970s the talk was of introducing a tenth year, and towards the end of the decade this gradually became compulsory for all' (Zinnecker, 1981, p. 111).

16 First introduced in 1971, regular grants were received in 1978 by 26 per cent of all college students and 37 per cent of all students (Zinnecker, 1981, p. 84).

17 Pross's study (1969) is symptomatic of the new political and research interest.

18 The comprehensive educational reform that Willy Brandt promised in his government declaration in 1969 was supposed to affect women in particular.

19 Seventy-one per cent of women aged 65 to 69 were unskilled, compared with 34 per cent of 20 to 21 year olds (the corresponding figures for men were 29 per cent and 25 per cent) (Gottleben, 1981, p. 102).

20 Girls/women as percentage of total in:

	High school (upper forms)	First year of college	Later years of college
1960	36.5%	27.0%	23.9%
1970	41.4%	28.8%	25.6%
1981	49.7%	41.6%	37.6%

Source: Grund- und Strukturdaten 1982/83, pp. 34, 116f.; Schmid-Jörg et al., 1981, pp. 413, 415.

21 In 1960 only 26 per cent of 18-year-old women were in full-time education; by 1979 the figure was 64.5 per cent (Seidenspinner and Burger, 1982, Bericht, p. 12).

22 Ibid., p. 9.

23 It cannot be excluded, of course, that future budget cutbacks will lead to a worsening of the situation, especially as they mainly hit socially weaker groups and those 'more remote from education'.

24 Brehmer, 1982; Schultz, 1979.

25 Quoted from *Basler Magazin*, No. 22, 4 June 1983, p. 11.

26 Scharmann, 1974.

27 Bernstein, 1974.

28 The following table from Seidenspinner and Burger (1982, p. 10) compares the highest educational level reached by 15 to 19-year-old girls with that of their parents:

	Father	Mother	Respondent
Basic secondary school	679 (61%)	785 (71%)	369 (33%)
Higher secondary without Abitur leaving certificate	240 (22%)	252 (23%)	370 (34%)
Abitur/college	166 (15%)	56 (5%)	*361 (33%)
No reply	20 (2%)	8 (1%)	—

*The college mention refers to entrance applications.

29 See, for example, Lempp, 1981; Reiser, 1981.

30 See, e.g. Elkind, 1981; Hengst, 1981.

31 Hengst, 1981, pp. 33ff.

32 See, e.g. Brinker-Gabler, 1979; Gerhard, 1978; Honegger and Heintz, 1981; Tilly and Scott, 1978; Willbrandt and Willbrandt, 1902.

33 Honegger and Heintz, 1981, p. 22.

34 See, e.g. Brinker-Gabler, 1979 and Schenk, 1980, pp. 26ff. Some dates may serve to illustrate this point: 1865, founding of the Association for Employment of the Female Sex and the German Women's Association; 1872, first training college for kindergarten workers in Leipzig; 1889, founding of the General Association of Women Office Workers; 1890, founding of the German Association of Women Teachers.

35 The prevailing attitude is apparent from the 1908 edition of *Meyers Großes Konversationslexikon*: 'The W. [woman question] mainly refers to *unmarried women*, since married women have their upkeep and sphere of activity within the family' Quoted from Hausen, 1983, p. 9.

36 Schenk, 1980, pp. 63f.

37 Ibid., p. 66.

38 Ibid.

39 Ibid. See also Glass, 1979; Lüders, 1979.

40 Schenk, 1980, pp. 68ff.; Reichenau, 1979.

41 Schenk, 1980, pp. 74ff.

42 In the German Federal Republic the percentage of married women with a paid job nearly doubled from 34.6 per cent in 1950 to 60.9 per cent in 1979 (*Frau und Gesellschaft*, 1981, p. 17). For more figures, see Schwarz, 1981.

43 Müller, 1983.

44 Höhn, 1982.

45 Beck-Gernsheim, 1981, 1983, and Höhn et al., 1981.

46 For example, Schmid, 1982, p. 63.

47 See, e.g. Friedrich et al., 1973 and also the report of the Study Commission on the Family (1983): 'In recent decades, successive groups of women... have returned more quickly to work after the birth of their children. Whereas the 1971 Census showed that only 9 per cent of mothers with new babies were economically active twelve months after the birth, the national survey of... 1979 showed that nearly one quarter were economically active by the time their babies were eight months old' (pp. 17f.).

48 'Roughly a third of all women are economically active all the time until they retire; another third interrupt their economic activity because of family responsibilities; and a further third end it definitively after the birth of a child' (Bundesministerium für Jugend, Familie, Gesundheit, 1980, p. 16).

49 See the preamble to the Equal Rights Act of 18 June 1957: 'One of the man's functions is to be the family's main provider and supporter, while the woman's primary task is to be the heart of the family.'

50 Article 1356 of the German Legal Code: 'The spouses manage the household by mutual agreement... Both spouses are entitled to be economically active.'

51 The scale of the change in attitudes over just a few years becomes clear if one considers what Helge Pross wrote on the basis of her studies of women workers (1971) and housewives (1973).

52 See, e.g. Brinker-Gabler, 1979; Gerhard, 1978; Willbrandt and Willbrandt, 1902.

53 See, e.g. Müller, 1981 (on domestic servants), Ostner and Krutwa-Schott, 1981 (on nurses) and Sauermann, 1979 (on women working in agriculture).

54 Tilly and Scott, 1978, pp. 114f.; Schulte, 1983; Wierling, 1983.

55 Precise comparisons are lacking, but already 'in 1975, 15- to 24-year-olds had more than twice as much money at their disposal than the 1953 generation' (Zinnecker, 1981, p. 80) and data from more recent studies of young people confirm the trend (Fuchs, 1981, p. 198; Seidenspinner and Burger, 1982, *Bericht*, p. 58 and tables, pp. 91f.).

56 Diezinger et al., 1982, esp. pp. 71ff.

57 See Becker-Schmidt et al., 1982; Ferree, 1983; Tilly and Scott, 1978.

58 See, e.g. the study by Kalmus and Straus (1982), 'Wife's marital dependency and wife abuse'.

59 See, e.g. Becker-Schmidt et al., 1982; Brown, 1982; Ostner, 1978; and Rerrich, 1983.

60 For women factory workers, the maximum length of the working day was fixed by law at 11 hours, for a six-day week, but this was exceeded on a large scale (Willbrandt and Willbrandt, 1902, pp. 170ff.). For women in domestic service there was no legally determined upper limit, only an 'unconditional duty to work according to the will and instructions of the master and mistress' (ibid., p. 139).

61 It is true that girls are still enlisted much more than boys to help with work in their parents' home (Fuchs, 1981, pp. 332ff. and Seidenspinner and Burger, 1982, tables, pp. 38ff.), but the demands are considerably less than in earlier decades.

62 See, e.g. the results of Seidenspinner and Burger, 1982. To the question whether they would prefer to spend more free time at home or outside the home, girls aged 15 to 19 replied: 'at home' (24%); 'outside' (37%); 'both more or less the same' (39%) (tables, p. 70).

63 See Willms, 1983.

64 From an interview in Becker-Schmidt, 1982, p. 24.

65 Gerhard, 1982.

66 See, e.g. Bundesministerium für Jugend, Familie, Gesundheit, 1980, p. 8; Meifort, 1979.

67 Möller, 1982.

68 For an overview see, e.g. Däubler-Gmelin, 1977.

69 See *Dritter Familienbericht*, 1978, p. 31.

70 From *Die Regierung handelt: Wir stärken die Familie*, CDU-Dokumentation 38 (12/1982).

71 Seidenspinner and Burger, 1982, *Bericht*, p. 11.

72 Diezinger et al., 1982, p. 152.

73 Ibid., p. 149; Fuchs, 1981, p. 197.

74 Seidenspinner and Burger, 1982, *Bericht*, p. 11.

75 Cramon-Daiber et al., 1983.

76 This was a major theme, for example, at the congress of the women's section of the Deutsche Gesellschaft für Soziologie, Munich, May 1983.

77 Pfeil, 1968.

78 Sigusch and Schmidt, 1973; Fricke et al., 1980; Jugendwerk der Deutschen Shell, 1981; Seidenspinner and Burger, 1982.

79 'Girls are entitled to sex only within a stable relationship. If she has had several sexual relationships – and often two are enough – she very soon becomes known as a tart or a slag. A number of sexual relationships increases a boy's attractiveness and his prestige (especially among other boys in his group). In the play *Was heißt hier Liebe*, there is the following ditty:

> *Leute! Hört das grosse Lied*
> *Von dem kleinen Unterschied!*
> *Fängt einmal ein Mädchen*

Mit einem Jungen was an:
Ist es gleich ein Flittchen!
Der Junge aber – ist ein Mann!
Das Leute, was das kleine Lied
Von dem grossen Unterschied!

[Good people, listen to the big song about the little difference! If a girl starts something with a boy, she is straight away a floozie! But the boy – is a man! That, good people, was the little song about the big difference!] (Fricke et al., 1980, p. 38; see also Woodhouse, 1982).

80 Fricke et al., 1980.

81 Quoted from Woodhouse, 1982. In this connection, Sigusch and Schmidt (1973) speak of 'resigned toleration'.

82 Fricke et al., 1980; Woodhouse, 1982.

83 See Woodhouse, 1982.

84 See, e.g. Cisler, 1970; Petchesky, 1980.

85 See Schwarz, 1982 and Study Commission on the Family, 1983, p. 11: 'What was generally unacceptable one generation ago and what is becoming more accepted today, despite the unease often felt among the parents of those involved, may possibly become commonplace by the turn of this century.'

86 Seidenspinner and Burger, 1982, tables, p. 9.

87 Ibid.

88 See, e.g. Douvan and Adelson, 1966. Characteristic of this attitude was what Carl Becker wrote in 1901 to his daughter Paula before her marriage to Otto Modersohn: 'Your duty is to be completely taken up with your husband, to devote yourself to him in complete accordance with his individual characteristics and desires… [and] not to let yourself be guided by egoistic thoughts.'

89 Seidenspinner and Burger, 1982, tables, p. 16.

90 Ibid., p. 83.

91 Schwarz, 1982.

92 See, e.g. Mitterauer and Sieder, 1980; Shorter, 1976; Wagnerova, 1982.

93 Wagnerova (1982) speaks in this connection of an 'individualization' of the marital relationship.

94 In an extreme form, this demand appears in many variants of modern psychology and psychotherapy. See, for example, the often quoted motto of Frederick Perls, the father of Gestalt therapy: 'I do my thing and you do your thing… I am not in this world to live up to your expectations, and you are not in this world to live up to mine. You are you and I am I; if by chance we find each other, it's beautiful. If not, it can't be helped.'

95 Ryder, quoted [and retranslated] from Schmid, 1982; Wagnerova, 1982.

96 Höhn et al., 1981; Schwarz, 1982; Wagnerova, 1982.

97 Beck-Gernsheim, 1980, pp. 176f.

98 Wagnerova, 1982.

99 See Fischer, 1983; Kohen, 1981; Wagnerova, 1982; Wiegmann, 1980.

100 In daily life the opposite is often assumed, but such a view is based on exceptional cases or on a confusion between alimony and claims to maintenance.

101 Wiegmann, 1980.

102 See the study by Greene and Quester (1982), 'Divorce risk and wives' labor supply behavior'.

103 Becker et al., 1977; Schumacher, 1981.

104 Wiegmann, 1980, p. 69 – also ibid., pp. 34 and 68 and Wagnerova, 1982, p. 106.

105 Wagnerova, 1982, p. 67. Cf. Diezinger et al., 1982, p. 209; Fischer, 1983, p. 50.

106 Friedan, 1983, p. 13.

107 Petchesky, 1980, p. 675.

108 Bock, 1983.

109 Friedan, 1983.

110 Friedan, 1983.

Bibliography

Anger, H. (1960) *Probleme der deutschen Universität. Bericht über eine Erhebung unter Professoren und Dozenten*. Tübingen.

Bäumer, G. (1902) 'Geschichte und Stand der Frauenbildung in Deutschland', in H. Lange, and G. Bäumer (eds), *Handbuch der Frauenbewegung*, vol. 3, *Der Stand der Frauenbewegung in den Kulturländern*. Berlin: Moeser. pp. 1–128.

Beck, U. (1983) 'Jenseits von Stand und Klasse', in R. Kreckel (ed.), *Soziale Ungleichheiten*. Special issue no. 2 of *Soziale Welt*. Göttingen: Schwartz (translated in this volume as 'Beyond Status and Class?').

Becker, G., Landes, E. and Michael, R. (1977) 'An economic analysis of marital instability', *Journal of Political Economy*, 85(6): 1141–87.

Becker-Schmidt, R. (1982) 'Entfremdete Aneignung, gestörte Anerkennung, Lernprozesse: Über die Bedeutung von Erwerbsarbeit für Frauen', in Sektion Frauenforschung in den Sozialwissenschaften (ed.), *Beiträge zur Frauenforschung am 21. Deutschen Soziologentag in Bamberg*. Munich: Verlag Neue Gesellschaft, pp. 11–30.

Becker-Schmidt, R., Brandes-Erlhoff, U., Karrer, M., Knapp, G., Rumpf, M. and Schmidt, B. (1982) *Nicht wir haben die Minuten, die Minuten haben uns. Zeitprobleme and Zeiterfahrungen von Arbeitermüttern in Fabrik und Familie*. Bonn: Verlag Neue Gesellschaft.

Beck-Gernsheim, E. (1980) *Das halbierte Leben. Männerwelt Beruf, Frauenwelt Familie*. Frankfurt/M.: Fischer.

Beck-Gernsheim, E. (1981) 'Neue Entscheidungsmuster im weiblichen Lebenszusammenhang: Beispiel späte Mutterschaft', in U. Schneider (ed.), *Was macht Frauen krank? Ansätze zu einer frauenspezifischen Gesundheitsforschung*. Frankfurt/M.: Campus. pp. 146–58.

Behrens, K. (ed.) (1982) *Das Insel-Buch vom Lob der Frau*. Frankfurt/M.: Insel.

Bernstein, B. (1974) *Class, Codes and Control*, 2nd edn. London: Suhrkamp.

Bilden, H. (1982) *DFG-Projektantrag Lebensentwürfe und biographische Realität junger Frauen*, hectograph copy. Munich.

Bock, G. (1983) 'Historische Frauenforschung: Fragestellungen und Perspektiven', in K. Hausen. pp. 22–60.

Bolte, K. M. (1983) 'Subjektorientierte Soziologie – Plädoyer für eine Forschungsperspektive', in K. M. Bolte and E. Treutner (eds), *Subjektorientierte Arbeits – und Berufssoziologie*. Frankfurt/M.: Campus. pp. 22–60.

Brehmer, I. (ed.) (1982) *Sexismus in der Schule*. Weinheim and Basle: Beltz.

Brinker-Gabler, G. (ed.) (1979) *Frauenarbeit und Beruf*. Frankfurt/M.: Fischer.

Brown, C. (1982) 'Home production for use in a market economy', in B. Thorne and M. Yalom (eds.), *Rethinking the Family. Some Feminist Questions*. New York: Longman. pp. 151–67.

Bundesministerium für Jugend, Familie und Gesundheit (ed.) (1980) *Frauen '80*. Bonn.

Cisler, L. (1970) 'Unfinished business: birth control and women's liberation', in R. Morgan (ed.), *Sisterhood is Powerful. An Anthology of Writings from the Women's Liberation Movement*. New York: Vintage. pp. 274–322.

Cramon-Daiber, B., Jaeckel, M., Köster, B., Menge, H. and Wolf-Graaf, A. (1983) *Schwesternstreit. Von den heimlichen und unheimlichen Auseinandersetzungen zwischen Frauen*. Reinbek: Rowohlt.

Däubler-Gmelin, H. (1977) *Frauenarbeitslosigkeit oder: Reserve zurück an den Herd!* Reinbek: Rowohlt.

Diezinger, A., Marquardt, R., Bilden, H. and Dahlke, K. (1982) 'Zukunft mit beschränkten Möglichkeiten. Entwicklungsprozesse arbeitsloser Mädchen', concluding report to the Deutsche Forschungsgemeinschaft, hectograph copy. Munich.

Dritter Familienbericht, Bundestagsdrucksache 8/31321, Bonn, 20 August 1978.

Douvan, E. and Adelson, J. (1966) *The Adolescent Experience*. New York: Wiley.

Ehrenreich, B. and English, D. (1976) *Complaints and Disorders: The Sexual Politics of Sickness*. Munich:

Ehrenreich, B. and Stallard, K. (1982) 'The "nouveau poor"', *Ms.*, August 1982, 11(1–2): pp. 217–24.

Elkind, D. (1981) *The Hurried Child. Growing up Too Fast Too Soon*. New York: Knopf.

Ferree, M. (1983) 'Sacrifice, satisfaction and social change', *Marriage and Family Review*.

81

Fischer, E. (1983) *Jenseits der Träume. Frauen um Vierzig.* Cologne: Kuepenheuer & Wutsch.

Frau und Gesellschaft (II), *Bericht 1980 der Enquete Kommission und Aussprache 1981 im Plenum des Deutschen Bundestages* (1981) Bonn: German Bundestag, Presse- und Informationszentrum.

Friedan, B. (1983) 'Twenty years after the feminine mystique', *New York Times Magazine,* 27 February, 13–19.

Friedrich, H., Lappe, L., Schwinghammer, I. and Wegehaupt-Schneider, I. (1973) 'Frauenarbeit und technischer Wandel', hectograph manuscript. Frankfurt/M.

Fricke, S., Klotz, M. and Paulich, P. (1980) *Sexualerziehung in der Praxis.* Cologne: Bunel-Verlag.

Fuchs, W. (1981) 'Jugendbiographie', in *Jugendwerk der Deutschen Shell,* vol. 1, pp. 124–344.

Gerhard, U. (1978) *Verhältnisse und Verhinderungen. Frauenarbeit, Familie und Rechte der Frauen im 19. Jahrhundert.* Frankfurt/M.: Suhrkamp.

Gerhard, U. (1982) 'Aus aktuellem Anlass: Über Frauenarbeitslosigkeit oder,Wenn uns die Zeit unter den Füssen brennt', *Feministische Studien,* 1(1): 127–36.

Glass, F. (1979) 'Der weibliche "Doppelverdiener" in der Wirtschaft', reprinted in G. Brinker-Gabler, (ed.), *Frauenarbeit und Beruf.* Frankfurt/M.: Fischer. pp. 345–8.

Gordon, L. (1977) *Woman's Body, Woman's Right. A Social History of Birth Control in America.* Harmondsworth: Penguin.

Gottleben, V. (1981) 'Nicht-formal Qualifizierte am Arbeitsmarkt', *Mitteilungen der Arbeitsmarkt- und Berufsforschung,* vol. 2.

Greene, W. and Quester, A. (1982) 'Divorce risk and wives' labor supply behavior', *Social Science Quarterly,* 63(1): 16–27.

Grund- und Strukturdaten 1982/1983 (1982) Bonn: Bundesminister für Bildung und Wissenschaften.

Hausen, K. (ed.) (1983) *Frauen suchen ihre Geschichte. Historische Studien zum 19. und 20. Jahrhundert.* Munich: Beck.

Hengst, H. (1981) 'Tendenzen der Liquidierung von Kindheit', in H. Hengst and E. Köhler *Kindheit als Fiktion.* Frankfurt/M.: Suhrkamp. pp. 11–72.

Herold, E. (1981) 'Contraceptive embarrassment and contraceptive behavior among young single women', *Journal of Youth and Adolescence,* 10(3): 233–42.

Höhn, Ch. (1982) 'Erwerbstätigkeit und Rollenwandel der Frau', *Zeitschrift für Bevölkerungswissenschaft,* 31: 297–317.

Höhn, Ch., Mammey, U. and Schwarz, K. (1981) 'Die demographische Lage in der Bundesrepublik Deutschland', *Zeitschrift für Bevölkerungswissenschaft,* 2: 139–230.

Holmstrom, L. (1973) *The Two-Career Family.* Cambridge, MA.: Schenkman.

Honegger, C. and Heintz, B. (eds) (1981) *Listen der Ohnmacht. Zur Sozialgeschichte weiblicher Widerstandsformen.* Frankfurt/M.: Europäische Verlagsanstalt.

Illich, I. (1973) *Deschooling Society.* Harmondsworth: Penguin.

Jugendwerk der Deutschen Shell (ed.) (1981) *Jugend '81. Lebensentwürfe, Alltagskulturen, Zukunftsbilder,* vols 1 and 2. Hamburg:

Kalmus, D. and Straus, M. (1982) 'Wife's marital dependency and wife abuse', *Journal of Marriage and the Family,* May: 277–86.

Kohen, J. (1981) 'From wife to family head: transitions in self-identity', *Psychiatry,* 44: 230–40.

Lempp, R. (1981) 'Schulangst', *Vorgänge, Zeitschrift für Gesellschaftspolitik,* 53: 55–8.

Lüders, M. (1979) 'Die Beamtin als Doppelverdiener', reprinted in G. Brinker-Gabler (ed.), *Frauenarbeit und Beruf.* pp. 348–53.

Meifort, B. (1979) 'Ausbildungsplätze nach Geschlecht. Über die Diskriminierung von Mädchen in der Berufsbildung', in M. Janssen-Jurreit (ed.), *Frauenprogramm – Gegen Diskriminierung.* Reinbek: Rowohet. pp. 56–68.

Mitterauer, M. and Sieder, R. (1980) *Vom Patriarchat zur Partnerschaft. Zum Strukturwandel der Familie,* 2nd edn. Munich: Beck.

Möller, C. (1982) 'Ungeschützte Beschäftigungsverhältnisse – verstärkte Spaltung der abhängig Arbeitenden. Konsequenzen für die Frauenforschung und die Frauenbewegung', in Sektion Frauenforschung in den Sozialwissenschaften (ed.), *Beiträge zur Frauenforschung am 21. Deutschen Soziologentag in Bamberg.* Munich: pp. 183–200.

Müller, H. (1981) *Dienstbare Geister. Leben und Arbeitswelt städtischer Dienstboten,* Schriften des Museums für Deutsche Volkskunde Berlin. Berlin: Museum für Deutsche Volkskunde.

Müller, W. (1983) 'Frauenerwerbstätigkeit im Lebenslauf', in W. Müller, A. Willms and J. Handl, *Strukturwandel der Frauenarbeit 1880–1980*. Frankfurt/M.: Campus pp. 55–106.

Münz, R. and Pichler, C. (1982) 'Aspekte des weiblichen Lebenszusammenhanges', hectograph manuscript. Vienna.

Myrdal, A. and Klein, V. (1956) *Women's Two Roles, Home and Work*. London: Routledge & Kegan.

Nave-Herz, R. (1972) *Das Dilemma der Frau in unserer Gesellschaft: Der Anachronismus der Rollenerwartungen*. Neuwied and Berlin: Luchterhand.

Ostner, I. (1978) *Beruf und Hausarbeit. Die Arbeit der Frauen in unserer Gesellschaft*. Frankfurt/M.: Campus.

Ostner, I. and Krutwa-Schott, A. (1981) *Krankenpflege – ein Frauenberuf?* Frankfurt/M.: Campus.

Petchesky, R. (1980) 'Reproductive freedom: beyond "a woman's right to choose"', *Signs*, 5(4): 661–85.

Pfeil, E. (1968) *Die 23jährigen*. Tübingen: Mohr.

Pross, H. (1969) *Über die Bildungschancen von Mädchen in der Bundesrepublik*. Frankfurt/M.: Suhrkamp.

Pross, H. (1975) *Die Wirklichkeit der Hausfrau*. Reinbek: Rowohlt.

Reichenau, Ch. von (1979) 'Frauenarbeit im Dritten Reich: Einschränkende Bestimmungen nach der "Machtübernahme" und ihre Auswirkungen', reprinted in G. Brinker-Gabler (ed.), *Frauenarbeit und Beruf*. pp. 364–76.

Reiser, H. (1981) 'Rüttelsieb mit Sackgassen/Veränderungen der schulischen Verhaltensbedingungen', *Vorgänge*, 53: 73–5.

Rerrich, M. (1983) 'Veränderte Elternschaft – Entwicklungen in der familialen Arbeit mit Kindern seit 1950', *Soziale Welt*, 4: pp. 420–449.

Sauermann, D. (1979) *Knechte und Mägde in Westfalen um 1900. Bericht aus dem Archiv für Westfälische Volkskunde*. Münster: Coppenrath.

Scharmann, D. (1974) 'Probleme der personalen Selbstentfaltung in der industriellen Arbeitswelt', in T. Scharmann (ed.), *Schule und Beruf als Sozialisationsfaktoren*, 2nd edn. Stuttgart: Enke.

Schenk, H. (1980) *Die feministische Herausforderung. 150 Jahre Frauenbewegung in Deutschland*. Munich: Beck.

Schmid, J. (1982) 'The family today: sociological highlights on an embattled institution', *European Demographic Information Bulletin*, 13(2): 49–72.

Schmid-Jörg, I., Krebsbach-Gnath, C. and Hübner, S. (1981) *Bildungschancen für Mädchen und Frauen im internationalen Vergleich*. Munich and Vienna.

Schulte, R. (1983) 'Bauernmägde in Bayern am Ende des 19. Jahrhunderts', in K. Hausen. pp. 110–27.

Schultz, D. (1979) 'Sexismus in der Schule', in M. Janssen-Jurreit (ed.), *Frauenprogramm – Gegen Diskriminierung*. Reinbek: Rowohlt pp. 22–9.

Schumacher, J. (1981) 'Partnerwahl und Partnerbeziehung, *Zeitschrift für Bevölkerungswissenschaft*, 4: 499–518.

Schwarz, K. (1981) 'Erwerbstätigkeit der Frau und Kinderzahl', *Zeitschrift für Bevölkerungswissenschaft*, 1: 59–86.

Schwarz, K. (1982) 'Bericht 1982 über die demographische Lage in der Bundesrepublik Deutschland', *Zeitsschrift für Bevölkerungswissenschaft*, 2: 121–223.

Seidenspinner, G., Burger, A., Brigitte and Deutsches Jugendinstitut (eds) (1982) *Mädchen 1982, Bericht und Tabellen*. Hamburg.

Shorter, E. (1976) *The Making of the Modern Family*. London: Rowohlt.

Sigusch, V. and Schmidt, G. (1973) *Jugendsexualität*. Stuttgart: Ferdinand Enke Verlag.

Study Commission on the Family (1983) *Families in the Future*. London: The Commission.

Tilly, L. and Scott, J. (1978) *Women, Work, and Family*. New York. London: Holt, Rinehart and Winston.

Wagnerova, A. (1982) *Scheiden aus der Ehe. Anspruch und Scheitern einer Lebensform*. Reinbek: Rowohlt.

Weltz, F., Diezinger, A., Lullies, V. and Marquardt, R. (1978) *Aufbruch und Desillusionierung. Junge Frauen zwischen Beruf und Familie. Forschungsberichte des Soziologischen Forschungsinstituts*. Göttingen: SOFI.

Wiegmann, B. (1980) *Ende der Hausfrauenehe*. Reinbek: Rowohlt.

83

Wierling, D. (1983) '"Ich hab meine Arbeit gemacht – was wollte sie mehr?" Dienstmädchen im städtischen Haushalt der Jahrhundertwende', in K. Hausen. pp. 144–71.

Willbrandt, R. and Willbrandt, W. (1902) 'Die deutsche Frau im Beruf', in H. Lange and G. Bäumer, (eds) *Handbuch der Frauenbewegung*, vol. 4. Berlin: Moeser.

Willms, A. (1983) 'Segregation auf Dauer? Zur Entwicklung des Verhältnisses von Frauenarbeit und Männerarbeit in Deutschland, 1882–1980', in W. Müller, A. Willms and J. Handl, *Strukturwandel der Frauenarbeit 1880–1980*. Frankfurt/M.: Campus. pp. 107–81.

Woodhouse, A. (1982) 'Sexuality, femininity and fertility control', *Women's Studies International Forum*, 5(1): pp. 1–15.

Woolf, V. (1929) *A Room of One's Own*. London: Hogarth Press.

Zinnecker, J. (1973) *Sozialgeschichte der Mädchenbildung*. Weinheim and Basle: Beltz.

Zinnecker, J. (1981) 'Jugend '81: Porträt einer Generation', in Jugendwerk der Deutschen Shell, vol. 1, pp. 80–122.

Translated from the German version **Vom Dasein für andere**, by Elisabeth Beck-Gernsheim.

6

On the Way to a Post-Familial Family

From a Community of Need to Elective Affinities

Prologue: Stages in a Controversial Debate

In Western industrial societies of the 1950s and 1960s, paeans were being sung to the family. In West Germany it was enshrined in the Constitution and placed under special state protection; it was the recognized model for everyday life and the dominant sociological theory regarded it as essential to a functioning state and society. But then came the student and women's movements of the late 1960s and early 1970s, with their show of resistance to the traditional structures. The family was exposed as ideology and prison, as site of everyday violence and repression. But on the opposite side, others appeared in the arena 'in defence of the bourgeois family' (Berger and Berger, 1984) or rediscovered it as a 'haven in a heartless world' (Lasch, 1977). A 'war over the family' broke out (Berger and Berger, 1983). Suddenly it was no longer even clear who or what constituted the family. Which types of relationship should be described as a family and which should not? Which are normal, which deviant? Which ought to be encouraged by the state? Which should receive financial support?

Meanwhile, at the beginning of the 21st-century, the discussion became still more confused. Many theorists perceived massive changes, perhaps even the end of the traditional family; others criticized what they called the constant talk of crisis and argued that the future belongs with the family; while a third group, lying somewhere in between, preferred to speak of tendencies towards pluralism. What made the debate particularly stimulating is the fact that all sides appealed to empirical data and especially to demographic statistics.

In this chapter I shall first look at two positions which emphasized continuity and stability of the family. In considering these, I will show that the black-and-white alternative 'end of the family' or 'family as the future' is not appropriate. The focus should instead be on the many grey areas or, better, the many different shades in the niches inside and outside the traditional family network. The main argument here will be that these forms signal more than just pluralism and contiguity, more than just a colourful motley thrown together at random. For a basic historical trend can be discerned in all this variety, a trend towards individualization that also increasingly characterizes relations among members of the same family. A shorthand way of saying this is that a community of need is becoming an elective relationship. The family is not breaking up as a result; it is acquiring a new historical form. Paradoxically, we could say that the contours of a 'post-familial family' are taking shape (Rosenmayr, 1992).[1]

The Construction of Normalcy

On the Handling of Figures

In the mid-1990s a respected daily paper carried a feature article under the programmatic headline 'The family is not a discontinued model' (Bauschmid, 1994). The first sentence already makes the point: 'Sometimes it is the normal situation which amazes the observer: 85 per cent of children and young people under eighteen in the Federal Republic grow up in complete families with natural parents who are still in their first marriage.'

The statistic is indeed surprising and it is therefore worthy of closer examination. Where does it come from? What is the basis of calculation? Three points immediately strike one. First, the cited figure takes children and young people in 'complete' families as its reference. The picture is therefore distorted in advance, because it excludes those who decide against a family. Two groups that have clearly grown in recent years are missing – men and women who do not marry in the first place and those who remain childless.[2] Second, the author writes that the figure comes from the year 1991, but in reality it covers a period stretching from 1970 to 1987.[3] And already within that period – even more in the years since then – a clear shift has taken place towards non-traditional forms of living. Since 1970, for example, the proportion of children born out of wedlock has been constantly rising;[4] and those born within it face an ever greater risk that their parents' marriage will break up (Nauck, 1991: 427). Third, population figures that give a picture of family life say nothing about whether people live willingly or unwillingly in such relationships. Neither do they say anything about the dynamic concealed behind these statistics. It is therefore necessary to look beyond the objective data and to investigate their subjective meaning. Then it becomes relevant to consider what sociological studies of the family show:[5] namely, that in many relationships there are partly open, partly submerged conflicts over the domestic division of labour and gender life projects, and that although traditional arrangements still largely prevail, there is increasing dissatisfaction on the part of women. In short, a considerable potential for conflict is visible beneath the surface normality.

What we find, then, is a screening out of groups which do not fit the image of normality (single persons, the childless); a disregard for the declining trend in the traditionally normal family (more children born outside marriage, more divorces); and also a disregard for the conflict potential within so-called normal families. One thing is obviously common to these three elements: they all lead to a picture that emphasizes the aspect of continuity and systematically underestimates the aspect of change. It is not so much normality as constructions of normality that are involved.

Redefinitions and Immunization

In an essay entitled 'Family in dissolution', the sociologist Laszlo Vascovics trenchantly criticizes those who point to radical changes in the family. He sees here just the long familiar talk of crises: 'Over the last two centuries, crisis and breakdown of the family have again and again been "detected" or predicted' (Vascovics, 1991: 186). And he is quite clear about his own conclusions:

> The family as nuclear or conjugal family has kept its dominance up to the present day... The 'normal chaos of love', as it has been called, continues to display quite clear and dominant patterns of the partnerships which... in most cases lead to a quite normal family. (Vascovics, 1991: 197)

In order to assess this view of things, it is important to know how Vascovics defines the 'normal family'. In fact, practically everything goes into his definition. With or without a marriage certificate, temporarily or for life, once or a number of times – everything is indiscriminately included in the nuclear family or its precursors. Even people living alone become 'partnership oriented' within this framework, because in Vascovics' view they do not in principle exclude a marital or non-marital partnership and even partly aspire towards one. Most non-marital partnerships are said to be 'at least geared to a medium-term perspective'. And if such couples separate, it can still be assumed 'that they will sooner or later enter into a non-marital long-term relationship with another partner'. It is true that there has been a decline in birthrates, but this changes nothing with regard to the normal family. 'Parenthood has not ceased to be an important aim for young women and men.' Developments such as later parenthood show nothing new:

> Why should there be a difference in how late and early parenthood, shorter and longer-lasting families, are regarded? It is in the nature of things that a family will be founded at one point in the life cycle and dissolved at another. (Vascovics, 1991: 188–94)

Within this conceptual schema, Vascovics is undoubtedly right that the normal family is alive and flourishing. But the series of redefinitions that allows him to argue this mostly discards what a short time ago constituted the essence of marriage and family: legal certification, binding force, permanence and so on. If, amid massive change, all this is simply disregarded, then obviously no change will be left. It is as in the race between the hare and the tortoise: the normal family is there already. Proof to the contrary is impossible, because everything that looks or could look otherwise is simply built into the original concept. This is what theory of science knows as immunization – explanations which cannot be refuted and so are not really meaningful.

The result is that the central questions are systematically left out. For example, it is well known from the data available that most men and women do indeed say that having children is one of their aims in life. The interesting question here is why do young people *fail* to achieve this aim more often than previous ones. What are the barriers, the resistances? Or do other goals in life nowadays have greater attraction? Furthermore, it is hardly surprising that most single people do not dismiss all thought of a partnership. But far more intriguing is the question of why they *actually* live alone. What are the resistances or the rival goals? Finally, not much can be said against the statement that every family starts at some point and comes to an end at another. It is as correct as it is trivial. What is not at all trivial is when the family is founded and especially why it is ended – through death or through divorce. How many go on to found another family? How many let it all drop? How many set up several families in succession?

If such questions are not asked, if instead all forms of private life (with or without children, with or without a certificate, with or without permanence) are bunched together under the heading of the 'normal family', then all contours go by the board. Change? The perspective does not allow for it. And so it nowhere comes into view. The conclusion is fixed in advance: 'Nothing new under the sun.'

Family and Individualization: Stages in the Process of Historical Change

The emphasis on continuity of the family will now be contrasted to an approach that consciously places new elements at the centre of analysis. To draw out what is new, we shall take the discussion on individualization as our reference, focusing first on the historical changes that can be located in the lifespan of the individual. Individualization is understood as a historical process that increasingly questions and tends to break up people's traditional rhythm of life – what sociologists call the normal biography. As a result, more people than ever before are being forced to piece together their own biographies and fit in the components they need as best they can. They find themselves bereft of unquestionable assumptions, beliefs or values and are nevertheless faced with the tangle of institutional controls and constraints which make up the fibre of modern life (welfare state, labour market, educational system etc.) (Beck and Beck-Gernsheim, 1993). To put it bluntly, the normal life history is giving way to the do-it-yourself life history. What does this imply about the family? How is the relationship between family and individualization to be conceived? Above all, what is new in all this?

The Obligation of Solidarity

It is advisable to start by glancing back at the pre-industrial family. As many studies from social history have shown, this was essentially a relationship centred upon work and economics. Men and women, old and young people each had their own place and tasks within it. But at the same time, their activities were closely co-ordinated with one another and subordinated to the common goal of preserving the farm or workshop. Members of the family were thus exposed to similar experiences and pressures (seasonal rhythms, harvest, bad weather etc.) and bound together by common efforts. It was a tightly knit community, in which little room was left for personal inclinations, feelings and motives. What counted was not the individual person but common goals and purposes. In this respect the pre-industrial family may be defined as a 'community of need' held together by an 'obligation of solidarity' (Borscheid, 1988):

> Family, household and village community made productive assets out of the estate, ensured that the many efforts were not just a labour of Sisyphus, partly

afforded the possibility of welfare and social prestige, and promised some security in the event of destitution, sickness and old age. Unless one was integrated
into a family and a village community, one was virtually nothing, an impotent
creature looked down upon by society... In this network of dependence, it was
not individual freedom but the material interests of one's own family, farm and
village that were uppermost in people's minds. For better or for worse, everyone
was tied to this community; it was at once their sheet anchor and their lead
weight. (Borscheid, 1988: 271f)

As many historical documents testify, family members were not bound to one
another only in love and affection; tension and mistrust, even hatred and violence,
were not uncommon. Yet the basic experience remained one of mutual dependence, to which personal wishes and dislikes had to be subordinated in case of
conflict. There was not much scope, then, for individuals to break out. To go
one's own way was possible (if at all) only at a high personal cost.[6]

With individualization came the decisive historical break. The family lost its
function as a working and economic unit and started up a new relationship with the
labour market. In a first phase, it was chiefly men who were involved in gainful
employment outside the home. The imperatives of the performance-oriented
society meant that what counted was now the individual person rather than the
community. Women, however, were initially relegated to the realm of home and
children, to the newly forming space of the private. (At least that was the model for
the rising bourgeoisie, institutionally underpinned through the administration of
justice, education, philosophy and so on). Within this framework of relations
between the sexes, which was geared in principle to a 'halved modernity' (see
Beck, 1986: 179), a new form of dependence began to assert itself: the woman
became dependent on the man's earnings, while he needed her everyday labour and
care to be capable of functioning in the workplace. The obligation of solidarity that
had characterized the pre-industrial family went on existing in a modified form.

The Welfare State and the Logic of Individually Designed Lives

A new stage in the history of the family and individualization began with the gradual development of the welfare state, first around the end of the nineteenth century
but above all in the second half of the twentieth. A series of social security mechanisms (old age pension, sickness and accident cover etc.) was introduced to give
some protection against the rigours of the market and various forms of material
assistance to weaker groups (income support, education grants, housing benefit,
help with buying a home etc.) were meant to assure greater social justice. One result
of such measures was that even if individuals could not function in the labour
market, or could do so only to a limited extent, they still became less dependent on
family, goodwill and personal favours. The beginnings of social security thus guaranteed a minimum existence beyond the family. Individual members of the family
were no longer unconditionally required to fit in and to knuckle under; they could
also get out in the event of conflict. The logic of individually designed lives was
thus given a boost, and ties to the family were considerably loosened:

Insofar as the state bestows its gifts upon individuals rather than the families to
which they belong, it becomes more likely that young people on a grant will

leave their family, that large households extending over several generations will split up, or that married couples in employment will be able to divorce. By reducing economic constraints, the state increases the scope for individual action and mobility. But it thereby also increases the probability that people's lives will move outside collective contexts. (Mayer and Müller, 1994: 291)

The Demand and Pressure for Women to have a 'Life of their Own'

Another major break occurs with the change in women's normal life history – something which also began towards the end of the nineteenth century but has greatly accelerated since the 1960s. Let us summarize this as concisely as possible (for a more detailed account see Beck-Gernsheim, 1983). As women move at least partly outside the family as a result of changes in education, occupation, family cycle, legal system etc. they can no longer rely on men as providers. Instead, in ways that are naturally often contradictory, a perspective of autonomy and self-sufficiency is held out to them. The 'subjective correlate' of such changes is that women today increasingly develop, and must develop, expectations, wishes and life projects which relate not only to the family but also to their own persons. At the level of economics first of all, they have to plan ahead for some security in life – if need be, without a man. They can no longer think of themselves just as an 'appendage' of the family, but must increasingly come forward as individuals with their own interests and rights, plans and choices.

The power of the family – above all, of the husband – has been correspondingly restricted. Unlike most of their forebears in previous generations, women are no longer referred to marriage as the route to economic security and social status. They can choose, perhaps not altogether freely but more than before, whether they really want to marry or to stay single and whether to seek a divorce rather than put up with endless conflicts if the marriage does not turn out as they hoped. This means that, in women's biographies too, the logic of individual design is gradually asserting itself and the obligation of solidarity is further breaking down.

Meanwhile, feminists have analysed this development with new categories and concepts. Whereas traditional sociology always conceived the family as a unit with homogeneous interests and positions in life, there is now a contrasting focus on gender difference. Whereas 'the family' always used to occupy the whole field of vision, now men and women are becoming visible as separate individuals, each linked to the family through different expectations and interests, each experiencing different opportunities and burdens. In short, the contours of distinctively male and distinctively female lives are now becoming apparent within the family.

Individualization and the Staging of Everyday Life

As a result of historical developments, then, a trend towards individualization has made itself felt. This increasingly affects relations between family members too, setting up a special kind of dynamic. A number of examples will help us to understand what is meant by this 'staging of everyday life', as we shall call it. More and more co-ordination is needed to hold together biographies that tend to pull apart from one another. At a number of levels, the family thus becomes a daily 'balancing act' (Rerrich, 1988) or a permanent 'do-it-yourself' project (see Beck and Beck-Gernsheim, 1993; Hitzler and Honer, 1994). The character of everyday family life is gradually changing: people used to be able to rely upon well-functioning rules and models, but now an ever greater number of decisions are having to be taken. More and more things must be negotiated, planned, personally brought about. And not least in importance is the way in which questions of resource distribution, of fairness between members of the family, have come to the fore. Which burdens should be allocated to whom? Who should bear which costs? Which claims have priority? Whose wishes have to wait?

The Divergence of Tempos and Abodes

In pre-industrial society, it was the demands of the family community centred on work and economics which directly set the course of everyday life. As the farm or workshop occupied the central place, each family member usually acted within a radius of which the others could easily keep track. And the distribution of tasks, having been practised for generations, followed a familiar rhythm that was tightly defined and co-ordinated.

Starkly contrasting with this is the everyday family life in highly industrialized societies. Most men are in employment outside the home and so are an increasing number of women. The children go to school and spend more and more of their leisure in organized activities outside the home (sports club, painting class, music lessons etc.), in the new forms of 'insulated childhood' spread right across the city (see Zeiher, 1994). Family life no longer happens in one place but is scattered between several different locations. Neither a fortiori is there a common temporal rhythm, for the family's life is structured by different social institutions: the timetable of kindergarten, school and youth organization, the working hours of the husband and wife, the opening hours of shops, the schedule of public transport and so on. Most important of all, the flexibilization of working hours directly intrudes upon family life, as it produces irregular and fluctuating tempos that do not correspond to such requirements of living together as continuity, stability and co-ordination.[7]

It is extremely difficult to tie together the threads of these different rhythms. The watchword is: 'Join together what is moving apart!' (see Rerrich, 1993) so that everyday family life becomes a kind of 'jigsaw' that is hard work rather than a game (Rerrich, 1991). The individual pieces have to be put together time and again, the temporal and spatial arrangements compared and collated. This is vividly shown by the results of a detailed empirical study (Jurczyk and Rerrich, 1993). The lives of individual family members, with their different rhythms, locations and demands, only rarely fit together naturally. Much more often, discrepancies appear and lead to repeated attempts to establish a balance. A harmonious everyday life is thus an 'achievement based on a great deal of preparation' (Rerrich, 1993: 311), which requires the family co-ordinator to be a skilful timetable juggler. Usually it is women who perform this task which entails considerable practical and emotional effort, often with the help of a grandmother, au pair or child minder. The need to plan, organize and delegate is thus growing all the time as the family becomes a kind of small business. 'Elements of rationalization and calculation are marching into private life' (Rerrich, 1993: 322). My, your, our time becomes the issue in a struggle between time of one's own and a quest for common time. And it is not uncommon for this to result in tension and competing demands – especially between men and women. Who will take responsibility for what? When and for how long? Whose need for time has priority? Who is free when?

Multicultural Families

In pre-industrial society, when a man and a woman got married they nearly always shared a wide repertoire of local experiences, values and attitudes. For lifeworlds were then far more closed than they are today and marriage opportunities were greatly limited by factors ranging from class and property to ethnic origin and religion. In comparison, the everyday lifeworld is nowadays much more thoroughly mixed: people from different regions and social strata meet and often marry one another. The old barriers erected by the law or by the wider family have not completely disappeared, but they are much weaker than they used to be. The principle of a free choice of partner has become generally accepted, so that people who live together (with or without a marriage certificate) often come from quite different backgrounds. Or, as Berger and Kellner put it in a classic text, the modern choice of partner is characterized by the meeting of two strangers:

> Marriage in our society is a dramatic act in which two strangers come together and redefine themselves... the term 'strangers' [does not] mean, of course, that the candidates for the marriage come from widely discrepant social backgrounds – indeed, the data indicate that the contrary is the case. The strangeness rather lies in the fact that, unlike marriage candidates in many previous societies, those in ours typically come from different face-to-face contexts. (Berger and Kellner, 1974: 160)

The marital relation thereby acquires new meaning, but also, of course, is subject to new strains. For the great opportunity of personally chosen togetherness – namely, the creation of a common world beyond the legacy of family and kin – requires that both participants make enormous contributions. Within the system of modern marriage, the partners are not only expected to construct their own form of togetherness; they *must* do so:

> Marriage and the family used to be firmly embedded in a matrix of wider community relationships... There were few separating barriers between the world of the individual family and the wider community... The same social life pulsated through the house, the street and the community... In our contemporary society, by contrast, each family constitutes its own segregated sub-world... This fact requires a much greater effort on the part of the marriage parties. Unlike in earlier situations in which the establishment of the new marriage simply added to the differentiation and complexity of an already existing social world, the marriage partners now are embarked on the often difficult task of constructing for themselves the little world in which they live. (Berger and Kellner, 1974: 162–3)

This is especially true of bi-national or bicultural couples, where each partner comes from a different country or culture. Such unions also existed in earlier epochs, of course, but their number has increased considerably in recent times, owing to migration of labour, political upheavals and political persecution, mass tourism and foreign travel for education or business. In Germany, every seventh couple marrying today is nationally mixed.[8] What Berger and Kellner saw as characteristic of modern marriage is here even more applicable. For in nationally mixed marriages, the strangers are 'even stranger and the differences in socialization are greater' (Hardach-Pinke, 1988: 116).

Today in every marriage, different lifestyles, values, ways of thinking and communicating, rituals and everyday routines have to be fitted together in one family world. In the case of bi-national/bicultural marriages, this means that both partners must achieve the 'construction of a new intercultural reality' (Hardach-Pinke, 1988: 217) , build an 'intercultural lifeworld' (Hardach-Pinke, 1988) or a 'bi-national family culture' (Scheibler, 1992: 87ff). They act within a space that has been little structured beforehand, as two different worlds meet. In this situation, for which there is no preparation and no specific rules, the partners have to work out arrangements of their own (Scheibler, 1992: 45).

Much that used simply to happen, without any questions asked, must now be weighed up and decided upon. Where shall we live: in your country or mine, or perhaps in a third where neither has the advantage of its being home? Shall we stay here or later move to your home country? Who has which opportunities where? Who must bear which burdens where? Who will be without legal status, job protection or pension cover? Do we communicate in your language or mine, or in a third, or in whichever suits the occasion? Which festivals and holidays will we celebrate? What shall we do about family visits and all the many branches of the family? What about the division of labour at home? How are the children to be brought up: in your religion or mine, in your language or mine? What forenames will we choose, reflecting which of our origins?

To repeat: there are no models for any of these decisions. Each couple goes its own way, seeks its own forms. Whether they choose to follow one or the other cultural tradition in its entirety; whether they try to find forms combining elements from both; whether they test out several options and perhaps keep switching around (Scheibler, 1992: 44ff) – all this will depend on their previous history, actual place of residence and plans for the future, as well as on the cultural preferences and prejudices in their surroundings. Each bi-national couple lives out its own story, its own distinctive version of bi-national family culture.

The biography of each partner is far from unimportant in this process. The one who comes from a different country is 'the stranger' here. Perhaps their background was one of poverty and hunger, or perhaps of torture, persecution and escape; anyway they have gone through experiences and anxieties quite different from those of people in their new surroundings. Their life is, to a greater or lesser degree, cut off from their own cultural roots, their socialization, their language. If their mode of expression, behaviour and appearance becomes noticed, they live with the stigma of 'the other' (see Goffman, 1963). They have to face humiliating treatment and mistrust at the hands of courts and officials, landlords and employers. They live without protection, and if their legal status is insecure they can have their work permit withdrawn and perhaps even be deported. True, the native partner is not unaffected by all this, but he or she is in a comparatively secure position and can take steps in self-defence. It remains completely open what attacks from the outside will mean for the couple's relationship: in one case it may be tested to the point of breakdown, while in another it may be made all the stronger. But whatever the outcome, the structure of their relations is typically such that one partner is more exposed than the other. So, differences between their social positions establish themselves. There is an imbalance, more or less pronounced, between their respective opportunities and dangers.

Finally, a bi-national/bicultural marriage also makes both partners confront their own origins, with sometimes paradoxical results. Someone who looked for the attraction of 'the other' in a relationship with a foreigner suddenly discovers the 'native' element in his or her own self. 'One sees how deeply rooted is one's own value system – indeed, in many respects one sees it for the first time' (Elschenbroich, 1988: 368). Contemplating the children's future brings memories back with particular force, making it necessary to confront one's own socialization and history, values and desires – one's own identity. The question 'Who am I, what do I want?' is posed anew in the course of a bi-national marriage. And it leads on to further questions that call for a crucial decision: 'What do I want to keep?', 'What can I give up?', 'What is important to me?'

Divorce and its Consequences

The number of divorces rose dramatically in the course of the twentieth century. Every third marriage ended in divorce in the Federal Republic of Germany, every second one in the United States.[9] Children too were increasingly affected. A German study that compared children born in 1960 and in 1980 came to the following conclusion: 'During these twenty years, the risk of being affected in childhood by parental separation has risen more than threefold' (Nauck, 1991: 427).

When divorce occurs, the situations of men and women, adults and children, develop in different directions. This is true first of all in a directly geographical sense: one partner (nearly always the man) moves to another dwelling and perhaps another town (so as to make a fresh start). Women and children stay behind, but it is not uncommon for them to move too at a later date (to cheaper accommodation, closer to grandparents and so on) – which means a change in surroundings, school and neighbours. New economic situations are especially important: a drop in income usually takes place, depending on the laws of the country concerned. In the United States the standard of living sharply declines for women and children, while it not infrequently rises for men (because they often pay no maintenance) (Cherlin, 1992: 73f). In Germany money, or lack of it, is more evenly divided and most men have to contend with a reduced budget, but still the women and children generally are worse off (Lucke, 1990).

In addition, a new organization of everyday life becomes necessary after a divorce. It has to be negotiated, often fought over, between the two who used to be a couple. Who keeps the apartment, who gets which share of the household goods, which keepsakes? How much maintenance will be paid for whom? And above all, who gets the children and what are the custody rights? Man versus woman: claims and demands are raised, rights and duties redistributed. New agreements are sought, often with a great deal of argument. Instead of a common daily life and a common abode, there are now separate 'access' times for the father. When should he come, and for how long? How much is he entitled to have the child at weekends and holidays? In extreme cases, the man or woman may even try to settle things by force: the number of child kidnappings has also been increasing.

Family therapists, lawyers and judges see every day how wounding and bitterness, rage and hatred can escalate between ex-partners after a divorce. But even when the separation is calm and reasonable, it inevitably leads to a new relationship among husband, wife and children. Much more clearly than before, they confront one another as individuals eager to assert their own interests and pursuits, their own wishes and rights. The ex-partners differ in how they think not only about the future but also about their time together in the past – often too about who was to blame and how the whole thing should be seen (he always had other women, she always threw their money around).

In between are the children (on their situation see Wallerstein and Kelly, 1980; Wallerstein and Blakeslee, 1989; Furstenberg and Cherlin, 1991; Cherlin, 1992). Naturally they have wishes of their own. As various studies have shown, they usually hope that the parents will get together again. Yet the parents still go their own ways regardless. The children then have to learn to live with divided loyalties. Where fights break out over who they should stay with, they are asked by the court whether they would prefer to live with the mother or the father. However carefully it is done, the child is being asked to make a statement against one or the other parent – and when little care is taken, the child directly experiences the parents' manoeuvres and attempts to gain influence. Where visiting rules are in force but the ex-partners cannot overcome their sense of hurt, the children become involved in a post-divorce battle in which they are sounded out about the lifestyle and new relationships of the former spouse or used as carriers of information between the warring fronts. But that is not always all. In some families, the children become split between the parents, as brothers and sisters too may divide against each other, Much more often, however, their relationship to the father rapidly tails off as he disappears from their immediate horizon. Relations with the paternal grandparents also grow weaker and more problematic, sometimes partly prevented by the mother as a way of wiping out all reference to the father (Cherlin and Furstenberg, 1986: 136ff).

What all this means for the growing child is a matter of dispute. Many studies indicate that children, being sensitive and vulnerable, often suffer lifelong disturbances when early relations are severed (see Wallerstein and Blakeslee, 1989). Others suggest that children are more flexible, robust, even thoroughly adaptable and that although the period after a divorce is certainly a dramatic crisis, the children usually get over it and settle into the new conditions (see Furstenberg and Cherlin, 1991; Cherlin, 1992). It may be that both interpretations are not completely wrong, but also not completely right; perhaps they are both too narrow. In keeping with what has been said so far, I would therefore like to propose a third interpretation. The series of events connected with separation may, that is, involve a special kind of socialization, the essence of which is a message of, and a hard lesson in, individualism. If children manage to come to terms with changing family forms, this means that they have had to learn to sever close bonds, to cope with loss. They learn early what it means to be abandoned and to part. They see that love does not last for ever, that relationships come to an end, that separation is a normal occurrence in life.

Conjugal Succession and Elective Family Relationships

Many divorced people later remarry or cohabit with a new partner who was also married before and may also have children of their own. More and more children thus grow up with one non-biological parent. On closer examination, these step-families appear in a sense to be a variant of the bicultural family. According to recent findings, they are a 'curious example of an organizational merger; they join two family cultures into a single household' (Furstenberg and Cherlin, 1991: 83). Here too, values, rules and routines, different expectations and everyday practices – from table manners and pocket money to television viewing and bedtime hours – have to be negotiated and agreed. In addition, many children move backwards and forwards between their different family worlds, between the 'everyday parent' who has custody and lives with a new partner and the 'weekend parent' who does not have custody and may also have a new family. This may well lead to complex relationship structures that can be presented only in diagrams with many ramifications. 'Marriage and divorce chains',[10] 'conjugal succession' (Furstenberg, 1989), 'multi-parent families' (Napp-Peters, 1993), 'patchwork families' – all these are concepts designed to make the new family forms easier to grasp. One key characteristic, of course, is that it is not clear who actually belongs to the family. There is no longer a single definition – that has been lost somewhere in the rhythm of separations and new relationships. Instead, each member has their own definition of who belongs to the family; everyone lives out their own version of the patchwork family:

> Let us consider the case in which a married couple with two children divorces and the wife retains custody of the children... If we ask the divorced mother who is in her immediate family, she certainly would include her children, but she might well exclude her ex-husband, who now lives elsewhere. If we ask her children who is in their immediate family, however, we might get a different answer. If the children still see their father regularly, they would probably include both their father and their mother as part of their family. And if we ask the ex-husband who is in his immediate family, he might include his children, whom he continues to see, but not his ex-wife. Thus, after divorce, mother, father and children each may have a different conception of who is in their immediate family. In fact, one can no longer define 'the family' or 'the immediate family' except in relation to a particular person. (Cherlin, 1992: 81)

In this constellation it is no longer the traditional rules of ascription (descent and marriage) which determine the family bond. The key factor now is whether the social relations stemming from it persist after the divorce. Where these relations are broken or gradually fade, there is also an end to the ties of kinship. What could be seen emerging in other family constellations of modernity is here fully displayed: maintenance of the family link is no longer a matter of course but a freely chosen act. In the situation following a divorce, kinship is worked out anew in accordance with the laws of choice and personal inclination – it takes the form of 'elective affinities'. As it is no longer given as a destiny, it requires a greater personal contribution, more active care. As one study of patchwork families puts it: 'From the huge universe of potential kin, people actively create kin by establishing a relationship – by working at becoming kin. And they have wide latitude in choosing which links to activate' (Furstenberg and Cherlin, 1991: 93). Many relatives by the first marriage continue to be 'part of the family'; many by the second marriage are added to them; and others remain outside or drop out.

The outcome no longer follows a predetermined model. For where there is a choice, personal preferences more and more become the yardstick; each individual draws his or her own boundaries. Even children growing up in the same household no longer necessarily have the same definition of who belongs to the family (Furstenberg and Cherlin, 1991: 93). What all this means is that 'conjugal succession implies greater fluidity and uncertainty in kinship relations. Cultivating family ties may become more important as less can be taken for granted about the obligation of particular kin to one another' (Furstenberg, 1989: 28f). This confronts everyone involved with new questions that need to be answered; new rules of solidarity and loyalty become necessary:

> It will be extraordinarily interesting to see the relative strength of consanguinal and affinal bonds within families whose members have been multiplied by successive marriages. How will grandparents divide their inheritance among biological grandchildren whom they barely know, stepgrandchildren acquired early in life, or stepgrandchildren acquired from their own second marriage who have helped to nurse them later in life? Do biological fathers have more obligation to send their biological children, who have been raised by a stepfather, to college or their own stepchildren whom they have raised? (Furstenberg, 1989: 29)

When such networks take shape, the net result of divorce for the children is an enlargement rather than a narrowing of their kinship boundaries. The character of the ties does, however, change in the process. No longer taken for granted, they become thinner and more fragile, more dependent upon personal co-operation and also upon external circumstances (such as a change of place). This kind of bonding contains special opportunities but also special risks. By the same token, we should not underestimate the value of bonding which, precisely because of its weakness, encompasses a wide kinship network. But 'this thinner form of kinship may not be an adequate substitute for the loss of relatives who had a stronger stake in the child's success' (Furstenberg and Cherlin, 1991: 95). Today, through divorce and remarriage, people are indeed related to more people than they used to be, but the obligations involved in the bond have been decreasing.

Prospects for the Future

Whereas, in pre-industrial society, the family was mainly a community of need held together by an obligation of solidarity, the logic of individually designed lives has come increasingly to the fore in the contemporary world. The family is becoming more of an elective relationship, an association of individual persons, who each bring to it their own interests, experiences and plans and who are each subjected to different controls, risks and constraints.

As the various examples from contemporary family life have shown, it is necessary to devote much more effort than in the past to the holding together of these different biographies. Whereas people could once fall back upon rules and rituals, the prospect now is of a staging of everyday life, an acrobatics of balancing and co-ordinating. The family bond thereby grows more fragile and there is a greater danger of collapse if attempts to reach agreement are not successful. Since individualization also fosters a longing for the opposite world of intimacy, security and closeness (Beck and Beck-Gernsheim, 1995), most people will continue – at least for the foreseeable future – to live within a partnership or family. But such ties are not the same as before, in their scope or in their degree of obligation and permanence. Out of many different strivings, longings, efforts and mistakes, out of successful and often unsuccessful experiments, a wider spectrum of the private is taking shape. As people make choices, negotiating and deciding the everyday details of do-it-yourself relationships, a 'normal chaos' of love, suffering and diversity is growing and developing.

This does not mean that the traditional family is simply disappearing. But it is losing the monopoly it had for so long. Its quantitative significance is declining as new forms of living appear and spread – forms which (at least generally) aim not at living alone but at relationships of a different kind: for example, without a formal marriage or without children; single parenting, conjugal succession, or same-sex partnerships; part-time relationships and companionships lasting for some period in life; living between more than one home or between different towns. These in all their intermediary and secondary and floating forms represent the future of families or what I call the contours of the 'post-familial family'.

Notes

1 Leopold Rosenmayr (1992) speaks of a 'post-familial family'.

2 These trends were more marked in West Germany, but they were also on the increase in East Germany. As to singles, the percentage of men and women who stay single over their lifetime has been increasing continuously, in West Germany since 1930, in East Germany since 1950 (Engstler, 1997: 85). As to cohabitation, in West Germany, the number of non-married couples living together rose tenfold between 1972 and 1996, from 137,000 to 1,408,000. In East Germany, this number rose from 327,000 in 1991 to 442,000 in 1996 (Engstler, 1997: 62). As to those without children, in West Germany, of women born in 1945, 13.3 per cent remained childless; of those born in 1960, approximately 23.3 per cent will remain so. In East Germany, until recently the number of women remaining childless was very low, but it is now also increasing (Engstler, 1997: 96, 103).

3 The figures quoted by Elisabeth Bauschmid evidently come from Bernhard Nauck's article (1991), based on research work carried out in 1988. The forms of family in question refer to the period from 1970 to 1987.

4 In West Germany, the number of children born outside marriage rose threefold between 1965 and 1997, from 4.7 per cent to 14.3 per cent (Statistisches Bundesamt 1990: 116; for 1997, data from the Federal Bureau of Statistics in Wiesbaden. In East Germany, nearly half of the children (44.1 per cent) were born outside marriage in 1997 (data from the Federal Bureau of Statistics in Wiesbaden).

5 See the survey contained in Elisabeth Beck-Gernsheim (1992).

6 See the example of an eighteenth-century divorce, in Bock and Duden (1977: 126).

7 For more data on the growth of flexitime working (weekend, shift, part-time work, etc.), see Gross et al., 1987, 1989.

8 According to the latest available figures, for the year 1996, from the Federal Bureau of Statistics in Wiesbaden. This points to a rapid increase in such marriages, which still only accounted for a twelfth of the total in the second half of the 1980s. See also Engstler (1997: 83).

9 For more recent figures see Engstler (1997: 88, 90) and Cherlin (1992: 7, 24).

10 The concept of 'divorce chains' originated with the anthropologist Paul Bohannan and was adopted by other authors such as Cherlin (1992: 83).

Bibliography

Bauschmid, E. (1994) 'Familie ist kein Auslaufmodell', *Süddeutsche Zeitung*, 4 January: 4.

Beck, U. (1986) *Risikogesellschaft. Auf dem Weg in eine andere Moderne.* Frankfurt M.: Suhrkamp.

Beck, U. and Beck-Gernsheim, E. (1993) 'Nicht Autonomie, sondern Bastelbiographie', *Zeitschrift für Soziologie*, 3: 178–87.

Beck, U. and Beck-Gernsheim, E. (1995) *The Normal Chaos of Love.* Cambridge: Polity Press. (Orig. 1990).

Beck-Gernsheim, E. (1983) 'Vom "Dasein für andere" zum Anspruch auf ein Stück "eigenes Leben" – Individualisierungsprozesse im weiblichen Lebenszusammenhang', *Soziale Welt*, 3: 307–41.

Beck-Gernsheim, E. (1992) 'Arbeitsteilung, Selbstbild und Lebensentwurf. Neue Konfliktlagen in der Familie', *Kölner Zeitschrift für Soziologie und Sozialpsychologie*, 2: 273–91.

Berger, B. and Berger, P. L. (1983) *The War over the Family.* Garden City and New York: Anchor Press/Doubleday.

Berger, B. and Berger, P. L. (1984) *In Verteidigung der bürgerlichen Familie.* Reinbek: Rowohlt.

Berger, P. L. and Kellner, H. (1974) 'Marriage and the Construction of Reality', in R. L. Coser (ed.), *The Family: Its Structures and Functions.* London: Macmillan.

Bock, G. and Duden, B. (1977) 'Arbeit aus Liebe – Liebe als Arbeit', in *Frauen und Wissenschaft. Beiträge zur Berliner Sommeruniversität für Frauen.* Berlin. pp. 118–99.

Borscheid, P. (1988) 'Zwischen privaten Netzen und öffentlichen Institutionen – Familienumwelten in historischer Perspektive', in Deutsches Jugendinstitut (ed.), *Wie geht's der Familie?* Munich: Kösel. pp. 271–80.

Cherlin, A. J. (1992) *Marriage, Divorce, Remarriage.* Cambridge, MA: Harvard University Press.

Cherlin, A. J. and Furstenberg, F. F. (1986) 'Grandparents and divorce', in *The New American Grandparent.* New York: Basic Books. Chapter 6.

Elschenbroich, D. (1988) 'Eine Familie – zwei Kulturen', in Deutsches Jugendinstitut (ed.), *Wie geht's der Familie?* Munich: Kösel.

Engstler, H. (1997) 'Die Familie im Spiegel der amtlichen Statistik. Aktualisierte und erweiterte Neuauflage 1998', in Federal Ministry for Family, Senior Citizens, Women and Youth (ed.), Berlin.

Furstenberg, F. F. (1989) 'One hundred years of change in the American family', in H. J. Bershady (ed.), *Social Class and Democratic Leadership: Essays in Honor of E. Digby Baltzell.* Philadelphia, PA: University of Pennsylvania Press.

Furstenberg, F. F. and Cherlin, A. J. (1991) *Divided Families: What Happens to Children when Parents Part.* Cambridge, MA: Harvard University Press.

Goffman, E. (1963) *Stigma: Notes on the Management of Spoiled Identity.* Englewood Cliffs, NJ: Prentice-Hall.

Gross, H., Pekuhl, U. and Thoben, C. (1987) 'Arbeitszeitstrukturen im Wandel', in Der Minister für Arbeit, Gesundheit und Soziales des Landes Nordrhein-Westfalen (ed.), *Arbeitszeit '87*, Part 2. Dusseldorf.

Gross, H., Thoben, C. and Bauer, F. (1989) *Arbeitszeit '89. Ein Report zu Arbeitszeiten und Arbeitszeitwünschen in der Bundesrepublik.* Cologne.

Hardach-Pinke, I. (1988) *Interkulturelle Lebenswelten. Deutsch–japanische Ehen in Japan.* Frankfurt/ M.: Campus.

Hitzler, R. and Honer, A. (1994) 'Bastelexistenz. Über subjektive Konsequenzen der Individualisierung', in U. Beck and E. Beck-Gernsheim (eds), *Riskante Freiheiten. Individualisierung in modernen Gesellschaften.* Frankfurt: Suhrkamp. pp. 307–15.

Jurczyk, K. and Rerrich, M. S. (eds) (1993) *Die Arbeit des Alltags.* Freiburg: Lambertus.

Lasch, C. (1977) *Haven in a Heartless World: The Family Besieged.* New York: Basic.

Lucke, D. (1990) 'Die Ehescheidung als Kristallisationskern geschlechtspezifischer Ungleichheit', in P. A. Berger and S. Hradil (eds), *Lebenslagen, Lebensläufe, Lebensstile.* Göttingen: Schwartz Verlag. pp. 363–85.

Mayer, K. U. and Müller, W. (1994) 'Lebensverläufe im Wohlfahrtsstaat', in U. Beck and E. Beck-Gernsheim (eds), *Riskante Freiheiten. Individualisierung in modernen Gesellschaften*. Frankfurt: Suhrkamp.

Napp-Peters, A. (1993) 'Mehrelternfamilien – Psychosoziale Folgen von Trennung und Scheidung für Kinder und Jugendliche', *Neue Schriftenreihe der Arbeitsgemeinschaft für Erziehungshilfe*, 49: 12–26.

Nauck, B. (1991) 'Familien und Betreuungssituationen im Lebenslauf von Kindern', in H. Bertram (ed.), *Die Familie in Westdeutschland*. Opladen: Laske und Budrich. pp. 389–428.

Rerrich, M. S. (1988) *Balanceakt Familie. Zwischen alten Leitbildern und neuen Lebensformen*. Freiburg: Lambertus.

Rerrich, M. S. (1991) 'Puzzle Familienalltag: Wie passen die einzelnen Teile zusammen?', *Jugend und Gesellschaft*, 5–6.

Rerrich, M. S. (1993) 'Gemeinsame Lebensführung: Wie Berufstätige einen Alltag mit ihren Familien herstellen', in K. Jurczyk and M. S. Rerrich (eds), *Die Arbeit des Alltags*. Freiburg: Lambertus.

Rosenmayr, L. (1992) 'Showdown zwischen Alt und Jung?', *Wiener Zweitung*, 26 June, 1.

Scheibler, P. M. (1992) *Binationale Ehen*. Weinheim: Deutscher Studienverlag.

Statistisches Bundesamt (ed.) (1990) *Familien heute. Strukturen, Verläufe, Einstellungen*. Stuttgart: Metzler-Poeschel.

Vascovics, L. (1991) 'Familie im Auflösungsprozess?', in Deutsches Jugendinstitut (ed.), *Jahresbericht 1990*. Munich: pp. 186–98.

Wallerstein, J. S. and Kelly, J. B. (1980) *Surviving the Breakup: How Children and Parents Cope with Divorce*. New York: Basic Books.

Wallerstein, J. S. and Blakeslee, S. (1989) *Second Chances*. New York: Ticknor & Fields.

Zeiher, H. (1994) 'Kindheitsträume. Zwischen Eigenständigkeit und Abhängigkeit', in U. Beck and E. Beck-Gernsheim (eds), *Riskante Freiheiten. Individualisierung in modernen Gesellschaften*. Frankfurt: Suhrkamp.

7

Division of Labour, Self-Image and Life Projects

New Conflicts in the Family

The Potential for Conflict

In recent studies of the family, there is hardly any topic with so much available empirical material as that of the domestic division of labour between the sexes (e.g. Metz-Göckel and Müller, 1985; Bertram and Borrmann-Müller, 1988; Nave-Herz, 1988a; Thiessen and Rohlinger, 1988; Deutsches Institut für Wirtschaftsforschung, 1990; Keddi and Seidenspinner, 1991; Künzler, 1992). And despite the great diversity of clients, institutions and research interests, the balance sheet always looks much the same. More and more women are economically active – but men's participation in housework is mostly still low, even among the younger generation. The same holds for other European countries (Nave-Herz, 1989) and for the United States (Hochschild, 1990; Blair and Lichter, 1991; Ferree, 1991; Thompson, 1991).

Here, for example, is the result of a study conducted by the Institut für Demoskopie: 'Detailed investigation of individual activities shows the daily routine of running the home to be largely the woman's responsibility' (*Einstellungen zu Ehe und Familie*, 1983: 129). Similar, although sharper in tone, is the conclusion of another study:

> A shorthand formula presents itself... for all the marriages in the period of observation, regardless of what work the two spouses did. The stereotyped gender roles do not break down over time... There is no changeover in household activities. 'Driving the car' and 'making breakfast' serve as alibi functions. These male concessions in the couple's everyday 'battle over work' cannot be considered really revolutionary. (Thiessen and Rohlinger, 1988: 656)

Much research also shows that a growing number of women are not prepared to accept such an unequal situation as normal or natural but express dissatisfaction with it. Thus, the division of domestic labour is becoming a source of frequent irritation and tension, and sometimes of constant dispute, within the marital relationship (e.g. *Einstellungen zu Ehe und Familie*, 1983; Metz-Göckel and Müller, 1987; Hochschild, 1990; Rerrich, 1991a). Even where there is evidence of relative harmony and acceptance of a division of labour, considerable potential for conflict is often visible beneath the surface (Bertram and Borrmann-Müller, 1988: 264, 267; Erler et al., 1988a, e.g. pp. 41, 47).

In this chapter I want to take this apparently trivial, because long-known observation as the starting-point for diagnosis rather than the conclusion. My question is why the division of labour is so important that it gives rise to such deep tensions. Why do conflicts always break out around it? Why are those involved not able to work out rational rules and compromises, which allow for the wishes of both?

My explanation will start from the basic idea that these conflicts between men and women must be seen at two interlocking levels. For if one considers only the content of 'mundane' household activities within the family (shopping, cooking, cleaning, washing, controlling expenditure, taking a child to the doctor etc.), one can hardly grasp the explosive force of things that really should be solvable. The deeper dimension of such conflicts becomes comprehensible only if one keeps in view a second level that is always also involved: that is, if one considers how the private labour and division of tasks are closely bound up with the self-image and the life projects of men and women.

The Conflict behind the Conflict: Self-Images and Life Projects

It would seem useful to begin by looking in very broad outline at the impetus to individualization which the female biography has received in the last few decades. Already in the late nineteenth century, but much more clearly since the 1960s, structural changes have occurred in various sectors of society – especially education and work, the family cycle and the legal system – which have reshaped the basic conditions of the female biography. However diverse these changes may seem, they have been operating in much the same direction: women have been at least partly detached from the family bond; they are less and less able to expect a man to provide for them; and they have to stand on their own feet and provide for themselves, in often contradictory ways.[1]

These are, so to speak, the 'external' givens of the female biography. Since the late 1960s they have been supported and reinforced by a newly emerging 'rhetoric of equality' – in politics, the media, public life and, not least, the educational system – which questions the polarity of gender roles and argues instead for equality of rights and opportunity (Diezinger et al., 1988; Geissler and Oechsle, 1990).

Empirical studies show that, as a result of this new basis of gender socialization, internal changes are also under way for women (e.g. Becker-Schmidt et al., 1981, 1983; Allerbeck and Hoag, 1985; Biermann et al., 1985; Geissler and Oechsle, 1990; Diezinger, 1991). Among the younger generation of women, new models are being at least partly internalized in the form of new self-images and life projects (timidly or resolutely according to the woman's background and educational level). To be sure, the family still plays an important role, but at the same time – and this is what is new – values of autonomy, independence or personal space are emphasized much more strongly than in the past. A job or career has become part of women's life project, because it promises recognition, money of their own and personal development beyond the family. Expectations of equality and fairness in relations between the sexes develop in the process – at least partially, at least implicitly, although sometimes quite explicitly.

But in everyday life there is little support for these expectations; in other words, not much has been done to follow up the rhetoric of equality with a reshaping of social practice. The unfavourable structures of work and attitudes of employers, together with the shortage of nurseries, all-day schools and other institutional support for young families, have been amply demonstrated (and summarized in *Familie und Arbeitswelt*, 1984). They represent massive obstacles to a combination of career and family and hence to the life project most favoured by women, insidiously establishing new inequalities and hierarchies in the relationship between the sexes.

So much for the younger generation of women. If we now turn to the evolution of the normal male biography, the first point to note is the small amount of directly relevant research (Pross, 1978; Metz-Göckel and Müller, 1985; Strümpel et al., 1988; and on the present state of research, Leube, 1988); most of the data have been presented in the context of other, thematically broader studies (e.g. Allerbeck and Hoag, 1985; Erler et al., 1988a; Burkart et al., 1989; Zoll et al., 1989; Hochschild, 1990). On the basis of this material, it may be said that changes are also occurring among young men with regard to their expectations and life projects, as well as an at least partial loosening of the old gender role models. But the material also clearly shows that such changes are much more hesitant and slowly paced among men than among women. What has mainly been noticeable up to now has been a 'conceptual emancipation of men' (Schneewind and Vaskovics, 1991: 171).

Principles of equality in relationships between the sexes are accepted in part, but often with a characteristic split between ideas and men's actual practice, more for society as a whole than with their own wife in their own home. According to Metz-Göckel and Müller: 'Men are divided in their reactions. They accept things with their head but do not translate them into action. They conceal actual inequality beneath words about mutual sharing' (1985: 18). Or, as Regina Simm concluded from a broadly based panel investigation of young families, most men 'want a stronger traditional conception of life – for women. They value women's economic activity less, and their traditional focus on family activity more, than women themselves do' (1989: 18). In short, it certainly seems that both men and women have changed their understanding of gender roles in relation to themselves and to the other sex – but on the whole women have done this more quickly, so that the experiences of difference remain and have even been growing (Wahl, 1989: 14).

These differently filled ideas of equality become active when men and women start to live together and set up a family. For the younger generation of women, this results in an explosive combination. The expectations of equality which they have at least to some extent internalized, so that they form part of their self-image, are now contradicted by experiences of inequality both at work and in private life.

Already in the 1980s a number of studies of young people were predicting the conflict we have just outlined. Klaus Allerbeck and Wendy Hoag, for example, wrote:

> When a girl chooses a job that is stimulating and interesting... but is not able to do it part-time or interrupt it for a few years, this means that a woman affected

by such a choice soon finds herself in a dilemma... It seems inescapable that this
will lead to considerable frustration. (1985: 120–123).

And a *Mädchen '82* study conducted by the German Youth Institute
concluded:

> Help and support can hardly be expected for a solution to the conflict between
> job and family; the existing structures in the labour market and the family do not
> allow of it. Even if some room for manoeuvre is present in the family, different
> laws prevail in the labour market... Today's 15 to 19-year-old girls do plan their
> lives, but it is questionable whether their plans will be realized. (Seidenspinner
> and Burger, 1982: 21f.)

The way in which gender-differentiated self-images, wishes and plans for the
future collide within the family is vividly demonstrated in a recent representative
survey of young couples conducted by Erler and others. One of the questions they
were asked was how each partner would like to change and how each thought the
other partner should change. The replies were significantly different. Whereas the
women mostly wanted to be more emancipated than they already considered themselves, the men wanted their partner to be less emancipated than she actually was,
to be a more traditional wife. A 'hidden front of future conflicts' – according to
Erler et al. – should therefore be expected 'if both partners seek to fulfil their
desires'. The same supposition arises when the men's self-images and wishes for
the future are contrasted with the women's expectations. The survey results suggest
that the men do want to change into becoming more like a 'new man'. Nevertheless,
'the wishes for change turn out to be rather meagre (that is, the differences between
self-image and desired ideal are minimal). Their partners, by way of contrast, wish
that they would change very much more' (Erler et al., 1988a: 46f.).

Couples from the younger generation may be said to be living through what
Hochschild calls a 'stalled revolution' (1990: 11ff.) or what Klaus Wahl terms the
'modernization trap' – that is, a split between myth and reality in modernity,
between 'internalized promises of, on the one hand, self-confident autonomy,
family happiness and social progress... and, on the other hand, actual experiences
of withheld recognition, contempt for human dignity, and damaged self-esteem'
(Wahl, 1989: 16). On the basis of what has been outlined, it may be assumed that
this modernization trap affects women in particular. The male partner from whom
she hopes to receive closeness and support displays attitudes and modes of behaviour which violate her understanding of a fair division of labour and equality
of opportunity; he takes privileges for himself and leaves her with most of the
burdens. For many women today, such conduct means not only a lack of help in
everyday life but also, I would argue, a daily experience of inequality within the
family, an offence against expectations and demands that are part of their life project, a display of contempt for their personality and indeed for their existential
desires and rights. The available studies suggest that such disappointed expectations give rise to rancour against husbands and dissatisfaction with marriage and
the family (Hochschild, 1990; Rerrich, 1991a). Here again is Klaus Wahl:

> If we take a finding about 'family discontent' (an index composed of various
> aspects of relations within the family), according to which women... are content

with family life significantly less often than men... then it becomes apparent that the promise of modernity that women may be self-confident and autonomous individuals... has for women in general been found considerably wanting. (1989: 280)

Various studies also show that for men the expectations and demands of women are not only uncomfortable but signal a cancellation of many privileges which they used to take for granted, an offence against deeply rooted elements of the male self-image and self-confidence. With a subjective sense that they have something to lose, men feel troubled and pressured by women (Erler et al., 1988a: 47; Hochschild, 1990). For both sexes, then, the issue of the household division of labour stirs much deeper layers of identity, planning for the future, and self-esteem.

The resulting thesis is that *when conflicts flare up in marriage or a relation-ship over the division of labour, more than housework is at issue*. For a job is not only a job, and housework is not only housework. Both also stand for ideas of what a family and a relationship between the sexes should be like. They therefore involve the self-images and identities of both men and women. They raise such questions as: Who am I? How would I like to be? What is a real man or a modern woman? – questions that concern the (partly conflicting) gender-specific ideas of equality, justice and the right way to live. This is, so to speak, the 'conflict behind the conflict' – and a constant source of tensions.

No doubt it is mainly women who bring such identity questions into a relation-ship. But their conflict potential and their characteristic intertwining of division of labour and identity has an exemplary character, as Giddens has shown in his *Modernity and Self-Identity* (1991). According to Giddens, the scope for deci-sion that opens up in late modernity not only concerns external questions but increasingly also matters of identity. At many levels of everyday life, including small details and all the things that used to be determined by routine and tradi-tion, we are now faced with decisions about who we are and how we want to be. 'What to wear, what to eat... all such choices (as well as larger and more conse-quential ones) are decisions not only about how to act but who to be' (Giddens, 1991: 81). Identity in late modernity is less and less an ascribed fate; it becomes dependent upon decision, risky and reflexive. And this is true not least of gender identity: 'What gender identity is, and how it should be expressed, has become itself a matter of multiple options' (ibid.: 217). In this sense, the negotiations over the household division of labour are also part of 'identity choice' (Lash and Friedman, 1991: 7). More, their very sharpness and bitterness comes from the fact that they are part of an ongoing *identity struggle* which always breaks out when external barriers and constraints become more fragile, when individuals are per-mitted, expected and compelled to shape the definition of themselves.

The argument here is not that the satisfaction of women with marriage depends only upon the household division of labour (or that of men only upon women's preparedness to accept the traditional division of labour without complaint). Even today marriages (with or without a certificate) are not merely work communities; they are not just a question of who takes the rubbish down or washes the floor. Precisely today, there are quite different measures, criteria and expectations bound up with living together – all the desires, for example, which arise out of the experiences of an individualized society, from the quest for security and inner stability to the secular religion of love (Beck and Beck-Gernsheim, 1990). It is therefore quite conceivable that, even among women with strong expectations of equality who get little support from their man around the house, a strong potential for conflict will not necessarily build up. This might be the case if they are very content in other areas of the marriage, if their partner has many other qualities that they value or regard as compensation (reliability or tenderness, a sense of humour, a number of shared interests, and so on).

We may assume, however, that such cases are likely to be rather rare in the long term. For if we look more closely at the social script for marriage in the individualized society, it becomes apparent at many points that it involves a kind of dual script: expectations of feelings *and* expectations of equality, whose combination can easily become like the squaring of a circle (Beck and Beck-Gernsheim, 1990). In any event, from the *woman's* point of view there may obviously be relations of interference between these two levels – which indicates a difference between the sexes that is fraught with consequences. When things are not going well with the division of labour, her feelings of love are also disturbed; and conversely, when the man does his share in the house, this is recognized by the woman and interpreted as a sign of love (Thompson, 1991: 185).

Hochschild spends a whole chapter on the story of Evan and Nancy to illustrate the tensions in modern marriage. In an interview, Nancy says: 'Evan and I look for different signs of love. Evan feels loved when we make love… I feel loved when he makes dinner for me or cleans up.' The author comments:

> For Nancy, feeling loved was connected to feeling her husband was being considerate of her needs, and honouring her ideal of sharing and equity. To Evan, 'fairness' and respect seemed impersonal moral concepts, abstractions rudely imposed on love. He thought he expressed his love for Nancy by listening carefully to her… And by consulting her on major purchases. But who did the dishes had to do with a person's role in the family, not with fairness and certainly not with love. In my interviews, a surprising number of women spoke of their fathers helping their mothers 'out of love' or consideration. As one woman said, 'My dad helped around a lot. He really loved my mom.' But… not one man I interviewed made this link between help at home and love. (1990: 49)

Pointing in a similar direction is a conclusion from the qualitative study of Burkart et al., of the changing meaning of relationships among different social groups. In the milieu of technical staff (ten interviewees, four of them women), a far-reaching division of labour with partners was found. One woman, whose partner did half the housework, said: 'I really know where I am with my partner. You don't find someone like that so easily.' And the researchers add: 'This is the point she really stresses; "love", on the other hand, is a secondary matter.' In this milieu, only one woman complained of an 'unfair' division of labour and this was precisely the couple about whom the researcher remarked, 'obviously a lot of other things weren't right in the relationship' (Burkart et al., 1989: 147). Both cases, then, indicate interference between love and work – one positive, the other negative.

One might say that the greater the expectations of equality with which women today approach marriage, the more other qualities the man must offer if he does not live up to those expectations. And, other things being equal, this makes it more likely that the man will be unable to display enough of such compensatory qualities that make for a contented marriage – more likely, in other words, that the potential for conflict will grow.

Conflict Reduction Strategies

It would now seem appropriate to ask how couples today tackle this potential for conflict in their different conceptions of housework, job and gender roles. To answer this question, I have examined some empirical material about marriage and relationships to see if and when the conflict over private labour is reflected in them. Before presenting my results, I would like to propose a way of structuring the various kinds of material, so that *'preventive' strategies* for the handling of conflict (chosen before the couple starts living together) are distinguished from *'acute' strategies* (developed only in the course of their living together and having children). Both stages may be further divided into three. First, there are attempts to reduce the material potential for conflict, to remove it in reality; I group these under the concept *'avoidance'*. Second, there are what I call *'negotiation'* models which aim to reduce the conflict potential intersubjectively; these involve efforts to get the partner to accept the other's point of view, through persuasion, talking and talking round. Third, there are models that aim to reduce the conflict potential subjectively, through what will here be called *'repression'*. These involve, in effect, attempts to redefine the cognitive field – from dissonance reduction to denial, defence, splitting, perceptual disturbance and the whole range of mechanisms that have been analysed by writers from Sigmund Freud to Leon Festinger.

These distinctions are summarized in Table 7.1.

Table 7.1 *Conflict reduction strategies*

	'Preventive' strategies (prior to living together and starting a family)	'Acute' strategies (after starting to live together and having a family)
'Avoidance': objective conflict reduction	Choice of partner Alternatives to traditional family model (e.g. cohabitation; childless marriage)	Reduction of man's outside work commitments Reduction of family labour (e.g. through delegation or foregoing of more children)
'Negotiation': intersubjective conflict reduction	Prenuptial agreements (e.g. marriage contract)	'Psychological warfare' (e.g. using selective yardstick of comparison, pretexts as argument)
'Repression': subjective conflict reduction	Unrealistic plans of women for a 'dual role'	Self-deception and family myths

Objective Preventive Strategies

The preventive strategy that seems most logical is to choose a partner whose views concerning housework, career and gender roles agree with one's own and do not threaten to cause lasting conflicts on this score. I suspect that such motives definitely do play a role, at least implicitly, in the choice of partner. In the material known to me, I have not found any direct references to this – for two obvious reasons. First, in the modern script relationships and marriage are supposed to be based mainly upon love, so by all means there can be heart flutters and passion but not any practical-prosaic calculations, particularly to do with ironing or the washing-up. Nevertheless, it is not rare to find in the lonely hearts columns various formulations that can be read as indirect signals for a suitable choice of partner. Men, for example, announce that they are looking for a 'sweet' or 'feminine' woman, 'no women's lib firebrands'; or women say they are hoping to find a 'new, open-minded man', no 'male chauvinist or macho types'.

The crucial barrier to the strategy of finding a suitable partner must, of course, be that supply and demand are far from balancing in the marriage market. 'There are not enough new men for new women' is a characteristic way of putting it (Diezinger et al., 1988: 143). In other words, if women insist on finding a man who shares their views of partnership and equal rights, they can wait a long time and still have little chance of success. For men the situation looks similar in reverse: there are not enough traditional women for the number of traditional men. There are probably solutions for men, however, such as the old model of 'marrying down' to women with a lower educational level. This gender difference in education is no longer as marked as it used to be (Ziegler, 1985), but it does still persist in weaker forms (e.g. Cooney and Uhlenberg, 1991). Since educational qualifications and job orientation are now clearly correlated for women, such a model of marriage offers men the chance of finding a wife who is less career minded and more prepared to take on housework.

It is nevertheless a precarious strategy, since the number of women with educational qualifications of their own has been growing. Other ways may therefore be tried out, and it is in this light that the statistics concerning mixed-nationality marriages should be considered. Thus, among German men who marry foreign women, the first preference is for partners from the Far East or Eastern Europe (Esteves, 1988: 17), whereas German women who marry foreign partners have quite different national preferences (ibid.). The conclusion suggests itself that, in some cases at least, female partners are sought who are prized both as being of exotic origin and as coming from a cultural background where women's responsibility for the home and family is still taken for granted. (Not for nothing do marriage bureaux recommend Bulgarian and Czech women as 'solid' and 'home loving'.)[2]

In another respect too, the empirical material suggests that the course is often set for conflict over household labour in advance of the couple's living together and starting a family. One thinks, for example, of current population trends relating to the family: the growing number of people living alone and of cohabiting couples; a tendency to 'living apart together' in two households; a rise in the average age at marriage; a postponement of children until later stages or a decision not to have children at all (see Deutsches Jugendinstitut, 1988; Lüscher et al., 1988; Nave-Herz, 1988b; Bertram, 1991; Engstler and Lüscher, 1992). This is a broad spectrum of lifestyles, but our earlier considerations suggest that there might be a common thread to them all: namely, a preventive strategy of not wishing to fall into the trap of the traditional family model, with its conflicts over the division of labour, and of opting instead for alternatives in which less domestic labour is involved or the responsibilities are not so clearly divided by gender.

In order to check this interpretation, it is necessary to go beyond the population trends and to investigate the *motives* of the people concerned, their desires and goals and conceptions of life. In the investigations presently available, one can find numerous indications that speak in favour of the perspective just offered. Let us take just a couple of examples.

Studies of unmarried couples have repeatedly established that 'insofar as they are resolutely opposed to marriage, the female partners make up the "hard core" of this hostility.' Thus an official study of cohabiting couples concludes that 'postponement or rejection of marriage often specifically [results] from the intention of women... to guarantee their career identity and to ensure that the man "behaves as a real partner".'[3] One constant finding is that in relationships of this kind such values as partnership and equal rights have a high priority, which entails, at least at the level of intentions, 'more rights and more options for women' (Spiegel, 1986: 112f.; see also Meyer and Schulze, 1988; Stich, 1988; Simm, 1989: 9f.; Keddi and Seidenspinner, 1991).

Rosemarie Nave-Herz's study of childless couples points in a similar direction: 'Career interests are by far the most common grounds given for intentional childlessness... especially by younger marriage cohorts. Three-quarters of them cited their career as the reason for deferring their wish to have children, and this applied more to women than to men.' Nave-Herz explicitly concludes from this that 'temporary childlessness' functions as a 'conflict resolution strategy' (1988b: 44, 56).

Intersubjective Preventive Strategies

If we now turn to what we have called 'intersubjective preventive strategies' – where men and women try to remove the potential for conflict by talking and negotiating about who will be responsible for running the home and family – we encounter contradictory findings. On the one hand, a growing number of couples conclude marriage contracts which, along with financial aspects, also stipulate how career and family work are to be divided.[4] Also interesting, at least as a symptom, is the advice found in popular books that the married couple should agree beforehand about who will be responsible for child care.[5]

Similarly, Geissler's and Oechsle's study of young women's plans for the future show that a majority believe they will be able to gain acceptance of those plans only through active negotiation with their partner. In the interview material:

It is explicitly stated that the space for autonomy has to be negotiated: young women today believe in the power of communication. Discussion serves in two ways to lessen dependence. Young women know that they must assert their ideas about the compatibility of career and family in couple relationships, that they must make them appear plausible to their partner, that their life together will look different from their parents.

That is, that their plans for life are different from those of their mother's generation. Furthermore, they suspect that men do not give much thought to the problem of autonomy and dependence in a relationship, that they will do so only if women themselves have the communicative skills to anchor the goal of "equality" in their partner's plans for life' (Geissler and Oechsle, 1990: 28).

Unfortunately this material cannot tell us how many of the women with such a belief in communication later actually practise it. One may assume, from the potential for conflict which builds up in new marriages, that the 'anticipations' described earlier are at least in some cases a kind of 'wishful thinking'. When the real thing later happens, and differing views become apparent at the beginning of a relationship, some women do not perhaps dare to risk bringing things up that might lead to a quarrel or even separation.

Such an assumption is supported by data from a study of young married couples, in which they were asked about any wish to have children and how this would affect their plans for the future. Here it was 'quite apparent that... there was often no consensus within the couple' about the woman's job after the birth of a child' (cf. Burkart et al., 1989: 138f.; Schneewind and Vaskovics, 1991: 61). There is also material illustrating evasive strategies in relation to looming problems – strategies of not talking with the partner or talking at cross-purposes. Here, for example, is an interview extract (Nave-Herz, 1988b: 55f.; cf. Burkart et al., 1989: 137f.):

Husband: If you're going to have a child, you should bring it up yourself and not give it away somewhere.

Wife: (at a later point in interview): Yes, if it happens, we've thought that I'll work half the day... so I didn't want to give up my job altogether.

Husband: Well, we've... by and large... I know... now... Anyway my view has been that you should give up your job altogether.

Wife: Yes, at first.

Husband: Yes! (laughs)

Hochschild observed similar avoidance strategies among her students (1990: xii): 'Nearly all... want to have full-time jobs and rear children... Sometimes I ask [them], "Do you ever talk with your boyfriends about sharing childcare and housework?" Often they reply with a vague "Not really." I don't believe these lively, enquiring eighteen to twenty-two-year-old students haven't thought about the problem. I believe they are afraid of it.'

Subjective Preventive Strategies

The empirical material suggests that many women – probably still a majority – choose a third kind of preventive strategy, in which conflict is reduced not through appropriate action or negotiation but in their own head – by looking away and not seeing or wanting to see. This group probably includes most of the women who refer to a dual orientation in questionnaires: a career of their own *and* the main responsibility for family and children. Whether in the studies of young people conducted by Seidenspinner and Burger in 1982 and Allerbeck and Hoag in 1985, or in Uta Meier's more recent study (1991) of young people in the new *Länder* of the Federal Republic, in the representative study by Erler et al. (1988a) of young couples today, or in data on American students provided by Machung (1989) and Hochschild (1990), the picture is always similar: many young people form plans for their life which clearly do not fulfil the conditions of reality.[6]

Thus Allerbeck and Hoag (1985: 128f.):

> Many girls appear to have contradictory role expectations: work activity (a modern woman has a career of her own etc.) *and* maternity. As answers to questions about the dual burden show, either the resulting conflict is denied or its solution is postponed through a continuation of education. Girls today have to choose between competing and contradictory models. They are not, however, prepared in advance for this choice. And the models they follow are ones whose incompatibility with the real world is all too plain.

Or Uta Meier (1991: 12):

> [M]ore than half the girls questioned say, with their future family and children in mind, that they can imagine later doing part-time work. Yet, according to the girls themselves, their willingness to admit this model of work should not be equated with a lack of interest in their job. When they first start it, they evidently do not realize that a satisfying and meaningful career... is closely bound up with a normal work history, and thus with a full-time job.

And Hochschild (1990: 263):

> Most [of the women students interviewed by Anne Machung] planned to interrupt their careers from one to five years to have the children but they didn't think this would disadvantage them at work. The students I teach fit this description too. When I show my students a picture of the woman with the flying hair, briefcase in one hand, child in the other, they say she is 'unreal', but they want to be just like her.

Objective Acute Strategies

After the preventive strategies, we should now consider the various acute strategies. These involve dealing at a later stage with the conflict potential, when a couple are already living together and have children. To begin with strategies that aim to reduce the conflict objectively, we can identify two main variants: either men may restrict the demands of their job in order to take on more work within the family; or both partners may choose to aim at keeping the demands of domestic labour as limited as possible. In both cases, we have empirical material to go on.

At present, there is a small but slowly increasing group of men who practise part-time work or periods of withdrawal from their job. As the study by Strümpel et al., demonstrates (1988: 6), they often give as their main reason 'a wish to make it easier for their partner to work... The ideal is an egalitarian definition of roles, an equal sharing of outside work, housework and childcare by both partners.'

In the case of the second variant (reduction of work in the family), we can start from the well-known population statistics showing a decline in the number of families with more than one child. The study by Urdze and Rerrich (1988) demonstrates that women very often want to have no further children because they do not want to become more tied to work in the family. 'Behind this are often desires whose fulfilment is for men... usually a matter of course: for instance, to have a child as well as a job appropriate to their education; or to have a family as well as a little time for themselves' (Rerrich, 1988: 66). Another possibility is to displace or delegate the work to other (mostly female) persons, such as a child minder, a granny or an au pair (see Beck-Gernsheim, 1980: 209ff.; Hochschild, 1990; Rerrich, 1991b). Yet another idea is to be more free and easy or even minimalist about the standards of domestic labour, buying ready-made meals instead of home-cooked three-course menus, inviting fewer people round, hoovering less often and so on (Beck-Gernsheim, 1980: 209ff.; Hochschild, 1990). Men, in particular, seem to prefer the last option; they have been described as having a 'higher dirt threshold' than women (Burkart et al., 1989: 151). Hochschild interprets this as deliberately defensive behaviour: 'Men... resisted by a strategy of "needs reduction"; they claimed they didn't need the bed made, didn't need a cooked meal' and so on (1990: 260). Hochschild suspects that in future more and more couples will attempt this solution, which would come down to what Burkart et al. (1989: 143) call a 'generalization of the male lifestyle'. In other words, 'women become like men, and men stay as they are' (Hochschild, 1990: 208). Such an outcome would, in her view, hardly contribute to greater humanity and a better quality of life: 'A strategy of "cutting back" on the house-work, the children, the marriage may be on the rise, with correspondingly reduced ideas about what people "need"' (ibid.).

Intersubjective Acute Strategies

When it does not prove possible to defuse objectively the conflict over gender roles and the division of labour, an intersubjective strategy of 'negotiation' and 'attempted persuasion' is often pursued. This includes efforts to get the partner to accept one's own view of things, whether by presenting arguments to back it up, or by using others that weaken the partner's position. I shall not offer here an exhaustive analysis of the arguments that are traded back and forth in such situations, but simply outline how both partners resort to elements of psychological warfare and employ a policy of changing the subject. Here are a few typical examples.

One strategic variable is obviously the yardstick of comparison. Thus when a wife reproaches a husband with not helping enough with the housework, his elegant retort is that other men do much less (Hochschild, 1990). Many men come up with a comparison that puts them in an even more favourable light – namely, the case of their father and grandfather (LaRossa, 1988).

When there are children to be cared for, the division of labour between the sexes is especially precarious – and strategically charged arguments are correspondingly more frequent. In the study by Metz-Göckel and Müller, men especially mention child care in referring to a norm that the mother belongs to the child – and therefore at home (1985: 26f, 81). According to Erler et al., a dispute arises in many marriages when the child is old enough for the mother to go out to work. 'The concern of mothers to return to their career, perhaps earlier than planned, encounters a whole battery of opposing or obstructive attitudes on the husbands' part... Fathers often consider the child to be still too young – a position that has a lot to do with ensuring an easy life for themselves' (1988a: 39f.). In the study by Urdze and Rerrich, it emerges that men often verbally leave to their wife the decision about whether to have another child or not. The researchers interpret this as a 'playing safe' strategy; the wife is supposed to take the decision, so that she has the responsibility for any further children and cannot demand any changes in the status quo (1988: 85). Women who are unhappy with the present division of labour and therefore do not want another child are often unable to express this directly (ibid.). They then fall back on the 'ruse of powerlessness' (Honegger and Heintz, 1981), a policy of displaced argument that invokes financial reasons rather than dissatisfaction with domestic arrangements. Urdze and Rerrich (1988: 85) see in this a typical case of 'rationalization': 'Often all they have left is to fall back on financial arguments against another child, since those are the most likely to persuade men.'

Subjective Acute Strategies

If all these strategies are of no avail, here too there is still the path of subjectively repressing the potential for conflict, of closing one's eyes to it. In her case studies, Hochschild has forcefully drawn attention to the many forms of self-deception that younger women practise in order to maintain their pride and self-confidence, in a family situation that more or less flatly contradicts their own ideals and measures of equality, fairness and sharing. Hochschild shows how such combinations give rise to 'family myths': for example, both partners may claim to have worked out a fair division of labour, when the objective evidence is that the 'half' supposedly done by the husband is really only a minimal share. According to Hochschild, these life lies fulfil a function mainly for the wife's psychical economy, so that she is able to retain an image of herself as a modern, open-minded woman but does not have to see those sides of everyday family life which do not fit the picture. By paring down her ideas of equality more and more, she manages to go on 'believing one thing and living with another'; it is a 'mental trick' whereby she conceives herself to be equal while living in peace with a man who practises different views (Hochschild, 1990: 55f.).

Now, other researchers have come to different conclusions in this respect (for a summary, see Thompson, 1991), namely, that even women who contribute to the family's upkeep through a job of their own do not consider the skewed division of housework as unfair. Linda Thompson explains this by the fact that conceptions of equality and fairness do not operate according to straightforward 'fifty-fifty' rules, and she shows in an impressive analysis how much more complex measures of comparison are employed. For example, many women compare themselves with other women rather than with their own husband; or they see their labours in the family only partly as work, and much more as an expression of loving care. Of course, this leaves open whether and why women arrive at more complex yardsticks of this kind. On the one hand, it seems quite plausible that elements of gender-specific socialization are still at work here, which the women internalized at an early age. But, by the same token, one cannot help suspecting that what appears here as contentment is in some cases, especially among younger women, a product of the more or less conscious repression identified by Hochschild and Machung, a kind of secondary contentment manufactured for their own inner protection because the discrepancy between ideal and reality could otherwise scarcely be maintained.

This might explain the relative contentment of young mothers in Schneewind's and Vaskovics's study, even though more domestic labour than ever fell on their shoulders after the birth of their child (a situation not at all in keeping with their original wishes). For 'since the women adjust their ideal image to the changed circumstances and no longer strive so hard for an equal division of labour, the discrepancy is reduced... This adjustment of the ideal image [leads] to a necessary reduction in the cognitive dissonance, which would otherwise eventually make the situation intolerable' (1991: 205).

Similarly, Hochschild describes the following combination under the section heading 'Suppressing the politics of comparison':

> In the past, Nancy had compared her responsibilities at home, her identity, and her life to Evan's, and had compared Evan to other men they knew. Now, to avoid resentment, she seemed to compare herself more to other working mothers – how organized, energetic, and successful she was compared to them. By this standard, she was doing great... Nancy also compared herself to single women who had moved further ahead in their careers, but they fit another mental category. There were two kinds of women, she thought – married and single. 'A single woman could move ahead in her career but a married woman has to do a wife's work and mother's work as well.' She did not make this distinction for men. (Hochschild, 1990: 48–49)

The costs of such repression and self-deception are evidently high. They require a huge expenditure of psychic energy – or, as Hochschild calls it, 'emotional work' – to maintain the illusion. 'Many women struggle to avoid, suppress, obscure, or mystify a frightening conflict... They do not struggle like this because they started off wanting to, but because they are forced to choose between equality and marriage. And they choose marriage' (Hochschild, 1990: 85).

At this point, of course, the high rates of divorce in the contemporary world come to mind. It is not a question of looking for monocausal explanations. But one suspects that women's growing dissatisfaction with the division of domestic labour must play a role in these trends. We might formulate the following correlation. If conflicts over gender roles and the division of labour are not reduced in one way or another – through avoidance, negotiation or repression – they can escalate to a point where the only thing left is to abandon the marriage.

Concluding Remarks

The question with which we started – who does what in the home? – has led to a number of deeper questions. These show how closely the family division of labour is bound up with the self-image and self-confidence of both sexes. Such an approach can explain why it is often so difficult for those involved to work out rules and compromises. It explains where the inner resistances lie and why the issue is so emotionally charged. To repeat our conclusion: what is at stake for both sexes is not just work but also the preservation of identity.

A model could therefore be sketched of the strategies that men and women might pursue to reduce the conflict in question. The approach presented here outlines only the range of variation; a further step might extend this to questions such as the following. Which conditions favour the selection of one or another strategy? Which social and political premises, which cultural and ethnic traditions, which individual experiences in life, induce people to take one or another course? What role is played here by such things as family policy, family law and divorce legislation, in their various historical and national forms? Or by the fact that a woman's own mother was or was not economically active? Or by other experiences in childhood, in the original family and in earlier relationships? Which groups of women choose alternatives to the traditional family, which bank on open negotiation with their partner and which construct family myths based on self-deception? Analyses that took up these questions would have to focus on such variables as educational qualifications and job position, as well as on differences between urban and rural milieux. Differences in attitude and behaviour between the generations are probably even clearer in this connection. And if this is so, it is possible that even where conflicts have remained hidden, they will in future become sharper and have major repercussions on the family and relationships between men and women. Perhaps, as Bertram and Borrmann-Müller suspect, there has been a 'modernization deficit in women's consciousness' – one which may 'be eliminated within the space of a few years and give way to novel forms of family organization' (1988: 267).

Notes

1 For a detailed account of this individualization process, see Beck-Gernsheim, 1983, 1986, 1988. On its contradictions and limits, see especially Bilden and Diezinger, 1984; Diezinger, 1991; Ostner, 1983, 1984.

2 See relevant advertisements in *Süddeutsche Zeitung*, 9–10 November 1991.

3 Bundesministerium für Jugend, Familie und Gesundheit, *Nichteheliche Lebensgemeinschaften*, Bonn, 1985, pp. 125f.

4 Naegele, 1987; Partner, 1984; *Der Spiegel*, No. 14, 1990; *Süddeutsche Zeitung*, 27 August 1991. See also *International Herald Tribune*, 24 September 1986: 'Leonore J. Weitzman, a Stanford University professor, said of the boom in prenuptial agreements, "Young idealistic couples want to form egalitarian relationships and want to be sure that marriage truly is an equal partnership".'

5 Joyce Brothers, a popular marriage guidance writer in the United States, has devised a 'children checklist' for couples to agree on their future plans for life. Here are some of the questions on the list (1985: 66):

- Will you [the wife] be the primary caretaker? If so, what share of the child's or children's care do you expect your spouse to assume? Do you plan to share fifty-fifty in their care, feeding, diaper-changing and all the rest? If so, how do you plan to arrange this?
- Will you, the wife, work after the baby is born? How soon after will you go back to work? How do you, the husband, feel about this?
- If you, the wife, go back to work, what arrangements will you make for the child care? Do you, the husband, agree with these arrangements?

6 To avoid any misunderstanding, it should be made clear that this is a statement not so much about what young women do or do not think, as about a society which assigns to them 'an underhand

dual mission' and thus 'increasingly unsettles women in every situation in life' (Erler et al., 1988b: 12). When structural conditions wreck in many ways the compatibility of job and family, women are implicitly required to give up either the one or the other. The 'rational' life plan that combines the two is a utopia. On this 'planning trap', see also Rerrich, 1988.

Bibliography

Allerbeck, K. and Hoag, W. (1985) *Jugend ohne Zukunft? Einstellungen, Umwelt, Lebensperspektiven*. Munich.

Beck, U. and Beck-Gernsheim, E. (1990) *Das ganz normale Chaos der Liebe*. Frankfurt/M.: Suhrkamp; *The Normal Chaos of Love*. Oxford: Polity.

Becker-Schmidt, R., Knapp, G. -A. and Rumpf, M. (1981) 'Frauenarbeit in der Fabrik – betriebliche Sozialisation als Lernprozeß? Über die subjektive Bedeutung der Fabrikarbeit im Kontrast zur Hausarbeit', *Gesellschaft. Beiträge zur Marxschen Theorie*, 14. Frankfurt/M.: Suhrkamp. pp. 52–74.

Becker-Schmidt, R., Brandes-Erlhoff, U., Rumpf, M. and Schmidt, B. (1983) *Arbeitsleben – Lebensarbeit, Konflikte und Erfahrungen von Fabrikarbeiterinnen*. Bonn: Basis.

Beck-Gernsheim, E. (1980) *Das halbierte Leben. Männerwelt Beruf, Frauenwelt Familie*. Frankfurt: Fischer.

Beck-Gernsheim, E. (1983) 'Vom "Dasein für andere" zum Anspruch auf ein Stück "eigenes Leben" – Individualisierungsprozesse im weiblichen Lebenszusammenhang', *Soziale Welt*, 3: 307–341; translated above as 'Living for others'.

Beck-Gernsheim, E. (1986) 'Von der Liebe zur Beziehung?', in J. Berger (ed.), *Die Moderne – Kontinuität und Zäsuren*. Special issue no. 4 of *Soziale Welt*. Göttingen: Schwartz. pp. 209–233.

Beck-Gernsheim, E. (1988) *Die Kinderfrage. Frauen zwischen Kinderwunsch und Unabhängigkeit*. Munich: Beck.

Bertram, H. (ed.) (1991) *Die Familie in Westdeutschland. Stabilität und Wandel familialer Lebensformen*. Opladen: Leske und Budrich.

Bertram, H. and Borrmann-Müller, R. 'Von der Hausfrau zur Berufsfrau? Der Einfluß struktureller Wandlungen des Frauseins auf familiales Zusammenleben', in U. Gerhardt and Y. Schütze (eds) (1988) *Frauensituation*. Frankfurt/M.: Suhrkamp. pp. 251–72.

Biermann, I., Schmerl, C. and Ziebell, L. (1985) *Leben mit kurzfristigem Denken. Eine Untersuchung zur Situation arbeitsloser Akademikerinnen*. Weinheim and Basle: Beltz.

Bilden, H. and Diezinger, A. (1984) 'Individualisierte Jugendbiographie? Zur Diskrepanz von Anforderungen, Ansprüchen und Möglichkeiten', *Zeitschrift für Pädagogik*, 2: 191–207.

Blair, S. L. and Lichter, D. T. (1991) 'Measuring the division of household labor: gender segregation of housework among American couples', *Journal of Family Issues*, 12(1): 91–113.

Brothers, J. (1985) *What Every Woman Ought To Know About Love and Marriage*. New York: Ballantine Books.

Burkart, G., Fietze, B. and Kohli, M. (1989) *Liebe, Ehe, Elternschaft. Eine qualitative Untersuchung über den Bedeutungswandel von Paarbeziehungen und seine demographischen Konsequenzen*. Wiesbaden: Bundesinstitut für Bevölkerungsforschung.

Cooney, T. M. and Uhlenberg, P. (1991) 'Changes in work–family connections among highly educated men and women: 1970 to 1980', *Journal of Family Issues*, 12(1): 69–90.

Deutsches Institut für Wirtschaftsforschung, *Wochenbericht 29/90*, Berlin, 19 July 1990.

Deutsches Jugendinstitut (ed.) (1988) *Wie geht's der Familie? Ein Handbuch zur Situation der Familien heute*. Munich: Kösel.

Diezinger, A. (1991) *Frauen: Arbeit und Individualisierung. Chancen und Risiken. Eine empirische Untersuchung anhand von Fallgeschichten*. Opladen: Leske und Budrich.

Diezinger, A., Jurczyk, K. and Tatschmurat, C. (1988) 'Kleine und große Experimente – die neue Frauen', in Deutsches Jugendinstitut (ed.), *Wie geht's der Familie? Ein Handbuch zur Situation der Familien heute*. Munich: Kösel.

Einstellungen zu Ehe und Familie im Wandel der Zeit. Eine Repräsentativuntersuchung im Auftrag des Ministeriums für Arbeit, Gesundheit, Familie und Sozialordnung, Baden-Württemberg durchgeführt vom Institut für Demoskopie Allensbach (1983) Stuttgart: Ministerium für Arbeit, Gesundheit, Familie und Sozialordnung.

Engstler, H. and Lüscher, K. (1992) 'Späte erste Mutterschaft. Ein neues biographisches Muster der Familiengründung?', *Zeitschrift für Bevölkerungswissenschaft.*

Erler, G., Jaeckel, M., Pettinger, R. and Sass, J. (1988a) *Kind? Beruf? Oder beides? Eine repräsentative Studie über die Lebenssituation und Lebensplanung junger Paare zwischen 18 und 33 Jahren in der Bundesrepublik Deutschland im Auftrag der Zeitschrift Brigitte.* Hamburg: Eigenverlag.

Erler, G., Jaeckel, M., Pettinger, R. and Sass, J. (1988b) 'Männerwelten – Frauenwelten, oder: Wer hat es besser?', *DJI-Bulletin*, 10: 9–12.

Esteves, V. (1988) 'Interethnische Ehen und Familien in der Bundesrepublik Deutschland', in IAF (Interessengemeinschaft der mit Ausländern verheirateten Frauen e.V.) (ed.), *Kindesmitnahme durch einen Elternteil. Ursachen, Lösungsmöglichkeiten und Prävention.* Frankfurt/M.: pp. 16–25.

Familie und Arbeitswelt. Gutachten des wissenschaftlichen Beirats für Familienfragen beim Bundesministerium für Jugend, Familie und Gesundheit (1984) Schriftenreihe des Bundesministers für Jugend. Familie und Gesundheit, vol. 143. Stuttgart: Kohlhammer.

Ferree, M. M. (1991) 'The gender division of labor in two-earner marriages: dimensions of variability and change', *Journal of Family Issues*, 12(2): 158–80.

Geissler, B. and Oechsle, M. (1990) 'Lebensplanung als Ressource im Individualisierungsprozeß', Sonderforschungsbereich 186 der Universität Bremen. Arbeitspapier No. 10. Bremen.

Giddens, A. (1991) *Modernity and Self-Identity. Self and Society in the Late Modern Age.* Cambridge: Polity.

Hochschild, A. (with Anne Machung) (1990) *The Second Shift. Working Parents and the Revolution at Home.* London: Piatkus.

Honegger, C. and Heintz, B. (eds) (1981) *Listen der Ohnmacht. Zur Sozialgeschichte weiblicher Widerstandsformen.* Frankfurt/M.: Europäische Verlagsanstalt.

Keddi, B. and Seidenspinner, G. (1991) 'Arbeitsteilung und Partnerschaft', in H. Bertram (ed.), *Die Familie in Westdeutschland. Stabilität und Wandel familialer Lebensformen.* Opladen: Leske und Budrich. pp. 159–92.

Künzler, J. (1992) 'Bedingungen für das Gelingen der Fusion von Partnerschaft und Elternschaft', report to the 'Partnerschaft versus Elternschaft' conference. University of Bielefeld, October 1991.

Lash, S. and Friedman, J. (1991) 'Introduction: subjectivity and modernity's other', in S. Lash and J. Friedman (eds), *Modernity and Identity.* Oxford. pp. 1–30.

LaRossa, R. (1988) 'Fatherhood and social change', *Family Relations*, 34: 451–7.

Leube, K. (1988) 'Neue Männer, neue Väter – neue Mythen?', in Deutsches Jugendinstitut (ed.), *Wie geht's der Familie? Ein Handbuch zur Situation der Familien heute.* Munich: Kösel. pp. 145–54.

Lüscher, K., Schultheis, F. and Wehrspaun, M. (eds) (1988) *Die postmoderne Familie. Familiale Strategien und Familienpolitik in einer Übergangszeit.* Konstanz: Universitätsverlag.

Machung, A. (1989) 'Talking career, thinking job: gender differences in career and family expectations of Berkeley seniors', *Feminist Studies*, 15(1).

Meier, U. (1991) 'Generation auf gepackten Koffern. Erste Ergebnisse einer Befragung von Ausbildenden in ostdeutschen Städten', *DJI-Bulletin*, 20: 9–12.

Metz-Göckel, S. and Müller, U. (1985) *Der Mann. Brigitte-Untersuchung 1985.* Hamburg: Brigitte.

Metz-Göckel, S. and Müller, U. (1987) 'Partner oder Gegner? Überlebensweisen der Ideologie vom männlichen Familienernährer', *Soziale Welt*, 1: 4–28.

Meyer, S. and Schulze, E. (1988) 'Nichteheliche Lebensgemeinschaften – eine Möglichkeit zur Veränderung des Geschlechterverhältnisses?', *Kölner Zeitschrift für Soziologie und Sozialpsychologie*, 40: 337–56.

Naegele, W. (1987) *Eheverträge, Individuelle Gestaltungsmöglichkeiten vor und nach der Eheschließung.* Munich: Roestel.

Nave-Herz, R. (1988a) 'Kontinuität und Wandel in der Bedeutung, in der Struktur und Stabilität von Ehe und Familie in der Bundesrepublik Deutschland', in R. Nave-Herz (ed.), *Wandel und Kontinuität der Familie in der Bundesrepublik Deutschland.* Stuttgart: Wissenschaftliche Buchgesellschaft. pp. 61–94.

Nave-Herz, R. (1988b) *Kinderlose Ehen. Eine empirische Studie über die Lebenssituation kinderloser Ehepaare und die Gründe für ihre Kinderlosigkeit.* Weinheim and Munich: Juventa.

Nave-Herz, R. (1989) 'Tension between paid working hours and family life', in K. Boh et al. (eds), *Changing Patterns of European Family Life*. New York/London: Routledge. pp. 159–72.

Nichteheliche Lebensgemeinschaften in der Bundesrepublik Deutschland (1985) Schriftenreihe des Bundesministers für Jugend. Familie und Gesundheit, vol. 170. Stuttgart: Kohlhammer.

Ostner, I. (1983) 'Kapitalismus, Patriarchat und die Konstruktion der Besondheit "Frau"', in R. Kreckel (ed.), *Soziale Ungleichheiten*. Special issue no. 2 of *Soziale Welt*. Göttingen: Schwartz. pp. 277–97.

Ostner, I. (1984) 'Arbeitsmarktsegregation und Bildungschancen von Frauen', *Zeitschrift für Pädagogik*, 30(4): 471–86.

Partner, P. (1984) *Das endgültige Ehebuch für Anfänger und Fortgeschrittene*. Munich: Rowohlt.

Pross, H. (1978) *Der deutsche Mann*. Reinbek: Rowohlt.

Pross, H. (1984) *Der deutsche Mann*. Reinbek: Rowohlt.

Rerrich, M. S. (1988) 'Kinder ja, aber… Was es Frauen schwer macht, sich über ihre Kinderwünsche klar zu werden', in Deutsches Jugendinstitut (ed.), *Wie geht's der Familie? Ein Handbuch zur Situation der Familien heute*. Munich: Kösel. pp. 59–66.

Rerrich, M. S. (1991a) 'Ein gleich gutes Leben für alle? Über Ungleichheitserfahrungen im familialen Alltag', in P. A. Berger and S. Hradil (eds), *Lebenslagen, Lebensläufe, Lebensstile*. Special issue no. 7 of *Soziale Welt*. Göttingen: Schwartz. pp. 189–205.

Rerrich, M. S. (1991b) 'Fortune et infortune de la femme salariée: la familie et les lois du marché', in IFRAS and Goethe-Institut (eds), *Affaires de la famille, affaires d'état. Sociologie da la famille*. Nancy: pp. 133–43.

Schneewind, K. A. and Vaskovics, L. A. (1991) *Optionen der Lebensgestaltung junger Ehen und Kinderwunsch. Endbericht*, hectograph. Munich and Bamberg: Eigenverlag.

Seidenspinner, G. and Burger, A. (1982) *Mädchen '82. Eine Untersuchung im Auftrag der Zeitschrift Brigitte*. Hamburg.

Simm, R. (1989) 'Partnerschaft und Familienentwicklung', report to the conference 'Berufsverlauf und Familienentwicklung von Frauen', organized by the Max-Planck-Institut für Bildungsforschung, Schloß Ringberg/Tegernsee, October 1989, hectograph.

Spiegel, E. (1986) *Neue Haushaltstypen: Entstehungsbedingungen, Lebenssituation, Wohn- und Standortverhältnisse*. Frankfurt/M.: Institut of Sozial Forschung.

Stich, J. (1988) '"Spätere Heirat nicht ausgeschlossen" – Vom Leben ohne Trauschein', in Deutsches Jugendinstitut (ed.), *Wie geht's der Familie? Ein Handbuch zur Situation der Familien heute*. Munich: Kösel. pp. 155–62.

Strümpel, B., Prenzel, W., Scholz, J. and Hoff, A. (1988) *Teilzeitarbeitende Männer und Hausmänner. Motive und Konsequenzen einer eingeschränkten Erwerbstätigkeit von Männern*. Berlin: edition sigma.

Thiessen, V. and Rohlinger, H. (1988) 'Die Verteilung von Aufgaben und Pflichten im ehelichen Haushalt', *Kölner Zeitschrift für Soziologie und Sozialpsychologie*, 40(4): 640–57.

Thompson, L. (1991) 'Family work: women's sense of fairness', *Journal of Family Issues*, 12(2): 181–96.

Urdze, A. and Rerrich, M. S. (1988) *Frauenalltag und Kinderwunsch. Motive von Muttern für oder gegen ein weiteres Kind*. Frankfurt/M.: Campus.

Wahl, K. (1989) *Die Modernisierungsfalle. Gesellschaft, Selbstbewußtsein und Gewalt*. Frankfurt: Suhrkamp.

Ziegler, R. (1985) 'Bildungsexpansion und Partnerwahl', in S. Hradil (ed.), *Sozialstruktur im Umbruch*. Opladen: Leske und Budrich. pp. 85–106.

Zoll, R., Bents, H., Brauer, H., Flieger, J., Neumann, E. and Oechsle, M. (1989) *'Nicht so wie unsere Eltern!' Ein neues kulturelles Modell?* Opladen: Leske und Budrich.

Translated from the German version, **Arbeitsteilung, Selbstbild und Lebensentwurf: Neue Konfliktlagen in der Familie**, by Elisabeth Beck-Gernsheim.

8

Declining Birthrates
and the Wish to have Children

From the Baby Boom to the Fall in Birthrates

When birthrates began to fall sharply after the baby boom of the 1950s and early 1960s, in Germany as in other industrially developed countries, it took demographers completely by surprise. In their model, industrializing societies were supposed to experience a small but steady population increase (Mackenroth, 1953), but instead they were undergoing a decline (apart from immigration). Even today, four decades and more later, there is no sign that the trend is changing: the latest figures show that, in nearly every country belonging to the Council of Europe, the birthrate is lower than required for the population to remain the same (*BiB-Mitteilungen*, No. 4, 1996: 31).

In the 1970s and 1980s diverse attempts were made to explain this unexpected development, varying widely according to the theoretical perspective and political position of the observer. There was talk of the hedonism and egotism of the younger generation, of women's drive for emancipation, of changing values and looser links to the church, as well as the influence of the pill, the higher costs associated with having children and the number and range of competing desires that make themselves felt in the contemporary world – to mention just a few of the explanations on offer (see Bolte, 1980). In some of these at least, it even began to seem that the wish to have children was old fashioned in the age of industrialization and modernization, a relic of past times now pushed aside by more powerful and competing pressures.

And yet there are a number of facts which do not readily fit into this picture. For example, both in Germany and in other industrially developed countries, specialists in reproductive medicine are treating a growing number of women clients who want to have children, often at considerable physical, psychological and financial cost to the women themselves. Or, according to the reports of adoption authorities, there are long waiting lists for people seeking to adopt a child – and when they have no prospect of achieving this legally, some turn to illegal means. Or again, the evidence of empirical studies is that even women with career jobs do not simply think of 'a career instead of a child', but often display a clear wish to have children.

The picture that emerges is one of contradictory trends. For all the statistical information confirming a persistent decline in birthrates there are also data giving clear indications of a wish to have children. How is this paradoxical combination to be explained?

Obviously we need an approach which does not highlight only the one or the other aspect but attempts to analyse both together: in short, which consciously examines the fractures and contradictions. My own explanation will thus relate trends in the birthrate to the ongoing discussion on 'individualization', locating the wish to have children in the chances and risks, desires and demands, which emerge under the conditions of growing individualization. The key thesis will be that a claim and a compulsion to have a bit of 'a life of one's own' have arisen in the wake of modernization and individualization and that since the late nineteenth century, but above all since the 1960s, these have affected women too in an ever greater measure (Beck-Gernsheim, 1983). But the desire to have children does not simply disappear in the individualized and thoroughly rationalized societies of the West. To some extent, in fact, it acquires new importance as a search for content and meaning in life, for closeness and warmth, for a counter-world of roots and familiarity (Beck-Gernsheim, 1988). If we take these two aspects together, we can see more clearly the nature of the conflict in which women find themselves, the manner in which they are torn this way and that between the wish to have a child and the wish for independence and a bit of a life of their own. Because these desires are so hard to reconcile under the existing social and institutional conditions, more and more women face the dilemma of the 'child question' (Beck-Gernsheim, 1988). And according to the most recent studies, this conflict is not going away but on the contrary is growing more intense. Here, first of all, are some findings from Germany's western *Länder* which illustrate how full of tension is the wish to have children.

When young women are asked about their views and plans in life, the great majority still say that having children is part of life for them. But as the population figures show, this wish is deferred until later and later in life; the average age of a woman at the birth of her first child has risen (Statistisches Bundesamt, 1995: 119). Often the desire itself is reduced, so that women who initially wanted two or more children have only one in the end. And for a growing number of women, the desire is not only deferred but eventually suppressed altogether. From generation to generation, the number of women who have no children has been on the increase – today it is about a quarter of the generation born after 1960 (Schwarz, 1996).

So much for present trends in Western Germany. But what of the new eastern *Länder*? To what extent does the perspective just outlined offer an explanation there? What happens if we take the life projects of young women, their wishes, fears and conflicts and relate them to the notions and demands associated with the new conditions in Eastern Germany since the end of the GDR? Or, to be even more specific, how far do the hopes and demands for 'a life of one's own' – which the individualization approach sees as contributing to the fall in West German birthrates – also apply to the situation in the 1990s in Eastern Germany? Or are they only Western themes, perhaps even a luxury that flourishes only in conditions of prosperity?

Birthrate Trends in the New Länder of Eastern Germany

As numerous studies show, reunification and the radical transformation of the political system in Eastern Germany also set in train deep changes in the social and economic structure there, with many consequences stretching into the family and private life. This is apparent, for example, in the evolution of marriage and divorce rates. But it is most striking of all in the 60 per cent drop in the birthrate over the five years from 1989 to 1994 – a dramatic collapse which has entailed a new low, even in international terms. The number of births did pick up again in 1995 and 1996, but it is still quite low and there is no clear sign of a change in the trend (*Statistische Monatszahlen*, 1996: 658). It remains the case that 'East German women have... as few children as anywhere else in Europe or even the world' (Richter, 1996: 3).

To appreciate the explosive nature of these findings, it is necessary to know the importance that was and still is attached to the family in the eastern *Länder*. In the days of the GDR, the family represented a kind of private refuge from political intervention by the state and its constant efforts to establish ideological control (e.g. Mau, 1994: 199) and previous surveys have repeatedly shown that the family occupied a place at the top of the scale of people's values and aspirations. In Eastern Germany today, the family and children continue to be important and are considered a self-evident part of human well-being and happiness (Störtzbach, 1993–1994; Richter, 1996; Seidenspinner, 1996). But if this is true, how are we to explain the fall in the birthrate, which is historically unprecedented in both scale and speed?

In demographic studies, various causes or explanatory factors are mentioned. One is the composition of the population – or, to be more precise, changes in the population structure – triggered by the large-scale migration from east to west; those who moved and later had children in the west left behind 'gaps' in the East German birth figures. This was significant above all because it was mainly young people, yet to start a family of their own, who headed west (Grundmann, 1995), while older people tended to keep living and working in the place familiar to them. It has been estimated that as much as 30 per cent of the decline in the East German birthrate can be attributed to this mass emigration of young people (Mau, 1994; Münz and Ulrich, 1993–1994).

More Options, More Demands

Another explanation points to the increased range of options, which quite simply compete with having a child:

> More young adults are able to study. If they find a job, they also have chances of a higher income and more opportunity to spend the money on such things as foreign travel, cars and various consumer goods. But anyone who can secure the necessary income must also put more energy into jockeying for position and planning a career. All this militates against an early family or in many cases against any children at all, because they undoubtedly mean a huge limitation of occupational and geographic mobility. (Münz and Ulrich, 1993–1994: 482f.)

Here we should bear in mind what many studies of the old GDR social structure have demonstrated: namely, that the course of life was much less open to individual decision, much more tightly controlled from above, than in the West (e.g. Geulen, 1993: 38f.). Whether in job assignment, place of study or housing allocation, many things depended less on one's own choice and more on social and political criteria. So long as one did not fall out of favour politically, one's basic needs were taken care of – and, of course, it was hardly possible to live it up. Now this is all very different:

> The whole attitude to life is different. The security you used to have as a family in the GDR is gone. You even fear for your job; you fear for your home. You are more afraid that things won't work out with children as you would like them to – so it has become more difficult. Before, the way was mapped out for you from above. When you married, you eventually got some housing, and you also got job training and qualifications – you got them so long as you made some effort and didn't make a negative impression at work. (Woman, b. 1955, trained as diet cook, correspondence course in economics, married with two children aged 4 and 16; from an interview in Böckmann-Schewe et al., 1994: 40).

What is discernible in such statements is a kind of inverted image of the chances and demands of 'a life of one's own' with which people grow up in the individualized societies of the West. In the days of the GDR, the scope for 'a life of one's own' before one had children was considerably narrower, so that parenthood therefore did not mean any sharp break. With reunification, however, the scope grew larger and competition suddenly appeared between the wish to have children and other options and demands. Patterns of behaviour that had long been taken for granted were no longer appropriate. Lives that could to some extent be calculated in advance now took on a labyrinthine complexity, becoming filled with tensions and dangers. Consequently, within the current perspective of insecurity plus increased options, the kinds of choices that shape people's lives for years ahead have become more and more of a wager; they are 'afflicted with a high risk of "faulty planning" [and] therefore tend to be avoided' (Menning, 1995: 147). So it is that the wish to have children is first deferred – and then, who knows?, perhaps later fulfilled, perhaps indefinitely postponed, perhaps eventually suppressed in favour of other goals.

Crisis and Radical Change – Particularly for Women

In many explanations there is also an idea that falling birthrates are the expression of a shock, of an upheaval in norms of conduct that used to be a matter of course, of a fundamental existential crisis affecting people in Eastern Germany (e.g. Mau, 1994; Münz and Ulrich, 1993–1994). This may apply at present to all sections of the population. And yet, if one looks more closely, it is especially women who are undergoing the dramatic changes that began with the end of the GDR, above all in the area of tension spanning job and family. It is true that, as we now know, equality between men and women was by no means assured in GDR-style state socialism (Nickel, 1993). It is also true that the official policy of equality was commanded from above in paternalist-patriarchal fashion, not least under economic pressures. Nevertheless, such a policy did exist and was not just a matter of verbal declarations and normative appeals; it had tangible practical effects, in the shape of social and political measures to make it easier for women to combine a job with a family. Among these measures was one day off a month for the household, generous leave to care for sick children and a wide supply of day nurseries, workplace creches, organized children's holidays and so on.

Consistent with this was the normative image of motherhood. Whereas the prevailing view in the West was that children (at least in the first few years) needed as much maternal care as possible, it was thought socially and politically desirable in the GDR, and was broadly accepted by the population, that the mother should return to work quite soon after the birth of her child. Public forms of child care were not considered detrimental to the child's development, but were seen as a normal part of life for women, children and families (Hildebrandt and Wittmann, 1996; Schröter, 1996).

As far as this model is concerned, little has changed even today in the new federal *Länder*. Young women there have scarcely allowed themselves to be made insecure by the spectre of uncaring working mothers. The generation which once went to nurseries, creches and day homes mostly wants the same facilities for its own children (Schröter, 1996: 26). It sees in daylong child care the solution to the problem of combining job and family (Hildebrandt and Wittmann, 1996: 41).

Contrary to what many expected immediately after reunification – for example, that East German women would be happy to shake off the dual burden and look to household and home as their main sphere of activity – more recent studies have generally shown that they remain strongly oriented to a job or career. Women writers from Eastern Germany repeatedly stress that this is due not only to a wish to earn money, but above all to a need for 'a demanding and recognized occupation' (Schröter, 1996: 22) and 'involvement in the process of social life' (Schorlemmer, quoted from ibid.: 26). That it is natural for both women and men to have a job, that this is fundamental to people's self-confidence, social recognition and financial security: these are basic assumptions with which East German women have grown up and which they have firmly internalized. A different kind of life limited to the private realm seems to most of them unthinkable (Hildebrandt and Wittmann, 1996; Schröter, 1996):

> So... well, work is certainly important... because I have to be with people all the time and do something – otherwise you wouldn't have anything to talk to your partner about. If you sit at home all day doing nothing, well, what is there left? Sooner or later, the joy goes out of your life – I mean, your relationship and all that. (22-year-old dental nurse, single, no children; from an interview in Richter, 1996: 19)

> You have to work anyway, just because of the money. But nor would I like to stay home all day. I'd want to be doing something. You've got to enjoy the work – I wouldn't want to scrub floors for eight boring hours. I do have a job where you can think for yourself a little, be a little creative. It also keeps you in touch with people – you need that too. (27 year old on maternity leave, single, one child; from an interview in Richter, 1996: 19)

The New Market Conditions

But whereas the life plans and aspirations of women in Eastern Germany show considerable continuity, there has been a radical shift at the level of institutions. As these adapted to the West German social system, what was on offer to women socially and politically shrank through a major series of cutbacks, reductions, substitutes and straightforward closures. At the same time, the introduction of a Western-style market economy led to deep restructuring in the field of employment and women were especially hard hit by the unemployment resulting from factory shutdowns and redundancies. Two-thirds of those without work in Eastern Germany today are women (Kommission für Zukunftsfragen, 1996).

Single mothers, who form a large group in society, are the most affected by the changes; their situation has taken a lasting turn for the worse (Großmann and Huth, 1995). Since divorce figures were very high in the GDR, the relationship with a man was always insecure – anyway too insecure to build anything on it alone. Women looked for other certainties, other reliable foci in life: above all, their job and their children, and the combination of the two made possible by a range of social and political measures. In the days of the GDR, then, a woman's decision to take sole responsibility for a child did not by and large mean a sharp break in her way of life. This is the very thing that has now changed. With the turn in social policy and the enforcement of a market economy, it has become a matter of private choice – and one with serious and far-reaching implications:

> Conditions then were obviously much better; children were simply more part of life. They could precisely be combined with a job – take all the nighttime facilities, the weekend nurseries, and so on, which are now closing down for the crazy reason that they don't fit into any bureaucratic structure, even though the need for them is very great. In a city like Berlin, where you have to reckon on an average of an hour to get to work and the nurseries are only open for eight hours... if the children can get a place in one at all. (27 year old on maternity leave, single, one child; from interview in Richter, 1996: 20)

Children as an Existential Risk

Now women have to learn how, in a market economy, motherhood limits their chances on the labour market and single mothers in particular are excluded and marginalized (Großmann and Huth, 1995). It is becoming clear that to have children is an occupational, financial and existential risk. The new message communicated to women is that the main priority is to make sure of your own way in life. Only then can one possibly, if things work out right, think of taking on the existential risk of a child:

> It makes me think that... if things had remained as they were socially – I mean in terms of both the labour market and social policy – it would now be easier to say, okay, I'm going to have a child, if that's what I wanted. But if the question came up now, with social policy and jobs being the way they are, I'd simply have to say, no, hang on, I'd better wait. If it was still like in the GDR days, I'd say better now than any other time. (23-year-old female student, single, no children; from an interview in Richter, 1996: 24)

> So, I always used to think you should have your first child around 22 to 25; that would have been quite normal in the GDR days and could also have been combined with studying... Well, the present situation means that by the time things are ready I'll be an older mother – which no one would previously have gone for, and... of course, it's not easy to combine three children with a career. (24 year old, single, no children; from an interview in Richter, 1996: 24f.)

Both the difficult labour market conditions and the withdrawal of social benefits affect women especially hard in Eastern Germany. Suddenly what appeared a matter of course – the possibility of combining children with other goals, especially a job – has become fragile and open to doubt. Most of them still want to have children, but they are learning that they must go about it carefully – through gradual approximations, as it were. An extensive empirical study, published in 1996, reaches the conclusion that for a majority of East German women 'the insecure job situation and the changed frame of reference… are the main things in the way of their wish to have children'. Moreover, since the prospects for the labour market situation are not looking good, 'it is to be expected that for some women a child will remain a "risk factor" that no longer has a place in their life project' (Hildebrandt and Wittmann, 1996: 41). Rather more trenchantly, one might say that a kind of dramatic social experiment is being conducted before our eyes, whereby a previously straightforward wish to have children suddenly becomes 'the question of children' requiring careful individual consideration and planning. As one reads through various interviews and personal accounts, this learning effect fairly leaps to the eyes.

A married woman with two children aged 6 and 14:

> And if I was today at the age to start a family, I'd give quite a lot of thought to whether I should or shouldn't have a child at all, and I do think it's a problem to cope with one nowadays, because there's also the question of do I earn enough money, how would it work out, and would I get back into my job. After all, they think to themselves: is that a woman with small children or not? That never used to be an issue. (From an interview in Böckmann-Schewe et al., 1994: 41)

A single woman with no children:

> Personally, I was single before the changes came and wanted to have a baby and… in fact I'd still like to have one today… but I'm afraid because of the financial and social situation about what it would mean practically if I dropped out; I don't know what would happen to me… if it happened that I can ditch my job. That would be the end of it for me, and so naturally I'm afraid and, on the one hand, there's the wish to have a child, and on the other hand my reason tells me to say 'no'. The difference is really huge, because then it was a matter of course and now it's become almost a luxury – I mean, whether you can afford to have a child. (From an interview in Böckmann-Schewe et al., 1994: 41)

In East Germany and Elsewhere

What these women articulate from their own experience refers not to the individual course of their lives but to changes in the *social framework* that women are experiencing today in Eastern Germany. It refers to institutional pressures and constraints and not least to institutional deficits and shortcomings in relation to women's so-called 'compatibility dilemma'. In this light, it is certainly appropriate to consider birth trends in Eastern Germany also from a subjective point of view, which includes the hopes, fears and conflicts faced by individuals (in this case, especially by women). In fact, it is said that such trends can today only be understood by looking at women's plans for life. Falling birthrates 'are symptoms of quiet resistance on the part of women for whom paid work has become "the natural thing to do" – resistance to a… family and social policy designed to bring them back into old patterns' (Nickel, 1993: 253).

The last question, which was also the first, is whether individualization and 'a life of one's own' are exclusively Western issues, remote from the reality of life in the East. The answer must be that it depends on what is meant by individualization. If we think of it not just as a growth in options and freedoms, but more as a way of life under certain institutional constraints and demands or, indeed, as pressure to put a life together under often contradictory and partly incompatible conditions – which poses manifold difficulties that many do not manage to resolve – if we understand individualization in this broader sense, then we can certainly say that people in Eastern Germany (and especially women) are today experiencing individualization.

This applies to the most diverse areas of life, and not least to having children. The basic thesis may be summarized as follows. The greater people's options and demands for a bit of 'a life of their own' and the greater the attendant risks, uncertainties and demands, the more does having children cease to be a natural part of life and become the object of conscious planning and calculation, hopes and fears – in short, the more it becomes 'the question of children'. Depending on the constraints of social policy, the structures of the educational system and labour market and the prevailing cultural norms and traditions, the question either remains concealed for a long time or soon bursts into the open with varying degrees of severity. But the general point is that what women are experiencing in Eastern Germany is not an exceptional case. Many women are faced with 'the question of children', both in other parts of Germany and in other highly industrialized and individualized societies.

Against this background, let us end by hazarding a rough prognosis. In the modern societies of the West, the desire to have children will not disappear but exert its own power of attraction and provide a framework for hopes and longings – not least on the basis of the constraints and demands to which women are today exposed. But this is only part of the story. For the counter-weights are also strong, sometimes even stronger.

So long as it is an individual task for women (through trial and error, balancing acts and ever precarious makeshift efforts) to resolve the tension between their wish to have children and to have a life of their own; so long as political measures to make these different spheres compatible remain skimpy or even non-existent; so long as men do not become noticeably more willing to take an active share in child care – so long as these things do not happen, it is hardly to be expected that birthrates will increase significantly. In Eastern Germany the situation may turn out to be somewhat different because, after the times of massive change and general loss of security, there might be a gradual revival of the birthrate. This would represent a 'settling down at a lower level', a return to something more like normality after the exceptional situation and extremely low figures of recent years. But despite the many motives for which women will still want to have children, the general tendency will remain the same. So long as the obstacles identified here are still in place, the news of falling birthrates will be with us as the stuff of everyday life – in Germany as well as in other highly industrialized and individualized societies.

Bibliography

Beck, U. and Beck-Gernsheim, E. (1994) 'Nicht Autonomie, sondern Bastelbiographie', *Zeitschrift für Soziologie*, 22(3): 178–87.
Beck-Gernsheim, E. (1983) 'Vom "Dasein für andere" zum Anspruch auf ein Stück "eigenes Leben" – Individualisierungsprozesse im weiblichen Lebenszusammenhang', *Soziale Welt*, 3: 307–341; translated above as 'Living for others'.
Beck-Gernsheim, E. (1988) *Die Kinderfrage. Frauen zwischen Kinderwunsch und Unabhängigkeit*, 3rd edn (1997). Munich: Beck.
BiB-Mitteilungen/Informationen aus dem Bundesinstitut für Bevölkerungsforschung beim Statistischen Bundesamt (1996), 17(4).
Böckmann-Schewe, L., Kulke, C. and Röhrig, A. (1994) 'Wandel und Brüche in den Lebensentwürfen von Frauen in den neuen Bundesländern', *Aus Politik und Zeitgeschichte*, 6(94): 33–44.
Bolte, K. M. (1980) 'Bestimmungsgründe der Geburtenentwicklung und Überlegungen zu einer möglichen Beeinflußbarkeit', in *Bevölkerungsentwicklung und nachwachsende Generation*. Schriftenreihe des Bundesministers für Jugend, Familie und Gesundheit, 93: 64–91. Stuttgart: Kohlhammer.
Geulen, D. (1993) 'Typische Sozialisationsentwürfe in der DDR. Einige qualitative Befunde über vier Generationen', *Aus Politik und Zeitgeschichte*, 26–27 (93): 37–44.
Großmann, H. and Huth, S. (1995) 'Sozialhilfeabhängigkeit Alleinerziehender als Folge des gesellschaftlichen Umbruchs', in H. Bertram et al. (eds), *Sozialer und demographischer Wandel in den neuen Bundesländern*. Berlin: pp. 3–46.
Grundmann, S. (1995) 'Die Ost-West-Wanderung in Deutschland (1989–1992)'. In Bertram, Hans u.a. (Hrsg.). *Sozialer und demographischer Wandel in den neuen Bundesländern*. Berlin: Akademie, 3–16.
Hildebrandt, K. and Wittmann, S. (1996) 'Lebensziel Kinder? Ein Ost-West-Vergleich', *Die Frau in unserer Zeit*, 25(4): 35–41.
Kommission für Zukunftsfragen der Freistaaten Bayern und Sachsen (1996) *Erwerbstätigkeit und Arbeitslosigkeit in Deutschland, Teil 1, Befunde*, hectograph report. Bonn.
Mackenroth, G. (1953) *Bevölkerungslehre. Theorie, Soziologie und Statistik der Bevölkerung*. Berlin/Göttingen/Heidelberg: Springer.
Mau, S. (1994) 'Der demographische Wandel in den neuen Bundesländern', *Zeitschrift für Familienforschung*, 6(3): 197–220.
Menning, S. (1995) 'Geburten- und Heiratsverzicht in den neuen Bundesländern – Abschied von der Familie?', in H. Sydow et al. (eds), *Chancen und Risiken im Lebensverlauf: Wandel in Ostdeutschland*. Berlin. pp. 137–50.
Münz, R. and Ulrich, R. (1993–1994) 'Demographische Entwicklung in Ostdeutschland und in ausgewählten Regionen', *Zeitschrift für Bevölkerungswissenschaft*, 19(4): 475–515.
Nickel, H. M. (1993) '"Mitgestalterinnen des Sozialismus" – Frauenarbeit in der DDR', in G. Helwig and H. M. Nickel (eds), *Frauen in Deutschland 1945–1992*. Berlin: Akademie. pp. 233–56.
Richter, K. (1996) 'Zum Wandel von Kinderwunsch und Familiengründung in den neuen Bundesländern', in *Demographie aktuell*. Vorträge – Aufsätze – Forschungsberichte, No. 8. Berlin: Humboldt University.
Schröter, U. (1996) 'Ostdeutsche frauen im "verflixten" siebenten Jahr', *Die Frau in unserer Zeit*, 25(4): 22–8.
Schwarz, K. (1996) 'Zur Debatte über Kinderzahl der Ehen und die Bedeutung der Kinderlosigkeit für die Geburtenentwicklung in den alten Bundesländern', *BiB-Mitteilungen/Informationen aus dem Bundesinstitut für Bevölkerungsforschung beim Statistischen Bundesamt*, 17(2): 10–13.
Seidenspinner, G. (1996) *Junge Frauen heute. Wie wir leben, was sie anders machen*. Opladen: Leske und Budrich.

Statistisches Bundesamt (ed.) (1995) *Im Blickpunkt: Familien heute*. Stuttgart: Kohlhammer.

Statistische Monatszahlen (1996) *Wirtschaft und Statistik*. November. pp. 630–59.

Störtzbach, B. (1993–1994) 'Deutschland nach der Vereinigung. Meinungen und Einstellungen zu Familie, Kindern und zur Familienpolitik in Ost und West', *Zeitschrift für Bevölkerungswissenschaft*, 19(2): 151–67.

Translated from the German version, **Gerburtenrückgang und Kinderwunsch** in *Zeitschrift für Bevölkerungswissenchaft*, by Elisabeth Beck-Gernsheim.

9

Apparatuses do not Care for People

Heading for a Demographic Revolution

In the Federal Republic as in many other industrialized countries, life expectancy has risen to an unprecedented level. This means an increase in the number of old and very old people, which will in turn change society not only quantitatively but also in its inner core. Together with this demographic recomposition, people's lives, needs, demands and rights have also been undergoing structural change. Questions concerning a fairer system of distribution are again being placed on the agenda, and bitter disputes are beginning to take place around them. Massive transformations are in store for the political, social and economic structure, with consequences that will sooner or later make themselves felt at levels ranging from the everyday conditions of life (family, gender relations, housing, leisure, transport) to the various constituent parts of society (labour market, education, medicine and health, social policy). The conclusion drawn by relevant studies is that we are 'in the midst of a demographic revolution that, sooner or later, will affect every individual and every institution in the society. This revolution is the inexorable aging of our population. By the middle of the next century, when this revolution has run its course, the impact will have been at least as powerful as that of any of the great economic and social movements of the past.'[1]

I would here like to consider more closely two questions that arise in connection with this demographic revolution:

1 What are the changes in old people's living conditions, especially with regard to everyday provision and, where necessary, personal care and attention?
2 What new questions, challenges and allocation conflicts do these pose for society?

Old Age and the Post-Familial Family

In pre-industrial society different generations lived closer together than they do today. This past is often nostalgically idealized as in a Karl Spitzweg painting: grandmother at the spinning wheel, grandfather in the armchair, a merry crowd of children at their feet, everything pervaded by an air of home, sweet home. The truth is, however, that the pre-industrial family was mainly a union born of necessity and compulsion.[2] For the sake of survival, it was the material interests of the farm and community, not the freedom of the individual, which had priority; little room was left for personal consideration, tenderness and empathy. And the strong social cohesion, praised in later times as an example of love of one's neighbour, stemmed mainly from an awareness of mutual dependence: 'For better or worse, everyone was tied to this community; it was at once their safety anchor and their lead weight.'[3]

Family Support Today

Since those times, the ways in which people live have fundamentally changed. Industrialization brought with it the rise of the bourgeois family, which was supposed to be primarily a community of feeling rather than of work. This form too, as we have long known, is not a locus of pure love and harmony; it produces its own frictions, irritations and conflicts, involving repression and even violence. Yet for all its defects, it is also a source of mutual support that is felt across the generations.

Some old people, of course, are shunted off into a home where no one bothers about them any more. There can be no doubt that the elderly often endure loneliness and isolation, as well as defective everyday care and provision. But for many the family is an important – indeed, the most important – support they have. As recent studies have shown, the emotional and practical support of old people and any necessary personal care and attention, are still provided mainly within the family.[4] When they are asked about the person who looks after them ('Who do you speak to when you have trouble with something?'), there is no contest. In a representative survey, 54 per cent of people aged over 60 named their children and a further 26 per cent other relatives.[5] For assistance with such things as shopping or small repairs, 68 per cent of old people turned to their children or other relatives. And when it came to illness, not least of a chronic kind, family members played an especially crucial role.[6] A study of care in old age concluded: 'Where the health is impaired, the ultimately decisive factor in the further quality of life is not the person's age but the presence or absence of family members in the household, whether in the same house or close by.'[7]

Individualization and Pluralization

Meanwhile, of course, another major upheaval is looming. At the close of the twentieth century there was much talk of pluralization and individualization of lifestyles. These keywords should not be taken to imply that the so-called traditional family (a lasting bond among husband, wife and children) has more or less disappeared. Rather, they signal that alongside this form – which continues to exist – other ways of living are today spreading and developing, especially among certain groups and milieux (depending on, for example, educational levels or town–country differences). These new forms include living alone, single parenthood, non-marital cohabitation, childless marriage, serial marriage or 'living apart together' with a partner in separate dwellings. They may differ greatly from one another, some consciously chosen, others involuntarily undergone, some intended to last, others only temporary. On the whole, however, increasing numbers of people find themselves, for varying lengths of time, leading a life which does not correspond to the classical model of the bourgeois family. Such men and women still live in relationships, but these are limited either in scope or in time. Not all or even most people, but certainly a growing number, live in 'part-time communities':[8] the 'negotiated provisional family';[9]

the 'part-life companionship';[10] and amid this multiplicity, the 'postmodern family'[11] or 'post-familial family'.[12]

The question therefore arises as to how old age will look in the future. Alternative ways of living may offer many advantages by releasing individuals from the straitjacket of the old-style family and creating new options and free spaces (which is not the least of the reasons why they are consciously adopted). But it is unclear how they will shape up in old age, in three or four decades from now. One can speculate that many relationships will be long past (a 'part-life companion' being almost by definition not a companion in old age), while others may prove less functional with the passing of the years ('living apart together' becomes more difficult when reduced mobility means that it is more of an effort to get out and about). For couples without children, the turning point will come when one partner dies and the other (more often than not, the woman) is left alone. One way or another, then, it has to be asked what options there are beyond the traditional family for care and support in old age. Where the old forms no longer exist, will new ones develop in their place?

Women and 'Living for the Aged'

Up to this point, the family has been spoken of as 'gender neutral'. But it is well known that it is mainly women's area of responsibility – or has been at least since that polarization between the outside world of society and public life and the inner realm of privacy which emerged with the transition to modern industrial society. Role models were then defined as complementary to each other: for the husband, a paid job with the toughness and self-assertiveness associated with it; for the wife, family, heart and feelings. That was the beginning of the 'halfway modernity',[13] which ascribed a special role to women as a counterweight to the laws of the market. This role was designed as providing a kind of refuge, an ambulance station for life's vicissitudes. While the husband grew used to asserting himself in the rat race outside the home, the wife was meant to 'live for others' – especially for her husband and children, for the sick and the elderly.

Recent studies of old people confirm that women still take on this task. We said earlier that care and attention are still provided for old people mainly within the family, but that was rather a loose way of putting it. To be more precise, it is primarily wives, daughters and daughters-in-law who perform this service, often with a considerable expenditure of time and energy.[14]

In the last few decades, however, major changes have taken place in women's lives.[15] The basic pattern is as follows. More and more women find their ties to the family loosened through education, a job, changes in the family cycle and the legal system and so on; fewer and fewer can expect a husband to provide for them; and the general trend, in however contradictory a form, is towards independence and self-sufficiency. The biographical result is that women increasingly develop – in fact, have to develop – expectations, desires and life plans which relate not only to the family but also to themselves as individuals. First of all economically, they must plan to make their lives secure, if necessary without their husband. They can no longer think of themselves only as an 'appendage' to the family, but must increasingly see themselves as individuals with their own interests and rights, plans and options.

The most visible expression of this are the life plans formed by girls and young women. Most of them do not want to spend all their lives as a housewife-cum-mother, but want a share in both a career and a family. But the organized world of work puts many obstructions in the way of this desire and little support comes from political institutions either. The postulate of the compatibility of job and family, though extolled on all sides and still affirmed in basic programmes and holiday speeches, has therefore remained little more than a postulate. Often, if women actually try to combine a career with children, they are worn down by excessive burdens in the running daily struggle. Then it is especially hard to care for the old ones as well, to fit their needs together into the constraints of a working career. And yet, many women are evidently still prepared to attempt this balancing act and feat of strength – or, if absolutely necessary, to give up their job:

> A 1985 survey by the Travelers Corp. found that about one employee in five over 30 was providing some care to an elderly parent, most often a widowed mother. Most of those workers were women, even where it was the husband's parent who needed the care. A Philadelphia study surveyed 150 families in which married women, about half of them employed, provided most of the care for their widowed mothers. More than a quarter of those who were not working had quit their jobs, and a quarter of those employed had considered resigning.
>
> The American Association of Retired Persons estimates that, in 1987, seven million US households included people responsible for the elderly, and 55 per cent of those overseers also had jobs. Its 1989 survey of working people who cared for the elderly found that 14 per cent had left fulltime jobs because of family responsibilities... 'One reason older women are so much poorer than older men is that the average woman spends 11½ years out of her working life on all forms of care giving, compared to six months for the average man'. (Joan Kuriansky, executive director of the Older Women's League, a non-profit advocacy group in Washington)[16]

It is uncertain, of course, whether women in the twenty-first century will be able and willing to take on this task, whether 'living for the aged' can be fitted into their life projects. The most recent studies suggest that major problems may soon arise in this respect: 'The fact... that with each new generation more and more women are economically active outside the home will not remain without consequences for the model of informal care and assistance, and it will lead to increased demands on formal service providers.'[17] This poses the question more sharply than ever, not only for particular groups but for everyone: How will older people be looked after a few decades from now? If women are not available as a reserve army for the family, who will carry out these tasks?

One thing is already clear today. If the traditional forms of the male-female division of labour that developed with the onset of industrial society begin to crumble, the relationship between the generations will also become precarious. Politicians can no longer tacitly assume that women will take over when necessary and anyone who hopes for 'stronger ties of solidarity between the generations' – as a German government report puts it[18] – cannot overlook the fact this also requires a new kind of solidarity between the sexes. In other words, in order to place the much-discussed inter-generational contract on a new footing, it will also be necessary to negotiate a new inter-gender contract. And solidarity between the generations will depend not least upon whether men are willing to take on some share of 'living for the aged'.

Who will Look after us in Old Age?

The 'kitsch idyll in the evening sun',[19] as a cultural model of old age, has found a modern variant in the effective media staging of fit, happy and active seniors skipping in the park. The evening of life as constant pleasure: today Flensburg or Blackpool, tomorrow Mallorca? Such images are not completely false, but even less are they completely true; they depict only part of the whole and all too often the reality may be quite different. What is developing before our eyes is, to be sure, an explosive combination of two tendencies that are likely to grow stronger. On the one hand, the number of people at an advanced or very advanced age in need of care and attention is growing apace, not least because of new achievements in medical technology. On the other hand, the 'personal resources' hitherto deployed in care of the aged are clearly becoming less dependable, because family lifestyles are changing and so too are women's own lives.

If this is an accurate diagnosis, it becomes essential to ask who will care for us in old age.[20] Or rather, what personal resources outside the traditional family can conceivably be deployed in ways that are both socially acceptable and economically feasible? Can, for example, social networks and types of relationship be constructed that involve new ways of living together in old age? Will men be prepared to share in solidarity between the generations, not only in words but in deeds? To what extent will the state and society be prepared to create a wide and flexible range of care facilities? Or will the rich simply purchase good and expensive care for themselves on the 'senior services market', while the less well off receive no help because they cannot pay for it? Will the social inequality of old age, already dramatically in evidence, take more open and brutal forms?[21]

Let us recall how Améry described this inequality:

> [I]t is not the same whether a poor devil dies alone in hospital, scarcely noticed by indifferent nurses, or whether a man of means gives up the ghost in a luxury clinic, with flowers on the table, with doctors showing personal touches of solicitude, and with relatives able to visit at all hours who, though perhaps not helping him when the time comes, lighten some of his pain-free moments and assure him of the good life even in dying.... It must be said over and over again: if we are all equal in the face of death... we are not all equal in the face of dying. 'Crying is easier when you have money', says an East European Jewish adage. Dying is also easier when you have money.[22]

We begin to see that it will cost not only money but also political and private imagination to give some dignity to the last stage of life. Otherwise, the achievements of medical technology in making life ever longer, seeing it through acute crises and chronic illness, will become a double-edged gift that leads into a social vacuum. This highlights a simple truth: apparatuses can prolong life, but they cannot care for people. What will become of the 'late freedoms' of old age,[23] if the next stage threatens to involve a permanent need for nursing care? The very word 'care' is dropping out of people's vocabulary, leaving only potential objects of medical intervention. What if it is not even a care ward that awaits us at the end, because society has at some point surrendered in an emergency? Or, to extrapolate a little from signs that are already visible, will many find a solution to indignity, dependence and isolation in the euthanasia movement, in self-administered death as a release from over-prolonged life? That too would be a paradox of modernity.

Such visions, which I have drawn here in a sharp way, must not become reality. But they indicate what might happen if alternatives are not found in time. The expansion of medical technology can prove its human value only insofar as a 'social infrastructure' of old age is built, or rebuilt, at the same time. Only if this is successfully done – in whatever form – will the 'newly gained years'[24] also bring a greater quality to life.

Society and Politics Confronted with New Choices

For a long time the issue of 'old age' remained on the margins of public, political and academic interest, but this has now changed appreciably with the increased life expectancy and the growing number of older people. Considerable discussion, often employing spectacular catch-phrases, is devoted to various aspects that concern the evolution of society as a whole – for example, the implications for pensions and social policy, health and welfare benefits, international relations and shifts in voter behaviour.

One question that often arises is whether the changing composition of the population will also result in changing relations of power. For example, will there be greater competition to secure older people's votes? Will they themselves organize or remain a politically neutral group? Will the value system and power structures of society be geared less to the young and more to the values and lifestyles of older people?

Other questions concern the role of the state and trends in the public provision of services to certain age groups. Again let us just mention a few examples. What will happen to facilities such as nurseries, schools, playgrounds and swimming baths, which mainly serve the requirements of a youthful population? Should workers who cater to the needs of the young and very young (nursery staff, for instance) be retrained to care for the old? Where will jobs and investment be cut back and according to what priorities? What struggles over living standards would then have to be fought out within society?

Medicine and Health

In order to make these questions more specific, let us focus on the health sector. As we have seen, more and more people survive illnesses which would earlier have proved fatal and even those with serious chronic conditions can expect to live longer as a result of new advances in medical technology. An ever increasing number of people are therefore reaching a great or very great age. But, of course, this also means that by the end of their life they have developed more and more chronic disorders:[25]

Of course we recognize in the back of our minds that a cure for cancer increases our chance of dying from stroke or heart disease, just as a cure for all of these enhances the likelihood of living out our days with dementia. But that ironic way of assessing medical triumphs is no more popular now than it was in those enthusiastic years during the 1950s and 1960s when the various wars against cancer and other diseases were initiated. Those wars continue, fought as always with the tubes, drugs, and machines so desperately dreaded as our possible personal fates. We thus spend an enormous and increasing amount of money to propel ourselves inexorably toward that which we most fear – hoping, of course, that in our own case the technology will be just enough to save us but too little to oppress us.[26]

The consequences are obvious: huge financial burdens on the health service, probably becoming so huge that the social and political system will be faced with urgent moral choices and questions. Thus, if the number of very old people and the heroic capacity of doctors to save them continue their rapid growth, will we have the economic means to provide everyone with all that is medically and technologically possible? If it is old people who make the greatest demands on the health system, will a struggle over its resources one day develop between the generations? Will old people in the twenty-first century face restrictions on their care and provision which are today unthinkable? And what are the moral, medical, political and economic principles with which to chart a course in this unfamiliar terrain?[27]

The State's Construction of Old Age

In the field of health provision, there is a tendency which we might call – following the terms of recent sociological discussion of life trajectories and the welfare state[28] – the 'state construction of old age'. What is meant by this is that, under the conditions of the welfare state and scientific-technological civilization, old age becomes less and less a 'natural' category and more and more dependent upon political decisions as to both the quantity (the average number of years) and the quality of life, as well as the resources available to maintain them. Many new questions are associated with this state construction of old age. For example, what is it technically possible to do for old people and what is it economically possible to do? Which restrictions are economically necessary and which are morally acceptable? Where will the priorities for state support lie within and between the generations? Which groups and which demands will be taken into consideration and which will be left out? Where does provision for old people lie in that long scale of political issues and objectives which stretches from nursery places to environmental protection, from development aid to unemployment benefit and financial support for the new *Länder* of Eastern Germany? Whose needs, demands and rights should come first – and whose will have to take second place?

The 'Life Politics' of Fundamental Choices

The state construction of old age may be placed in a broader frame of reference, such as that provided by Anthony Giddens in his social theory and contemporary analysis. One of the essential features of our epoch, he argues, is that what used to be laid down in advance (whether by tradition, class or nature) increasingly gives way as new spaces for decision open up. Reference points that previously appeared to be constants of human existence are now posed as variables: class distinctions, for example, or relations between the sexes or our biological make-up. Hence, more and more decisions become necessary, at the most diverse levels, about how we want to shape our lives. Intensive medicine and reproductive medicine are even posing anew the most basic questions of all: What is human life? Where does it begin? How is its end to be determined? At the extreme, medical decisions are required in which not only people's lives but the very definition of life and death are at stake. The inevitable question here is how much should be done and for how long. How many operations and courses of radiation treatment? How much invasive surgery and technology? How much artificial feeding and artificial respiration?

Explicitly or implicitly, such decisions always involve what Giddens calls 'life politics'.[29] 'The "end of nature" opens up many new issues for consideration.... Life-political issues call for a remoralizing of social life.'[30] This constellation carries a huge explosive force, for the processes of decision and negotiation that now become indispensable are anything but simple. In many cases there is not just one morally clean answer; each decision produces its own follow-up problems, curbing the existential needs of one group and imposing risks and burdens on another. When human intervention takes over from a rigid destiny, we are faced not only with new questions but also with moral dilemmas of a new kind. 'No one', Giddens concludes, 'should underestimate how difficult it will be to deal with these.'[31] With a view to the population statistics, the question is already posed today of whether good health provision and an ageing society are morally compatible with each other.[32] And in connection with the state construction of old age, the dilemmas and allocation battles are already taking shape and – to risk a prediction – will tomorrow be still more dramatic and unrelenting.

The Administration of Old Age

In conclusion, let us consider how the government is responding to the issues, challenges and conflicts of choice that have become unavoidable with the rising life expectancy and the rapidly growing number of old people. What ideas does it have to offer towards a social contract that will define the contours of the ageing society?

It has to be said that the answer is not very encouraging. There is a lack of money, but even more of political imagination and assertiveness. In 1986, when the German government published its fourth 'Family Report', it declared: 'The Federal Republic is... on the way to becoming a country that is friendly to older people.'[33] A number of years have since elapsed. The arguments over old-age care insurance had still not been settled by July 1992 and there were a variety of different proposals and approaches, including guidelines for a 'federal old-age plan'.[34] On reading it, one discovers a masterpiece on the administration of old age, with such key phrases as 'further development of the old people's assistance structures', 'central sporting events for older people' and 'measures to help older people meet one another'. The discussion of actual issues and political visions is skimpy in the extreme and correspondingly more elaborate is the consideration given to the most detailed financial points (for example: 'The daily rate for participants without accommodation away from their home area will be limited to

6.00 DM'). The only thing missing is a final sentence like: 'We have everything under control with regard to old age.'

Notes

1 A. Pifer and D. L. Bronte, 'Introduction: Squaring the Pyramid', *Daedalus*, special issue on 'The Aging of Society', 115/1, winter 1986, p. 1.

2 See P. Borscheid, 'Zwischen privaten Netzen und öffentlichen Institutionen. Familienumwelten in historischer Perspektive', in Deutsches Jugendinstitut (ed.), *Wie geht's der Familie?*. Munich: Kösel, 1988, pp. 271–280; and Arthur E. Imhof, *Reife des Lebens. Gedanken eines Historikers zum längeren Dasein*, Munich: Beck, 1988.

3 Borscheid, 1988, p. 273.

4 C. Attias-Donfut, 'Die Abhängigkeit alter Menschen: Familiale und gesellschaftliche Versorgung', *Zeitschrift für Sozialisationsforschung und Erziehungssoziologie*, 4, 1991, pp. 355–73; P. Gitschmann, 'Armut und Unterversorgung bei Krankheit und Pflegebedürftigkeit im Alter', in D. Döring, W. Hanesch and E. -U. Huster (eds), *Armut im Wohlstand*, Frankfurt/M.: Suhrkamp, 1990, pp. 270–85; J. Kytir, R. Münz, 'Wer pflegt uns im Alter? Lebensformen, Betreuungssituation und soziale Integration älterer Menschen in Österreich', *Zeitschrift für Familienforschung und Erziehungssoziologie*, 4, 1991, pp. 332–54; H. J. Schubert, 'Mitglieder der erweiterten Familie in persönlichen Hilfenetzen – Ergebnisse einer egozentrierten Netzwerkanalyse', *Zeitschrift für Familienforschung*, 3, 1990, pp. 176–210; *Vierter Familienbericht. Die Situation der älteren Menschen in der Familie*. Bonn: Bundesminister für Jugend, Familie, Frauen und Gesundheit, 1986.

5 U. Fink, 'Der neue Generationenvertrag', *Die Zeit*, 3 April 1987.

6 B. Badura (ed.) *Soziale Unterstützung und chronische Krankheit. Zum Stand sozialepidemiologischer Forschung*, Frankfurt/M.: Suhrkamp, 1981.

7 Kytir/Münz, 1991, p. 347.

8 Imhof, 1988, p. 57.

9 U. Beck, *Risikogesellschaft. Auf dem Weg in eine andere Moderne*, Frankfurt/M.: Suhrkamp, 1986, p. 205; *Risk Society: Towards a New Modernity*, London: Sage, 1992, p. 129.

10 K. Kister, 'Szenen einer wilden Ehe', *Süddeutsche Zeitung*, 2–3 December 1989.

11 K. Lüscher, F. Schultheis and M. Wehrspaun (eds), *Die 'postmoderne' Familie. Familiale Strategien und Familienpolitik in einer Übergangszeit*. Konstanz: Universitätsverlag, 1988.

12 L. Rosenmayr, 'Showdown zwischen Alt und Jung?', *Wiener Zeitung*, 26 June 1992.

13 Beck, *Risikogesellschaft*, p. 179.

14 Attias-Donfut, 1991; Kytir/Münz, 1991; *Vierter Familienbericht*, 1986.

15 E. Beck-Gernsheim, 'Vom "Dasein für andere" zum Anspruch auf ein Stück "eigenes Leben" – Individualisierungsprozesse im weiblichen Lebenszusammenhang', *Soziale Welt*, vol. 3, 1983, pp. 307–341; translated above as 'Living for Others'.

16 T. Lewin, 'U.S. Women Are Disrupting Careers to Tend to Aged Relatives', *International Herald Tribune*, 15 November 1989.

17 Schubert, 1990, p. 203.

18 *Vierter Familienbericht*, 1986, p. 180.

19 Jean Améry, *Über das Altern. Revolte und Resignation*. Stuttgart: Reclam, 1979, p. 134.

20 Kytir/Münz, 1991.

21 Gitschmann, 1990; M. Dieck and G. Naegele, '"Matthäus-Prinzip" kontra "Neue Alte"'. manuscript, 1991.

22 Améry, 1979, p. 114.

23 The phrase comes from L. Rosenmayr, *Die späte Freiheit. Das Alter – ein Stück bewußt gelebten Lebens*, Berlin: Severin und Siedler, 1983.

24 A. E. Imhof, *Die gewonnenen Jahre*. Munich: Beck, 1981.

25 See J. L. Avorn, 'Medicine, health, and the geriatric transformation', *Daedalus*, 115(1): 211–26.

26 D. Callahan, 'Adequate health care and an aging society: are they morally compatible?', *Daedalus*, 115(1): 249.

27 See Avorn, 1986, p. 220.

28 K. U. Mayer and W. Müller, 'Lebensverläufe im Wohlfahrtsstaat', in A. Weymann (ed.), *Handlungsspielräume. Untersuchungen zur Individualisierung und Institutionalisierung von Lebensläufen in der Moderne.* Stuttgart: Enke, 1989, pp. 41–60.

29 A. Giddens, *Modernity and Self-Identity: Self and Society in the Late Modern Age.* Cambridge: Polity, 1991, p. 215.

30 Ibid., p. 224.

31 Ibid., p. 231.

32 Callahan, 1986.

33 *Vierter Familienbericht,* 1986, p. Xv.

34 *Gemeinsames Ministerialblatt,* published by the Federal Minister of the Interior, year 43, no. 7, 21 February 1992, pp. 129ff.

Translated from the German version, **Apparate pflegen nicht: Zur Zukunft des Alters**, in: H.U. Klose (ed.) 1993, *Altern der Gesellschaft.* Published here, in English, by kind permission of Bund-Verlag Köln.

10

Health and Responsibility
in the Age of Genetic Technology

Technological research in the social sciences frequently focuses on the relationship between technological change and social change. Roughly summarized, two positions have initiated the debate.[1] On the one hand, there is a technological determinism which sees technology as destiny: technology dictates whether and in what way it will be applied. On the other, there is the position of social reductionism. Here it is the users who decide whether and in what way technology will be applied. Cultural influences, social norms and interests play a crucial role in the shaping and use of technology.

Meanwhile, of course, the deficiencies and lacunae of both positions have become evident. Both perceive only segments, not the whole, as sociologist Peter Weingart puts it: they are 'the two great traditions of one-eyedness'.[2] Consequently, recent research focuses on the relationship between the cultural prerequisites of technology and what it offers. Here technology may be seen as a spiral-like process.[3] It appears as both the product and the instrument of social needs, interests and conflicts. Technology is effect and cause at the same time.

In this chapter, I want to explore this spiral-like process for the sphere of genetic engineering – or, more precisely, for genetic engineering as applied to human beings through genome analysis, predictive medicine and prenatal diagnosis. I will start by considering the concepts of 'health' and 'responsibility', two basic values of the individualized society. After briefly sketching their social genesis and historical ascendance, I shall analyse their two-way relationship with genome analysis and its possible applications. My central question is simply: what happens when the demands of the individualized society combine, or even ally, with the new possibilities opened up by technology? What is the shape of the future that may be in store for us on this basis?

In the case of genome analysis, I want to show that three mutually supporting trends are becoming apparent. Processes of individualization have given 'health' and 'responsibility' the character of guiding values and these greatly influence the culture and prepare the ground for public acceptance of genome analysis. Once this acceptance is won, the values themselves begin to change through a surreptitious shift in their content. The expansion of medical technology also brings an expansion of what is called 'health' and 'responsibility'. This gives rise both to new opportunities for action and new burdens of action, to new social norms and controls as well as new dilemmas and conflicting choices. As the possibility of genetic prediction grows, so too, paradoxically, does biographical uncertainty.

Health as a Guiding Value of the Individualized Society

The Task of Keeping Healthy

In pre-industrial society, the dominant ways of living and securing a livelihood were communal. Day to day this meant the family acted as an economic unit pooling its labour;[4] in emergencies it meant support by the village or clan.[5] With industrialization, such modes of provision grew more and more fragile and individuals became primarily responsible for their own livelihood, to be obtained through personal achievement and self-assertion in the labour market. Active self-management was increasingly required, as individuals were expected to make advance plans that pinpointed the chances open to them as well as the potential risks and dangers. Martin Kohli has summed this up as follows: 'Life is no longer... "God's wondrous gift" but an individual property, to be defended continuously. More, it becomes an individual task or project.'[6]

In these circumstances, care and provision for one's health are among the biographical models promoted and required by the individualized society. To keep one's head above water in a competitive labour maket, it is necessary to be fit, healthy and capable. Now health, too, is not so much a gift from God as a task and achievement of the responsible citizen, who must protect and look after it or face the consequences. Anyone with health problems has fewer chances in the labour market and is soon placed in the 'hard to find work for' category. This is a danger that potentially threatens all of us. It gives rise to a new morality of health, enjoining us to arm ourselves in advance. Citizens, protect yourselves against illness, accident and disability, against germs and viruses! Do it in time, by measuring and weighing yourself, by getting into shape and having the right jabs, by taking your vitamin pills and drops! Whereas health used to be something given to us that only required repairs in an emergency, it now has to be constantly produced.

Health as Salvation

Of course, people in previous centuries also hoped for good health and a life without pain. But then their horizon was strongly determined by religion, which promised life after death and redemption from suffering. Earthly existence was always measured against this and felt to be less important. What did it matter if you lived for two or 20 or 70 years, if then came eternity?

This entailed a different way of handling illness and suffering.[7] Although often an oppressive burden, they were also given a meaning as part of the infinite cosmos, a trial sent by God to lead people towards purification and reflection. This idea of a higher meaning can be found in all the philosophies and world religions; again and again, thinkers have seen a redemptive power in suffering or even maintained that life's only real cure comes from emptying the cup of suffering. Illnesses, wrote Novalis two centuries or so ago, 'are years of apprenticeship in the art of life and development of character'. The Romantic poet, who died of consumption when he was barely 29, well knew that 'pain can harden the heart', but also that 'whoever flees pain no longer wishes to live'. And Schopenhauer concluded his famous chapter 'On the Doctrine of the Denial of the Will to Live' with a saying of the Dominican of Cologne, Meister Eckhart, which was much quoted in the Middle Ages: 'Suffering is the fleetest animal that bears you to perfection.'

In the course of secularization, this belief in God, eternity and redemption broke down among broad sectors of the population. What remains is the individual, in a here and now to which all his or her hopes and efforts are related. When the belief in an afterlife is lost, health acquires a new meaning and a higher value; it becomes a secular expectation of salvation. Historical and sociological analyses draw a similar conclusion. 'What can no longer be expected from an afterlife is now... projected on to life here below: freedom from cares and afflictions, illness and suffering – and thus ultimately happiness and immortality.'[8] The value of the body and everything connected with it is hugely enhanced. For good health and a smoothly functioning body are now 'the one and only guarantee of our existence, *all through* our lives. When the body withers away, so too does our life.'[9] Health 'acquires, so to speak, a transcendental meaning; without it everything else is nothing.'[10] A pithy formula might be that healing [*Heilung*] has been throned in the place of salvation [*Heil*].[11]

Health as a secular expectation of salvation and health as pressure to perform in individualized market society, are two of the driving forces behind the rise of the 'health project'. The characteristic striving for health in the modern world – for what critics describe as a cult fetish or a phantom[12] – is thus not merely an expression of personal inclinations, compulsions or neuroses. Rather, it is part of the global project of modernity, of the new malleability of life with all its opportunities, checks and pressures.

Health and Genome Analysis

With the rise and spread of the new biotechnologies, the malleability of life has gained further scope and thrust. A combination of medicine, biology and genetics has brought novel ways of intervening in the stuff of human existence, so that it is becoming an open question what man is, should be and can be. The new biotechnologies 'turn qualities of human nature that have hitherto represented limits of action into objective fields for human action. Man can in a new sense make himself.'[13]

The Promise of Health

In Germany genetic technology is still the object of heated debate; it is even the problem child for those who see it as their task to gain acceptance for modern technology in general.[14] Memories of eugenics soon spring to mind, with the deadly, indeed murderous, consequences of a policy that distinguished and selected between the genetically 'good' and the genetically 'inferior'. It is this past which makes politicians and even some human geneticists rather alarmed about the scale of biological intervention that will become feasible.

If, nevertheless, there is a growing clientele for the supply of genetic advice, both in Germany and internationally, one contributory factor is certainly the fundamental value placed on health. Survey results suggest, for example, that 'as medical applications are more clearly spelled out... ethical reservations connected with eugenics and human breeding, as well as images of what human genetics meant in the past, tend to drop out of the picture.'[15] Health is the magic word that wins acceptance – in the media and politics, among men and women in the street. Health – or rather, the promise of health – opens doors, removes obstacles, draws in public support and money. If health is riding high and if it has been closely associated in people's minds with genome analysis, then the popularity of genome analysis will also rise.

Of course, it is a matter of dispute how close the association between health and genetic technology really is. While some scientists expect enormous progress, others express doubts or even regard such expectations as grossly inflated. So far, we know for certain only that there is a huge gap between the possibilities of diagnosis and those of therapy. When and indeed whether this gap will disappear, whether the major therapeutic breakthroughs will ever happen, whether the great promises will ever be kept – this is all hotly debated even within the natural sciences.

Those who have entered the lists on behalf of genetic technology (one thinks not least of the pharmaceuticals industry) have consciously used the promise of health to paint a glowing picture of a better and happier future. One example comes from the book that Nobel prizewinner Renato Dulbecco wrote together with the journalist Riccardo Chiaberge:

> Meanwhile the complete decoding of the genome has moved within reach. We are on the eve of a Copernican revolution in medicine. Once many of the conventional methods are laid aside, we shall completely revise our ways of diagnosing and treating illnesses. Any pathological change in the organism – whether hereditary, chronic or due to an infection – will be analysed and combated by reference to the genes that cause or at least assist its growth. Health will find new and invincible allies, life will last longer, and a future of greater well-being will open up for us.[16]

Here we see a model of assertiveness that might be called the bridgehead strategy. According to Weingart, the introduction of a new technology always requires 'a kind of bridgehead within the social system from which it can then spread out':

> [A] 'situation of at least partial acceptance' is extremely useful from this point of view. 'One may evoke the image of colonization: the triumphal march of the colonizers, even overcoming the superior strength of the "old cultures", can be explained only by the fact that these are internally divided and ambivalent in the face of the intruders.'[17]

In the case of genetic technology, we can expect such a partial acceptance for the very reason that health is a major value of modern society. References to health may thus be seen as establishing a bridgehead from which expansion may follow. One cannot argue against health, especially in a society that no longer recognizes any god, any generally binding morality, any settled traditions. In the wake of a technology that can claim for itself the secular salvation expected from health, barriers continue to fall and norms to change. Erosion of the remaining taboos and boundaries soon sets in.

Expansion of the Concept of Health

In 1992 a keynote essay entitled 'Changing your genes' appeared in *The Economist*.[18] The opening sentence quoted Freud's famous dictum that biology is our destiny and a future was then drawn in which this no longer held because people consciously selected and recombined their own genes. Today, it is said, therapies target malignant genes. But tomorrow they may work on genes which not only turn a badly functioning body into a well-functioning one, but also turn a well-functioning body into one that is even better, even faster, even stronger, even more beautiful. The article touched in passing on a couple of ethical objections, then launched into a plea of its own. Freedom of choice above everything, for everything, even for genes! Genetic choice will bring a new era of freedom! This tone is kept up until the logical final sentence: 'With apologies to Freud, biology will be best when it is a matter of choice.'

In an issue of *Newsweek* devoted to new medical possibilities, an article by the medical writer Michael Crichton offers an even more glowing account of what the future holds in store. The title 'Greater expectations', borrowed and intensified from Dickens, is meant to be taken quite literally:

> The physician as lifestyle expert, as wellness adviser, has already begun to appear. And as genetic profiles and other predictive tools improve, the art of prevention will grow far more sophisticated. Physicians will administer tests and, armed with the results, prescribe preventive measures just as precisely as they now dispense medications... Even more fundamental will be gene-replacement therapy, in which missing or defective genes are supplied by the physician. Such procedures are now being developed to treat serious illness, but they will even be used to boost enzyme levels and hormone production to retard aging and to increase vigour... What all this means is that our present concept of medicine will disappear... Medicine will change its focus from treatment to enhancement, from repair to improvement, from diminished sickness to increased performance.[19]

We shall not discuss whether genetic intervention of this kind could happen in the foreseeable future; what interests us more is the concept of health presented as desirable in such statements, which points to a truly epochal shift. For the promises here associated with gene technology insidiously, but no less radically for that, expand the concept of health beyond its previous limits. Biology, understood as the basic genetic endowment, is no longer destiny but starting point. Expectations of indefinite change and improvement are now the order of the day. Nature is not completely passé, as it still supplies the necessary raw materials, but technology will fashion it into a work of art. From the old body, a new one will arise that is much better and healthier. The 'rationalization of the conduct of life',[20] the 'in order to' mentality that is the hallmark of modernity and stretches into ever more spheres of life,[21] is now directly applied to the human body. 'The body is becoming a phenomenon of choices and actions.'[22]

Voluntary Compulsion

One of the main respects in which genetic diagnosis differs from traditional kinds is its predictive dimension.[23] Whereas conventional diagnostics identifies pathological change only when it has already appeared (at however early a stage), its genetic counterpart is able to spot an illness long before it begins.

Genetic technology thus carries the tendency to planning and rationalization into new dimensions, making it possible for people to know their own risk factors (such as a predisposition to heart disease or diabetes) and to use them as reference points in planning their lives. Preventive care, according to Daele, is 'an element of self-management expected of modern individualized persons. When a methodical way of life becomes established practice – from the planning of education... to provision for a "successful" old age – then preventive health care must become a priority.'[24]

This 'must' does not imply direct compulsion, but still less does it mean a purely free choice. One might speak paradoxically of voluntary compulsion or, as Daele does, of 'preventive compulsion'.[25] In his view, preventive measures easily obtain a status of legitimacy and rationality today, barely allowing for objections to be raised. For options to avoid health risks count both as resources of self-planning and as claims for public facilities directed towards the state. The individual seeks security from the vicissitudes of life (illness and accident, disability and need for permanent nursing care) in all kinds of publicly funded insurance. Underutilization of preventive facilities – that is, the fact that many people reject a health-oriented way of life – therefore becomes a problem:

> In general, the social role of the sick person includes a corresponding expectation of those around that he or she will make every reasonable effort to get well soon. This expectation is the quid pro quo for such privileges as being excused from work or provided with extra care. Claims on community services in the event of illness are matched by an obligation to be healthy. Obviously, this idea can be transferred to well people who "irresponsibly" fail to take advantage of preventive facilities.[26]

Bräutigam and Mettler, two prominent champions of high-tech medicine, argue that 'knowing our genes should induce us to a responsible lifestyle'.[27] Similar statements occur frequently in the debate, the word 'responsibility' appearing almost as a refrain. Like health, responsibility ranges among the major values of modernity. Who can be against it? Who would put forward a case for irresponsible behaviour? The question is only what is meant by responsibility. And perhaps, with the march of genetic technology, it is not only the concept of health but also that of responsibility which has changed.

Expansion of Tesponsibility

In order to highlight the direction of the trend, we shall single out the sphere of prenatal and genetic diagnostics, where the possibilities have increased most rapidly and the concept of parental responsibility has been changing in the same degree.

First a couple of examples. A pregnant woman: 'I felt caught in a horrible dilemma. All the time I was asked: Have you had the test done? You really should, now that it's possible... But what if you have a handicapped child? You've already got two children. You must think of them, and of your husband!'[28] A gynaecologist to a 35-year-old patient: 'A woman – at your age – it's essential. From 35 on, you *must* do it.'[29] A popular book about the advantages and risks of prenatal diagnosis: 'You should definitely read this book if you... take responsibility for your pregnancy and want to take well-founded decisions... [With this information] responsibility is put where it belongs: with you.'[30]

A New Tune

There is ample evidence that these examples are not haphazard examples. What they express is an insidious change in the meaning of the concept of responsibility. The more that safe methods of contraception become available, the more widespread becomes the idea of responsible parenthood. Once this referred to the quantitative aspect: only as many children as you can properly bring up and provide for.[31] Now, with the new possibilities in reproductive medicine and prenatal diagnostics, the concept of responsibility has been moving in the direction of a qualitative choice that begins before birth or perhaps even before conception. The actual formulations, borrowed from the language of government administration, do not directly spell out the aim but speak of 'prevention'[32] or 'prophylactic measures'.[33] Such terms have a positive connotation in our society. They sound up to date, rational, hygienic, as much part of publicly promoted health care as brushing your teeth morning and night. They refer to goals that receive wide support, serving the interests both of the individual (preservation of health, avoidance of pain) and of society (cost saving).

More is at stake here, however, than oral hygiene. In plain language, it is a question of avoiding the birth of a handicapped child, either by way of forgoing biological parenthood altogether or (more likely) by a 'tentative pregnancy' and abortion in the event of a genetic deficiency.[34] Tendencies are already in the air to praise such conduct as an expression of responsibility. Here, for example, is Hubert Markl, former president of the Deutsche Forschungsgemeinschaft, in a lecture on 'Genetics and ethics': 'I want to state very clearly – because the opposite is sometimes argued – that to renounce for such reasons the idea of having children of one's own is at least as praiseworthy as the decision taken out of relentlessly fatalistic piety to allow a possibly cruel fate to take its course.' Or further on: 'To prevent the birth of handicapped children should never be the task of a human polity; such considerations belong exclusively in the private moral domain of the individual.'[35]

And that seems to be where they go. Does ethics in the age of genetics mean that citizens of sound judgement are expected to prevent the birth of handicapped children? Hardly anyone, at least in Germany, would say this publicly (what one says to one's mates around a pub table is another matter). But thoughts like those of the German philosopher Martin Sass are already gaining ground. High-risk reproductive decisions are, in his view, 'irresponsible towards the society that accepts and supports severely handicapped children in its midst'.[36] And in everyday life, we can also see a change of attitudes creeping in. Increasingly, women who do not undergo prenatal testing are seen as selfish, ignorant or stupid: 'They prefer to stick their head in the sand rather than to learn the truth.'[37] In recent questionnaires, 26 per cent of respondents were of the view that 'everyone should be obliged' to have their hereditary disposition investigated, so that they are informed about any predispositions to illness among their offspring.[38]

A New Guilt

It is not hard to see the logic behind these trends. Responsibility, like health, is a primary value, a lodestar on the horizon of modernity based on the philosophy of the Enlightenment. Responsibility is presented as meaning greater autonomy, much as Kant once defined enlightenment as the 'emergence from self-inflicted immaturity'. Already in that formulation, however, there was a double meaning that pointed to a reverse side: anyone who did not take responsibility counted as irresponsible; any dereliction counted as 'guilt'. Not by chance does the phrase 'reminding someone of their responsibilities' have a threatening undertone. It is precisely this which we can now observe in the field of prenatal diagnostics. On the one hand, in the medical profession as well as in political boards and committees, freedom of choice is declared a basic right and any compulsion on people to undergo tests is constantly forsworn. Everyone must be free to act as they see fit. But on the other, in the slipstream of technological advances, a number of small and at first barely noticeable steps attach new meaning to the concept of responsibility by adapting it to what is technically feasible. Anyone who does not play along thus appears as irresponsible – suspect, if not downright guilty.

The responsibility at issue has many addressees and reference points. First, as we have just seen, there is the responsibility to society. Then, as quoted earlier, there is the responsibility to one's family, husband and other children (perhaps even to grandparents hoping for a healthy, cuddly and presentable grandchild). Neither should we forget the responsibility to the unborn child; should it really be burdened with a life of suffering, rejection and dependence? One can imagine what goes through the mind of a woman who decides to terminate a pregnancy after 'Down's syndrome' has come up in a test: 'As we ourselves age, to whom would we leave the person XYLO would become? In a society where the state provides virtually no decent, humane services for the mentally retarded, how could we take responsibility for the future of our dependent... child?'[39]

So many levels of responsibility, so much potential guilt. So much fuel for reproach and self-reproach, for social and moral pressure. As we know from similar situations, this pushes people into taking the tests on offer, 'so we won't have to blame ourselves later on'.[40] Of women whose age put them in a risk group, a good half were opting a few years ago for a prenatal diagnostic test.[41] And the latest estimates are that the rate has considerably increased since then.[42]

Changes in Women's Plans for Life

A contributory factor in the rapidly increasing demand for prenatal testing is that not only the child's future but also the mother's is directly at stake – a fact related to the far-reaching changes that have occurred in women's lives over the past few decades, at least partly loosening their ties to the family and forcing them to provide for themselves.[43] Whereas young women today express a wish to combine a job and a family, the society around them sees things differently: the world of work outside the home takes no account of family tasks and duties; social ministries and local authorities lack the money or the will to provide an adequate supply of nurseries and creches. Having children today is thus the number-one risk to women's job or career aspirations – more, an actual hindrance by the standards of the market. In taking up the offer of prenatal tests, women seek to 'compensate' for their age-related risk so that they can forget the fear of a handicapped child and all the disadvantages it would entail at work and in life.

This link comes over loud and clear in a number of interviews. For example: 'Imagine a handicapped child – how terrible and how much work it would mean. I could kiss my job goodbye straight away.'[44] Or: 'My main reason for having the test was that I have a job I'd like to keep on doing... A handicapped child would tie me up for years. For years I've worked to get away from the traditional woman's role, and I wouldn't want to slip back into it. Having a mongoloid child would mean looking after it for 20 years or more at the level of development of a small child. It would fix you once more to the woman's role.'[45]

What of the Future?

A number of different, but not at all mutually exclusive, trends are shaping up for the future. If the predictive possibilities of genome analysis continue to grow, there may be a gradual 'individualization of health-related risks'.[46] Such a tendency is already apparent independently of genetic risks, as the costs explosion leads to calls in the most varied quarters for greater 'individual responsibility in health care'. With regard to the use of DNA analysis, this interest of the health system in cost saving may interact with the interest of individuals in discovering their personal risk to curtail still further the principle of socialized care in favour of greater individualization – and even set up a compulsion to prevention. As the legal theorist Wolfram Eberbach writes: 'The growing individual calculability of health risks leads... to the allocation of ever wider personal responsibility – and... not suddenly, but over a certain length of time, insurance advantages and legally prescribed health obligations [may result in] a growing compulsion to behave in accordance with one's genes.'[47]

If things develop along such lines, genome analysis could become an influential factor in lifestyle standardization.[48] The function of steering behaviour, formerly exercised by the traditional agencies of social control (such as religion), would then be at least partially taken over by medical technology. The health system would increasingly assume the role of institutionalized monitor of people's lifestyles, and doctors that of a 'health police'.[49] Thus, not only are care and provision for one's health among the precepts of the individualized society; forms of institutional surveillance will also be introduced to ensure that those precepts are observed. Of course, the compulsion that is brought to bear is subtler than the punishments meted out in pre-industrial society to those who did not conform to often strict rules. Nevertheless (or for this very reason), the constraints imposed today by medical technology are rather more effective and people voluntarily accept them for the sake of the magic word: health.

All this means that women and men today are taking their fate into their own hands. They plan, look ahead, check and optimize. They no longer obey God and the stars. Their genes now tell them how they should arrange their lives.

But *what do* the genes say? *How much* do they tell us? Genetic technology brings with it new spaces for human action and intervention, but also a need for new 'life-political' decisions and conflicts about decisions.[50] Characteristically, the old concept of politics – which used to denote statecraft, the art of managing the public weal – here acquires a new meaning. For politics, in the sense of Giddens's 'life politics', no longer recognizes the polarization between those above and those below, between government and people, but includes everyone, even the woman or man in the street. The lowly spheres of everyday life in which ordinary citizens operate may now throw up dramatic constellations and the processes of negotiation and decision required are often fraught with incalculable consequences and unsuspected burdens. Suffering must be weighed up against suffering, life against life and abstract statistics or probabilities must be translated into existential judgements (to terminate or continue a pregnancy, to decide what is likely to happen and to whom). Here the possibility and the necessity of making choices can lead to a veritable 'moral odyssey'.[51] As Giddens puts it:

> The capability of adopting freely chosen lifestyles, a fundamental benefit gener-
> ated by a post-traditional order, stands in tension, not only with barriers to
> emancipation, but with a variety of moral dilemmas. No one should under-
> estimate how difficult it will be to deal with these.[52]

Here, as in other domains, the chances opened up by modernity come together with new questions and conflicts. And the traditions from which answers could be drawn began to break up a long time ago. The basic feature of modernity, then, is not autonomy but do-it-yourself biography and perhaps also do-it-yourself morals – in short, 'biographical uncertainty' at more and more levels.[53]

Notes

1 See B. Joerges (ed.), *Technik im Alltag*. Frankfurt/M.: Suhrkamp, 1988; P. Weingart (ed.), *Technik als sozialer Prozeß*. Frankfurt/M.: Suhrkamp, 1989.

2 P. Weingart, 'Differenzierung der Technik oder Entdifferenzierung der Kultur', in Joerges, 1988, p. 145.

3 B. Mettler-Meibom, 'Mit High-Tech zurück in eine autoritäre politische Kultur?', *Essener Hochschulblätter*. Essen, 1990, p. 61.

4 A. E. Imhof, *Die verlorenen Welten*. Munich: Beck, 1984.

5 P. Borscheid, 'Zwischen privaten Netzen und öffentlichen Institutionen. Familienumwelten in historischer Perspektive', in Deutsches Jugendinstitut (ed.), *Wie geht's der Familie? Ein Handbuch zur Situation der Familien heute*. Munich: Kösel, 1988, pp. 271–80.

6 M. Kohli, 'Gesellschaftszeit und Lebenszeit. Der Lebenslauf im Strukturwandel der Moderne', in J. Berger (ed.), *Die Moderne. Kontinuitäten und Zäsuren*. Special issue no. 4 of *Soziale Welt*, Göttingen: Schwartz, 1986, p. 185.

7 I. Illich, *Medical Nemesis: The Expropriation of Health*. London: 1975.

8 U. Mergner, E. Mönkeberg-Tun and G. Ziegeler, 'Gesundheit und Interesse. Zur Fremdbestimmung von Selbstbestimmung im Umgang mit Gesundheit', *Psychosozial*, 2, 1990, p. 18.

9 Imhof, 1984, p. 223.

10 W. van den Daele, 'Das zähe Leben des präventiven Zwanges', in A. Schuller and N. Heim (eds), *Der codierte Leib. Zur Zukunft der genetischen Vergangenheit*, Zurich and Munich: Schuster 1989, p. 208.

11 Cf. J. J. Rohde, *Soziologie des Krankenhauses*, Stuttgart: Enke, 1974, p. 130.

12 H. Ernst, 'Das Phantom Gesundheit', *Psychologie heute*, January 1991, pp. 20–26; Mergner et al., 1990.

13 W. van den Daele, *Mensch nach Maß? Ethische Probleme der Genmanipulation und Gentherapie*, Munich: Beck, 1985, p. 11.

14 L. Hennen and T. Stöckle, *Gentechnologie und Genomanalyse aus der Sicht der Bevölkerung*, results of a population survey conducted by the TAB (Bundestag's Office for the Evaluation of the Consequences of Technology), TAB discussion paper no. 3, December 1992, p. 53.

15 Ibid., p. 16.

16 R. Dulbecco and R. Chiaberge, *Konstrukteure des Lebens. Medizin und Ethik im Zeitalter der Gentechnologie*. Munich: Piper, 1991, p. 117.

17 P. Weingart, '"Großtechnische Systeme" – ein Paradigma der Verknüpfung von Technikentwicklung und sozialem Wandel?', in Weingart (ed.), 1989, p. 190.

18 *The Economist*, 25 April 1992, pp. 11f.

19 M. Crichton, 'Greater expectations: the future of medicine lies not in treating illness but in preventing it', *Newsweek*, 24 September 1990.

20 M. Weber, *Gesammelte Aufsätze zur Religionssoziologie*, vol. 1. Tübingen: 1986, pp. 113, 115.

21 B. Sichtermann, *Leben mit einem Neugeborenen*. Frankfurt/M.: Fischer, 1981, pp. 34ff.

22 A. Giddens, *Modernity and Self-Identity: Self and Society in the Late Modern Age*. Cambridge: Polity, 1991, p. 8.

23 Institut für System- und Technologie-Analysen, *Perspektiven der Anwendung und Regelungsmöglichkeiten der Genomanalyse in den Bereichen Humangenetik, Versicherungen, Straf- und Zivilprozeß. Eine Studie im Auftrag des Büros für Technikfolgenabschätzung des Deutschen Bundestages*, hectograph. Bad Oeynhausen: 1992, p. 43.

24 Daele, 1989, pp. 207f.

25 Daele, 1989.

26 Ibid., p. 208.

27 H. H. Bräutigam and L. Mettler, *Die programmierte Vererbung. Möglichkeiten und Gefahren der Gentechnologie*. Hamburg: Hoffmann und Campe, 1985, p. 138.

28 From an interview in Eva Schindele, *Gläserne Gebär-Mütter. Vorgeburtliche Diagnostik – Fluch oder Segen*. Frankfurt/M.: Fischer, 1990, p. 64.

29 From an interview in ibid.

30 B. Blatt, *Bekomme ich ein gesundes Kind? Chancen und Risiken der vorgeburtlichen Diagnostik*. Reinbek: Rowohlt, 1991, pp. 16f., 25.

31 M. Häußler, 'Von der Enthaltsamkeit zur verantwortungsbewußten Fortpflanzung. Über den unaufhaltsamen Aufstieg der Empfängnisverhütung und seine Folgen', in M. Häußler, C. Helfferich, G. Walterspiel and A. Wetterer, *Bauchlandungen. Abtreibung – Sexualität – Kinderwunsch*. Munich: Frauenbuchverlag, 1983, pp. 58–73.

32 W. Schmid, 'Die Prävention des Down-Syndromes (Mongolismus)', *Neue Zürcher Zeitung*, 20 January 1988, p. 77.

33 'In families with a genetic risk, the aim should be to give human genetic advice before conception. If necessary ... prophylactic measures should be aimed for' H. Bach, W. Göhler, H. Körner, H. Metzke, J. Shöneich, V. Steinbicker, 'Orientierung humangenetischer Betreuung – genetische Beratung in der DDR', *Medizinische Genetik*, 4, 1990, p. 41.

34 See B. Katz Rothman, *The Tentative Pregnancy: Prenatal Diagnosis and the Future of Motherhood*. London: Pandora, 1988.

35 H. Markl, 'Genetik und Ethik. Rede anläßlich der Verleihung des Arthur-Burkhardt-Preises 1989'. Stuttgart, 26 April 1989, hectograph.

36 Bundesministerium für Forschung und Technologie (ed.), *Ethische und rechtliche Probleme der Anwendung zellbiologischer und genetischer Methoden am Menschen. Dokumentation eines Fachgesprächs im Bundesministerium für Forschung und Technologie*. Munich: 1984, p. 123.

37 From an interview in Schindele, 1990, p. 66.

38 Hennen and Stöckle, 1992, p. 36.

39 R. Rapp, 'XYLO: A True Story', in R. Arditti, R. Duelli Klein and S. Minden (eds), *Test-Tube Women: What Future for Motherhood?* London: Routledge and Kegan Paul, 1984, p. 319.

40 On experiences in the field of reproductive medicine, see H. Kentenich et al., 'Am schlimmsten ist das Warten. Wie Paare die In-vitro-Fertilisation erleben', *Sexualmedizin*, 16, 1987, pp. 364–70.

41 T. Schroeder-Kurth, 'Medizinische Genetik in der Bundesrepublik', *Medizinische Genetik*, 4, 1990, p. 39.

42 Institut für System- und Technologie-Analysen 1992, p. 26; P. Bradish, G. Gräning and T. Kratz, *Reproduktionsmedizin, Gentechnologie, Pränatale Diagnostik und ihre Bedeutung für Frauen*. Hamburg: Senatsamt für Gleichstellung, 1993, pp. 68f.

43 For a more detailed account, see E. Beck-Gernsheim, 'Vom "Dasein für andere" zum Anspruch auf ein Stück "eigenes Leben" – Individualisierungsprozesse im weiblichen Lebenszusammenhang', *Soziale Welt*, vol. 3, 1983, pp. 307–341; translated above as 'Living for others'.

44 From an interview in Schindele, 1990, p. 9.

45 From an interview in M. Leuzinger and B. Rambert, 'Ich spür' es – mein Kind ist gesund', in C. Roth (ed.), *Genzeit. Die Industrialisierung von Pflanze, Tier und Mensch*. Zurich: Limmat, 1987, p. 87.

46 Institut für System- und Technologie-Analysen, 1992, pp. 47f.

47 W. H. Eberbach, 'Genomanalyse und Prävention', in H. M. Sass (ed.), *Genomanalyse und Gentherapie. Ethische Herausforderungen in der Humanmedizin*. Berlin. 1991, p. 84.

48 Institut für System- und Technologie-Analysen, 1992, pp. 48f.

49 Ibid., p. 49.

50 Giddens, 1991, p. 215. Cf. Chapter 9 in this volume.

51 Blatt, 1991, p. 9.

52 Giddens, 1991, p. 231.

53 M. Wohlrab-Sahr, *Biographische Unsicherheit*. Opladen: Leske und Budrich, 1993.

Translated from the German version, **Gesundheit und Verantwortung im Zeitalter der Gentechnologie**, by Elisabeth Beck-Gernsheim, in: Ulrich Beck and Elisabeth Beck-Gernsheim (eds.), *Riskante Freiheiten, siehe oben*. Published here, in English, by kind permission of Suhrkamp Verlag, Frankfurt.

11

Death of One's Own,
Life of One's Own

Hopes from Transience

In *Eigenes Leben*, a collectively authored book published in 1996,[1] we attempted to show that the desire, myth and reality of a life of one's own arise when industrial society and its group forms (class, family, gender roles) are caught up in the solvent of modernization ('reflexive modernization'). Then people are forced to conceive of themselves as do-it-yourself producers of meaning and biography, to play a part in shaping both their own lives and the life of society (including their possible failure). The various chapters of *Eigenes Leben* analysed a number of partly contradictory conditions and determinants, which together add up to a rather paradoxical picture.

A 'life of one's own' is a highly socialized existence, utterly dependent on institutions. Indeed, we can understand the 'logic' of this historically late form of existence, of its distinctive possibilities and compulsions, only if we recognize that it follows certain institutional objectives. The training system, labour market, welfare state, legal system and so on, presuppose and release individual actors. What we call a life of one's own is thus neither the expression of a bubbling indivi- dualism and egoism that has reached epidemic proportions, nor a life in which individuals float free in determining themselves, but rather a life of thorough *conformity* that is binding on more and more groups within the context of labour markets buffered by the welfare state. It is a conformity, however, which produces its opposite in the *incalculability of the social*; a normalization of deviations which cancels the criteria for both normality and deviance. In other words, the open spaces of a life of one's own are created by a society that is highly differentiated by function. How those spaces are filled can no longer be dictated from above or outside, neither can it be predicted in advance. The overtaxing demands on individuals that become the general rule are ambivalent; they facilitate opposite things – emancipation *and* power, to use the classical terms. For the character of everyday life also changes, becoming detraditionalized and individualized but also *palpably globalized*. What happens on other continents directly enters the circle of experience that makes up the life of one's own. Isolationist and fundamentalist tendencies – the revival of ethnic identities and local nationalisms – are from this point of view reactions to dangers posed to them by advancing individualization and globalization.

These and other illustrations of the life of one's own – the struggle for one's own space or money, the compulsion to self-staging and self-responsibility (with the possibility of shifting the blame for social crises on to the individual), the globalization and informalization of the social, the paradoxes of a social morality associated with the life of one's own – remain incomplete if the existential significance of *death* is not also considered in this context. The distinctive meaning of the life of one's own will become understandable only from its end, only from death.

The more personal and unique life is, the more it is irreplaceable. The price for far-reaching individualization is a confrontation with one's own past that is by no means gentler than before. The uniqueness of life makes this experience precious but also inherently hard to handle. For it is a life that cannot live on in anyone or anything else; it ends with oneself.

No previous historical epoch was so light minded as to allow life to end when it ended. In religious cultures death was like a change of costume or a change of stage. Often the promise of liberation was bound up with this; people passed from the world of appearance and torment to 'the true life'.

In the secularized societies of socialism or communism, the individual also 'lived on' in the sacrifices made for a better world – only now this world was to be built and achieved here on earth. The Communist apparatus of power was most elaborately interwoven with human and humanitarian ideals, so that the maximization of state power and repression appeared to be in the service of liberty, equality and fraternity. The individual was nothing, society everything. Extreme availability and extreme seductibility complemented and reinforced each other. Individual existence was completely absorbed in 'the creation of the new man', in a secular religion of social redemption. The transcendence of one own's life was relocated here below; 'faith' was invested in a life beyond capitalism.

Death as the end – not a passage but an absolute and irrevocable end – first emerged with the form of existence we have called 'a life of one's own'. It is, in the most radical sense of the word, *past* life. It has lost all the certainties of transcendence. Both the cosmic-religious and the social-political belief in redemption have had their magic and their self-evidence destroyed. This is also true precisely when any means are used to break out of the immanence of one's own life, through an escape into mysticism, esotericism, new religious movements and so on.

The life of one's own is by definition an attempt, a temptation, to find in oneself the ground, strength and purpose of the shaping of oneself and the world. This attempt, when looked at from the other end, is threatened with failure. This gives the life of one's own its peculiar features: its volatility, its hunger for life, its taste of bitterness and disconsolation, its irony and lightness, which grow out of the incomprehensibility of its ceasing to exist. This is the basis for its arrogance, mania and adventurousness, for its combination of ebullience and mortal distress.

The meanings of death and dying now change around. Death becomes unfathomable. Dying becomes the ubiquitous threat to one's own life.

Death begins when the life of one's own has ended, when one is no longer there to be found. There is no bridge, no communication between the two. Death is not perceptible: it knows no feelings, no knowledge, no pain, no suffering. But now its place has been taken by dying. The life of own's own is from the start distinguished, indeed tormented, by a fear of dying. *This* end begins early; it can be experienced and it is always present. It provides a living for insurance brokers, doctors, pharmacists, the cosmetics and pharmaceuticals industry, salvationists and drug peddlers in both the literal and extended senses, and all the specialists in precare and aftercare who promise to erase the minutest signs of decay from one's body and one's life. Fear of dying installs itself in the new cathedrals of security and insurance, which are supposed to protect mere earthly existence from the traces of its past. What happens in the end is not that you die but that medicine stops working.

This is the first step to eternity *here below*, on which those born into a life of their own work with all the power at their command. It is true that our knowledge is not yet so advanced, but one fine day we will all be able to prevent our circulation from breaking down – and then the real jubilation will start! Death is the residual risk, the one thing at the end of the life of our own which we still cannot outsmart. But if our demands for control keep growing as they should, the archaic insecurity of having to die will become as restricted and armoured in, and therefore as uncertain, as nuclear power stations already are today!

The first great insurance policy against the end of one's own life was the Church's promise of *eternal* life. At the height of the Middle Ages, the death of one's own life was only a transformation into the *real* life in and with God. Death as a *trial before God* was an invention which, beginning in the thirteenth century, unsettled souls – and separated them off. Death thus meant to give an account of oneself before God. So began the original sin of individualism – as a demand of the Church.

You can actually hear the theologians quarrel as they wrestle with the paradox: individual life is valuable and, in principle, self-determining; it can go wrong; freedom comes into the world as a human potential for sin. But is this not sheer heresy? What is God doing if man can go wrong? Individual culpability is the first step both into godlessness and into the life of one's own.

Here, too, Church doctrine is strangely undecided. On the one hand, the world and all human strivings count for naught; they are but a fleeting shadow before God. On the other, the conduct of one's own life now determines everything: eternal bliss or eternal damnation. This is decided in death. Death is therefore not an end but an examination, *the* examination, on the career ladder towards eternal life (rather like the higher level examination that opens the door to a permanent post in the civil service).

The scale of the threatened punishment – the fires of Hell – was an attempt to make up for the theological blunder of consigning man to the godlessness of a life of one's own. The freedom, lack of restraint or anarchy of life centred upon itself was both facilitated and annulled by the threat of eternal damnation under which it was placed. Accordingly, it was the fear of Hell, not so much fear of dying or death, which then tormented people at the thought of their end.

To this very extent, however, life became centred on itself; the trials of paid labour became the examination before God. As Max Weber shows in his celebrated study of protestantism, the unrelenting way in which modern man conquers the traditional world and strips it of its mystique has its original justification in this secular testing of man before God. To lead a life of one's own becomes a divine command. This self-inflicted loss of power on God's part, this digging of its own grave on the part of theology, is remorselessly spelt out through all the stages of secularization.

At first death still remains a trial – no longer before God, however, but before society, before the common interest, before man's mission in the world. 'Both Hegel and Marx – the former through his concept of knowledge, the latter through his concept of social change – celebrate the death of the individual in the interests of the future of humanity. Here everything is inverted. The point is no longer to be reconciled with one's ancestors at a religious or mythical level, but to become the midwife of future humanity at a profane historical level' (André Dumas).

Only the life that is confronted with itself alone becomes a revolt against its end. Opposite 'existential' responses are possible to this. The thought of death and the experience of dying *can* kindle or strengthen the pleasure of being alive. At the great feasts of the ancient Egyptians, Death danced beside the Jester. He heightened the fun, he was the real power in the music. He added a transcendental taste to the transience. On a clock above a church portal, we can see it written: 'Each wounds, the last kills.' The last minute, that is. The ticking of life's clock challenges the here and now. The sting and the thrill of transience make the moment infinitely precious.

The thought of death can also clear the way to freedom. Or anyway, it can call into question all the constructions of the social hierarchy. So that's why they all fought and lied, deceived themselves and others, held them down or raised them high! For the sake of that absurd nothingness. All truth and duty, all searching, fretting and fleeing, all striving, suppressing, loving, wrangling, lying and hiding: all runs its course into one and the same absolute end. 'To philosophize means learning to die', wrote the wise Montaigne. Awareness of one's own life can grow out of a clear knowledge of one's transience.

And yet the dominant response of modernity is to forget and suppress, to bury death, to lock it up in the deepest vaults, the darkest memorial chambers of the self. May it rest there, until it rises again and the life of one's own ends. The ideal death of *this* life of one's own is a completely sudden death without dying, a death without any thought of death. This death, in which even one's own absolute end is forgotten, is the radical form of ideal death for the life of one's own.

If not death, then at least dying can be abolished. And this will happen insofar as the thought of death disappears and the passage from life to death is over in a flash. Sudden death in an accident is the perfect way out.

This is still not enough, however, if the abolition of one's own dying awakens a terrible indifference *of others* to one's death. If I suddenly cease to be there, others are no longer able to keep the end of the end under control. The solution is collective death by accident in a big bang. That is the ideal way to abolish dying.

Hence there are only two directions in which to work towards the abolition of dying: either endless prolongation of one's own life or a sudden common ending of life. In both directions a lot of progress has been made.

Note

1 Beck, U., E. Ziegler and W. Rautert, *Eigenes Leben*. Munich: Beck Verlag, 1996.

Translated from the German version. © **Eigenes Leben. Ausflüge in die unbekannte Gesellschaft, in der wir leben** von Ulrich Beck, Wilhelm Vossenkuhl and Ulf E. Ziegler. 105 Fotos von Timm Rautert, München, 1995.

12

Freedom's Children

The Berlin Wall has collapsed. But a chorus of criticism is shaking and blocking the West. Are we a society of egoists? One might almost think so if one reviewed the slogans echoing through the public sphere: the dissolving of solidarity, the decline of values, the culture of narcissism, the egoism trap, entitlement thinking, hedonism. Franz Kamphaus, the Catholic Bishop of Limburg, Germany, writes:

> Every moment on the infinite playing field of freedom is accompanied by crises of relationships, the renunciation of loyalties and cracks in the chain of tradition. Does a person who wants to live out his freedom ultimately only live out himself? Will modern societies fail from their atomization, their exhaustion of solidarity?[1]

The enemy stereotypes of the East–West conflict are relinquished and replaced by the diagnosis of neo-Spenglerism that solidarity is exhausted. The environmental crisis comes to mind here. Modern society lives from natural resources that it has consumed and destroyed, but also from moral resources, which it is equally unable to renew. The transcendental 'values ecology', in which communalism, solidarity, justice and ultimately democracy are 'rooted', is decaying.

In contrast to that, the sceptic of democracy, Alexis de Tocqueville, wrote as long ago as 1848 in *Democracy in America* that 'fighting against freedom means fighting against God himself'. What might that wanderer between the worlds of the feudal and democratic ages have meant by this? A self-authorization of the individual was characteristic of European modernity from the very beginning. Its origin does not lie in capitalism, not even in humanism and certainly not in the 'death of God' (Nietzsche), but in the world of changing religious experiences of ancient and early Christianity, as well as in the discovery and the release of the power of reason in Greek philosophy.

A few chapters later in de Tocqueville, one finds this sentence, which is hardly less shocking to many people today: 'The Americans battled individualism, the fruit of equality, with freedom, and they have vanquished it.'[2] Applied to the present debate, this implies that the symptoms of the 'me generation' cannot be opposed with less freedom; they must be opposed with more freedom, but *political* freedom. Freedom, if seized and actively filled out, fosters commitments in the public space and is thus the exact opposite of the neoliberal idolization of the market.

This prescription, opposing decline with public freedom, is so important because it is in such dramatic opposition to the view almost dominant today that modernity needs, indeed uses up, ties (Dahrendorf's 'ligatures') which it cannot itself renew. In this conception, modernity is inherently counterproductive. It permanently undermines its indispensable moral prerequisites. This self-concept of modern society (and its philosophy and sociology) is completely false. Christianity and political freedom are not mutually exclusive, but mutually inclusive, even if this builds an insoluble contradiction into the Christian traditions.

The point is to give a simple, comprehensible answer to a complicated question. The question is: what is modernity? The answer is: not just 'instrumental rationality' (Max Weber), 'optimal use of capital' (Marx) or 'functional differentiation' (Talcott Parsons, Niklas Luhmann), but supplementing and conflicting with these, it is *political freedom*, citizenship and civil society. The point of this answer is that meaning, morality and justice are not preordained and, as it were, extraterritorial variables for modern society. Quite the reverse is true. Modernity has an independent, living and simultaneously ancient and highly up-to-date wellspring of meaning in its midst: political freedom.[3] The latter is not exhausted by daily use; instead, it bubbles up with greater life and vigour. Modernity accordingly means that a world of traditional certainty is perishing and being replaced, if we are fortunate, by legally sanctioned individualism for everyone.

Just Stay at Home

Young People Practise a Highly Political Disavowal of Politics

We Western Europeans are not living in a crisis of culture and certainly not in a decline of values; instead, we are threatened by something much 'worse'. Our words of freedom are beginning to become deeds in everyday life and are thus calling into question the bases of our previous coexistence, which relied on the precondition that we would only talk of political freedom, not act according to it. The 'catastrophe' is therefore that we must understand, acknowledge and put up with more and different types of freedom than those foreseen in the picture book of democracy as spoken of and promised, but not lived up to. Being freedom's children thus means that we are living under the preconditions of *internalized* democracy, for which many of the concepts and formulae of the first modernity have become inadequate.

No one knows how the traditional authority structure of the family can be connected to the new demands for freedom and self-realization for men and women. The high divorce rates and the figures on single-person households all speak this language.

No one knows how individualism and Christian faith can be reharmonized. And yet sociologists demonstrate that, along with individualization, the willingness to exist for others, indeed to believe, is growing and not disappearing.[4] No one knows how the needs of mass organizations (political parties and trade unions, but cities and communities as well) to obligate the individual are compatible with claims for self-participation and self-organization. No one knows how this immense variety can be mobilized and concentrated for politically necessary decisions.

We are therefore 'suffering' from freedom and not from a crisis. More precisely, we are suffering from the unintended consequences and expressions of a now customary increase in freedom, which was invoked at least on the level of lip service. Kant and Hegel were the first in Germany to set foot firmly in the land of modernity. We owe them the insight that even 'concretizing freedom' is a revolution, albeit a quiet one, occurring because the foundations of the previous social order must be renegotiated.[5]

If this interpretation can be supported, then the talk of a 'decline of values' contains something else, namely the fear of freedom, including the fear of freedom's children, who must struggle with new and different types of problems raised by *internalized* freedom. How can the longing for self-determination be brought into harmony with the equally important longing for shared community? How can one simultaneously be individualistic and merge with the group? How might the variety of voices which vie within each of us in a confusing world be combined into a political statement and action pointing beyond the present day?[6]

The spaces in which people think and act in a morally responsible manner are becoming, on the one hand, smaller and more intensive in that they comprise one's own immediate surroundings, and here the demands increase to the point where they cannot be fulfilled. On the other hand, they are becoming more voluminous and difficult to manage, even immune to any action at all. Young people are moved by that which (established) politics largely rules out: how can global environmental destruction be resolved? How can the death of hope signified by unemployment, a threat to prosperity's children, be prevented and overcome? How can one love and live, with the threat of AIDS? All these are questions that slip through the screens of the large political organizations. The consequence is that freedom's children practise a highly political disavowal of politicians.

They hate organizations for their formalism and their convoluted and dishonest call for 'selfless' commitment and they practise the kind of voting with their feet that was so profoundly underestimated some time ago by the leaders of East Germany. They simply stay at home. The members of Britain's Conservative Party have already reached the venerable (average) age of over 60. One of these days, people in Germany will also have to face up to the question of whether grandpa's mega-organizations will really be justified in their lament over the 'decline of values' when the last member resigns.

Those who want to get involved go to Greenpeace. According to a survey of the German Youth Institute, more than 60 per cent of young people consider the environmental activists credible. The parties, contrariwise, rank right at the bottom of the scale in the same survey, in eighth place, well behind trade unions, the press and the church. The scepticism of young people applies to parties of all stripes. While 6.8 per cent of the members of the (conservative) Christian Democratic Union were under 30 years old in 1991, the same group accounted for only 4.9 per cent in 1995. In the same period, the average age of CDU members rose by two to nearly 54. The typical Social Democrat does not look much younger. He too has almost half a century behind him. Only 7.4 per cent of his comrades are under 30. The (middle of the road) Free Democratic Party is also losing more and more of its younger generation. Its youth group has lost more than 2,000 members since 1991.

All parties are suffering because the 'me generation' may participate in demonstrations and in circulating petitions, but it finds the business of organized politics, with its debates on agendas and proposals, intensely boring. 'The loyal party soldier, who first pastes up posters for years and finally manages to make it into the town council, is a dying species,' says social researcher Helmut Jung.[7]

Young people have finally discovered something for themselves, something to make adults panic: fun, fun sports, fun music, fun consumption, fun life. But politics, as currently practised and represented, has nothing at all to do with fun. On the contrary, it acts like a dead-certain killjoy and hence young people are unpolitical, according to superficial impressions and in their own understanding, but in a very political way. Freedom's children regroup in a colourful rebellion against tedium and obligations that are to be complied with without reasons being given for them and even if no one can identify with them.

Thus there is a subterranean connection between wanting to have fun and grassroots opposition, which has so far been little noticed but which constitutes the actual core of what one could call the 'politics of youthful antipolitics'. Those who (whatever their intentions) refuse to care about institutionalized politics (parties, organizations etc.), but playfully follow the attractions of, for instance, advertising, are unintentionally acting very politically by depriving politics of attention, labour, consent and power. Ultimately, one can spare oneself the detour through membership meetings and enjoy the blessings of political action by heading straight to the disco. There is no need to raise the issue of power long-windedly by actual attendance. It gets raised, and more effectively so, the more decisively, mutely and numerously young people simply stay away.[8]

Freedom's children sometimes betray a winking awareness of this subliminally very effective connection, its subversive energy and irony, which would be more at home and better expressed in the art of the novel than in sociology. Everyone, the elite of the institutions as well as the young people, seems to sense that this policy of conforming withdrawal calls the system into question, once it is practised consistently enough.

This is how and where freedom's children display an unarticulated 'double strategy'. They are an actively unpolitical younger generation because they take the life out of the self-involved institutions and thus force upon them the Hamlet question: to be or not to be? This Western variant of 'antipolitics' (Gyorgy Konrad), which also opens up the opportunity to enjoy one's own life with the best conscience in the world, is supplemented and made credible by a self-organized concern for others which has broken free from large institutions. Freedom's children practise a seeking, experimenting morality that ties together things that seem mutually exclusive: egoism and altruism, self-realization and active compassion, self-realization as active compassion. Ultimately this amounts to questioning the monopoly of the custodians of the public interest on defining the public interest.

Robert Wuthnow has shown that all modern societies would collapse without voluntary activities for others.[9] Eighty million Americans, roughly 45 per cent of those above the age of 18, are involved for five or more hours a week in voluntary service for charitable purposes. In monetary terms this amounts to some 150 billion dollars.

The astonishing thing is this: for more than 75 per cent of the American population, solidarity, willingness to help others and concern for the public interest have a prominence equal to such motivations as self-realization, occupational success and the expansion of personal freedom. The real surprise is that self-assertion, enjoying oneself and caring for others are not mutually exclusive; they are mutually inclusive and strengthen and enrich one another. Insight into this seemingly paradoxical situation is blocked by four prevailing fundamental assumptions in public and scholarly debate:

1 The equation and confusion of commitment with membership – if membership lists are the only things that show commitment, then non-members are of necessity egotists.
2 The self-sacrifice assumption, that only by ignoring oneself can one live for others.
3 Silent help or the *housewife syndrome*, conveying that the dignity of serving others is that it remains invisible, that is, unpaid and unacknowledged, done at the behest of others who are in control.
4 A clear separation of roles between helpers and needy – it never occurs to anyone that those who commit themselves to others also need help and receive it from their service, that perhaps the enrichment might lie precisely in the experience of mutual helplessness.

If one puts together these four assumptions of the equation of commitment and membership, the principles of selflessness and invisibility and the image of the heroic helper-and-nothing-but, then one has (albeit in a rather crude distortion) the intimidating image that forces freedom's children to *flee* organizations. The latter equate commitment with selflessly performed service. Accordingly, the individual becomes anonymous in hierarchical dependency, a foot soldier in a 'public interest army', a mere executing agent in predetermined 'sacrificial' cases.[10]

The much Maligned Decline of Values is Generating New Value Orientations for the Second Modernity

At heart, we are thus concerned not with a decline of values but with a conflict of values, with two images of society, politics and democracy which are different in style and content. Those who lament the decline of values are very much up on their high horses as they complain about the 'ungrateful society' and the ungrateful younger generation who are simply unwilling to recognize how well our institutions (and those who control them) are managing everything.

Many young people (one must be very careful with generalizations, because these are freedom's children, after all) find themselves confronting completely changed global situations and problems, on both the large and the small scale, in their own life milieu and in global society. The adults and the institutions they direct have no answer to these because they have never experienced them and do not take them seriously. Freedom's children:

> find they face a world that no longer falls into two camps, but rather into a vast group of fracture lines, cracks and gaps among which no one any longer knows the way. The future has become multidimensional; the patterns of explanation offered by older people are no longer effective... There are many more riddles

than solutions, and even the solutions, looked at more closely, prove to be sacks full of riddles.[11]

The danger of the new diversity is not the alleged confusion it brings. It lies in the inability of political parties, trade unions, churches, organizations and so on to deal with this increased diversity. Those in charge must give themselves a kick in the pants: stop demonizing individualism, which has already become a reality and instead acknowledge it as a desirable and inevitable product of democratic evolution. They should realize that this is an expression of the Western heritage. Only then can one convincingly ask what political orientations and degree of accommodation are emerging in the individualized and globalized society of the second modernity.

What astonishes and angers me is that the conservative wailing about the alleged decline of values is not only completely false, it also obstructs the view of precisely the sources and movements from which can be created a readiness to take on the tasks of the future. The much demonized decline of values actually *produces* the orientations and prerequisites which, if anything can, will put this society in a position to master the future.

The basic idea is that without the expansion and strengthening of political freedom and its social form, civil society, nothing will work in the future. In this regard, it is important first of all to recognize that changing values and acceptance of democracy go hand in hand. An inner kinship exists between the values of self-development and the ideal of democracy. Many of the findings that research into the changes in values has brought to light, such as the spontaneity and voluntarism of political activism, self-organization, the resistance to formalism and hierarchies, contrariness, tentativeness, as well as the reservation of getting involved only where one can remain in control of the activity, may indeed collide with the party apparatus, but they certainly make sense in the forms and forums of civil society.

One can elaborate this in relation to a number of challenges. The major figures in the study of values (Helmut Klages and Ronald Inglehart, Gerhard Schmidtchen, Daniel Yankelovich, Robert Wuthnow and Helen Wilkinson) all agree that the change in attitudes does not amount to an inflation of material demands. On the contrary, the old and apparently eternal pattern of 'more income, more consumption, more career, more conspicuous consumption' is breaking up and being replaced by a new weighting of priorities, which may often be difficult to decipher, but in which immaterial factors of the quality of life play an outstanding part. What does this imply? For one thing, control over a person's 'own time' is valued higher than more income and more career success, because time is the key that opens the door to the treasures promised by the age of self-determined life: dialogue, friendship, being on one's own, compassion, fun and so on.

This means that the struggle over the distribution of material goods, which still monopolizes public and social scientific attention, has been undermined for some time by a struggle over the distribution of scarce immaterial goods that can hardly be offset by (expressed in) money, such as rest, leisure, self-determined commitments, the love of adventure, interchanges with others and so forth. In the endangered ways of life of our highly civilized world, these are gaining urgency and attractiveness.

In the age of the self-determined life, the social perception of what constitutes 'wealth' and 'poverty' is changing so radically that, under certain conditions, less income and status, if they go hand in hand with the opportunity for more self-development and more ability to arrange things personally, may be perceived as an advance and not a setback. This should not be celebrated without reservation, since it is certainly the underlying cultural perception explaining why the dramatic exacerbation of material social inequality has (so far!) been accepted without a political outcry. Conversely, however, this shows an unexpected opportunity to turn less into more: material sacrifices are tolerable if they go hand in hand with a guaranteed increase of self-developed society. A freedom society, not a leisure society, could perhaps allow us to say goodbye to growth-oriented labour society.[12]

People are better adapted to the future than are social institutions and their representatives. It is important to recognize that the secular change also creates the preconditions for mastering it, but preconditions (and only partial ones at that), not a guarantee. The decline of values which cultural pessimists are so fond of decrying is in fact opening up the possibility of escaping from the creed of 'bigger, more, better' in a period that is living beyond its means ecologically and economically. It is particularly the apostles of the status quo who grumble that individualization means egocentrism; this expresses more about themselves than about those whom they claim to criticize. While in the old values system the ego always had to be subordinated to patterns of the collective (also always designed by individuals), these new orientations towards the 'we' create something like a *co-operative or altruistic individualism.*[13] Thinking of oneself and living for others at the same time, once considered a contradiction in terms, is revealed as an internal, substantive connection. Living alone means living socially.[14]

Research also shows that, in contrast to the distortion implied by the term 'dog-eat-dog society', tolerance for other types of people and marginal groups, whether foreigners, homosexuals, handicapped people or the socially disadvantaged, has steadily increased as values have changed.[15] An epoch in which global society finds itself disturbingly refracted in personal life is finding in the alleged 'decline of values' precisely the willingness to appropriate external things which, as Georg Simmel shows, gives birth to the miracle of the new.

One final example: it is often asserted in gloomy tones that today's 'mobile people' have become devoid of commitments. A recent study of singles (not a group, but a category that comprises a number of very heterogeneous situations) shows that mobility is indeed highly valued. The idea of having to practise a 'lifetime profession' is considered a burden rather than something desirable, while change, in work as well as in relationships, is considered natural and desirable by many. Who could fail to recognize here that one core promise of modernity, mobility, is being turned against another, the ideal of a lifelong profession as internalized in primary modernity? No one is saying that this can occur painlessly and succeed without contradictions. One does not need to read the leaves, however, to recognize that the structural transformation creates preferences that enhance the status of the imperative to deal with diversity and mobility.

Here too, one sees that the age of the self-determined life is not populated entirely by people demanding benefits, people quarrelling, making trouble, shirking. Quite the contrary, orientations and priorities come into being here that surreptitiously meet the challenges of the second modernity. Personal responsibility, self-organization and personal politics are getting an enlightened and realistic chance to redistribute responsibility and power in society, but this opportunity must now be seized by a politics that is hitting its limits in every respect.

The Short-Lived Dream of Everlasting Prosperity

The poet Hölderlin may have believed that danger is the mother of salvation, but none of the rest of us should be swept away by such sentiments. For freedom's children encounter a world in which prosperity, once considered certain, is eroding. Even though some would like to deny it, it remains true that freedom presupposes security, as shown most impressively and emphatically by T. H. Marshall in his famous study, *Citizenship and Social Class*. Accordingly, the former prime minister of Spain, Felipe González, observes:

> Freedom is, generally speaking, not a primary striving of people, but something people seek when their other needs have been met... I believe that security is the primary emotion, so that we are closer to the instinct of animals... When security is lost, the sense of freedom becomes weak and fragile.[16]

The faster and more thoroughly social transformation changes the operating principles of living, working and running a household, the more probable it is that people will feel overburdened and the more the fear of freedom will spread. Thus studies show that more and more people consider their life and well-being under threat, even though the number of violent crimes (in Germany) is not increasing, but stagnating at a relatively low level or even decreasing slightly. It is important to distinguish between crime and fear of crime, which does not feed on crime itself but on the general feeling of uncertainty.[17]

'The more freedom we have, the more troublesome and threatening it seems,' writes Zygmunt Bauman. 'I believe that people today are not so much concerned with the need to belong to a community as with liberation from the compulsion of constantly having to choose and decide.'[18] Where freedom becomes a cage, many choose the freedom of a cage (new or old religious movements, fundamentalism, drugs or violence).

How is one to understand this paradox of 'imposed freedom', which so many are seeking to escape? A self-determined life is not a self-chosen form of existence, but rather a structural principle based on the entire society and it can be influenced only to a limited extent. 'Programmed individualism' is the slogan, which becomes more comprehensible if one connects Kafka's worldview to that of Sartre. The age of the self-determined life is produced by a dense fabric of institutions (law, education, the labour market and so on) which 'condemn' everyone 'to freedom' (Sartre) on pain of (economic) disadvantage.

The crucial point is that paid labour, the cornerstone that integrated people socially and materially into society, is eroding in the context of 'institutionalized individualism (Parsons). Unemployment no longer threatens only marginal groups, but also the middle sections of society, even groups (such as doctors and executives) which, until a few years ago, were considered the very quintessence of middle-class economic security. Moreover, this is happening on such a massive scale that the difference between unemployment and threatening unemployment is becoming insignificant to the affected parties. To understand the extent of this transformation of the foundations of modern society ('reflexive modernization'), it makes sense to distinguish three phases of development since the Second World War.

For the first phase (extending into the 1960s) the necessity and obviousness of rebuilding a destroyed world meshed together with the fear that what had been achieved might again collapse and consequently classical virtues such as willingness to sacrifice, diligence, self-denial, subordination and living for others mutually reinforced one another.

'The short-lived dream of eternal prosperity' (Burkart Lenz) could be the key phrase for the second phase, which reached into the 1980s. The earned wealth was considered certain; the 'side-effects' (environmental crisis, individualization), which call the foundation of primary modernity into question, were repressed (by the established order) and brought to public awareness by varying protest movements. Political freedoms developed then and radiated out into the overall society.

In a third phase, which I have described as the 'global risk society', there is a return of uncertainty, which did not just shake public trust in the ability of key institutions of the industrial world, of business, law and politics, to tame and control the threatening effects they produce; there is also a sense that, across all income groups, prosperity biographies become risk biographies, losing their social identity and material faith in future security:

> Against the background of economic decline, the dominant fear is now that the prosperity once considered secure could collapse. People have lost their orientations and have reached the conclusion that it might make sense after all to think about the future. They worry about their chances in the labor market, the level of their income, the four walls around them, the education of their children and the security of their old-age pensions.[19]

When advanced capitalism in the highly developed countries breaks up the core values of work society, a historic alliance between capitalism, the welfare state and democracy shatters. Democracy arose in Europe and America as a 'democracy of work' in the sense that political freedom relied on participation in paid labour. The citizen had to earn a living one way or another in order to fill the political freedoms with life.

The consequence is that 'citizens mobilize more and more often and more and more self-confidently against rowdies of both right and left, against criminals, against disruptive and annoying elements, against drug dealers and hustlers; and against their own anxieties for the future,' writes Ronald Hitzler.[20] A citizens' initiative movement for security and order appears to be succeeding the environmental, women's and peace movements and setting off on its own 'march through the institutions'. Here, conversely, the risks of freedom, that is, of liberality and the decline of standards, are denounced and self-help and other remedies are being put into practice.

We have to shout to be heard by neoliberals worldwide, given their ignorance of historical experience: the market fundamentalism they worship is a form of democratic illiteracy. The market does not have an inherent justification. This economic model is capable of surviving only in an interplay of material security, social-welfare rights and democracy. Counting only on the market implies destroying democracy along with the economic mode.

Emphasizing this publicly is one thing, but opening people's eyes to the realities is something quite different. Large and growing groups of the populace are excluded *inside* modernity from the prerequisites for making a living and the safety nets of modernity. The crucial point is not only that radical collapses and splits are occurring or impending, but that these are brought about against the background of *fully established* modernity as a 'modernization of modern society'. The key issue is therefore: how do self-confident citizens who are aware of their freedoms react when they see the security of their world tottering and see themselves subject to radical inequalities?

In this third phase into the 1990s and beyond, cutbacks of fundamental rights, fear of the future and demands for and awareness of freedom coincide. This is the constellation that gives birth to what I have called elsewhere the *ugly citizen*. Where it is necessary to put up with threatened or lost social security in a milieu of perceived political freedom, civic virtues turn ugly and aggressive.

The face of the second modernity will therefore not resemble the ideal image of the citizen in all his or her kindness and beauty. Instead, it will be necessary to bid farewell to wide-eyed hopes for an ideal marriage of self-organization and reason, not out of some culturally pessimistic sense of inevitable failure, but as an ever present possibility. This loses its terror when one sees that precisely the abuse of freedom is freedom's most reliable indicator.

Anyone who would like to know how free a country and its people are should not look only at the constitution and should leave debates in parliament and governmental programmes aside. Instead, attention should be paid to how people behave with respect to excesses of freedom (pornography, criminality by 'foreigners', violence among young people); if they react with composure, then freedom is in good hands.

It is a simple statement, but nonetheless true: freedom also has an ugly side. This is not a refutation, but a proof of freedom, of its really human, that is to say fallible, dimension.

Political Responses

Neoliberalism, Communitarianism and Cosmopolitan Republicanism

What political responses are struggling with one another here? To mention just the keywords: neoliberalism, communitarianism, protectionism.

The neoliberals of the world have most clearly gathered their ranks under the banner of the *market* and are rehearsing an attack on the crumbling foundations of primary modernity, such as the welfare state, the nation-state, trade union power or 'ecological inhibitions on inhibitions on investment'. The consequences are fatal for the individual as well as society, because an antihuman image of humanity is elevated here to the status of a foundation for social intercourse. Social exclusion becomes the rule. Success in the market ultimately decides existence or non-existence. Consequently, adaptation becomes the highest goal of character formation. The political concept of society fades or disappears.[21]

The French sociologist Pierre Bourdieu recommends that anyone professing allegiance to neoliberalism be set down by helicopter in the ghettos of the outcasts in North and South American cities. He is certain that, after at most a week, such a person would come back as a convert to the welfare state.

The opponents of the neoliberals, the *communitarians*, march against the flag of the market with that of the *community*, and most powerfully, interestingly enough, in those countries where neoliberalism has raged the longest and most devastatingly, namely the USA and Great Britain. Markets and contracts, according to the intellectual code here, do not create any social cohesion in and of themselves. They require and use up the active identification of citizens with their communities as 'social mortar'. In that sense, the communitarian movement can be understood only as a movement in opposition to the 'neoliberalism of greed'. But while the new idolizers of the market *act*, and very effectively at that, the communitarians are satisfied in essence with *cosmetic measures*. They are attempting in the final analysis to exorcize the evil of egoism with a sanctimonious rhetoric of community spirit, a home remedy from grandma's medicine cabinet which, as we know, costs nothing and is worth every penny.

Many communitarians confuse moralizing with analysing. They forget that there is not just the danger of too little community, but that of too much as well, as the history of Germany in this century notably attests. The German-born American historian Albert O. Hirschman writes:

> During the Weimar Republic there was often complaining in Germany about the lack of certain social qualities that a society was supposed to have according to the understanding of the times. A sense of mission, a feeling of belonging together and a certain warmth – in short, community spirit – were missed. The Nazi movement owed its success in no small part to its promise to satisfy these alleged 'needs' in abundance by creating a newly strengthened *Volksgemeinschaft*.[22]

The majority of communitarians take the existing institutions as a constant and thus fail to see that these are being changed down to their very foundations by reflexive modernization.[23]

The (still) silent majority of *protectionists* is meandering aimlessly in the no man's land between the neoliberals and the communitarians. Despite widely varying political objectives, the protectionists are united in the attempt to defend the old worldview and order of battle intellectually and politically against the onslaught of the realities of the second modernity. Beneath the surface layer of agitated debates on globalization, an all-party coalition of protectionism is forming. The conservative protectionists bemoan the decline of values and the loss of significance of the national. The left-wing protectionists are shaking the dust out of the old costumes from the class struggle just in case they might be needed. The green protectionists are discovering the charms of the nation-state and its range of weapons for defending environmental standards against the encroachment of the global market.

The irony is that Germany, occupied with itself and the problems of unifying West with East Germany, has thus far largely slept through these warring solutions: neoliberalism, communitarianism and protectionism. Rather than hopping on a train that other countries are already leaving, it could therefore now tie together opposing movements, articulate them and convert them into practical politics. I would like to call this continental European position the cultural policy of a *cosmopolitan republicanism* and characterize it by five principles.

First is the new significance of the *individual*, with whom the right and the left, all varieties of communitarianism and the environmental movement have such difficulties. Second is the centrality of *cosmopolitan* agents, identities, networks and institutions. Third (and only apparently contradicting this) is the new significance of the *local*, the magic of place in world society. The two latter aspects run deeply against the grain of those who view the national and the nation-state as the *non plus ultra* of (primary) modernity. Fourth, there is the crucial significance of *political freedom*, that is, an active civil society, for the cohesion and self-responsibility of democracy beyond labour society, as well as for how it might become possible to respond to the ecological crisis. Fifth is the concluding insight that derives from all of this, the necessity for deep-seated *institutional reforms*, indeed a reformation of primary industrial modernity that would affirm diversity and 'cultivated conflict' (Helmut Dubiel). A few explanations of these points will be given using the example of municipal politics.

The Redefinition of the Local in the Age of Globalization

In the late 1930s, two Jewish émigrés in Paris are discussing their plans. One wants to emigrate to Uruguay. 'So far away?' asks the other in astonishment. 'Far away from where?' the first man replies. The fate of the rootless, the homeless and the stateless bursts forth in this question, as Hannah Arendt has depicted so incisively. Especially in global society, the citizen needs an (imaginary) place. But the problem of what that means is now coming up again, since place must be defined directly and autonomously in global society, while the national framework loses its significance.[24]

'City' and 'citizenship' have more than just an etymological kinship. Civil society and political freedom have their social origin and their locus in a tangible local area. Strengthening civil society therefore implies strengthening local politics and identity, strengthening cities against the national centres. Large cities can no longer be just destinations in a shunting yard of the great problems. Everyone shifts everything imaginable and unimaginable on to cities and there is even a lovely word for it: the mature citizen.

The revaluation of the local as a response to globalization will therefore not be possible without reform of, for instance, municipal finances and a revised distribution of power and problems between national and local politics. Are there models and conceptual targets for this in political philosophy and theory? Indeed there are.

If one asks us Germans for our admission ticket to the democratic age, we do not have a French, an American or even an English revolution to show off, but we do have Immanuel Kant. Our revolution occurred in the realm of thought, bears the noble name of *Critique of Pure Reason* and can gather dust on bookshelves. If one blows away the dust and begins to read, one notes with some displeasure that, to put it ironically, Kant, our officially licensed philosophical revolutionary, was outside the boundaries of our constitution. He took on himself the freedom to label parliamentary democracy 'despotic', because the principle of representation contradicts the self-determination of the individual. 'Among the three forms of the state, democracy, in the strict sense of the word, is necessarily a despotism,' because it is the foundation for an executive power in which '*all*, who indeed are *not all*, *decide* against one who agrees or dissents, which is a contradiction of the general will with itself and with freedom.'[25] This is the German way of revolution led by its 'purest reason'.

I consider this contrast between national majority democracy and a cosmopolitan republicanism of the local to be one of the crucial themes being placed on the agenda in the transition to the second modernity by a grand coalition of necessity and reason. The shrinking labour society, the overburdened and unaffordable welfare state, but also the terrible efforts, in the truest sense of the word, that are demanded of us all to alleviate the ecological crisis in that new focus of globalization, all of these overtax the nation-state and institutionalized politics based on it. How then can the political system – parliament, parties, government – be unburdened and how can the self-responsibility of civil society be supported and expanded? How can these two sites and regulative agencies of politics share the load of future problems and power and still be attuned to one another? No one will be able to avoid this question. The answer is: only by upgrading the local area of democracy, the towns and cities.

All this presumes, among many other things, a repoliticization of municipal policy, indeed a rediscovery and redefinition of it by mobilizing programmes, ideas and people to make the incomprehensible and impossible real and possible, step by step.[26]

I am afraid that civil society is in such poor repute among politicians partly because it does not meet the efficiency standards of a professional politician. A rational-democratic self-misunderstanding of politics lies concealed here and must finally be expressed. Politics must not be merely rational in a democratic society, it must also be emotional. Efficient solutions are important, but so are passions, the ability to listen, justice, interests, trust, identities, and conflict when necessary; these involve, moreover, materials that are objectively so complex that the concept of the single optimal path which still haunts so many minds is completely illusory.

Politics is language, language is politics. Someone who wishes to inspire must speak inspiringly. This reveals a close relationship between art and politics. Language is what has remained for us. *Community spirit*, which many obviously miss so painfully, is formed only in the symbols created and reaffirmed in public speaking and listening. That is why the technocratic plastic speech of so many politicians is a cancer on democratic culture. Language is the site and the medium for creating and caring for the social sphere. We live in language. And who would care to live in the utterances of politicians? Not even politicians themselves, I fear.

Like so many other things, it has become unclear what really constitutes a 'city'. The criteria for creating an identity, such as a river, a group of historic buildings, the seat of government, a cathedral or other features that refer to a specific geographical point, have lost meaning because of the intensification of mobility, travel and information. Even cities can no longer rest in the security of a firmly emplaced geographical identity. They must be reinvented, as it were. Inventing does not mean designing on a draftsman's table; the public image of a city, its identity, which determines so many other things, must instead be created, shaped and coloured as a magic intoxicated with and tested by reality. Municipal politicians, at least the good ones, are urban magicians who shape the identity of their city, in competition with others, by public stage management, the development of urban projects and urban architecture.

What is considered an attractive and identity-fostering symbol in this regard is by no means arbitrary. An opera house might work, but not a six-lane multilevel highway intersection or a radio tower with a revolving restaurant on top. Low crime rates might be useful, but they do not create magic in and of themselves. A nuclear fusion reactor for research purposes that provokes international mistrust would probably also have the opposite of the intended effect. By the same token, exemplary solutions to urban problems are certainly capable of developing such a magical attraction. One need only think of the idea of a zero-emission industrial park, in which factories are so interlocked that one reuses the wastes of another, as has been done in the United States. In this way, the frog no one wanted to kiss turns into a sought-after prince.

On Curiosity about the Unknown Society in which we are Living

Two epochal processes above all others, individualization and globalization, are changing the foundations of living together in all spheres of social action.[27] Both only superficially appear to be threats; they force but they also permit society to prepare and reshape itself for a second modernity. People are not to blame for the immobility; indeed it is essential to recognize that cultural individualization and globalization create precisely that historical orientation and those preconditions for an adaptation of institutions to a coming second modernity that are obstructed by the institutions (or those controlling them). The problem is obstacles in perception. Thinking has to change.

The conservative bemoaning of the decline of values (in all social camps) is not only self-righteous, it is also stricken with historical and empirical blindness. In Germany we have managed to put two dictatorships behind us, both of which stood under the motto: 'You are nothing, your class is everything.' Against this background, the amount of individualization that has been achieved is a decided advance. This is all the more true since it is completely false to equate individualization with unpolitical behaviour, indifference and egoism. Instead, the conceptions of what is political and what is not are changing. We are dealing with 'freedom's children', for whom the traditional patent remedies for living together (in marriage, parenthood, family, class and nation) have lost their practicability.

The two key concepts that characterize the situation after the collapse of the East–West enemy stereotype in what is now 'democracy without enemies' are *ambivalence* and *vacuum*. Ambivalence designates the simultaneity of relief and fear, initiative and fear. The loss of clarity is the paralysing thing, intellectually and politically. In quite superficial terms, there has never been such a remarkable increase in the number of liberal democracies, in the East but also in the south of the world. It is too quickly forgotten that a thoroughly militarized system of orthodox communism imploded *peacefully*. At the same time, however, nationalism, wars and civil wars have re-erupted everywhere. In Europe, the madness of 'ethnic cleansing' is winning victories and founding states. Even dyed-in-the-wool pacifists find themselves forced to reconsider the connection of freedom, human rights and war. Is there a right or a duty to go to war when human rights are being barbarically violated? Where does this have a limit? In Europe? Are genocides in Africa and Asia in the blind spot of this new 'global domestic policy'? Will we have to choose in the future between two unbearable alternatives, shocking indifference or global wars for human rights?

Vacuum means that even the victorious institutions of the West, NATO, the free market, the welfare state, multiparty democracy and national sovereignty, can no longer be taken for granted historically; indeed, they have lost their historical foundations. What is NATO without its anticommunism? The growth economy and consumer society with the knowledge of their ecological destructiveness? The welfare state in the global competition of the world economy and in view of the erosion of the old standard labour relationship? Multiparty democracy without its milieu of social and moral consensus? The nation-state in the network of global economic, ecological and security policy dependencies?

Taken together, ambivalence and vacuum mean that the system is not simply hopeless, it is also more open than ever, intellectually and politically.

Notes

1 Quoted in *Frankfurter Allgemeine Zeitung*, 4 June 1994. In a letter to the editor of the *Süddeutsche Zeitung*, Kamphaus has subsequently attacked the misinterpretation of his essay as cultural criticism and pleads for an understanding of freedom's children.

2 A. de Tocqueville, *Democracy in America*, New York: Knopf, 1945, p. 591.

3 This view is also directed against the brilliant argumentation of Lash (in U. Beck, A. Giddens and S. Lash, *Reflexive Modernization*, Cambridge: Polity 1994), where he consistently inquires into possibilities of post-traditional 'reflexive community formations', but does not mention or consider the ancient and highly modern tradition of a political Europe of individuals.

4 See, for example, U. Beck, 'The democratization of the family, or the unknown art of free association', in U. Beck, *Democracy without Enemies*, Cambridge: Polity, 1998, Chapter 6.

5 See U. Beck, 'The renaissance of politics in reflexive modernity: politicians must make a response', in ibid., Chapter 8.

6 See H. Wilkinson, 'Kinder der Freiheit', in U. Beck (ed.), *Kinder der Freiheit*, Frankfurt/M.: Suhrkamp: 1997.

7 Quoted from 'Opas Tante', *Der Spiegel*, 43, 1996, pp. 41f.

8 The example of the United States shows, however, that it is difficult to determine the limit where loss of membership (or failure to turn out to vote) becomes a threat to the continued existence of the political system.

9 R. Wuthnow, 'Active compassion', in Beck, *Kinder der Freiheit*. See also H. Wilkinson, 'Kinder der Freiheit', in ibid.

10 Similarly, W. Dettling ('Und der Zukunft nicht zugewandt', *Die Zeit*, 30, 1994) describes how the 'culture of helping' has changed: 'The volunteer fire brigade and the army, parties and charitable organizations certainly still represent social activities, but there is a growing number of (young) people whose social commitment overshoots these offers and seeks other forms. They do not want to become the executive organ of some set ideal of service (Gerhard Schmidtchen). Today it is a different group of people who become social activists.'

11 Barbara Sichtermann in a commentary on North German Broadcasting (NDR), Hamburg, September 1995.

12 See U. Beck, 'The democratization of the family'.

13 'Increasing individualization does not demolish solidarity relationships wholesale; it creates a new type of solidarity. It is exhibited voluntarily and not so much from a sense of obligation. It is also less inspired by a morally charged pathos of helping. The price of a high degree of self-determination and a diversity of opportunities appears to be a loss of orientation. This in turn leads to a demand for binding social networks that create a sense of belonging and a meaning in life.' (H. Keupp, 'Solidarisch und doch frei – für eine kommunitäre Individualität', *Psychologie Heute*, 7, 1995.)

14 Hondrich and Koch-Arzberger write: 'But where the compulsoriness of power, the cold contractual character of the market, the emotional elevation of love and the kind condescension of unilateral help do not suffice or are not accepted and lose their binding force, that is where solidarity finds its place as a binding and regulating force of a unique type. More emotional than contracts but more sober than love, it does not dissipate itself in selfless charity, but assumes mutuality of support at least for an indeterminate future. It is inspired by the idea of some sort of equality between givers and receivers, despite the differences between them and their mutual distress, it originates voluntarily and can be dissolved the same way.' K. -O. Hondrich and C. Koch-Arzberger, *Solidarität in der modernen Gesellschaft*. Frankfurt/M.: Fischer, 1992, p. 114.

15 See H. Klages, 'Der schierige Bürger', in W. Weidenfeld (ed.), *Demokratie am Wendepunkt*. Berlin: Suedler, 1996.

16 From an interview on South German Broadcasting (SDR), 13 November 1996.

17 See R. Hitzler, 'Der alltägliche Machiavellismus'. Forthcoming, Munich: (manuscript, 1996).

18 Z. Bauman, 'Wir sind alle Vagabunden', *Süddeutsche Zeitung*, 10 September 1996.

19 D. Yankelovich, 'Wohlstand und Wertewandel – das Ende der fetten Jahre' (extract from a report to the Clinton administration), *Psychologie Heute*, 3, 1994.

20 See 'Der alltägliche Machiavellismus', op. cit.

21 On the contradictions of conservatism, see A. Giddens, *Beyond Left and Right*. Cambridge: Polity, 1994.

22 *Leviathan*, 2, 1994, p. 283.

23 See U. Beck, *The Reinvention of Politics*, Cambridge: Polity, 1996; and Beck, Giddens and Lash, op. cit.

24 See M. Albrow, *The Global Age*. Cambridge: Polity, 1996.

25 I. Kant, *Zum ewigen Frieden*, quoted here from *On Perpetual Peace and Other Essays*. Cambridge: Suhrkamp, 1983, p. 207 [emphasis added].

26 See Beck, 'The renaissance of politics', op. cit.

27 On controversies regarding the challenges of 'global society', see U. Beck, *What is Globalization?* Cambridge: Polity, 2000.

Translated from the German version, **Freedom's Children: Wider das Lamento über den Wertezerfall**, in Ulrich Beck, *Riskante Freiheiten, siehe oben*. Published here, in English, by kind permission of Suhrkamp Verlag, Frankfurt.

13

Freedom's Fathers

The Age of Equality: Alexis de Tocqueville

However sudden and momentous the events which we have just beheld so swiftly accomplished, the author of this book has a right to say that they have not taken him by surprise. His work was written 15 years ago, with a mind constantly occupied by a single thought – that the advent of democracy as a governing power in the world's affairs, universal and irresistible, was at hand.

These two sentences are a quotation, written not in the heady days of 1989 to celebrate the collapse of the Berlin Wall and the despotic Communist regime, but in the year 1848 as a triumphant opening to the 12th edition of Alexis de Tocqueville's *Democracy in America*.[1] When I read them, however, the same paradoxical feeling occurs to me that I have when I reread the whole book: one of being enlightened about the most recent miracle of history by something written a century and half ago.

'The gradual development of the principle of equality', de Tocqueville wrote in the original introduction, 'is a providential fact. It has all the chief characteristics of such a fact: it is universal, it is durable, it constantly eludes all human interference, and all events as well as all men contribute to its progress.' Does this mean that equality asserts itself not because human beings assert it but because it *escapes* their power? Is de Tocqueville claiming that democracy is an unintended side-effect of all attempts to check it? Yes, he is. 'The whole book that is offered here to the public has been offered under the influence of a kind of religious awe produced in the author's mind by the view of that irresistible revolution which has advanced for centuries in spite of every obstacle and which is still advancing in the midst of the ruins it has caused.'[2]

De Tocqueville, who in Germany is usually copied out at length as a cultural critic of democracy, saw before him something which is today often overlooked: that, in the democratic age, religious themes from Christianity and Judaism combine with others from ancient Greek philosophy in a virtually unstoppable modern political movement. Or as he put it: 'To attempt to check democracy would... be to resist the will of God'[3] – which for him is not an overblown analogy but the most succinct way of expressing his theory of democracy. He wanted to show the overwhelming power that is concealed in European modernity and its principle of individual self-organization. This basic theme of political freedom always goes unrecognized when people are sure of freedom; it develops its hugely subversive force when it is withheld from them.

At the same time, de Tocqueville is in no doubt that the idea of political freedom endowed with power of its own is nothing but empty sentimentality, which has been refuted in the most terrible way down the centuries. It is precisely he who looks ahead with such clear eyes and sees the despotism of the democratic age:

> I seek to trace the novel features under which despotism may appear in the world. The first thing that strikes the observation is an innumerable multitude of men, all equal and alike, incessantly endeavouring to procure the petty and paltry pleasures with which they glut their lives. Each of them, living apart, is as a stranger to the fate of all the rest; his children and his private friends constitute to him the whole of mankind. As for the rest of his fellow citizens, he is close to them, but he does not see them; he touches them, but he does not feel them; he exists only in himself and for himself alone... Above this race of men stands an immense and tutelary power, which takes upon itself alone to secure their gratifications and to watch over their fate. That power is absolute, minute, regular, provident, and mild. It would be like the authority of a parent if, like that authority, its object was to prepare men for manhood; but it seeks, on the contrary, to keep them in perpetual childhood: it is well content that the people should rejoice, provided they think of nothing but rejoicing. For their happiness such a government willingly labours, but it chooses to be the sole agent and the only arbiter of that happiness; it provides for their security, foresees and supplies their necessities, facilitates their pleasures, manages their principal concerns, directs their industry, regulates the descent of property, and subdivides their inheritances: what remains, but to spare them all the care of thinking and all the trouble of living? Thus it every day renders the exercise of the free agency of man less useful and less frequent; it circumscribes the will within a narrower range and gradually robs a man of all the uses of himself... I have always thought that servitude of the regular, quiet, and gentle kind which I have just described might be combined more easily than is commonly believed with some of the outward forms of freedom, and that it might even establish itself under the wing of the sovereignty of the people... Every man allows himself to be put in leading-strings, because he sees that it is not a person or a class of persons, but the people at large who hold the end of his chain.[4]

Are both communism and consumerism expressed in this? Who in the old West does not glimpse in this picture the society in which he or she lives?

De Tocqueville, then, is anything but a romantic democrat. Here is an aristocrat who, with wistful detachment both from the values of faded aristocratic rule and from those of the nascent democratic age, climbs to a vantage point from which to discern the traces of the new. This curiosity without illusions of someone passing through no man's land puts him in a good position to say more things of substance about Europe after the end of the East–West conflict than we hear from all those who jabber on about the various 'ends' (of history, democracy, the nation-state, politics, solidarity, decency and public spiritedness). De Tocqueville tries to release and draw out the categories of the new age from beneath the certainties of the old decayed world. In doing this, he creates a language in which the democratic age can observe, judge and criticize itself. It is the sceptical gaze of a non-democrat sympathetic to democracy which we find so fascinating.

The End of the Alien

We late democrats of little faith, we democratic atheists who think we know all the tricks, learn from de Tocqueville that democracy is more ancient than our own particular branches and more powerful than our own weak capacity to sustain and develop it beyond the intermediate stage of the national state. What does he regard as the basis of the superior strength of the democratic age?

The living conditions of various nations, classes and individuals are becoming increasingly similar. In the past, different continents, cultures, ranks, trades and professions inhabited *different worlds*, but now they more and more live in one world. People today hear similar things, see similar things, travel back and forth between similar places for the daily grind. Of course, the contrasts between rich and poor are growing. But in the course of modernization, which embraces more and more countries and niches around the world, these contrasts themselves become more alike. Any extension of education and training promotes such change. Any improvement in transport promotes it. Science and technology promote it. The globalization of the economy promotes it, as does the emergence of global telecommunications networks.

The birth of equality means the end of an economy where everyone is different, the end of a system where people are enclosed in their differences. A new way of perceiving alterity has emerged which is completely new for everyone and rests upon an opening up of how people identify one another. One gives the orders, okay – but it must be clear that it could just as well be the other. Superiority no longer rests upon superiority in *kind* – in race, nature, origin, divine choice – but must be exercised and earned under conditions where it can in principle be taken by someone else.

In the global rivalry between cultural alternatives, everything must be debated out before it is selected and established. Whether it is a question of celibacy, scientific truth, the nuclear family, the white, male, heterosexual understanding of civil rights or the priorities of economic growth and a professional career, the mode in which they are established is changing from internal to external discursiveness. For traditions are losing their circular self-evidence; they can be substantiated only by passing through each other, so to speak, only through the change of perspective that comes with distance. In the everyday global collision of mutually exclusive certainties, everyone one must – or, more cautiously, should – step outside himself and adopt the other's standpoint, as husband and father, as ecological sceptic or enthusiast, as Central European, as car driver and so on. This self-verification through clashing with others requires a huge change in everyday life and every aspect of social activity and this is another reason for the turmoil and anxiety of this age of homogenization.

The consequences are often a walling off from others, perhaps with guns in hand or, as Anthony Giddens puts it, fundamentalisms of every kind (including in the very milieu of 'enlightened' Western modernity, of masculinity, feminism, market idolization, no-let-up-on-socialism and so on). The demand for a change in perspective is thus turned by moral militancy into its opposite. Although it took a long time to realize it, the age of equality is above all the age of *involuntary global dialogue between cultures* (in a perfectly everyday sense of dialogue) and of a deep resulting loss of security. It signifies not the end of difference but a universal struggle for its recognition.

Occidental Identity

This has its roots first of all in the (often mentioned) alliance between antiquity and the second modernity. For de Tocqueville, democracy does not begin with eighteenth-century humanism. Neither is it essentially linked to the political theories of natural law and social contract which began in the sixteenth century to displace the Church and theology from the centre of culture, then continued in the metaphysical and scientific systems of Suarez and Bacon, Galileo, Kepler, Descartes, Grotius, Hobbes, Spinoza, Pascal, Leibniz and Newton, and finally converged in the seventeenth and eighteenth centuries in the birth of the Enlightenment, Rousseau's *contrat social* and the contractualism of a Puffendorf. The triumphal march of equality, then, does not begin *after* religion and the Church, with the victory of humanism and what Max Weber called 'occidental rationality' (the combination of bureaucracy, law, capitalism and faith in technological progress). It is not borne only by an Enlightenment conception of modernity in which God – as Kant's system has been rather crudely accused of implying – appears as a mere 'parasite of ethics'; every word in the title 'Critique of pure reason' – critique, pure and reason – is a stricture against dogma, metaphysics and ontology. The future of equality, as it first appeared to de Tocqueville for the first time in America in the early nineteenth century, is all these things: critique of pure reason, humanism, social contract, the newly independent rationality of science, technology and bureaucracy. But it is not only these things. It has its roots in the Old and the New Testaments, in the sources of the Jewish and Christian religions, and in the philosophy of ancient Greece. Equality – this is de Tocqueville's central message – is the basic theme that has maintained itself through the ages and the contradictions of European intellectual history. It is the spirit of occidental modernity in which the origin and the future of Europe are associated with each other. In the demand for equality, a religious, philosophical, metaphysical, humanist, romantic and rationalist summation of European culture finds both expression and outlet.

But just a moment! De Tocqueville's contemporary John Stuart Mill already objected that Christian morality was and is a theologians' morality. Its ground is neither the radical egalitarianism of the early-Christian sects which rebelled against the representatives of the earthly power of their time nor what is actually written in the Bible, but rather the medieval orthodoxy of scholasticism. It is less through Christianity than through various heresies that Europe has become a cultural space in which equality and individuality have a relatively high value. The aphorism that equality is an unintended consequence of all attempts to turn it into its opposite may thus even be one of those obliging falsehoods which all experience refutes.

Hannah Arendt also pointed to the sharp break between Christian tradition and political modernity, showing that the phenomenon of a this-worldly justification of political domination was something new in history. The French and American revolutions accomplished a shift from a sacred to a secular basis of legitimation, whose full scope was not at all grasped by those living at the time.

Freedom as the Ability to Begin

The real starting-point for de Tocqueville, however, is that the remedy for the anomalies of freedom is *more (political) freedom*. 'I contend that in order to combat the evils which equality may produce, there is only one effectual remedy: namely, political freedom.'[5] De Tocqueville learnt from the Americans that only the construction of democracy can avert the dangers of democracy.

This thesis – political freedom creates attachments – may be developed *against* communitarianism. Freedom does, of course, presuppose *some* human society; otherwise it would not be possible at all. But it does not presuppose the very society that exists now, even if some claim it to be necessary just because it exists. Political freedom does not presuppose any particular religious or class order – not the community structures of the American Mid-West in the 1960s, not the forms of association and party rivalry prevalent in the 1990s in Germany. These are all 'wishful' necessities, derived from a tendency to perpetuate the status quo. But why do so many moral apostles of communitarianism not take seriously the tradition of political freedoms, which, right from the beginning, has been an intrinsic part of modernity and the source of what is new and creative in it?[6] After all, as Kant said, the survival chances of modernity lie in creative reason.

Politics, Hannah Arendt argued, means essentially *the ability to begin*. But each new beginning 'becomes a miracle when seen and experienced from the point of view of the processes that it necessarily terminates'. Hannah Arendt, that resolute champion of a consistently secular concept of politics, transfers the 'miraculous' from religion to politics. 'A quite extraordinary understanding of freedom and of the power inherent in human liberty finds expression' in the person of Jesus of Nazareth. But 'the human capacity which corresponds to that power, and which, in the words of the Gospel, is able to move mountains, is not will but faith… To consider this miracle as an exclusively religious phenomenon seems to me to rest on a prejudice.'[7]

The implosion of communism restores to the collective memory this 'miraculous power' of political action. The term 'madness' that was everywhere used to describe the dancing on the Berlin Wall makes this quite clear; it was madness as a break with normality and the resulting sense of terror. This is the magic formula with which the huge capacity for renewal inherent in human action is celebrated and exorcized.

What Does 'Equality' Mean?

What then is the meaning of 'the age of equality' in de Tocqueville? It is easier to say what it does not mean. It is not the cancellation of hierarchies or the achievement of material equality (in the sense of an equal income for all, for example). Neither is it the overcoming or abolition of differences between people, in the sense that the same clearly identifiable range applies to what everyone has to wear, eat and say, to how everyone furnishes their home and thinks about the world, in short, to how they conduct themselves. This dystopian confusion of equality with uniformity is still quite widespread, not least because of the absurd misunderstanding that made it a conformist duty in the socialism which is now really no longer existing.

The age of equality identified by de Tocqueville may be understood as the exact opposite: it is the origin of a multiplication of multiplicity; it makes the unexpected, incalculable and unverifiable become the norm that everyone expects – in clothing, opinions, food, speech, affiliations, housing, relationships, political involvement, and all the other attributes of life. Equality severs the pre-dictable connection between the fundamentals of social existence, whereby sociologists can take your education, job and income and say how and where you live, what are your attitudes, affiliations, clothing, make of car or artistic interests.

De Tocqueville, to be precise, speaks not of an age of equality but of an age of likeness. Equality is conceived in opposition to social inequality, and alikeness or homogeneity in opposition to social heterogeneity. The age of likeness is thus perfectly compatible with material inequalities, with multiplicity and non-conformism, domination and obedience, poverty and wealth. What counts is equality before the law and hence the possibility for every citizen to perceive himself or herself beyond the categories of class and status, job, gender, race, religion, appearance, income, unemployment, homelessness and so on and to act politically in accordance with that perception.

The historical originality of modernity as the age of equality becomes truly visible, however, only when one compares it with what it excludes: that is, the ages of heterogeneity. For example, the aristocratic and all previous constitutions defined others as radically other. Social distance and the command–obedience relationship were conceived as eternal by virtue of natural differences between people. The other was considered and treated as alien, in a sense as an absolute stranger. Other (natural) laws applied to him, so that he was excluded from the laws and certainties of one's 'own' existence. This wall of heterogeneity was insurmountable. Perhaps it could be crossed in the field of cognition, but even there the other remained ultimately in the dark. To put oneself in his place, or even to take his place, was an obscene and blasphemous thought. Ages of hetero-geneity, then, exist in divided worlds (even if master and slave, for example, live under the same roof). Heterogeneity means an *ontologization* of difference, so that likeness comes to signify the *ending* of ontological differences.

In Praise of Heterogeneity

'I shall never accept,' wrote de Tocqueville, 'that people form a society only because they recognize the same leader and obey the same laws. There is a society only when people view a host of things in the same way; when they have the same opinions about a huge number of things; and when the same facts trig-ger the impressions and thoughts in them.'[8] Otherwise 'human opinions [would be] reduced to a sort of intellectual dust, scattered on every side, unable to col-lect, unable to cohere'.[9]

No society can exist without a lively imagined unity of the mind, de Tocqueville argues. 'How could society escape decline if the moral bond did not grow stronger and the political bond grew slacker? And what can be done with a nation that is master of itself and not subject to God?'[10] Thus, only those who recognize divine authority can oppose to human presumption a support that escapes the clutches of themselves. 'For my own part, I doubt whether man can ever support at the same time complete religious independence and entire political freedom.

And I am inclined to think that if faith be wanting in him, he must be subject; and if he be free, he must believe.'[11]

It has often been said, and shown, that religion can create and strengthen the social bond – usually with special reference to the way in which divine perfection transcends domination and inequality. Not only are all equal before God; they are all equally powerless. Since earthly life is but a shadow and the true life begins after death, all that death involves is a change of scene to a kind of supraterrestrial pan-communism.

The ingenuity of religious integration thus lies in the special logic of compensatory exchange: brief earthly misery for eternal heavenly bliss. Cohesion is thus created by the fact that the contractual conditions are unequal for the two parties: human beings are obliged to consent to their misery here below, whereas the promise of salvation can be redeemed only in another life that comes after this one.

This gives religion its power as a source of cohesion. Don't look too closely! Don't compare your situation with that of others! For your earthly misery is only an illusion. The reality is supernatural harmony. People's actual situation vanishes in the mists of transience.

To use a modern terminology, the unity of society is here assured through the derealization of social reality. Justification of the social order involves changing the 'Remember your position!' formula into 'Forget your position!' What are hunger, disease, hate, yearning, injustice, death, murder, war, weariness and cruelty, or even pleasure, passion and human love, when compared with the ineffable bliss that begins with death? The birth defect of democracy is a short-sightedness due to the originating spirit of Christianity. The faith may have been fading, but not the need for a *oneness* to guarantee community and cohesion.

Heterogeneous, ontologically separate worlds contain and sustain a threshold of inhibition, vision and responsibility which may well constitute something like an unquestioning sense of community. *Believed* heterogeneity conserves and pacifies social contradictions by making them acceptable in the pack ice of eternity. The difference between diverse people and heterogeneous people is that the former have a lot of questions and an unquenchable thirst for explanation and justification, whereas the latter can live isolated among each other in the silence of accepted relations of violence and exploitation (which precisely do not appear to them as such). The difference between a bondsman or slave in the Middle Ages and the unemployed, homeless, illiterate or ghettoized in present-day Manhattan, Rio or Berlin is – to be quite blunt about it – that slaves and bondsmen did not have endless trouble explaining to themselves and others why they were in such dire and hopeless straits. This need for justification was eliminated, as it were, by Church dogma.

In our own world, the rich derive a sense of identity and a confirmation of their self-esteem from the fact that they are seen as responsible for their own success; while poverty is forged as a new set of chains binding the poor hand and foot. This polarity of wealth and poverty does not apply in the unchallengeable realm of heterogeneity. The ontology of difference can be read as a semantics in which various elements – integration, legitimation, foundation – negatively reinforce each other in a kind of 'social cement' that holds opposites together within narrow confines. Here there is no empathy: it is not necessary to think either of those placed below or of those from whom orders and kicks are to be expected; the otherness saves on having to think about others or the consequences for them of one's own actions. Just imagine what a delightful world this is. Someone orders something – and it is carried out!

Misunderstandings of Equality

Three misunderstandings prevent access to the new issues connected with like-ness or homogenization. First there is the *socialist* misunderstanding, based upon a confusion of the issues of likeness with the issues of equality. Second there is a *conformist* misunderstanding, which equates likeness with the end of multiplicity, individuality and variation, when in fact the age of equality is the age of incalculable diversity, subversive incalculability and undifferentiability of individuality.

The 'democratic movement', writes Friedrich Nietzsche in confusing likeness with conformity, is 'the social form of the autonomous herd'. He senses and denounces the fact that things are still developing at 'much too slow and sleepy' a pace for the sick addicts of the democratic herd instinct:

> [This] is attested by the ever more raging howls, the ever more open baring of the teeth of the anarchist-dogs who are now flitting through the alleys of European culture. They are seemingly opposed to the peaceable and hard-working democrats, to the ideological revolutionaries, and even more to the bungling philosophasters and brotherhood-visionaries who call themselves Socialists and desire a 'free society' – but in actuality the anarchists are of the same breed, of the same thorough and instinctive hostility against any social structure other than that of the autonomous herd... They are one with all the others in their tough resistance against any special claim, any special privilege and special right (basically this means they are against all rights, for when all are equal no one needs any more 'rights'); they are one in their distrust of punitive justice... they are one in their religion of compassion, of fellow-feeling that extends to every feeling, living, suffering thing (down to the animal and up as far as 'God': the extravagance of 'compassion for God' belongs to a democratic age); they are one in the shriek, the impatience of their compassion; one in their deathly hatred of suffering as such, in their almost feminine inability to remain spectators at suffering, to *allow* suffering to take place; they are one in the involuntary depression and molly-coddling under whose spell Europe seems threatened by a new form of Buddhism; they are one in their faith in the morality of *commonly felt* compassion as though this feeling constituted morality itself, as though it were the summit, the *attained* summit of mankind, the only hope of the future, the consolation of the living, the great deliverance from all the guilt of yore – they are all one in their faith in fellowship as that which will *deliver* them, their faith in the herd, in 'themselves'.[12]

This wildly malicious scolding of the democratic age gathers together *all* the misunderstandings. Nietzsche confuses the question of homogeneity with those of social equality and inequality (the *socialist* misunderstanding); he equates homogeneity with uniformity in a 'herd movement' (the *conformist* misunderstanding), although in reality the democratic age brings forth subjective diversity.

The third, *humanist* misunderstanding is also present here in pure form. It is true that homogenization is marked by empathy and self-recognition, but it also brings with it beating and biting, hatred and violence – not from a lack of homogeneity but from its very invincibility. Where men and animals and nature are different 'agents' (Bruno Latour), rage grows against the *loss* of heterogeneity.

This background makes it easier to see the historical originality of the second modernity. It is *the epoch in which the ontology of difference is exhausted.* Perhaps it is part of the greatness of a thinker that he can be right even against himself. De Tocqueville sees and – in this respect a true child of his time – invokes three limits of equality: the heterogeneity between men and women (their role being to perform 'as well as possible' and with social recognition the tasks assigned to them in the family); the 'close association of politics and religion'; and the limited malleability of nature. But why should the movement towards equality, whose power de Tocqueville depicts as so overwhelming, stop at just those limits which appeared self-evident in the nineteenth century? To reverse one of his formulations, we might say that the second modernity is the age which compels people to understand everything and to dare everything.

Ideas Towards a Republican Modernity with Cosmopolitan Intent: Immanuel Kant

Now that the unification of the two German states is largely complete, the question arises as to what should be done next. Many intellectuals have ardently denounced the turn away from politics in recent times and been satisfied with the certainty that no bright prospects lie ahead for political endeavours. But now this very certainty is coming to an end and the shape of the future can no longer be viewed from the armchair as something impossible to determine in advance. In Europe's vacuum of ideas at the turn of the millennium, it may be useful to focus again on Immanuel Kant and his vision from Königsberg of a world republic. What do his ideas on republican modernity with cosmopolitan intent mean today? What is their value? Who are their enemies? What are their chances?

Kant speaks of the constitution of the republican state in his philosophical essay *Perpetual Peace.* This title has an ironic sparkle to it, for it appeared in Kant's own time on the signboard of a Dutch innkeeper.[13] 'Perpetual peace' is a place where we meet for a few beers. But along with this inscription, Kant tells us, the signboard also had the picture of a graveyard and he asks whether it applies 'particularly to heads of state (who can never have enough of war), or only to the philosophers who blissfully dream of perpetual peace'. Perpetual peace, then, occurs in inns, graveyards and philosophers' heads. Kant anticipates objections based on defence of the constitution (as we would say today). The author 'will consider himself expressly safeguarded… against all malicious interpretation' that sees 'a danger to the state' in the theorist's 'abstract ideas'. For in fact, he may be allowed to 'fire off his whole broadside, and the worldly-wise statesman need not turn a hair'.[14]

Nevertheless, 'perpetual peace' (in the dual sense of a philosopher's dream and a graveyard) everywhere entices and threatens. The relationship between nation-states is ultimately anarchic in nature, because it has no central court of appeal to bring about peace. It therefore breeds insecurity on all sides, with its fateful cycle of competitive arming. If this anarchy is not restrained, it will lead to 'a war of extermination, in which both parties and right itself might all be simultaneously annihilated [and which] would allow perpetual peace only on the vast graveyard of the human race. A war of this kind... must be absolutely prohibited.'[15]

Kant was already arguing, then, that the threat of human self-annihilation created an obligation to perpetual peace. Whereas the old right of nations (theorized by Hugo Grotius, for example) regulated the conditions of *war*, Kant sketched out a pure right of nations to *peace*. His considerations on perpetual peace had in mind a regulated, law-governed coexistence between states, which would outlaw wars instead of accepting them as an eternal destiny.

In other words, perpetual peace will arise anyway – either as a 'sweet dream of philosophers' or as 'the graveyard of the human race'. So that it should be the former and not the latter, Kant sketched in 1795 a still unfulfilled idea for a republican modernity with cosmopolitan intent, a radical-pacifist pamphlet written in a charming philosopher's German.

In this respect, it may be compared to an essay whose political force (unlike that of Kant's pamphlet) has long been apparent: namely, Henry D. Thoreau's *On Civil Disobedience*. Widely resonant in the American civil rights movement of the 1960s and 1970s, its impact was so great that young Americans opposed to the war in Vietnam sent back their call-up papers to the authorities with a copy of Thoreau's book in which the words 'Mexican war' had been replaced with 'Vietnam war'. Activists invoked Thoreau's name to blockade military transport ships at West Coast ports, and arrested demonstrators read out to policemen and judges his famous statement that prison was for the time being the only honourable place for a morally upright citizen.

Kant's talk of a 'graveyard of the human race' came long before Hiroshima and Nagasaki and before the widespread awareness of a threat of ecological devastation resulting from the industrial onslaught on nature. And yet, more than almost anyone else, his idea went beyond destruction in the physical sense to encompass the erosion of law, of the political and social rights of citizenship, which guarantee such things as individual dignity and freedom of action. The 'perpetual peace of the graveyard' is a danger when basic rights are trampled upon or left devoid of life. A lack of rights is the way not only to war but to barbarism.

The evidence for this view has become so overwhelming in the twentieth century, in the wake of Auschwitz, two world wars, fascism and communism, that Kant's categorical stand in favour of constitutionalism must be considered exceptionally clear sighted. The beginning or the end of civilization will be indicated by the development or the eradication of basic rights. Such rights are not 'granted' but grasped; it is the free union of individuals, the everyday practice of civil society, which grounds and facilitates social coexistence based upon constitutional rights.

This constitutional order grounds the modern community in two senses. First, it converts the state of menacing hostility between people into one in which peace is possible – although this should not be confused with a mature state of peace. The farewell to hostile heterogeneity opens the difficult path of *civil disagreement*, of dispute and argument over the contours and goals of living-together-against-one-another within modernity. Possible peace and fundamental rights are two sides of the same coin.

Second, fundamental rights are the ultimate foundation of social individualization; they open up spaces for action by people who are alike – not the same![16] –
which are in turn the prerequisite for the art of free association to be discovered
and developed. This space for free action is established where the humblest
person has the right and possibility to speak with the most powerful in the
language of equality – that is, not only to face up to him with pride, but to feel
sure that their two situations are, or could become, exchangeable with each other,
to know that his own word and conscience and, if necessary, his resistance to the
superior power of state actors can gain some response. This homogeneity of written civil rights finds its highest expression in the promise not only of equal value
at a level of principle, but of equal influence of the powerless and the powerful,
the individual and the state. As Rosa Luxemburg finely put it, freedom is always
freedom for those who think and behave differently. More, it is freedom for the
powerless in relation to powerful people and apparatuses, freedom for the individual in relation to the majority and the state. The highest expression of this freedom is the fundamental right to civil resistance.

Kant himself linked the farewell to the peace of the tomb to the *universalism*
of the rights relationship. This involves, on the one hand, a graduated system
of rights between citizens of different nationalities, right up to the guarantee of
world civil rights; and, on the other hand, an inward gradation of the content of
various rights. Civilization is (provisionally) protected against barbarism, then,
only if the rights relationship is *globally* valid, in both a horizontal and a vertical
sense. Kant's *Perpetual Peace* refers precisely to this *cosmopolitan* challenge to
national democracies, which is even more topical today than it was 200 years ago
when Kant's essay was written.[17]

At the same time, one finds in Kant a number of half-open, half-hidden references to antinomies of the constitutional freedom of the individual. Fundamental
rights are never guaranteed by the individual, but always by the law-based state
and its institutions of power, which in turn threaten those rights. State power and
the individual are born as twins. Without the state there is no individualization.
More individuality means more of the state. But this also means that state power
is both in one: a source of security *and* of danger to individual rights and freedoms.

This connection between rights, individuals and a public political space may
be illustrated by two extreme historical cases: stateless citizens and the Stalinist
show trials.

In her *Origins of Totalitarianism*, Hannah Arendt opposes the widespread view
that people can claim and achieve human rights simply as individuals. She writes:
'All societies for the protection of the Rights of Man, all attempts to arrive at a
new bill of human rights were sponsored by marginal figures... The groups they
formed, the declarations they issued, showed an uncanny similarity in language
and composition to that of societies for the prevention of cruelty to animals.'[18]
Talk of the inalienability of human rights is thus misleading in a twofold sense:
first, because the right to be human reckons with 'man in general' who does not
exist anywhere; and second, because human rights have their root not in a human
nature or essence but in the human community – or rather, in the rule of law
within a national state which defends them in case of need.

This right to have a right at all is denied to the group of *stateless persons*, so that they fall outside the system of legality. They are the walking refutation of 'pure' human rights, for they live in a bird-like freedom modernized through wars and catastrophes. They live, that is, in a situation without rights; they have ceased to be juridical persons. Political opponents or criminals who find themselves facing the most draconian punishment still move within a legal space in which a connection exists between what they have done and what is done to them. Stateless persons, however, are outside any laws, and there is no inner connection between their situation or their actions and what others do to them. Statelessness means the loss of all means of socially and legally building up one's individuality and politically showing it to advantage; it has 'a desperate affinity with the freedom of the hare in the hunting season'. In a sense, Hannah Arendt remarks, the modern stateless person is excluded from humanity more radically and definitively than slaves, 'who belonged to some sort of human community; their labour was needed, used and exploited, and this kept them within the pale of humanity.'[19]

A civilization that abounds in war produces tribes of placeless barbarians: people without a state who, stripped of all civil rights, are reduced to their mere physical existence. 'The danger is that a global, universally interrelated civilization may produce barbarians from its own midst by forcing millions of people into conditions which, despite all appearances, are the conditions of savages.'[20]

Stateless persons must experience talk of inalienable human rights as a sick joke. The abstract nakedness of their being nothing but human even appears as their greatest danger. Hannah Arendt writes of the fear of those without rights, who still cling desperately to their nationality because it is their only hope of ever being able to live a social existence again. 'Their lack of a relationship to the world is like an invitation to murder, since the death of people who stand outside any kind of legal, social and political references does not have any consequences for those who survive. If they are killed, it is as if no injustice or even suffering is inflicted on anyone.'[21]

Darkness at Noon

The second case is that *active* loss of self, that galloping obedience of self-destruction, which communists demanded from other communists and which was publicly celebrated in the Stalinist show trials. The psychology of communist despotism has rarely been depicted with such clarity and force as in Arthur Koestler's *Darkness at Noon*, whose central character, the convinced communist Rubashov is caught up in the mechanism of the Stalinist purges. But here the true communist is the one who gradually executes his own prosecution, sentencing and elimination. In a dialogue tapped out with the prisoner in the next cell, Rubashov reports a destructive probing of his readiness for self-abandonment:

I AM CAPITULATING.
He waited curiously for the effect.
For a long while nothing came; No. 402 was silenced. His answer came a whole minute later:

I'D RATHER HANG...
Rubashov smiled. He tapped:
EACH ACCORDING TO HIS KIND.
He had expected an outbreak of anger from No. 402. Instead, the tapping sign
sounded subdued, as it were, resigned:
I WAS INCLINED TO CONSIDER YOU AN EXCEPTION. HAVE YOU NO SPARK OF HONOUR LEFT?
Rubashov lay on his back, his pince-nez in his hand. He felt contented and
peaceful. He tapped:
OUR IDEAS OF HONOUR DIFFER.
No. 402 tapped quickly and precisely:
HONOUR IS TO LIVE AND DIE FOR ONE'S BELIEF.
Rubashov answered just as quickly:
HONOUR IS TO BE USEFUL WITHOUT VANITY.
No. 402 answered this time louder and more sharply:
HONOUR IS DECENCY — NOT USEFULNESS.
WHAT IS DECENCY? asked Rubashov, comfortably spacing his letters. The more
calmly he tapped, the more furious became the knocking in the wall.
SOMETHING YOUR KIND WILL NEVER UNDERSTAND, answered No. 402 to Rubashov's
question. Rubashov shrugged his shoulders:
WE HAVE REPLACED DECENCY BY REASON, he tapped back.
No. 402 did not answer any more.'[22]

The difference with the Inquisition and the public burning of witches is the
inwardly assumed, inwardly shifted self-judgement. The individual is not only abandoned without rights to the agents of the totalitarian state; he is actually cast as pro-
secutor, judge, detective and executioner in relation to himself. Thus, his role is not
to defend *his* individual rights against the demands and charges of the state power,
but *voluntarily to carry out the other's judgement on himself*. In every respect this
is the exact opposite of the role of the self-empowered (world) citizen, which Kant
outlined as the premise for a political society within a republican form of state.

A society of political individuals or a political society of individuals is, therefore, paradoxically bound up with *systemic* conditions for individualization, such
as political rights, citizenship rights, but also social and economic rights.[23]

Republican Freedom

Kant's handling of the question of 'perpetual peace' raises two possibilities:
either a descent into barbarism or the development of rational political action. His
wonderfully clear conclusion is that a space for rational political action, in which
inwardly directed tyranny as well as outwardly directed hostility and war become
excluded or at least less likely, can be provided only through the assertion of fundamental civil rights, only through the constitutional definition of the individual
as the subject of such action. The individual, then, is not a primordial category;
individualization does not at all conflict with forms of public political action
geared to the community. Already for Kant, a key question is *how* the communal
character of 'free individuals' is to be secured, which forms, standards and principles are to apply. This, in his view, is the crux of the distinction between the
democratic form of state (which always has a tendency to despotism) and the
republican constitution (which is possible only in accordance with the claims to
self-determination of all contractually regulated action).

In relation to democratic modernity, republicanism crucially asserts that fundamental rights must be conceived and assured not only from the top down but also from the bottom up. It is in political society that fundamental rights are guaranteed as a living reality. There is only one way of really defending political rights – and that is through their use. Unlike in the case of everyday objects of consumption, such rights are not used up through daily appropriation but filled with greater content and life. In case of doubt, it is not parliament, government or competing political parties, or even the constitutional court, which is the guarantor of liberty, but rather the political will and self-confident action of citizens.

Whereas democracy concentrates power (especially legislative power) in the government and subordinates the individual to majority decisions, the republic rests upon a division of labour and power between state and society and thus for the first time establishes the space of a political society of individuals. Not an institutionalized system of rules but a free association of individuals is the guarantee of a republican constitution. Kant's 'first definitive article of a perpetual peace' is accordingly:

> The civil constitution of every state shall be republican. A republican constitution is founded upon three principles: firstly, the principle of freedom for all members of a society (as men); secondly, the principle of the dependence of everyone upon a single common legislation (as subjects); and thirdly, the principle of legal equality for everyone (as citizens). It is the only constitution which can be derived from the idea of an original contract, upon which all rightful legislation of a people must be founded... [in a footnote] Freedom should be defined as a warrant to obey no external laws except those to which I have been able to give my own consent. Similarly, external and rightful equality within a state is that relationship among the citizens whereby no one can put anyone else under a legal obligation without submitting simultaneously to a law which requires that he can himself be put under the same kind of obligation by the other person.[24]

To put this the other way around, we might say that freedom is expressed in the possibilities and even laws, but also institutions of all kinds, which permit the *withholding* of consent – that is to say, in the right to *dissent*. No government or parliament or political party has the right to blanket loyalty. Consent is indissolubly bound up with the consent of one's own rational faculties and one's own conscience. The possibility of saying yes only arises together with and out of the possibility of saying no. Citizens remain unpredictable even in obedience and their unpredictability grows as fundamental rights become an integral part of their lives. We may therefore say that republican modernity is the most unpredictable society of all.

Michel de Montaigne, another independent thinker who lived before Kant, worshipped Epaminondas of Thebes as a symbol of such independence and civil courage. Once, this Theban general and statesman noticed a friend of his in the opposing ranks, leapt from his horse and – oblivious to the battle still raging around them – clasped him in an embrace. Thinking and acting for oneself are, in fact, shorthand for Kant's classical definition of enlightenment. Freedom is blocked by 'the inability to use one's own understanding without the guidance of another. This immaturity is self-incurred if its cause is not lack of understanding, but lack of resolution and courage to use it without the guidance of another. The motto of enlightenment is therefore: *Sapere aude!* Have courage to use your own understanding.'[25]

The republican constitution, Kant argues, necessarily underlies all societies based on the rule of law. But is it also a defence against the threat of perpetual peace? Yes, he replies. For:

> The republican constitution is not only pure in its origin (since it springs from the pure concept of right); it also offers a prospect of attaining the desired result, i.e. a perpetual peace, and the reason for this is as follows. If, as is inevitably the case under this constitution, the consent of the citizens is required to decide whether or not war is to be declared, it is very natural that they will have great hesitation in embarking on so dangerous an enterprise. For this would mean calling down on themselves all the miseries of war, such as doing the fighting themselves, supplying the costs of the war from their own resources, painfully making good the ensuing devastation, and, as the crowning evil, having to take upon themselves a burden of debt which will embitter peace itself and which can never be paid off on account of the constant threat of new wars. But under a constitution where the subject is not a citizen, and which is therefore not republican, it is the simplest thing in the world to go to war. For the head of state is not a fellow citizen, but the owner of the state, and a war will not force him to make the slightest sacrifice so far as his banquets, hunts, pleasure palaces and court festivals are concerned. He can thus decide on war, without any significant reason, as a kind of amusement, and unconcernedly leave it to the diplomatic corps (who are always ready for such purposes) to justify the war for the sake of propriety.[26]

The possibility and actuality of peace always also depend upon who is the potential aggressor. But precisely amid the uncertainty that can always build up through suspicions, threats and rumours (not to speak of hereditary animosities and deliberate propaganda), the opportunities for action contained within the very form of the state play a role that cannot not be overestimated. Kant's distinction between democratic and republican government applies here too. For the point of view of democracy concerns how the people governs or participates in government; and in this respect Kant attributes princely, noble and popular power to autocracy, aristocracy and democracy respectively. But this 'form of sovereignty' is not the same as the 'form of government'. The way in which the state makes use of its supreme power can be 'either republican or despotic'. Republicanism is 'that political principle whereby the executive power (the government) is separated from the legislative power'; whereas despotism bundles the two together, so that 'the ruler treats the will of the people as his own private will'.[27]

But now comes a statement that is hardly to be expected from an 'official philosopher' (to use Nietzsche's term). 'Of the three forms of sovereignty', Kant argues, democracy in the true sense of the word 'is necessarily a despotism, because it establishes an executive power through which all the citizens may make decisions about (and indeed against) the single individual without his consent, so that decisions are made by all the people and yet not by all the people; and this means that the general will is in contradiction with itself, and thus also with freedom.'[28] By this yardstick, even the latest democracy in Germany is *despotic* – and will be all the more insofar as it erodes fundamental rights and invokes 'the will of the majority' against the diversity of individuals.

For the crucial dividing line between despotic (not 'demos-political') democracy and the free republic is the line between the supposed popular will and individual rights and freedoms and thus between the modernity of consensus and the modernity of dissent. Democracy is based on broad forms of social consent that can be summoned up and represented: religious affiliation, status group, class, 'the people', the 'middle ground', the 'majority'. Republicanism, by contrast, starts out not from such units that bind individuals together, but from *the sovereignty of the many*. Here the existence and resolution of disagreement are ultimately the only possible form of consent. Freedom is measured by the freedom to express and act upon a heretical opinion.

In the age of equality, the mere example of failure to conform and bend the knee performs a valuable service. Precisely because the tyranny of the average is so great that eccentricity becomes a flaw, it is desirable that individuals should be eccentric in order to break the tyrannical hold. We can say, then, that the degree of eccentricity is a measure for the spirit of freedom prevailing in a society. When a man does not march in step with his comrades, Thoreau pointed out, it may be because he hears a different drummer – and he should be allowed to go on following the music he hears, wherever it comes from.

Belief in a collective authority ready on call (the authority of classes, the public weal, technological progress, the nation, and so on) clashes with the fact that epochs are more prone than individuals to error and that the prevailing views in each epoch have been considered false and even absurd by later ones:

> If all mankind minus one, were of one opinion, and only one person were of the contrary opinion, mankind would be no more justified in silencing that one person, than he, if he had the power, would be justified in silencing mankind... But the peculiar evil of silencing the expression of an opinion is, that it is robbing the human race; posterity as well as the existing generation; those who dissent from the opinion, still more than those who hold it. If the opinion is right, they are deprived of the opportunity of exchanging error for truth: if wrong, they lose, what is almost as great a benefit, the clearer perception and livelier impression of truth, produced by its collision with error.[29]

For Kant, the language of rights is the language of freedom – the 'lingua franca of democracy' (Agnes Heller). This clearly distinguishes him from Rousseau. He sees that, if political legitimacy results from the will of all, then no free constitution can ever come into being. The hallmark of republican modernity is not the general will but the possibility of a sovereign many who, in Thoreau's phrase, hear and follow different drummers.

These are the three principles of freedom upon which any republic is based: the inalienable and ultimately non-representable freedom of all individuals as members of society; the homogeneity of all persons as subjects; and the independence of each member of the commonwealth as a political citizen. In the first principle Kant argues for the negative (liberal) concept of freedom; in the third for the positive, democratic concept; and in the second for freedom as equality before the law.

On the Idea of an Ecological Republic

For Kant, there is an insoluble contradiction between freedom and happiness. This may serve (both with and against Kant) as a preview for the basic idea of an ecological republic: *freedom unifies, happiness divides*. A more cautious formulation might be that freedom can be lost, but that it can also be increased through use. When freedoms are exercised, both conflicts and the overcoming of conflicts are possible. Anyone who fights for the expansion of political freedoms may be often disappointed, but he or she may also experience an 'individualism of solidarity'. In the matter of bliss, however, there are always distribution conflicts over goods, possession, power and standing – and they are always *negative* sum games. In other words, there is a *growth logic of freedom*, which could mitigate or even overcome the ecological dangers that people inflict upon themselves through economic growth.

The eternal more – or, in old-fashioned terms, the idea of industrial progress – should be turned around so that it applies to the growth not of economic but of political freedom. Instead of a framework of material happiness, there would be one in which the main question is how freedom will be possible, liveable and productive of community? This, in short, is the question of *freedom as happiness*.

Were everyone on earth organized in free republics, everyone would also accept the three principles so splendidly formulated by Kant. This is rather more likely than in Kant's time, if we consider that since the three principles were worked out, they have probably also aroused needs for freedom. The principles qua principles do not define the character of a republic, but they do create the framework in which conflicts over needs and over differing interpretations of freedom can be resolved and they do allow for procedures whereby such conflicts and disputes can be settled through dialogue and negotiation (and not through power and violence). If conflicts both within and between states could be handled in this way, then even Kant's dream of perpetual peace would no longer be a utopia.

But is that dream still worth dreaming? Does it not mean duty-free shopping trips and provision for retirement as the ultimate bliss? In this connection, Nietzsche puts forward an ardent plea for perpetual *discord*.

Creative Individualism – Knowledge is Creation: Friedrich Nietzsche

If it is true that the Enlightenment cannot be refuted because any attempted refutation ultimately serves to confirm it, then it may be said to have in Nietzsche one of its greatest confirmers. His passion for freedom made even the Enlightenment suspect in his eyes as a substitute for action, as ersatz freedom, as a secularized Inquisition.[30] 'The categorical imperative reeks of cruelty.'

What is Nietzsche doing in a discussion of freedom's fathers and freedom's children? He is one of the freest minds in the German language:

> At home, or at least a guest, in many lands of the spirit; escaped many times from the stuffy pleasant corners into which preference and prejudice, youth, origin, accidental meetings with men and books, or even the weariness of our

wanderings have seemed to pin us down; full of malice against the bait of dependence that lies hidden in honours or money or offices or sensuous enthusiasms; grateful even for distress and vicissitudinous disease because it always frees us from some kind of a rule and its 'prejudice'; grateful to God, the devil, the sheep and the worm in us; curious to a fault; investigative to the point of cruelty; with impetuous fingers for the impalpable; with teeth and stomachs for the indigestible; ready for any trade demanding sharp-wittedness and sharp wits; ready for any venture thanks to an excess of 'free will'; with fore-souls and back-souls whose ultimate intentions are not easily fathomed; with foregrounds and backgrounds that no foot can explore to the end; concealed beneath cloaks of light; conquerors, though we may look like inheritors and wastrels; arrangers and collectors from early till late; misers of our wealth and our full stuffed drawers; economical in learning and forgetting; inventive of schemes; occasionally proud of tables of categories; occasionally pedantic; occasionally night owls of work in the midst of daylight; scarecrows, even, when necessary – and today it is necessary insofar as we are the born, sworn, jealous friends of solitude, our own deepest midnight and midday solitude: this is the type of man we are, we free thinkers! And perhaps you too, you coming new philosophers, perhaps you too belong to this type.[31]

This 'free thinker' moves not only 'beyond good and evil' but also – no less dangerously – *beyond truth and scepticism*. Belief in scientific truth is, in his view, comparable to belief in the Virgin Mary, since it too is based upon the fiction of virgin birth. The children of knowledge are children of God. They are conceived in a pure, bloodless, pleasureless, ideally even subjectless mode, in the absence of their progenitor. Scientific (that is, managed) truth rests upon the error of *designing* the act of knowing as something passive, while at the same time concealing from itself in a sham of dedication and acceptance this birth of knowledge out of a design imprisoned in error. The scientist writes letters to himself as if they have been commissioned by reality and truth; he pretends to be their recipient and calls these written-and-received messages 'knowledge'.

But, Nietzsche continues, the epistemological nihilist also deceives himself. A pessimist is someone who not only says and wills No but does it as well. 'Against such a type of "good will", the will to a real, active negation of life, there is no better-known or more successful soporific or sedative today than scepticism, the gentle, sweet, lulling poppy-juice called scepticism.' Indeed, the sceptic is 'the friend of peace and quiet, the security policeman. "This subterranean 'no' is frightful! Be quiet, now, you pessimistic moles!"'[32] Nietzsche is not only one of the first but still the most determined *constructivist*. 'Today it is dawning on perhaps five or six minds that physics, too, is only an interpretation of the universe, an arrangement of it (to suit us, if I may be so bold!) rather than a clarification.'[33]

Even the civil servant's *Critique* misses the truth. For:

The intellectual, the average man of science, has something of the old maid about him. Like the old maid, he does not understand the two most valuable functions of mankind. To both, as a matter of fact, to both the intellectual and the old maid we concede a kind of respectability, by way of compensating their deficiency... what is the scientific man?... The worst and most dangerous thing of which the intellectual is capable stems from the mediocrity of his type: from that Jesuitical mediocrity which instinctively labours to destroy any unusual man; which seeks to break every tight-drawn bow, or better yet, to slacken it.[34]

> Be on your guard, too, against the learned! They hate you: for they are unfruitful! They have cold, dried-up eyes, before which all birds lie stripped of their feathers. They boast that they do not tell lies: but inability to lie is far from being love of truth. Be on your guard! Freedom from fever is far from being knowledge! I do not believe frozen spirits.[35]

And then comes this sentence: 'He who cannot lie does not know what truth is.'[35]

The comparative of 'critique' is *creative* reason. Critique labours under a twofold misapprehension caused by the apparent self-evidence of that which currently exists. It criticizes what exists, not on the grounds that it is important or even correct to do so, but only because of its power. Subjugation to what exists therefore precedes the critique of it. Here we can see the inner bond between importance and reality, which are two sides of power.

But critique serves what currently exists also in the sense that it only criticizes and does not *replace* it. The creation of something new, on the other hand, develops its own field of force and power. A critique of what exists is entailed in the living contradiction between things currently taken for granted and the new certainties – or the light that these cast upon matters. At the same time, however, the amazing new alternative brings pressure to bear on the existing system of beliefs, putting it to the test both intellectually and politically. A new thematic forcefield, a new source of light, makes its appearance. The very existence of the alternative, with all its charm and eroticism, leads to all kinds of love trading, divorce and remarriage, perhaps opening up new insights and prospects along the way. *The comparative of critique is the besieging of what exists with provocative alternatives.* Creative reason – or, in the jargon of the contemporary philosophy of science, *active* (not reconstructive) constructivism aimed at the central nervous system and the heart of the age – redeems the promise of independent thought.

There have been and still are individuals who break the magic spell of custom. Nietzsche's life and work are just one reminder that nothing has ever been done that someone has not been the first to do and that every good thing in existence is the fruit of originality which at first was usually mocked, often hated and persecuted. In this sense, Nietzsche's talk of 'the death of God' means death of the *inner* god, of *self*-subjection to authority per se; it means post-religious self-affirmation, as opposed to Christian self-denial. Nietzsche is not – as many have claimed – conjuring up self-deification, self-idolization, a dance around the golden self. The 'superman' of whom he dreamt refers to two things: to the native affinity between freedom and innovative capacity, such that creative energies are released only when the yoke of authority (God) is broken; and, as a negative consequence, to the gravitational pull of human ordinariness, man's proneness to and love of error.

The superman symbolizes or embodies the huge effort required to break the power of the average. If we understand the superman as a symbol of this feat of self-liberation – or self-animation of freedom, to use a modern idiom – then this also implies the need for a good deal of self-confidence. Nietzsche teaches this self-confidence to secular humanity. What is necessary, then, is a creative redefinition or refoundation of modernity that overcomes its historical narrowness (industrial dangers to itself, national state, international class society). Zarathustra bursts the chains of the past. How? Not through critique but through the sketching of an alternative that is more than alternative, because it questions what exists in the name of the new thinking of the future.

Anyone who wants a different basis must have gone through all the fires of doubt and despair – only then will he be historically weatherproof. But doubt does not establish any structure. A reform of modernity requires the capacity to rethink and repose objectives. This self-legislation – the question of structure – is for Nietzsche essentially a question of *style*, of language, and is therefore bound up with agreement in public. *His* will to power is essentially a will to *linguistic* power.

Nietzsche is a virtuoso of language that no longer merely reproduces. The shaping of language is the shaping of reality; the creation of language is creation of the world. In this sense, Nietzsche supplies the basis of his assertions not after but in the shaping of language. The fascination of language produces its own conviction – a phenomenon long dismissed as 'mere rhetoric'. But this fails to recognize that it is 'creation' which appears in the place of truth and scepticism. Nietzsche's medium is the fascinating word, his catechism 'sentence construction' (Gottfried Benn).

Creative Constructivism

Nietzsche ascribes to Nietzsche this act of free thinking, this creation of the new, which knocks thought sideways. Or, to use his words, he ascribes it to the 'philosophers of the future' (which leaves it unclear whether 'the future' is the object of philosophizing or the location of the philosophers or both). In any case, they will be 'experimenters':

> By the name with which I ventured to christen them, I expressly emphasized their experimentation and their delight in experimentation. Did I do this because, as critics in body and soul, they will love to make use of experimentation in a new, perhaps wider, perhaps more dangerous sense? In their passion for new insight, must they go farther in bold and painful experiments than the emasculate and morbid taste of a democratic century can approve?[36]

In Nietzsche's vision the 'new philosopher' is an inventor, an experimenter, one who does not let himself be intimidated by authority – by the classics, by institutions, religions or other keepers of eternal verities – but freely creates his authority out of himself. This kind of self-empowerment is democractic in a primal sense, even if it clashes with that 'sissy-democracy' whose image Nietzsche constantly had before him. However one considers the revolt of the individual that Nietzsche rehearses in his figure of the 'new philosopher', its spirit is that of a republican Europe of individuals.

Creative constructivism requires qualities that distinguish the creator of structures from the sceptic:

> I mean a sureness as to standards of value, a conscious employment of a single method, a wary courage, an ability to stand alone and be responsible for themselves. But philosophers of this type are not critics... It seems to them no small indignity to philosophy when it is decreed, as happens so readily today,

> 'Philosophy itself is criticism and critical science – and nothing else besides.'
> Let this evaluation of philosophy enjoy the applause of all the Positivists of
> France and Germany (it might even have flattered the heart and taste of Kant –
> let us remember the titles of his principal works!), our new philosophers will
> nonetheless say: Critics are instruments of the philosopher, and being instru-
> ments, are precisely for that reason far from being philosophers themselves!
> Even the great Chinaman of Königsberg was only a great critic... The task itself
> is something else: it demands that he *create values*... But the real philosophers
> are commanders and legislators. They say, 'It shall be thus!' They determine the
> 'whither' and the 'to what end' of mankind – having the preliminary work of all
> the workers in philosophy, the overpowerers of the past, at their disposal. But
> they grope with creative hands toward the future – everything that is and was
> becomes their means, their instrument, their hammer. Their 'knowing' is *creat-
> ing*. Their creating is legislative. Their will to truth is – *will to power*.[37]

In place of the dualism of knowledge and doubt appears the imperative of creative shaping. Or, to use the latest epistemological jargon, the synthesis of truth
and scepticism is *creative constructivism*. Philosophers have hitherto unsuccess-
fully assumed and reconstructed a logic of science; now they have to design it.
The rationality of science is not already there; it is a utopia that has to be facilitated and conveyed through the creation of an image and a normative system.
Philosophers of science have hitherto sought only to explain the world of science,
but now the point is to change it.

Democratization of Zarathustra

This claim is not at all as extraordinary as it sounds at first. In the catastrophic
self-consciousness of the end of the twentieth century, there were many remarkable features but also trivializations of the superman of which Nietzsche would
never have dreamt. Almost everyone carried around a plan to rebuild the world.
So we saw a kind of democratization of Zarathustra. There are managerial
Zarathustras, scientific Zarathustras, ecological Zarathustras, perhaps even feminist Zarathustras.

You had only to open any page in a newspaper to see the spirit of upheaval
haunting the world: everything had to be turned upside down or downside up; we
were all at our wit's end; X, Y or Z will fall apart if things go on like this; in the
year two thousand and something, such and such a cause will bring about such
and such a situation: whether it is the population explosion (one can hear, for
example: 'Children are weapons, life is war!'), or climatic disasters, or the
destruction of work, the ozone hole, poisoning of the food supply, raw unadul-
terated capitalism or some other heartwarming piece of news. Recently I have
been able to watch one of these 'peddlers of the West's decline' (Karl Kraus)
doing his lecture work behind the scenes. It was a chef's special of hopelessness.
Knowledge of danger lends authority: it makes men into supermen. As endgame
scenarios were announced with the joy that comes from an awareness of decline,
every last hiding place was broken open and exposed to the refinements of
despair. But once he had snuffed out the last ray of hope, he ended the performance with sadistic charm by offering a final note of hope.

People respond in the most contradictory ways to forebodings of disaster. Most
common is a neanderthal type of 'adjustment reaction', as if to news of a ruined

summer. In the face of an inevitable end, a crocodile skin of indifference is developed against the cruel news.

But there is also a reaction that might be described as straightforward schizophrenia: to be an ecological convert in one's mind and a walking chemicals corporation in one's actions.

Then there are the virtuous ones who smelt trouble long ago and poured forth their donations; well-established dangers are almost blank cheques for public spending, on the principle that something must be done to put things right, whatever it costs. Deserts, or anyway man-made ones, can be skillfully turned into sources of money.

Of course, there are also the reformers who thrive on catastrophe. For them, the little red light starts flashing when the news suggests that disaster may *not* be coming. Non-catastrophe is here the ultimate catastrophe.

If truth is not set in advance, then it is elective. Everyone who sees disaster daily approaching must ask what he or she can do about it, unable to take advantage of any truth in itself and compelled to justify one interpretation rather than any other. Is there any point in arranging one's life on the assumption that disaster is imminent? Disaster fatalism can certainly be productive – for example, in overcoming an old faith in activity which has since become a hindrance, and which now, with greater knowledge of the hopelessness of all action, is to be at once excused and cultivated as a youthful transgression.

But the option of pessimism does not exactly testify to a strong passion for the cause of liberty. It is more a reward for intellectual old-age pensioners.

Hopelessness is not exactly a comfortable foundation. But neither is it as bad as its reputation. If one's own efforts are most unlikely to have any prospects, they are also freed of much that is tied up and endangered by efforts which can barely stir themselves when the prospects are good. For example, in a hopeless situation it is not worth writing another sentence, let alone another book; hopelessness punctures vanity. But if the hopelessness is finely measured, even the reservations that make thought small and subservient can be broken down. If everything is pointless anyway, why should one not strive for it without restraint? What could possibly stop one? Hopelessness, perhaps? But that spectre no longer instils fear.

By the same token, the flags do not wave for joy either. Hopelessness is simply a bad occasion for converting or subjugating others. There is no reason to drum anything into anyone. That impulse subsides. How? Into hopelessness.

Moreover, anyone who has experienced hopelessness can no longer be disappointed. Everything that now happens is more than one could ever have dared hope. In this sense hopelessness is liberating, perhaps even encouraging. Anyway, the post-utopia launched by hopelessness is the only one which also offers a hope of overcoming the violence that the lure of utopianism can unleash. It is possible to start something when you have nothing to lose and nothing to gain, when you know that all endeavour is probably in vain. It is the roaming sleepwalkers who pick up the scent when things are beginning to change. Friedrich Schorlemmer, a man with some experience of opposition to the GDR regime, wrote: 'Hopelessness does not frighten us. It was our daily bread.

Everything we wanted and demanded was hopeless.' Only perhaps the end of hopelessness is still a long way off, even now that the Berlin Wall has come down.

The Power of Language or the Role of Intellectuals in the Second Modernity: Gottfried Benn

Gottfried Benn is an artist of language, perhaps the greatest in German of the twentieth century. 'The word is the encounter of creation with itself, its self-movement. In the beginning was the word, and it will be at the end too – what is left of it.'[38] Benn is not what many see in him; he is not a nihilist but someone who believes in language, a priest of the religion of language, a language-utopian, almost a naive language-realist. 'Words, words – substantives! They need only open their wings and the millennia cease their flight.'[39] For Benn, language is not a means of expression but a means of discovering the world, of inventing the world. It is the *only* medium and goal which is left to the age of dissolution. Self-questioning modernity does not have language; it *is* language. 'Sentence construction' is the law of the second modernity. 'Those thinkers with their *raison d'être* that no one sees, completely formless, nothing but contributions, contributors – they turn on the tap and it is mostly some Plato that comes out, then they splash around a little, and then the next one appears in the bath.'[40]

Themes are empty – cultural dross:

> Existential – that is the death blow for the novel. Why work ideas into someone, into a figure or shapes, when there are no longer any shapes? Why invent characters, names, relationships, just when they are becoming insignificant? Existential – that aims backwards, draws a veil back over the individual and ties him down, makes demands which past centuries and generations of descendants were not equipped to fulfil.[41]

Writers 'who are not linguistically a match for their view of the world are called in Germany seers'.[41]

How does the age of dissolution produce community? The answer: through the *art* of free association, takes on a literal meaning in Benn. Language is not only able to explain, analyse and represent; it can also, with the strength of its conviction and the light of its imagery, generate common ground. 'Through words,' writes Benjamin Barber, 'we convey information, articulate interests and pursue arguments, but it is through tone, colour, volume and inflection that we feel, affect and touch each other. We reassure, we frighten, we unsettle, we comfort, we intimidate, we soothe, we hate and we love by manipulating the medium rather than the content of speech.'[42]

Language is always the language of many. It opens or closes space for common feelings and oppositions, for ideas and activities, for the development of oneself and of others. 'My language is the sum total of myself,' writes Peirce, 'for the man is the thought.'[43] He who shapes language, shapes a We. If the definition of democracy as the sovereignty of the many makes sense, it crucially includes sovereignty over language as the socially bonding semantic material of self-evidence acquired through the history of the world:

Democratize language, give each citizen some control over what the community will mean by the crucial terms it uses to define all the citizens' selves and lives in public and private, and other forms of equality will follow. We may redistribute goods and make power accountable, but if we reserve talk and its evolution to specialists – to journalists or managers or clerics or packagers or bureaucrats or statesmen or advertisers or philosophers or social scientists – then no amount of equality will yield democracy.[44]

The art of free association is thus above all else the art of language.

Without art nothing works any more – as Joseph Beuys succinctly put it. The socially creative significance of language gives the term 'art' a new primary political meaning. It is not the artist's intent which is political (it may actually get in the way) but the linguistic nesting places of the social that he or she opens up and moulds. 'The point,' Beuys tells us, 'is simply the principle which many still find hard to grasp':

Art today can no longer be art if it does not go to the heart of our predetermined culture and work its transforming effect there... this means that an art which cannot shape society and act upon its key questions, ultimately the capital question, is not art... Funnily enough, this does not seem like art to most people. They say: he's doing politics! But it can be shown that precisely this is not politics but *formal principle*... This is the crucial point.[45]

As social constructs and institutions are made by people, it is understandable that the art of creating social connections should be first and foremost a linguistic art. In classical antiquity – in Cicero, for instance – this was the seen as the task of rhetoric. But in this early conception, rhetoric as art does not at all simply reproduce situations; rather, situations and things are produced or moulded in the space of language and draw on its various possibilities. Language sets up specific combinations and thus creates the world in time. As is well known, Cicero saw the statesman as the embodiment of the art of rhetoric, understood not only as the art which creates world and self but as the power which opens up the space of human society as a political space, makes it become a political space. Language serves rhetoric as the power which creates and moulds human situations as *civilitas et urbanitas*, by transporting them from the barbarism of isolation into the world of shared forms and meanings.[46]

Lyotard, for example, sees the grand narratives of modern progress as a monolithic language game which contains and releases a totalizing political practice and undergoes a shackling incarnation in the institutions of industrial society.[47] In this sense, language becomes *the institution of institutions* (Schelsky), ultimately the one political meta-institution. 'Its power does not consist only of compulsion; language is also capable of freeing itself from the cage of language in a postmodern, fragmented and fragmentary political practice within the broken and scattered institutions.'[48]

When language and reality become indistinguishable and social connections are actually moulded in language, then, as Gottfried Benn says, reverence becomes the inner law of linguistic action: 'God is form.'[49] This artistic gospel of 'sentence construction' is the coming law:

For in my view, the history of man – his jeopardization, his tragedy – is only just beginning. Until now the altars of the saints and the wings of the archangel stood behind him and there was a leakage from the churches and baptismal fonts over his weaknesses and wounds. Now begins the series of great inescapable disasters that spell man's undoing. Nietzsche will prove to have been no more than a prologue.[50]

Furthermore: 'Ideas kill, words are more criminal than any murder, ideas take their revenge on heroes and herds.'[51]

Fatalism is a Language Disorder

If the moulding of reality becomes the moulding of words, this creates obligations but is also dangerous. 'We will have to learn to live with the fact that words have a latent existence which works like magic on those tuned in to them and enables them to pass on the magic. This seems to me the ultimate mystery at which our weak, overanalysed consciousness, interrupted only by occasional trances, senses its limits.' What does Benn mean by 'latent existence', 'magic' or 'ultimate mystery'? Or rather, *how* will the magic be worked, how will it become workable? What is fascinating here is that, to quote Beuys again: 'Art goes to the heart of our predetermined culture and works its transforming effect' – that is, it poses and gives form and expression to 'the core questions'.

In sociological terms, this means: Who sets the agenda? Who defines the issues and priorities, and how? Who focuses collective attention how and on what? This assumes an ability to speak in a *representative* manner, an ability to listen and to gain access to the public media. At the same time, the 'huge danger of the word' is apparent here, 'its multiple consequences, its inflammatory depths, its activity which exceeds everything that the harmless ions and isotopes could yield by themselves' (Benn).

Is it not the terror of newspeak which threatens here? 'The word itself thrills me, its purely associative motif, without regard to its descriptive character and then I feel quite objectively its quality of logical concept as a selection from concentrated catastrophes.'[52] Benn knows his Pappenheimer: 'Epic *is* a fix. Of course!'[53]

Yet Benn dodges the question of where the taboo areas lie in the fluid transitions between poetry and propaganda. His case for the defence is professional ideology; he wagers on exclusion through artistic talent. 'You can learn balancing feats, high-wire acts, walking on nails – but to position a word in a fascinating way, that you either can or you cannot do. The word is the phallus of the spirit, centrally rooted. Nationally rooted, then. Pictures, statues, sonatas, symphonies are international – poems never.'[54] The linguistic power that someone does or does not have protects against misuse – or so we might hope, together with Benn.

This does not interest Benn, however. His theme is different: 'Style is superior to truth', since 'it carried within itself the proof of existence'. Creative language does not point science or religion towards something lying outside it from which it derives its authority. Rather, the effect, the reality of language has its ground in itself. 'The form of feeling will be the great transcendence of the new epoch, the structure of the second age. God made the first in his image, man the second in accordance with his own forms – the in-between world of nihilism is over. In the first it was causality, original sin, primal sigh, psychoanalysis, resentment and reaction which prevailed; in the second it is plastic principles, constructions within set horizons.'[55]

The word facilitates the 'establishment of connections', 'inflammation of the self'. It has the power to loosen and to put together. The word overcomes frontiers and existences, binds together past and future. 'Botanical and geographical, peoples and countries, all these historically and symbolically lost worlds, here their blossoming, here their dream – all foolishness, all wistfulness, all hopelessness of the spirit becomes palpable from the layers of a representative selection of concept.'[56]

What is decisive is not just the word but its giving of form, the will to power of form, 'the wresting of form from the European collapse'. Social structures are moulded, materialized structures of meaning and language. Of greatest importance, then, is the craftlike work on ideas that is often wrongly described as 'unartistic' – the 'sentence construction' that Benn describes as 'intellectualistic'. 'Intellectualism, historically speaking, is Hegel when he says... that he will recognize nothing in the way of belief which is not justified by ideas. Kant, who separated the world of ideas from the world of experience. Nietzsche, all of him, who more than anyone else depicted the conscious and figurative element, the constructive element of creativity, the element that sets up, demolishes, masters and binds together forms... Intellectualism, then, means finding no other way out of the world than to bring it under concepts, to purify both it and oneself in concepts. This does not belong to any particular political or moral system; it is a basic anthropological impulse.'[57]

Is poetic language not here being confused with political language? The latter is supposed to be unambiguous and to convey information; the former to be ambiguous, to transcend, experiment and revolutionize. Politicians who speak in iambics and know how to display figuratively their innermost thoughts are hardly likely to inspire much confidence.

However great the gulf may be between artistic and political experimentation with language, both agree on one central point: language creates and fashions reality. Words and sentences are the building blocks for those self-evident truths which equip and orientate man's knowledge of the world and action within it.

Kant actively construed this origin as a 'transcendental framework' and removed it from the clutches of those who came after him. 'Transcendentality' is thus a technique of conceptual domination, with which creators of language try to protect themselves from the rebellion of their successors. The sentence constructor moulds self-evident truths which owe their magic, their rousing and contagious effect, precisely to the curious bacillus of self-evidence, but which for that very reason are not recognized as having their origin in the laboratory of language. *Language politics is metapolitics as non-politics.* Through linguistic moulding, the course of thought and action is set in the invisible material of self-evidence.

If everything appears hopeless, meaningless and fragmented, one should really see a language doctor before jumping from the Eiffel Tower. Fatalism is a language disorder. Concepts are empty; they no longer grip and illuminate. The greyness that lies over the world, the routine, the boredom, the melancholy, the inhuman and the superhuman that people choke down inside them, may also have its roots in a verbal mildew. When words die the slow, quiet death of empty repetition, when language is drained of blood, the self-evident truths with their own peculiar self-evidence have become deaf and dumb. The iron cage of serfdom is thus not bureaucracy – that is, as it were, a naively realistic inversion in which bureaucracy is glorified as creating language through its concept – but rather bureaucratic thinking about bureaucracy, which sees itself as the only alternative. That is where the weeping begins. The iron cage of serfdom is the *thinking* of the iron cage of serfdom, with all its attributes of hopelessness, linearity and rationality. If many of today's central social and political concepts preserve dead realities, this is the reason for the dominant sense of *déjà vu*. We keep circling around the past, because we lack the language to give meaning and structure to the new reality that is overtaking us.

The Public Welfare Silence

Questions of style are key questions of the second modernity. Anyone who wishes to create forcefields of action must break the spell of the ruling categories and open up the old-rooted meaning of words, in order to adjust the suggestive effect of language to the changed situation. Reformation of democracy presupposes a reformation of the language of democracy.

This is not at all novel. Different epochs have different key concepts in which the semantic transformations of the political can be read off. It is true that this fundamental change in the meaning or evaluation of words takes place gradually and almost unnoticeably for people alive at the time, but the alteration or even replacement of contents and semantic rings is also an object of literary studies, a result of classical texts and public debate about them.

> Major shifts in ideology and political power are always accompanied by such paradigmatic shifts in language usage – so much so that historians have begun to map the former by charting the latter. The largely negative meaning that the classical and early Christian periods gave to such terms as *individual* and *privacy* was transformed during the Renaissance in a fashion that eventually produced the Protestant Reformation and the ethics of commercial society. Eighteenth-century capitalism effected a transvaluation of the traditional vocabulary of virtue in a manner that put selfishness and avarice to work in the name of public goods... The history of democracy itself is contained in the history of the word *democracy*... *Poverty* was once a sign of moral weakness; now it is a badge of environmental victimization. *Crime* once proceeded from original sin; now it is an escape from poverty. *States' rights* once bore the stigma of dishonor, then signified vigorous sectionalism, then was a code word for racism, and has now become a byword for the new decentralized federalism. *Busing* was once an instrument of equal educational opportunity; now it is a means of destroying communities. The shifts in the meaning of these and a dozen other keywords mirror fundamental national shifts in power and ideology. The clash of competing visions – of social Darwinism versus collective responsibility and political mutualism, of original sin and innate ideals versus environmentalism, of anarchism versus collectivism – ultimately plays itself out on the field of everyday language, and the winner in the daily struggle for meaning may emerge as the winner in the clash of visions, with the future itself as the spoils of victory.[58]

This revaluation of categories should not, however, be thought of as an arbitrary act. 'To be bewildered and unable to write is not the same as surrealism.'[59] In order to break the magic of words and reset their internal clocks, it is necessary to refashion in accordance with rules of one's own the historical system of rules from which the meanings proceeded. Language politics is mining labour. You have to climb down into the massif of self-evidence, hollow it out and burrow through it, be able to live and work under the ground, so that you can scratch up something glittering until it eventually flashes and gleams like a polished ruby that carries its power of persuasion inside itself.

Much as the decline of the world can have its roots in gastric hyperacidity, the fatalism of an epoch can have its origin in an extinct language. Wherever one looks, the problems of the future are first and foremost problems of language, problems of a language that is not equal to the impending challenges and the possibilities they open up. We think in categories of *economic growth*, yet we know that this does not express the public interest but obscures the dangers to it. Anyone who rejoices over economic growth is being hypocritical, and not only privately but also publicly, because no one who is part of this world of ours can suppress the fact that the indicators of economic growth are also indicators of collective self-destruction. But a language which makes this public exists, if at all, only as a language of minorities, not as one carried along by the whole society. The newly minted phrase *sustainable development* is a step in the right direction, although it presses into a verbal formula the very contradiction that has to be resolved: development (economic growth) *and* sustainability (sparing of nature)! How can they go together?

So long as this contradiction remains insoluble, we are faced in public space with language forms of a *poisoned* commonwealth which hush up and therefore maintain the poisoning. This must be said loud and clear, because the communitarians seem to have stopped listening. There is no language of public welfare. No group, and certainly not the political, economic and scientific elites, can claim the right to speak *the* public welfare language for the future. But this means that the power of language to create common ground is in danger. The crisis of community which many find disturbing is a crisis of language and thought. For there is no sign anywhere of public welfare visions that are capable of becoming part of people's real lives and gaining their consent. On all sides things are suppressed or the old is conjured up again. The first necessity is to open up and invent the language which will make it possible to remove the national limitations and the progress fatalism of the first modernity and to pose and debate the issues of a second global modernity in a dialogue of cultures. The further development of democracy requires a worldwide opening of its languages to one another and to the issues of 'homogeneity' in the single world.

That language defines the horizon of modernity, is one of its basic insights and convictions. What Nietzsche and Benn added was the will to power of language. Is language power only a word indicating the empowerment of intellectuals, perhaps a kind of professional ideology or disorder? Who would deny it!

But we should not neglect the fact that those who forge concepts to guide people in their lives steer thought and action onto paths of self-evidence whose effectiveness derives precisely from the lack of knowledge embodied in the self-evident. The cosmopolitan reformation of modernity, which Kant already had in mind, is also a reformation of the language of nation-state democracy. Its method might be ironically described as the method of 'as if': to construct sentences *as if* the truth is contained in them; to bite into the word 'apple' so that the juice spurts from it; to eat the printed menu; to be unable to put the word 'disgusting' in your mouth, because the disgust would be unbearable; to scream *pain*; to switch on the word 'light' because it is getting dark. 'Reality – Europe's demonic concept', wrote Gottfried Benn.[60] But this unreal reality, alive and shapeable through language, is now really the only true reality.

Notes

1 The quotation appears on p. lxiii of the Everyman edition of *Democracy in America*, London: Campbell, 1994. The interpretation contained in this article owes a great deal to Marcel Gauchet's 'Tocqueville, Amerika und wir: über die Entstehung der demokratischen Gesellschaften', in U. Rödel (ed.), *Autonome Gesellschaft und libertäre Demokratie*. Frankfurt/M.: Suhrkamp, 1990, 125–206.

2 *Democracy in America*, vol. 1, pp. 6–7.

3 Ibid.

4 Ibid., vol. 2, pp. 318–19.

5 Ibid., p. 105.

6 Important exceptions are the writings of M. Walzer (e.g. *Civil Society and American Democracy*) and R. Rorty (e.g. 'Solidarity or objectivity?'), which themselves are strikingly ambivalent in assigning themselves to the communitarian movement. See also B. R. Barber, *Strong Democracy: Participatory Politics for a New Age*. Berkeley: Univers. of Calif. Press, 1984.

7 H. Arendt, 'Freiheit und Politik', in H. Arendt, *Zwischen Vergangenheit und Freiheit*. Munich: Piper, 1994, pp. 221f.

8 Quoted [and retranslated] from Gauchet, pp. 136f.

9 De Tocqueville, vol. 2, p. 7.

10 Quoted [and retranslated] from Gauchet, op. cit.

11 De Tocqueville, vol. 2, p. 22.

12 F. Nietzsche, *Beyond Good and Evil* (§ 202). Chicago: Hanser Verlag Munchun 1955, pp. 113–114.

13 I. Kant, 'Perpetual peace: a philosophical sketch', in *Political Writings*, 2nd edn., ed. by H. Reiss. Cambridge: Cambridge University Press, 1991, p. 93.

14 Ibid.

15 Ibid., p. 96.

16 See the considerations on de Tocqueville in the first part of this chapter.

17 On this point, see J. Habermas, *Die Einbeziehung des Anderen*, Frankfurt/M.: Suhrkamp, 1996.

18 H. Arendt, *The Origins of Totalitarianism*. London: Allen & Unwin 1967, p. 292; *Elemente und Ursprünge totaler Herrschaft*. Munich: Piper, 1993, pp. 453–70.

19 *The Origins of Totalitarianism*, p. 297.

20 Ibid., 302.

21 *Elemente und Ursprünge*, pp. 453–70.

22 A. Koestler, *Darkness at Noon*. Harmondsworth: Penguin, 1947, pp. 140–41.

23 For a more detailed discussion of this point, see U. Beck, *Das Zeitalter des eigenen Lebens*, Frankfurt/M.: Suhrkamp, 1997.

24 'Perpetual peace', pp. 99–100.

25 I. Kant, 'An answer to the question: "What is enlightenment?"', in *Political Writings*, p. 54.

26 'Perpetual peace', p. 100.

27 Ibid., p. 101.

28 Ibid.

29 J. Stuart Mill, 'On liberty', in *On Liberty and Other Essays*. Oxford: Oxford University Press, 1991, p. 21.

30 As Foucault or Zygmunt Bauman would later describe it.

31 *Beyond Good and Evil* (§ 44), p. 51.

32 Ibid. (§ 208), pp. 126–7.

33 Ibid. (§ 14), p. 15.

34 Ibid. (§ 206), pp. 122–3.

35 *Thus Spoke Zarathustra*, Harmondsworth: Penguin, 1961, pp. 300–1.

36 *Beyond Good and Evil* (§ 210), p. 132.

37 Ibid. (§ 210–211), pp. 132–5.

38 Gottfried Benn, here quoted from *Das Gottfried-Benn Brevier*. Munich: Klett-Cotla und Deutsche Taschenbuch Verlag, 1986, p. 27.

39 Ibid., p. 20.

40 Ibid., p. 60.

41 Ibid., pp. 57, 60.

42 B. R. Barber, *Strong Democracy*, p. 187.

43 Quoted from ibid., p. 193.

44 Ibid., p. 193.

45 Joseph Beuys, quoted from J. Stüttgen, *Im Kraftfeld des erweiterten Kunstbegriffs von Joseph Beuys*. Stuttgart: Urachhaus, 1988, p. 46.

46 See A. Thumfahrt, 'Rhetorische Sprache – Ein Kriterium zur Differenzierung von politischen und sozialen/soziologischen Institutionenbegriffen', in G. Göhler (ed.), *Die Eigenart der Institutionen*. Baden-Baden: Nomos, 1994, p. 226.

47 J.-F. Lyotard, *The Post-Modern Condition*. Manchester: Manchester University Press, 1984.

48 Thumfahrt, 'Rhetorische Sprache', p. 224.

49 *Das Gottfried-Benn Brevier*, p. 18.

50 G. Benn, *Prosa und Autobiographie – Gesammelte Werke in der Fassung der Erstdrucke*. Frankfurt/M.: Fischer Taschenbuch Verlag, 1984, p. 392.

51 *Das Gottfried-Benn Brevier*, p. 19.

52 Ibid.

53 Ibid., p. 57.

54 Ibid., p. 19.

55 Ibid., p. 15.

56 *Prosa und Autobiographie*, pp. 274f.

57 Ibid., p. 385.

58 Barber, *Strong Democracy*, pp. 195–6.

59 Benn, *Prosa und Autobiographie*, p. 140.

60 *Das Gottfried-Benn Brevier*, p. 69.

Translated from the German version **Freedom's Fathers 1,2,3,4**, in Ulrich Beck, *Kinder der Freiheit* (1997). Published here, in English, by kind permission of Suhrkamp Verlag, Frankfurt.

14

Zombie Categories:
Interview with Ulrich Beck

[This interview with Ulrich Beck was conducted in London by Jonathan Rutherford on 3 February 1999.]

JR Your concept of individualization provides a convincing explanation for what is happening in society – the transformation of work; the decline of public authority and increasing personal isolation; a greater emphasis on individuality and self-reliance; the changing balance of power between men and women; a redefinition of the relationship between men and women; a redefinition of the relationship between private life and the public sphere; the emergence of a culture of intimacy, informality and self-expression. You describe it as the 'disembedding of the ways of life of industrial society' (class, family, gender, nation) without re-embedding. Can you explain what you mean by individualization?

UB There is a lot of misunderstanding about this concept of individualization. It does not mean individualism. It does not mean individuation – a term used by depth psychologists to describe the process of becoming an autonomous individual. And it has nothing to do with the market egoism of Thatcherism. That is always a potential misunderstanding in Britain. Nor, lastly, does it mean emancipation as Jurgen Habermas describes it.

Individualization is a concept which describes a structural, sociological transformation of social institutions and the relationship of the individual to society. It is not simply a phenomenon of the second half of the twentieth century. Earlier historical phases of individualization occurred in the Renaissance, in the courtly culture of the Middle Ages, in the inward asceticism of Protestantism, in the emancipation of the peasants from feudal bondage and in the loosening of inter-generational family ties in the nineteenth and early twentieth centuries. European modernity has freed people from historically inscribed roles. It has undermined traditional securities such as religious faith, and simultaneously it has created new forms of social commitment. I use the concept of individualization to explore not just how people deal with these transformations in terms of their identity and consciousness, but also how their life situations and biographical patterns are changed.

Individualization liberates people from traditional roles and constraints in a number of ways. First, individuals are removed from status-based classes. Social classes have been detraditionalized. We can see this in the changes in family structures, housing conditions, leisure activities, geographical distribution of populations, trade union and club membership, voting patterns etc. Secondly, women are cut loose from their 'status fate' of compulsory housework and support by a husband. Industrial society has been dependent upon the unequal positions of men and women, but modernity does not hesitate at the front door of family life. The entire structure of family ties has come under pressure from individualization and a new negotiated provisional family composed of multiple relationships – a 'post-family' – is emerging. Thirdly, the old forms of work routine and discipline are in decline with the emergence of flexible work hours, pluralized underemployment and the decentralization of work sites.

At the same time as this liberation or 'disembedding' occurs, new forms of reintegration and control are created ('re-embedding'). With the decline of class and status groups the individual must become the agent of his or her own identity making and livelihood. The individual, not his or her class, becomes the unit for the reproduction of the social in his or her own lifeworld. Individuals have to develop their own biography and organize it in relation to others. If you take as an example family life under conditions of individualization, there is no given set of obligations and opportunities, no way of organizing everyday work, the relationship between men and women, and between parents and children, which can just be copied.

Alongside the freeing of individuals from traditional constraints, a new standardization occurs through the individual's dependency upon the employment market. This simultaneous individualization and standardization of our lives is not simply a private experience. It is institutional and structural. The liberated individual becomes dependent upon the labour market and because of that, dependent on, for example, education, consumption, welfare state regulations and support; possibilities and fashions in medical, psychological and pedagogical care. Dependency upon the market extends into every area of life. As Simmel noted, money individualizes, standardizes and globalizes.

The individual is removed from traditional commitments and support relationships, but exchanges them for the constraints of existence in the labour market. In spite of these new forms of constraint, individualized cultures foster a belief in individual control – a desire for a 'life of one's own'. There is a paradox here. On the one hand epochal changes are occurring – especially in the area of sexuality, the law and education. On the other – except for sexuality – these changes exist more in people's consciousness, and on paper, than in behaviour and social conditions. This historically created mixture of new consciousness and old conditions sharpens in people's minds the continuing and intensifying inequalities between men and women, rich and poor.

JR What's changing here, people or institutions?

UB I'm talking about zombie categories.

JR Zombie categories? Sociology and horror?

UB Because of individualization we are living with a lot of zombie categories which are dead and still alive.

JR Can you name some?

UB Yes. Family, class, neighbourhood.

JR Zombies are the living dead. Do you mean that these institutions are simply husks that people have abandoned?

UB I think people are more aware of the new realities than the institutions are. But at the same time, if you look at the findings of empirical research, family is still extremely valued in a very classical sense. Sure there are huge problems in family life, but each person thinks that he or she will solve all those problems that their parents didn't get right.

JR You write a lot about the family and relationships.

UB Yes. The family is a good example of a zombie category. Ask yourself what actually is a family nowadays? What does it mean? Of course there are your children, my children, our children. But even parenthood, the core of family life, is beginning to disintegrate under conditions of divorce. Families can be constellations of very different relationships. Take, for example, the way grandmothers and grandfathers are being multiplied by divorce and remarriage. They get included and excluded without any means of participating themselves in the decisions of their sons and daughters. From the point of view of the grandchildren the meaning of grandparents has to be determined by individual decisions and choices. Individuals must choose who is my main father, my main mother and who is my grandma and grandpa. We are getting into optional relationships inside families which are very difficult to identify in an objective, empirical way because they are a matter of subjective perspectives and decisions. And these can change between life phases.

If you ask what is a household, the answer seemed quite straightforward ten or 20 years ago. Today there is no simple answer. It can be defined as a geographical unit of one place, an economic unit in which individuals are economically supported and dependent upon one another, or a social unit of individuals who want to live together. And of course these definitions can contradict one another. There is also the dramatic increase in single households in the last 20 years. In cities like London and Munich, more than 50 per cent of all households are single households and it is a tendency which is increasing. But this category is not singular. There are old widows, men after divorce, maybe before remarrying and you have single households where people are living in quite close relations with others or not.

We are living with a rhetoric about the crisis in family life, but the family is not the cause of the historical conflict between men and women, it is the surface upon which this conflict becomes visible. Everything which strikes the family from outside – for example the contradiction between the demands of the labour market and the needs of relationships, the employment system, the law – is distorted into the personal sphere. The tension in family life today is the fact that equalization of men and women cannot be created in an institutional family structure which presupposed their inequality. In personal relationships conflicts are initiated by the opening up of possibilities to choose: in conflicting needs over careers, in the division of housework and child care. In making decisions people become aware of the contrasts in the conditions of men and women. With the lack of institutional solutions people are having to learn how to negotiate relationships on the basis of equality. This is transforming what we mean by the family.

JR I want to ask you what you think has determined these changes. I ask because you've tipped the conventional Marxist view that material conditions determine people's consciousness onto its head. You talk about how people's consciousness has changed but the institutions they live within, even their actual practices, haven't to the same extent.

UB Yes, that's true.

JR I accept that. I find it a paradox which is very interesting.

UB Let me pick up the question of this paradox. Marxist sociologists argue that capitalist societies, despite the changes I mention, are relatively stable structures of social inequality. They point out that the differences between the groups occupying the bottom, middle and top of society haven't really changed. They argue that this proves we are still living in a class society and that class remains the dynamic of modern capitalism. I argue that the dynamism of the labour market backed up by the welfare state has dissolved the social classes within capitalism.

JR You've called this transformation of society, capitalism without class.

UB It is true that in Germany, patterns of social inequality have remained relatively stable. Yet at the same time the living conditions of the population since 1960 have changed dramatically – which has set in motion the diversification and individualization of lifestyles and ways of life. This development is related to the expansion of education, the increase of social security and wealth, even the patterns of inequality. I want to think about these changes in terms of democratization. I would make a distinction between political democratization, social democratization related to the welfare state and what I would call cultural democratization. Individualization relates to this third description. If you look closely at the changes we are living through you find that principles of democracy are being picked up and at least believed in, as principles for the organization of everyday life and relationships. We are living under the preconditions of internalized democracy: the belief in equality in relationships, in dialogue not violence or the imposition of authority as the main element for reaching agreement. The capitalist market of instrumental relations under the conditions of the post-welfare state has produced something no one really imagined it would – an individualization which is infused with ideas of cultural democratization.

The situation is different now in the late 1990s, but let us stick with the 1970s and 1980s. I don't think you can make sense of what has happened in all Western European countries in terms of social movements, changes in family life, sexuality and love, a growing interest in the politics of everyday life and more direct forms of democracy, if you do not accept at least a part of this interpretation of cultural democratization.

JR I agree with you broadly speaking. What seems to be crucial to your analysis is this notion of culture – something which is not, as the more conventional Marxism has argued, a determined activity but is rather a relatively autonomous and transformative experience and activity in which human beings act upon and create their material world. This Marxism would argue that against the power of capital, cultural practices are relatively incidental and incapable of producing the kind of ideological political blocs which could resist exploitation, the globalization of capital, the commodification of society.

UB I would agree to some extent. First of all it is right that these changes in the family are only one part of the picture of what is happening in modern society. It is not the whole picture but I wouldn't agree with the old mechanical Marxist picture of capitalism which provides a too singular description of the way society is constructed and one which has to be understood as a natural law. There is something more significant going on which this old type of Marxist analysis cannot recognize. Over the last few hundred years we have been living in modernity, an experience of industrialization, democratization and modernization. We are now in a situation where this first modernity is being transformed into a second modernity. The first modernity is based upon a nation-state society, on given collective identities such as classes, families, ethnicities. Central to it was the principle, if not the practice, of full employment, and a mode of production based on the exploitation of nature. This modernity is being challenged by four developments. First of all by individualization. Second, by globalization as an economic, sociological and cultural phenomenon. Third, by underemployment or unemployment, not simply as the consequence of government policy or a downturn in the economy, but as a structural development which cannot be easily overcome. And fourth it is being challenged by ecological crisis. In this second modernity, we are heading for not only minor changes in, for example, personal relationships, but for a different form of capitalism, a new global order, a different type of everyday life. We have to begin again by asking very basic questions about how we live, how we can respond to these changes and how we can analyse them in sociological terms.

JR   In your books you talk about the global conflict between societies like ours, which are entering a second modernity and those that are either in, or entering, their first modernity. Do you think there is a similar uneven development within societies?

UB   Of course. We shouldn't simplify this process. There are very different speeds of development and individualization in different societies or subcultures and these are happening simultaneously. In the most developed countries you find undeveloped areas.

JR   And these different formations in society must each give rise to different politics and values? I just wonder whether individualization is not describing the culture of a metropolitan-educated elite, perhaps the emergence of a new knowledge-based class?

UB   No. I do think class is a zombie category. The discussion about individualization got started in the early 1980s in Germany too, after I published an article 'Beyond status and class'. Why did I do this? In the late 1970s and 1980s I had more and more trouble explaining class categories to my students. The conventional Marxist analysis of class bore no relation to their own experience and they could not make sense of it. I had to translate class to a more individualized culture which was concerned with quite different basic questions. The students did not think of themselves in an unconscious way as members of a class. Their cultural self-perception was somehow different from the picture presented by a class analysis of culture and society.

In Britain you still have a sociology which believes in the centrality of class as an explanatory category. You find this even in the writings of Anthony Giddens. Relativized yes, but still believing that we cannot say goodbye to the class category. Maybe this is related to experiences in Britain which I am not aware of. But if you look at how a class-based sociology defines class categories, you find that it depends upon what is going on in families and households. Empirical definitions of class identity are founded on categories of household defined by either a male head of household, or at least the leading person of the household. This is a completely fictitious way of defining class. No one can really say what a household or a family is nowadays, not in economic or social terms.

Let me give you an example of how the individualization debate has been picked up in Germany. First of all there has been very important research on the individualization of the poor. This challenges the misunderstanding that individualization is a matter for the rich. Research has shown that there is a much greater degree of mobility in and out of poverty amongst a wide range of people and at different periods of people's lives. There is still, of course, an increasing number of people who are poor in the long term. But in the middle there is a coming and going. Because of individualization, there is a lack of political organization of the poor. Capitalism without classes does not mean less inequality in the future, it will mean more. The current idea of exclusion can only be properly understood against the background of individualization or to be more precise atomization. It creates institutional circumstances under which individuals are cut off from traditional securities, while at the same time losing access to the basic rights and resources of modernity.

JR   Are you using the term poverty in the sense of material deprivation to describe something which is new? Perhaps it has to be redefined for this second modernity?

UB   Yes, I agree. Even poverty to some extent is a zombie category because we don't know what hides behind this term. This does not mean that these people are not poor, but it does mean that we cannot predict by one indicator what kind of life they lead and what kind of consciousness is going to develop out of this condition.

It is very difficult to work in a rich empirical way with class categories. You can only develop them on an objective income basis or on structures of work and employment. You can't relate them to how people live and think, eat, how they dress, love, organize their lives and so on. If you are interested in.what is going on in people's minds and the ways of life they are leading, you have to get away from the old categories. And if you want to know what this all means politically, again you have to get away from objective class categories. Then you can draw a picture of a differentiated society with different cultures of individualization and different reactions to it. It is possible to identify a variety of not classes, but what I will call collective life situations and each of these has a different political meaning.

Such an analysis differs from the old class analysis by concentrating on changes in everyday life. In the 1980s and early 1990s this analysis identified between 30 per cent and 40 per cent of the population in Germany who were interested in some form of experimental way of life and who were at the same time highly political in a new sense. No one could understand this for quite a while because they were not involved in any political party, not the liberals, the SPD, the conservatives or the Greens, nor were they part of union membership.

Nevertheless they were still active politically in a very direct way, both around their personal relationships and around wider issues. It is these individualized subpolitical cultures which helped to alter the political landscape of Germany. Nobody expected it. They want an experimental politics to happen. They want politics to adjust to the new realities they perceive.

JR You don't think that this 30 or 40 per cent is the formation of a new class category and consciousness?

UB No. If it is, you have to think of class in a different way.

JR I'm quite happy to. Your work reminds me of the humanist, cultural Marxism of E. P. Thompson, which describes how working people organized around the shared experience of exploitation and created their own class cultures and a class consciousness. It seems absolutely right that class cultures and consciousness under different conditions will change or disappear. What takes their place?

UB I think it relates to this tradition of cultural Marxism quite well – at least in terms of the importance of what people think and believe, and how they organize their lives. But there is one big difference which we probably have to debate about – the need to acknowledge the individual as the basic unit of democracy, the republic and political organization. All old class conceptions and politics presupposed that the individual and individualization were a basic illusion which had to be overcome in order to rebuild collective identities, to organize political life and to represent the individual in political democracy. I think this is a basic mistake. Just the opposite is necessary. Political parties nowadays have to recognize and acknowledge individualization, not as something to overcome, but as a new form of cultural democratization and self-consciousness of society. A new form of society in which politics is related to individual freedom, and the political freedoms and rights of groups in their everyday life. If political parties fail to understand this situation and always try to go back to a given collectivity or class, they will completely misunderstand the political forces and ideas of this society. The basic mistake of communitarianism is to react to individualization. It is 'reactionary' in its attempt to recuperate the old values of family, neighbourhood, religion and social identity, which are just not pictures of reality anymore.

JR There are residues of class identity and discrimination in British society which remain immensely powerful. I wonder whether this emergence of a second modernity could ever break away entirely from the institutions and categories of the first modernity. The psychological residues of class identity provide people with a personal history, a way of making sense of their own life experience or at least the experience of their parents. I'd extend this to the level of a society's perception of itself. Even if we now aspire to leave our class, it still remains as something which defines where we came from. It still appears to hold water in terms of defining the unequal distribution of educational opportunities and social and cultural capital.

UB Of course there are different situations in different countries. I am aware of Britain being a more everyday class-bound society than for example Germany. Again it is different in France. In the second modernity there are new powerful, transnational actors changing the social and political landscapes. There will be winners and losers, so maybe we will need redefined class categories to understand the relationships and dynamics of a cosmopolitan society. But a society and politics which only reacts to globalization and individualization and which tries to reactivate old values, is failing to understand the process of 'reflexive modernization' and the historical changes we are living through.

JR   Do you think it's simply about political parties not understanding? Surely they can't do anything. They are first-modernity institutions trying to grapple with a landscape beyond their language.

UB   Yes. Take the example of full employment, which is a zombie category. We are living with two models of employment. One is the welfare, post-war model of full employment, characterized by very low unemployment, a male family wage-earner, normal, usually secure work contracts, the idea of a career for the middle classes, a job for life. The other model is what we could call fragile or flexible employment – which means flexitime, part-time work, short-term contracts, people juggling different types of work at the same time. This second category of fragile employment is increasing rapidly in developed countries worldwide. We don't have the categories to describe it. Politics, and governments in Britain, Germany and France, are reacting to this pluralization and flexibilization of work – even in relation to the most advanced areas of the information economy – by trying to enforce the full employment principle. It is one example of an outmoded politics trying to engage with the new conditions of individualization.

JR   You describe an emerging society in which family and personal life has become individualized, employment has become less secure and more fragmented and the political system appears to be incapable of engaging with these processes. Is representative liberal democracy one of your zombie categories?

UB   This is a very difficult question to answer. I think we need to democratize democracy. For Germany our admission ticket to the democratic age lies with Immanuel Kant, who took it upon himself to label parliamentary democracy 'despotic'. Representative democracy contradicts the self-determination of the individual. It is founded upon the rule of the common will against the individual which, as Kant says, is a contradiction of the general will with itself. The alternative to national majority democracy is what I call a cosmopolitan republicanism. By this I mean the revaluation of the local and the self-responsibility of civil society – an active society where political processes are not simply organized in parliament and in the government but at a local and everyday level of the citizen. Civil society is in poor repute amongst politicians because it does not meet their standards of efficiency. The technocratic plastic speech of so many politicians is a cancer on democratic culture. Politics cannot be simply rational. Efficient solutions to problems are important, but so is passion. Politics has to be about emotional life. It is about the ability to listen, justice, interests, trust, identities and conflict when necessary; these involve more than a belief in some optimal path. We need a society which is not simply centred on work but is willing to finance, by for example a citizen's income and work, those forms of self-organization and experimental life forms which are already going on. Such a democraticization of democracy also needs to happen on a transnational level. We need a European civil rights movement which, with regard to foreigners, brings Europe's political identity into focus and helps develop it further. The more successful the Euro becomes, the more urgent is the question of Europe's soul and the need to democratize the Union.

JR Who are the enemies of this process of democratization?

UB Individualization doesn't automatically mean that people want to live as individuals and relate to one another as individuals. It could mean a new form of reflexive fundamentalism as well, which attempts to redefine collective identities – nationalism for example – and use them to resist or attack this process of individualization.

JR Do you see where this might be happening?

UB If you look back at history, Hannah Arendt explained German fascism as a reaction to an earlier phase of individualization (or again, more accurately, the atomization of society). A picture book example of creating a collective identity by politics. I am not saying this is being repeated today, but there is a fundamentalist reaction to individualization in all parties and social groups which may become a more open conflict in the future. There will be resistance in the second modernity to individualization and to the way globalization deterritorializes national cultures. It will come in particular from religious movements, the revival of ethnicity and counter-modern movements, paradoxically using the information technology of the second modernity to organize themselves globally.

JR You say in your writing that we are living in a crisis of freedom and choice.

UB Yes.

JR The second modernity seems to be founded upon freedom, choice, the individual, an existential uncertainty – and it is this last one that people draw back from and seek those old collective identities and certainties.

UB Yes, of course, you have to see this in the institutional context of the welfare state, the nation-state and a work-oriented society. There is not a simple choice between the new and the old. For example, in Germany the politicization of the ecological crisis is part of individualization and the second modernity. And yet out of this there is the possibility of a reflexive ecological fundamentalism as a reaction to this new culture of freedom.

JR What comes to mind in the relationship of the first modernity to the emerging second modernity is an antagonism between a large majority of the world's poor who might adopt a fundamentalist view of the world and a liberal minority of the rich societies. An antagonism which would also exist within the rich societies. I'm thinking about Islam both in Europe and in Britain where there are certain strands which mobilize fundamentalist interpretations of Islam to articulate an anti-imperialist politics and the grievances of Moslems against racism and injustice. The Islamic tradition of religion as central to everyday life and as a source of political expression poses a challenge to the secular pluralism of the second modernity.

UB Yes, indeed, this is one of the plausible future scenarios.

JR Second modernity against the first modernity. Privileged against the poor?

UB No, I wouldn't agree to just opposing first modernity to second modernity. It isn't that easy. The experimental cultures I speak about are not universal, but a part of European culture. There are what I will call 'divergent modernities' and 'contextual universalisms' in Asia, Africa, South America to be recognized as well. This means we cannot think about societies as we did before, as existing within the container of the nation-state with clear boundaries and relationships to others. We have to think globally. People are no longer living even simply local cultures any more. The poor population, even in a worldwide perspective, is changing. The meaning of being poor is changing. In the first modernity, poverty as Marx said, was determined by class or group access to the labour market. The situation today is dramatically different because nobody needs the poor anymore. Capitalism is creating joblessness and excluding swathes of populations. The second modernity is not simply a positive development. We in Western Europe are highly individualized but at the same time we are confronted – in a world which doesn't have the same borders any more – with people who are excluded and yet still living inside our lives. They are excluded but a part of our life. We have to relate to them. There are really dramatic challenges coming up. We have to rethink society in a cosmopolitan order, redefining the essential notions of justice and solidarity. At the moment, most of the philosophical debate is preoccupied by the assumption of the national container model of society and its self-definitions of community, justice and democracy.

JR   Going back to the seventeenth and eighteenth centuries, when society was radically changing with the emergence of capitalism and the first modernity, there existed a similar preoccupation with the self and with individual values and ethics. What do you think will be the values and ethics which emerge in this second modernity and which will lay the foundations for a different kind of politics?

UB   They will not be the ethics from those periods of early individualization. The late-eighteenth and early-nineteenth centuries witnessed the emergence of subjectivity and romanticism in everyday life. It was a dramatization of romantic love which created not only an individual biography, but also a moral and emotional complex that helped to create the couple and their history, as opposed to society. If you look at the cultural artifacts of the time – love letters and diaries – you are persuaded how people invented themselves and their relationships through love. The secular religion of love was invented at this time. You will also discover in these same love letters the invention of divorce as well. Today both romantic love and divorce have become ordinary and democratized.

The first impression one might have of individualized subcultures today is that they are similarly centred on the dramatization of their own egos. But research by Robert Wuthnow, a US sociologist of religion, has challenged the idea that we are living in a 'selfish society'. His study showed that for 75 per cent of the American population, solidarity, helpfulness and concern for the general welfare are as important as self-actualization, professional success and expansion of personal freedom. Individualized cultures do develop their own altruistic ethics. Being an individual does not exclude caring about others. In fact, living in a highly individualized culture means you have to be socially sensible and be able to relate to others and to obligate yourself, in order to manage and to organize your everyday life. In the old value system the ego always had to be subordinated to patterns of the collective.

A new ethics will establish a sense of 'we' that is like a co-operative or altruistic individualism. Thinking of oneself and living for others at the same time, once considered a contradiction in terms, is revealed as an internal, substantive connection.

JR   And are you willing to give up for others?

UB   Yes, willing to give up and having a lot of dilemmas and paradoxes about it. Let's think about it on the level of personal relationships. On the one hand, you want someone who will always support you in your own development. On the other, you have to support their own development if they are to support yours. More than this, you have to acknowledge the other's freedom and also his or her need to be loved. This is the dilemma: you must allow your beloved to be free, but in wanting them to love you, you restrict their freedom. Each partner wants his or her freedom and at the same time to be chained in the hands of the beloved. Out of the struggle with this dilemma between love and freedom a new ethics will emerge about the importance of individuation and obligation to others. No one has the answer as to how this will work.

JR   This is the business of growing up as children, learning the give and take of life, learning to be with others, reconciling our desire for autonomy with our need for dependence on others. Always that negotiation. Is this the ethical experience out of which a new politics will emerge?

UB   Yes. We have to understand that individualization presupposes a conscience and a reflexive process of socialization and intersubjectivity. You have to construct and invent your intersubjectivity in order to be an individual. But it is not a Robinson Crusoe society where everyone is for himself. It's the opposite. It is in the everyday experiments in living that we will find out about a new ethics that combines personal freedom with engagement with others and even engagement on a transnational basis. I think we are living in a highly moral world despite what the cultural pessimists try to tell us. But it is not a world of fixed obligations and values. Rather, it is one which is trying to find out how to combine individualization with obligations to others, even on a global scale.

JR   Does this ethical impulse have a political expression?

UB   It does.

JR   Where?

UB   First of all, on a subpolitical level where changes in attitudes do not amount to an inflation of material demands for more income, more consumption, more career. At the centre of the new ethics is the idea of the quality of life. What does this imply? For one thing, control over a person's 'own time' is valued more highly than more income or more career success. So, for example, providing there are basic securities, a lack of waged work means time affluence. Time is the key which opens the door to the treasures promised by the age of self-determined life: dialogue, friendship, being on one's own, compassion, fun, subpolitical commitment. In some ways this marks a shift away from the struggle for the distribution of material goods which still dominates public politics, toward a demand for the distribution of scarce immaterial resources which cannot be expressed in the exchange of money. I'm thinking of rest, leisure, self-determined commitments and forms of working, relationships, family life. Of course, these are the values of a self-oriented culture which is sensitive to ecological concerns.

An ethics of everyday life is developing its own subpolitics, which is often very local and concrete and which politicians don't recognize because they don't know the cultural nerve systems of these individualized cultures. It is an 'antipolitics'. We are witnessing today an actively unpolitical younger generation which has taken the life out of the political institutions and is turning them into zombie categories. This Western variant of antipolitics opens up the opportunity to enjoy one's own life and supplements this with a self-organized concern for others that has broken free from large institutions. It is organized around food, the body, sexuality, identity and in defence of the political freedom of these cultures against intervention from outside. If you look at these cultures closely, what seems to be unpolitical becomes politicized.

JR   Your vision of a positive outcome to an individualized society relies upon there being a moral impulse. I can see an alternative to this optimism here in Britain as we have moved away from the European model of social democracy toward the American model of a flexible, deregulated market economy. A more libertarian culture certainly, but one in which the poor and excluded and those needing support and help (and that means all of us at some time in our lives) are left to flounder alone. If the market is left to distribute freedoms in the way it distributes wealth then we're in deep trouble. There will be none of the social democratic institutions created in the first modernity left to defend people.

UB   This is very true. Arguing for the centrality of risk to understand the dynamics of our time, I am aware of the dark sides of individualization and globalization as well. But I can't help feeling bored by the habit of concentrating on the catastrophes ahead. It doesn't challenge us to think. How do we know that everything is getting worse? Neither the pessimist nor the optimist can foresee the future. It is very difficult and therefore intellectually challenging to open up a mode of thinking and acting for realistic utopian opportunities. Maybe I underestimate the threats of the second modernity, because I am still very much connected to the continental political movements of the 1970s and 1980s.

JR   I like that. It gives your work an optimism and hope for the future.

[The full version of this interview was published in Jonathan Rutherford (ed.) (2000) *Art of Life*. London: Lawrence & Wishart.]

Published here by kind permission of Ulrich Beck and Jonathan Rutherford.

Index